P9-BYF-144

INSIDERS' GUIDE® TO
MADISON, WI

HELP US KEEP THIS GUIDE UP-TO-DATE

We would love to hear from you concerning your experiences with this guide and how you feel it could be improved and kept up-to-date. Please send your comments and suggestions to:

editorial@GlobePequot.com

Thanks for your input, and happy travels!

INSIDERS' GUIDE® SERIES

INSIDERS' GUIDE® TO

MADISON, WI

FIRST EDITION

KEVIN REVOLINSKI

INSIDERS' GUIDE

GUILFORD, CONNECTICUT
AN IMPRINT OF GLOBE PEQUOT PRESS

All the information in this guidebook is subject to change. We recommend that you call ahead to obtain current information before traveling.

To buy books in quantity for corporate use or incentives, call **(800) 962–0973** or e-mail **premiums@GlobePequot.com.**

INSIDERS' GUIDE ®

Copyright © 2010 Morris Book Publishing, LLC

ALL RIGHTS RESERVED. No part of this book may be reproduced or transmitted in any form by any means, electronic or mechanical, including photocopying and recording, or by any information storage and retrieval system, except as may be expressly permitted in writing from the publisher. Requests for permission should be addressed to Globe Pequot Press, Attn: Rights and Permissions Department, P.O. Box 480, Guilford, CT 06437.

Insiders' Guide is a registered trademark of Morris Book Publishing, LLC.

Editorial Director, Travel: Amy Lyons
Project Editor: Kristen Mellitt
Layout Artist: Kevin Mak
Text Designer: Sheryl Kober
Maps by Sue Murray © Morris Book Publishing, LLC

Library of Congress Cataloging-in-Publication data is available on file.

ISBN: 978-0-7627-5696-4

Printed in the United States of America
10 9 8 7 6 5 4 3 2 1

CONTENTS

ABOUT THE AUTHOR

Kevin Revolinski grew up in Marshfield, a small Wisconsin town two hours north of Madison, and as a child he considered the capital city as magical as the Big Apple. He first moved to Madison in 1992 and, with the exception of a few teaching years overseas, has made his home base there since. His articles have appeared in the *New York Times* and *Chicago Tribune* and locally in *Isthmus* and *Wisconsin State Journal*. He is the author of several guidebooks such as *Wisconsin's Best Beer Guide, 60 Hikes Within 60 Miles Madison, Backroads and Byways of Wisconsin, The Wisconsin Beer Guide: A Travel Companion,* and *The Yogurt Man Cometh: Tales of an American Teacher in Turkey.* He lives in Madison when he is not on the road seeking material for his blog and Web site, The Mad Traveler Online (www.themadtraveleronline .com).

ACKNOWLEDGMENTS

As with writing any guidebook, a list of people a writer comes in contact with could fill the volume itself. I have to thank all the cooperative souls at the museums, businesses, and other listed entities here for their assistance and readiness with valuable information. In the big picture of things I—and we all—have the founders, builders, and workaday folk of this fair city to thank, because their foresight, vision, and hard work have combined to create such a wonderful place to be, from the exemplary park system to the revitalized downtown to the endless celebrations of our community and its great mix of cultures and viewpoints. We may never arrive at "perfect," but the longstanding progressive ambitions will hopefully keep moving us "Forward" as the state motto recommends. A big thanks to fellow travel writers Matt Forster, Kim Grant, and Lori Baker who are always there when I need a Rob Schneider-esque "you can do it" and to my Madisonian friends and neighbors for all their valuable input and mental support – Michele Harper, Jeffrey Price, Kristin Abraham, Marty and Mary Statz, Renee Lajcak, and Brian Babler. And finally, my wife, Peung, deserves a medal for putting up with my Neurotic Finish-the-Book Syndrome.

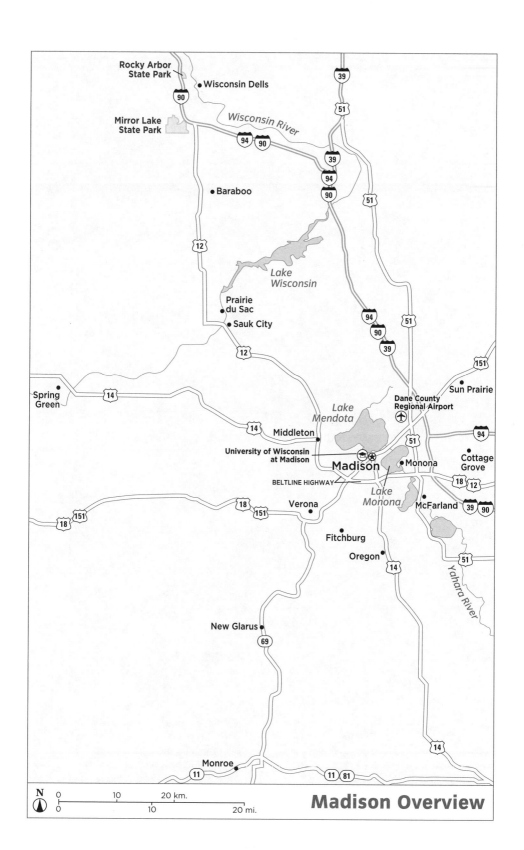

Madison Overview

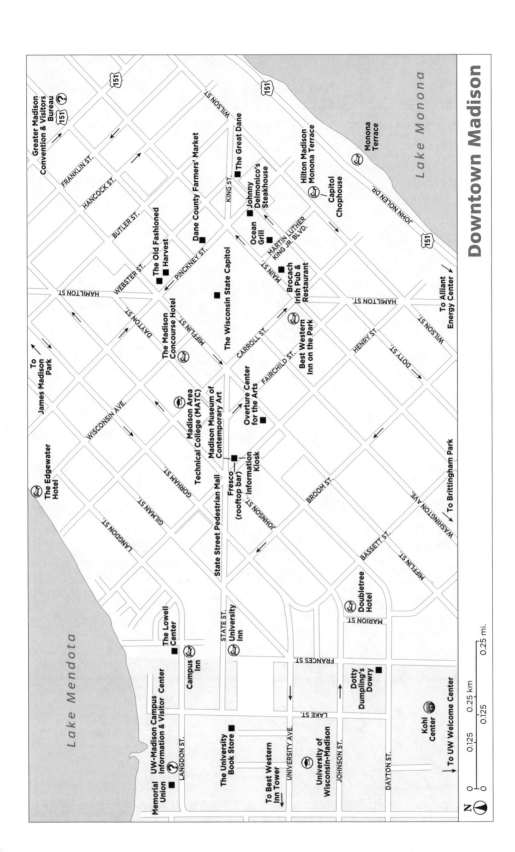

Downtown Madison

N

0   0.125   0.25 km
0   0.125   0.25 mi.

Lake Mendota

Lake Monona

Memorial Union
UW-Madison Campus Information & Visitor Center
The Lowell Center
Campus Inn
The University Book Store
To Best Western Inn Tower
University of Wisconsin-Madison
Kohl Center
To UW Welcome Center
Dotty Dumpling's Dowry
Doubletree Hotel
University Inn
The Edgewater Hotel
To James Madison Park
The Madison Concourse Hotel
Madison Area Technical College (MATC)
Madison Museum of Contemporary Art
State Street Pedestrian Mall
Fresco (rooftop bar)
Information Kiosk
Overture Center for the Arts
The Old Fashioned
Harvest
Dane County Farmers' Market
The Wisconsin State Capitol
The Great Dane
Johnny Delmonico's Steakhouse
Ocean Grill
Best Western Inn on the Park
Brocach Irish Pub & Restaurant
Hilton Madison Monona Terrace
Capitol Chophouse
Monona Terrace
To Alliant Energy Center
To Brittingham Park
Greater Madison Convention & Visitors Bureau

Streets:
FRANKLIN ST.
HANCOCK ST.
BUTLER ST.
WEBSTER ST.
PINCKNEY ST.
HAMILTON ST.
DAYTON ST.
MIFFLIN ST.
WISCONSIN AVE.
GORHAM ST.
GILMAN ST.
LANGDON ST.
STATE ST.
UNIVERSITY AVE.
JOHNSON ST.
DAYTON ST.
LAKE ST.
FRANCES ST.
MARION ST.
BASSETT ST.
BROOM ST.
HENRY ST.
FAIRCHILD ST.
CARROLL ST.
KING ST.
WILSON ST.
MAIN ST.
MARTIN LUTHER KING JR. BLVD.
DOTY ST.
WASHINGTON AVE.
JOHN NOLEN DR.
151

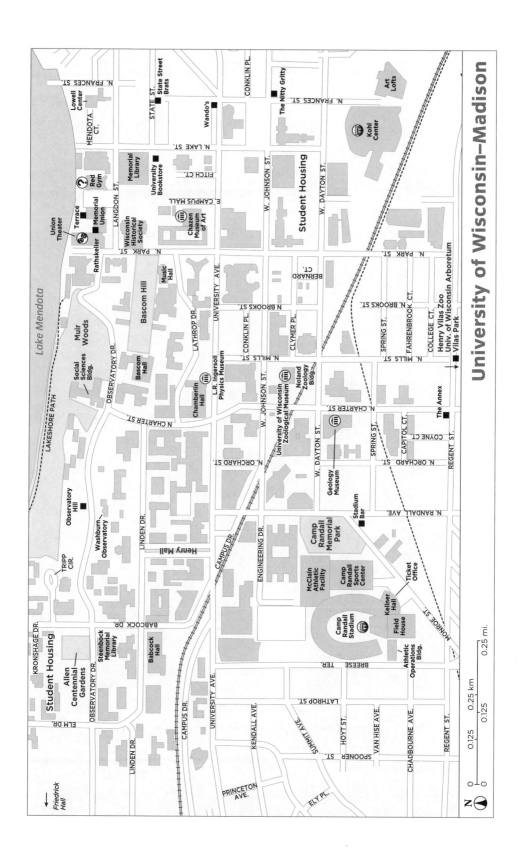

University of Wisconsin–Madison

PREFACE

Life is good here. Madison represents that perfect university city—a city that is not too big and not too small and carries a strong pulse maintained by the idealism and energy of such a large body of students while drawing intellect and culture from so many outside sources. But there is more to it than that. As the capital of Wisconsin and the seat of the University of Wisconsin, Madison brings together a lot of sophistication and an idea that education and smarts should be brought to bear on the community and society at large for the betterment of all. The proof is in the pudding. Every year Madison appears in a variety of publications' top-ten lists, and the subjects run the gamut from education, employment opportunity, family living, and outdoor recreation, to good farmers' markets, good health, and even good teeth.

The University has brought people from all walks of life, from all parts of the country, and even from around the world. Many of them never left. Restaurants hail from all parts of the globe bringing a variety of ethnic cuisines uncommon in such a modest-sized community. Young professionals are drawn here by a healthy job market, while families come for the highly rated education system and quality of living.

Madison is a city that loves the outdoors, with miles and miles of biking and walking paths and an inordinate amount of green space. Figure over 200 parks, an acre of them for about every 39 people. The heart of the city straddles an isthmus between two beautiful lakes, and a person is never more than 15 minutes from being surrounded by farmland, fields, or forest. The connection to its rural surroundings is expressed by the numerous farmers' markets, a hankering for locally grown foods, and the area's artisan cheeses.

Madison, or "the Mad City," has been compared to Austin, TX; Boulder, CO; and Ann Arbor, MI; and its volatile atmosphere and protests during the Vietnam War were as intense as those of Berkeley, CA. The Mad City's history of Progressivism, and in some cases radicalism, hasn't always been met with enthusiasm. A state governor once referred to Madison as being a certain number of square miles surrounded by reality. It was meant as an insult, but the city wears it like a badge. (In true Madison fashion, debate and discussion are continual about just how many square miles former Governor Lee Dreyfus actually quoted, with numbers ranging from 15 to 85.) There are two basic kinds of Madisonians: those who gush with love for their fair city and those who roll their eyes a bit, shake their heads, carry an itemized list of cynical complaints, and yet never seem to move away or miss it when they do. You just can't shake the place.

Watch the sun set over Lake Mendota down at the Memorial Union Terrace or take a stroll along a lake in summer or down State Street on a winter evening. Buy fresh vegetables, flowers, or artisan cheese at the nation's best farmers' market, or sip a cold local beer at one of the brewpubs, clubs, or taverns or a brewed cup of locally roasted coffee at the neighborhood coffeehouse. Catch Badger fever at a football game or hockey match, or enjoy an evening of culture and art at the multimillion dollar Overture Center. Listen to an indie rock band in a club, a jazz concert in the street, or a free symphony orchestra performance right out in front of the magnificent Capitol. Whether you prefer an old-school fish fry at a supper club, a vegetarian dish from a faraway land, the best hamburger and deep-fried cheese curds you ever had, or a meticulously prepared meal at an organic, locally sourced gourmet restaurant, Madison has you set up. Indeed, Mad Town is now 68.7 square miles (not counting 16 square miles of lakewater) and perhaps it is surrounded by reality.

Reality is overrated. Madison rocks.

HOW TO USE THIS BOOK

This book breaks Madison down into detailed chapters about the various aspects of the city. The list of traditional attractions may not overwhelm as it might in a major metropolis, but Madison does have its fair share of those—museums, a zoo, historical buildings. When the wide variety of recreational and entertainment options—a solid theater and arts community, and the impressive number of restaurants—are thrown in, the charming midwestern city rises to a level far beyond its size.

The included area maps give you an idea of how the city and its surroundings lay out. Throughout the book you can find Insiders' Tips , little hints and trivia bits that only a local might know, as well as some Close-ups that go more in depth on some characteristically Madison aspects.

Getting Here, Getting Around has all the information you need about negotiating a few of the tricks of travel from air travel to biking around and everything in between. The Accommodations chapter is divided geographically and shows price codes so you can stay closer to whatever you came to Madison to see or do at the price you can afford, while the Restaurants are listed by cuisine and also offer indicators of price. Nightlife pulls together everything from live music to book readings and is arranged by genre. Performing Arts stand on their own, while the Attractions, including more in-depth information about the University of Wisconsin, get their own separate chapter as well. The university contributes to the youthful energy as well as the diverse population of Madison, and its campus and some off-campus properties are must-visit attractions, not just student facilities. The Parks section, as one might expect, is a summary of the major city, county, and state parks in this park-loving community. The Recreation chapter is organized by activity and in many cases refers back to the Parks chapter as its venue guide.

Madison has a kid-friendly vibe and so a whole chapter pays attention to Kidstuff. Shopping ideas can be found in their own chapter, from the touristy to the practical, and the Spectator Sports section may show more options than one might expect from a city without a professional sports team. Check the Annual Events chapter for the city's activity-laden yearly schedule and see what's happening the next time you're in town. Be aware that the event dates are estimates (in many cases merely the month) as organizations jockey for position on the calendar. The chapter on Day Trips and Weekend Getaways expands the scope of this book. No one should miss the view from the towering rocky bluffs at Devil's Lake State Park or Wisconsin Dells and its collection of water parks just a short drive away.

Certain attractions don't always fit nicely into categories. Fine dining restaurants might also have exceptional seafood. Certain great nightlife spots might also be restaurants. The zoo or the geology museum are attractions for everyone and shouldn't be overlooked by parents who go immediately to the Kidstuff chapter. Explore the book a little just as you should the city itself. Discovery—be it a trivia bit or just a darn good hamburger—is the best part about visiting and exploring a destination. In many cases, crossover sites will be written up in one category but listed in one or two others with basic contact information, perhaps a line or two of tips specific to the category, and directions to its original long listing in another chapter. Things are always changing in a dynamic place like Madison, especially in the restaurant and bar business, so it is never a bad idea to call ahead just to make sure.

Lastly, are you moving to Madison or already live here? Be sure to check out the blue-tabbed pages at the back of the book, where you will find the **Living Here** appendix that offers sections on relocation, education, and health care.

AREA OVERVIEW

Madison is what some might term a modest midwestern city. It lies among the major metropolises of Milwaukee, Chicago, and the Twin Cities and is connected to them by the Interstates that run right along its east side. Three factors make Madison exceptional: state government, a massive state university, and its lakes. It's hard to say which makes the greatest impact. Lakes Mendota and Monona dictated the layout of the city streets. The Capitol and government rest between the two on a hill on an isthmus. Just a short walk to the west of the Capitol are the downtown area and the sprawling University of Wisconsin, which runs along the shore of Lake Mendota. What this combines in the heart of the city is the constant energy of bright young people who want to test the possibilities and limits of their lives and the world around them, and of the tumult of politics and public debate. It's a potent mix and never boring.

The natural environment contributes equally to the atmosphere of the city. The lakes and the abundant city parks—including the small, spring-fed Lake Wingra and the central forest preserve of the university's arboretum—bring beauty in every season. Beyond the city limits is a scattering of small towns and developing suburbs and a whole lot of rolling farmland and dairy farms, county and state parks, and a terrain shaped by the glaciers of the last chapter of the Ice Age.

Geographically speaking Madison is quite compact, and as you can read in the Getting There, Getting Around chapter, even getting all the way across town does not require much time. Listed here is a general breakdown of the city into sections followed by some comments on the seasons and weather.

THE ISTHMUS

The center of the city rests along this strip of land between Lakes Mendota and Monona just over a half a mile wide at its narrowest point. From the easterly edge of the University of Wisconsin campus in the west to just past the Yahara River in the east, the isthmus encompasses much of downtown, the Capitol, and some of the residential areas on the near east side.

DOWNTOWN & THE CAPITOL

The area surrounding the Capitol starts with office buildings and high-rise condos giving way quickly to old houses, some of which date back to the 19th century and are dominated by the university's student population. Washington Avenue enters the Capitol Square from the east and the

west, and State Street, which begins from the square and heads west to campus, is really the heart of downtown.

THE UNIVERSITY OF WISCONSIN CAMPUS

The University of Wisconsin occupies nearly 1000 acres or 2.5 square miles along the south shore of Lake Mendota. The campus stretches west about 1.75 miles from downtown to University Hospital and south across Johnson Street with the occasional buildings scattered like islands beyond what appears to be the edge of campus. Camp Randall Stadium is a popular westerly landmark as is Bascom Hill which begins just past the end of the State Street pedestrian mall. Campus housing extends into Eagle Heights which is north of the hospital on the bluffs overlooking the lake.

THE EAST SIDE

Starting on the isthmus on the near east side is the Willy (Williamson) Street area, one of the city's most eclectic neighborhoods. Some will say old hippies, new hipsters, artsy types, alternative lifestyles, free spirits, down to earth, or what have you. All labels may apply in some way, but it definitely has an inclusive friendliness and is characterized by old multistory, multiflat houses with small shops, restaurants, and bars clumped here and there throughout. Continuing east across the Yahara is more of the same in the Atwood–Schenk neighborhood and the surrounding areas passing through Olbrich Park and Olbrich Botanical Gardens to reach the far east side and the city of Monona. The far east side is primarily single-family dwellings less than 50 years old, getting newer as you move east. The big box stores cluster around East Towne Mall right before the Interstate. Suburban style development continues from there.

THE NORTH SIDE

This might generally be considered the area north of East Washington Avenue and extending up and over the easterly lobe of Lake Mendota to Governor's Island, Farwell's Point, and Cherokee Marsh along the upper Yahara River. The airport falls within this area to the east, while to the west the Village of Maple Bluff, a suburb engulfed by the city, sits on the east shore of Lake Mendota and functions as sort of the beginning of the north side off the isthmus.

THE WEST SIDE

From campus heading west, the closer neighborhoods on the near west side are of course the oldest. Neighborhoods such as University Heights or Vilas contain some magnificent old homes, many of which were "out in the country" back in the early days of Madison. A few golf courses are tucked in here and houses become newer and more modest as you head west while four-unit and larger apartments begin to appear.

On the far west side the malls, strip malls, and big box stores emerge amid a housing boom of condos and apartments as well as bigger, newer, single-family homes set along curving suburban streets and cul-de-sacs. Even farther west beyond the **Beltline Highway** are more condo developments and shopping centers.

THE SOUTH SIDE

South of the lakes and the Beltline Highway are more residential areas and apartment compounds. Several neighborhoods show some very large expensive houses, while others not so very far away are in a state of urban decline. Parks nevertheless abound throughout and a bit farther south, Fitchburg, the part-urban, part-rural community, begins.

MIDDLETON

Like Madison, Middleton has received some attention for being one of the top places in the country to live. Situated to the west a bit north of Madison, Middleton can be reached by following University Avenue west right into its heart. A revitalized town center has made it attractive not just for residents but for west-side Madisonians looking for a place to eat or meet.

MONONA

Almost indistinguishable from the east side of Madison, Monona nevertheless has its own assortment of businesses spread along Monona Drive and Stoughton Road. The city nestles up against the east shore of Lake Monona and extends down to the Beltline Highway.

SEASONS AND WEATHER

How you'll find Madison of course depends on the season. Summer is arguably the best time to be in town. The bulk of the students are out of town, the neighborhood festivals get going, and the outdoor activities are really in full swing. The weather is generally sunny and mild with occasional thunderstorms or the odd heat wave

Madison Vital Statistics

Mayor/Governor: Dave Cieslewicz (D)/Jim Doyle (D)

Population (2008): City: 231,916; Metro area: 543,022; Wisconsin: 5,627,967

Area: City: 67.3 square miles; Wisconsin: 65,498 square miles

Nicknames: Mad City, Mad Town, Cap City, The People's Republic of Madison, The Left Coast of Wisconsin, Athens of the Midwest, 68 Square Miles Surrounded by Reality

Average temperatures: July: 84ºF; January: 27ºF

Average rainfall: 36.6 inches per year; June is the rainiest with 4.6 inches per year

Average snowfall: 44 inches per year; January is the snowiest with 10.6 inches per year

Founded: 1848

Major colleges & universities: University of Wisconsin, Edgewood College, Madison Area Technical College

Major area employers: Alliant Energy, American Family Insurance, CUNA Mutual Group, Epic Systems Corporation, Oscar Mayer (Kraft Foods), Spectrum Brands (formerly Rayovac), The Douglas Stewart Company, University of Wisconsin, UW Health

of upper-80s and lower-90s temperatures. The fall carries some heat after Labor Day, with the occasional "Indian Summer" in October but typically is cool and comfortable. School is back on and it is football season for the Badgers, so a new energy is injected into the scene. Colors change through October and the leaves are gone by mid-November when the temperatures are decidedly jacket worthy or worse. Snow before Thanksgiving is not common and when it happens, it rarely sticks. More likely the great white comes in December in time for the holidays bringing with it the occasional subzero periods in both December and January. During winter, expect at least one or more "snow days" when the plows simply can't keep up or get a start, and the schools and some businesses close and life slows a bit. The lakes should be frozen over by January and may remain so on through March. In spring pasque flowers poke through the snows, and the relief of residents is palpable when the first no-jacket days arrive. The occasional snowstorm stubbornly blows through in March, less commonly in April but still possible even into May. By mid-May all should be green. May and June can vary from really warm to disappointingly cold and gloomy. Optimism dictates June is gorgeous and with a bit of luck, and depending on the harshness of winter, the mosquitoes don't take hold until at least halfway through the month.

HISTORY

In modern times, Madison may be nearly 68 square miles "surrounded by reality" but almost 20,000 years ago it was buried under 1,600 feet of ice. The Green Bay lobe of the glaciers that descended on Wisconsin during the last performance of the Ice Age came to a grinding (literally) halt just about 10 miles southwest of the Capitol.

The first immigrants arrived in the Madison area around 9500 B.C. to the best of current knowledge, originally coming across a land bridge from Asia several thousand years before that. Spear points and other archaeological evidence support that belief. So humans were already here hunting mastodon and bison while the big ice was melting its way back into Canada. As the trees and landscape changed with the changing climate, so did the Paleo-Indians who lived in the area, adapting hunting patterns with the disappearance of large Ice Age mammals. Madison's three lakes—Mendota, Monona, and Wingra—were all part of one big lake held back by glacial deposits blocking the Yahara River, but the water levels dropped over the centuries forming three separate lakes.

Woodland cultural traditions from the east influenced the midwestern people, and they too picked up practices such as pottery and building earthen mounds, which grew bigger by the Middle Woodland Period on up to around 500 A.D. The conical mounds of these Native Americans evolved into effigy mounds, built in simple geometric shapes or the forms of animals. At one time there were at least 1,000 of them in the area as counted by a 19th-century archaeologist. Many of these have fallen to farmer plows and development, but respect for the sacred ground and the historical significance of them led to their preservation. There are still some to be seen in the area such as those at Forest Hill Cemetery and a bird with a 624-foot wingspan on the grounds of the Mendota Mental Health Institute. Perhaps more impressive than the mounds was the development of agriculture. The Native Americans had learned how to cultivate corn, squash, potatoes, and tobacco and to harvest wild rice.

The lakes were as much of a prominent feature of the area as they are now and it was the Ho-Chunk people who gave them their first recorded name: *Taychopera,* meaning "land of the four lakes." Even after the European settlers arrived, Lakes Mendota to Kegonsa were known by their blasé surveyor names: First Lake (Kegonsa) to Fourth Lake (Mendota). The modern names with Ho-Chunk origins were actually given by State Governor Leonard Farwell and his associates in 1855.

The arrival of the European settlers created quite a stir of course. Initially the settlements in the east pushed eastern tribes such as the Sauk, Fox, and Ojibwe into Wisconsin. French explorer Jean Nicolet arrived in the Green Bay area in 1634, and soon after, French fur traders, who expanded into the territory via the Great Lakes and the state's rivers and who often married into local tribes. The French were the dominating European presence even after area forts changed hands after the 1763 Treaty of Paris, which granted Great Britain the rule of the land. The fur industry expanded down into the Four Lakes region in search of more supply. But the British influence also hung on longer than treaties would have suggested; after the American Revolution, they stuck around in what became known as the Northwest Territory. After the War of 1812, however, the Brits were sent back beyond the border of British Canada.

The lure of farmland and a boom of lead mining in what is now southwestern Wisconsin increased the arrival of pioneers. In 1830 fur trader Wallace Rowan constructed the first recorded permanent cabin on the north shore of Lake Mendota. The first shop on the hill of today's capitol, however, was made of brush and canvas. Oliver Armel had abundant business trading whiskey and odds and ends with the Native Americans for furs. There may be some argument as to who got the better part of that deal.

THE BLACK HAWK WAR

As the new nation methodically spread west, the lands of the Native Americans were being ceded to the encroaching settlers by treaties at an increasing rate, and tribes were pushed toward and across the Mississippi River. The Sauk people in what is now northern Illinois were none too pleased with their deal and reluctant to leave their summer croplands. Sauk warrior chief Black Hawk, at odds with Keokuk, the Sauk leader who had signed the land treaty with the U.S. government, returned to his village of Saukenuk (today, Rock Island, Illinois) for the growing season in 1830 and again in 1831. The muscle of Federal troops forced Black Hawk to agree to stay west of the Mississippi. But in 1832, believing he had support from other area tribes, Black Hawk returned with over 1,000 of his people. Militia was called up to confront him and they burned a village along the way, forcing Black Hawk to reconsider once again. But when emissaries of Black Hawk's band, presumably offering a truce, met the militia on May 14, 1832, one was shot in an alleged misunderstanding. Violence erupted and 11 militiamen were killed as their disorganized group made a frantic retreat. Exaggerations of the size of Black Hawk's group of warriors and some unaffiliated regional conflicts with other tribes fueled panic and the war was on.

For the next two months, Black Hawk's band was involved in several raids and skirmishes, and by July the entire group of warriors, elders, and women and children was heading north into Wisconsin pursued by Generals Henry Dodge (who would become the first territorial governor of Wisconsin) and James Henry. The chase passed across the Madison isthmus and its marshy area around the Yahara River. At the Battle of Wisconsin Heights on July 21, 1832, near today's Sauk City, Black Hawk and his warriors made a costly stand, successfully holding off the militia while their people crossed the Wisconsin River. As many as 70 died either in battle or by drowning.

Eleven days later, however, their flight ended at the bank of the Mississippi River near the Bad Axe River. Caught between the steamboat *Warrior* and pursuing troops, many of Black Hawk's people—women and children included—were killed in a one-sided, two-day confrontation. Even by the mid-19th century, the Battle of the Bad Axe River was being referred to as a massacre. Black Hawk escaped to the north but surrendered weeks later and was taken to Washington, D.C., to meet President Andrew Jackson and then on to prison. Shortly thereafter Black Hawk traveled back west displayed as a prisoner on a public tour before being released to his people now permanently west of the Mississippi.

> **i** Notable names turn up in a history of the Black Hawk War. Abraham Lincoln served in the militia in Illinois, while Zachary Taylor commanded troops under General Henry Atkinson. Eventual president of the Confederacy, Jefferson Davis, returned from leave to escort the surrendered Black Hawk to a military post in Missouri.

A CAPITOL IDEA

Of all the comings and goings around that time, the visitor most influential on the destiny of Madison was just someone passing through in 1829. The beauty of the lakes and the land—and the potential profit of land speculation—didn't go unnoticed by territorial judge James Duane Doty.

In 1834, surveyors marked out the town that would soon become Madison City, and just eight months later a road was constructed, connecting the forts in Portage to the north and Prairie du Chien to the west on the Mississippi River. The road passed just north of Lake Mendota. The man behind that first road across southern Wisconsin? James Duane Doty. Doty bought land on either side of the Yahara River in 1835, and with a partner bought up much of the center of the isthmus including the hill on which the Capitol now rests. When the territorial delegates from throughout the newly formed Wisconsin Territory met in the first capital, Belmont (Wisconsin), it was to decide where the permanent capital might be. Doty was careful not to miss being there. The competition was stiff, and in the end 19 alternative sites had been proposed and defeated before the legislature declared Madison City, named for the recently deceased and beloved former president, the winner. But what of the swampland along the proposed site's isthmus or the distance from either Lake Michigan or the Mississippi? It is true that Madison's east-leaning location in the territory would become more central when the territory would most certainly be split in half, as was in fact done just two years later. But surely the selection had more to do with Doty's knowledge of the region and his knack for persuasion. He purchased buffalo robes for the legislators who found the accommodations in Belmont a bit on the cold and drafty side. He also sold some land in the proposed capital to various influential individuals at a good price—some sources say free, but it appears prices were agreed upon at least on paper. Regardless of the shenanigans behind it, the new capital was approved and the government held its first session in 1838.

Madison City was a paper city even as the decision was made. The streets would be named after signers of the *U.S. Constitution* and arranged in a radial fashion, much as the nation's capital, but for now the place was empty. The first permanent structure on the isthmus—not canvas and brush—was a public house (i.e., tavern and lodging) consisting of two cabins joined by a lean-to kitchen owned by Eben and Rosaline Peck and completed in 1837. Nothing but a plaque on King Street and a commemorative pilsner at the Great Dane Brewpub across the road remain. The same year a saw mill opened on Lake Mendota at the end of North Hamilton. But by 1846 the population had grown to a whopping . . . 238. Motions were growing to move the capital, perhaps to Milwaukee. The modest first capitol building did little to impress lawmakers and, in fact, the pigs in the basement could be manipulated to drown out debate. The new Madison Hotel, however, offered luxuries to politicians who would remain in support of Madison City, and the *Wisconsin Enquirer,* the city's first newspaper, did its part to influence readers. The capital stayed.

A NEW STATE AND ITS CAPITAL

In 1848 Wisconsin was granted statehood and the University of Wisconsin, set on what was already known as College Hill, also came to fruition firmly establishing Madison as the star on the map. Leonard J. Farwell, the second governor of Wisconsin, was instrumental in the initial development of the city. He bought up all of Doty's unsold lands, eventually donating the land for the asylum that would become the Mendota Mental Health Institute. Governor's Island was also his. He built a dam to capture the river power for a mill and thus raised the level of Lake Mendota and lowered that of Lake Monona. He had the Catfish (now Yahara) River straightened and officially renamed the generically numbered lakes. During Farwell's time in Madison, the muddy roads were paved with gravel, sidewalks were put in, and marshy areas on the east side were drained. Madison soon doubled in size, and the wealthy built impressive homes along Big Bug Hill, what today is Mansion Hill. The railroad gave Madison an additional boost in 1854 connecting the capital with Milwaukee and the Mississippi River. In 1857, construction of the second capitol building began, taking 12 years to complete but putting a proper dome at the center of the state's capital.

i For an outstanding account of the early history of Madison, check out *Madison, a History of the Format.*

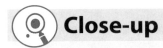 **Close-up**

Fighting Bob

One of the most influential U.S. Senators in history, **Robert Marion La Follette Sr.** was born on June 14, 1855, in rural Dane County, not far from Madison. He worked his way through college by teaching on the side and graduated in 1879 from the University of Wisconsin establishing a reputation as a brilliant orator along the way. He married Belle Case, a fellow orator at UW who shared his passion for politics and was an active supporter of women's suffrage. In 1880 he passed the bar, and as the Republican nominee was elected to be the Dane County District Attorney. From local government he went on to national government, serving three terms in the U.S. House of Representatives. His support for the controversial McKinley Tariff Act, which aimed to protect American manufacturers but ended up bringing hardship to farmers, cost him his next election.

He returned to Madison.

While in Washington, La Follette learned how much big business, especially the railroad industry, was influencing members of the Wisconsin-founded Republican Party. When a fellow party member attempted to bribe him, La Follette had had enough and he decided to start his own party within the party. They were known as The Insurgents by the detractors, but many saw his point and joined him.

These Progressives wanted reform including consumer rights and protections and direct voting of senators. Questionable railroad financing and overbuilding led to a failure of banks in 1893, and many Wisconsinites began to see La Follette's point of view. The Progressives proposed La Follette for governor in 1896 and 1898. To fight corporate influence they demanded direct election of nominees in primaries, and in 1900 the Progressives rallied enough support to take the nomination. La Follette traveled almost the entire state giving long speeches often lasting over three hours. His knack for persuasion nabbed him the governorship for the next six years.

Opposing Republicans, known as The Stalwarts, tried to roadblock everything he wanted to accomplish. In a time when the media did not have instantaneous access to information and a national audience, La Follette had to take to the road himself drawing publicity with his "roll calls," public readings of a list of politicians and their votes against his populist policies, such as direct election of U.S. senators, progressive taxation, women's suffrage, a minimum wage, and workers' compensation.

One of La Follette's beliefs was that good government could be obtained by developing smarter public policy based on research. His close relationship with the University of Wisconsin exem-

THE CIVIL WAR

The subject of the spread of slavery was heatedly debated in the city and its newspapers, with the Republicans—a party founded in 1854 in Wisconsin—firmly against expansion of it. When South Carolina seceded from the Union on December 20, 1860, some were hesitant to pick up arms. Crowds gathered outside the telegraph office to get news of what was happening in the south. At the fall of Fort Sumter in 1861, however, most hesitation dissipated and the volunteers came quickly. Two out of three men in Madison served in the Union army. One out of four never returned. The 30-acre state fair grounds on the west side of the city became Camp Randall, named for then Governor Alexander Randall, a Republican and supporter of Lincoln. Seventy-thousand troops trained here during the war and at one point the camp even held prisoners from the south. Some of the war dead, including prisoners who died of disease at Camp Randall, are interred at Forest Hill Cemetery. After leaving

plified what has become known as The Wisconsin Idea. The School of Public Affairs at the University of Wisconsin–Madison is named in his honor.

He nominated himself for Wisconsin's empty U.S. Senate seat in 1905, and after finishing off his gubernatorial term in January 1906, he left for Washington. He took his "roll calls" with him, becoming a gadfly for senators on the national level.

His popularity grew, but then came World War I. La Follette did not want to have any part of it, and this put him head to head with President Woodrow Wilson. When the Associated Press misquoted one of his speeches in St. Paul, La Follette became labeled as a German sympathizer. The situation reached a boiling point, and Fighting Bob was allowed to address Congress publicly in October 1917. He defended the right of free speech during wartime and so overwhelmed the crowd that they burst into applause when he was finished. But he didn't get the last word, and the rebuttals by three senators were scathing. In particular, Arkansas senator Joseph Taylor Robinson broke Senate tradition and addressed La Follette directly, heaping on him such criticism and eventually abuse that the audience fell silent and even the press made note of it in print.

For the presidential election of 1924, several smaller parties proposed to unite under progressivism, and one faction proposed to nominate La Follette. But when a Communist-controlled party took control of the coalition, La Follette denounced them and stepped out, leaving the coalition to collapse. A second attempt at a coalition came together just one time as the Progressive Party, and in his 1924 run, La Follette won 17% of the popular vote, won his home state of Wisconsin, and came in second in several other states. Since the Civil War, only the third-party performances of Theodore Roosevelt in 1912 and Ross Perot in 1992 have been more successful with popular voting percentages of 27% and 19%, respectively. La Follette remained in Washington until his death on June 20, 1925. The Congressional Reading Room in the Library of Congress is named in his honor.

But Fighting Bob did eventually come back to Madison: his remains lie in Forest Hill Cemetery. A bust of La Follette is on display in the State Capitol rotunda, and the Post Office at 215 Martin Luther King Jr. Blvd. was renamed for him and features a mural of his life and times.

Fighting Bob Fest, a political picnic-cum-powwow for progressives from across the country, is held every September just north of Madison in Baraboo. (www.fightingbobfest.org)

the governorship, Leonard Farwell had moved to Washington, D.C., to work in the U.S. Patent Office. He was present at the Ford Theatre when President Lincoln was assassinated and the first person to warn Vice President Johnson of the possible danger to him as well.

THE GROWTH OF A CITY

In 1894 Madison Parks and Pleasure Drive Association was formed by well-to-do Madisonians, thus beginning an era of beautification and preservation that continues to this day. The city bought Tenney Park in 1896 and built a boat lock (and updated it in 1959) making traffic between the two big lakes easy. The second capitol burnt to the ground in a winter fire in 1904, and construction on the current capitol (third time's a charm) began in 1906. Its completion in 1917 gave the city a glorious building as its centerpiece, and to this day its grandeur and beauty are praised. In 1908 nationally famous landscape architect and city planner John Nolen was hired to give his guidance to healthy city development with a focus on aesthetics and green space.

Industry and commerce continued to grow. Many small businesses came and went, and the old brick buildings and shop fronts can still be seen along State Street and other locations. Bigger businesses found a home in Madison. The French Battery and Carbon Company, better known by the name Rayovac (now part of Spectrum Brands), opened in 1907. A German sausage company, known to all as Oscar Mayer, built a plant in Madison in 1919, eventually moving its headquarters here as well. The plant remains but is now owned by Kraft Foods. By the end of the 1920s, the city had several theaters showing stage acts and moving pictures. Four theaters from that era are still open for entertainment. German immigrants opened breweries such as Hausmann's Capital Brewery as well as Fauerbach's Brewery which survived Prohibition but closed in 1966. (Both Hausmann's and Fauerbach's beers are being brewed again by a regional microbrewery.) Madison seemed the typical prosperous midwestern city, with the usual ups and downs of economy, but generally that nice hardworking down-to-earth kind of place. That is, until the 1960s.

THE VIETNAM WAR

In 1963, Madison was voted the Best City to Live in the USA. Business was up, the university was prosperous. But national politics had set a kettle to brewing. A group of students gathered in October 1963 to protest the presence of U.S. military advisors in Vietnam. The size and volatility of the crowds grew as the war did. In the spring of 1965 protestors were arrested at the airbase in Madison participating in a bit of civil disobedience. When Dow Chemical Company came to campus to recruit professionals from the University of Wisconsin, the event didn't go unnoticed. The company's position as a military contractor and provider of Agent Orange, the controversial defoliant used during the war, made them the focus of the protestors in 1967. In October of that year, the students engaged in a sit-down on campus. Police moved into the crowd. Suddenly, billy clubs were swinging and soon after, the tear gas came out. Sixty-five students were sent to the hospital. A city referendum in 1968 showed that 48% favored a pullout from Vietnam, and the protestors were not about to be silenced. Today's Mifflin Street Block Party was first held in 1969 in defiance of local authorities. When the police arrived and arrests were made, rocks and bottles started to fly, fires were started, and tear gas—a now common scent in the air—clouded the street.

Protests turned their focus on the U.S. Army Math Research Center on campus. By 1969, the protestors had increased efforts of sit-downs and obstruction, and the National Guard was called in. The shooting deaths of four students at Kent State in Ohio by the National Guard in May of 1970, and two more by police several days later at Jackson State University in Mississippi, shocked the nation and sobered protestors, but it was the bombing of Sterling Hall that represented the climax of the violence in Madison. Four protestors wanted to destroy the Army Research Center on the hall's 2nd through 4th floors. At 3:24 a.m. on August 24, 1970, they parked a stolen van full of ammonium nitrate and fuel oil and detonated the payload. While damage was tremendous to surrounding buildings and the physics lab in the hall's basement, the research center was not destroyed. Unknown to the four perpetrators, however, was that postgrad researcher Robert Fassnacht, a husband and father of three, was in the basement finishing up some work. Two of the bombers eventually served prison time for Fassnacht's murder, while one of the four disappeared and has never been heard from again.

The 1979 documentary *The War at Home* captures the intensity of the antiwar movement in Madison, and the film garnered an Oscar nomination. Another documentary *Two Days in October* and the books, *RADS: The 1970 Bombing of the Army Math Research Center at the University of Wisconsin–Madison and Its Aftermath* by Tom Bates and Pulitzer Prize-nominated *They Marched into Sunlight* by David Maraniss, are also good resources.

THE MODERN CITY

From the 1970s on, Madison has seen a lot of changes that transformed it to the first-class city that it is today. Paul Soglin, once one of the student protestors on campus, became mayor from 1973 to 1979 and again from 1989 to 1997. Under Soglin the State Street Mall and Capitol Concourse were developed. Soglin helped improve the public bus system and pushed for a city performing arts center. The Madison Civic Center was completed in 1980. The Monona Terrace Community and Convention Center, a concept put forth by Frank Lloyd Wright before his death in 1959, finally came to be built in 1997, albeit with modifications to Wright's design, and inspired another surge in downtown construction. In 2004, the first phase of the multi-million dollar Overture Center for the Arts opened on State Street, and several years later the State Street Mall and Capitol Concourse received another makeover. Today a stroll downtown shows just how far Madison has come from a marshy isthmus with muddy streets and a rickety capitol with a pig sty in the basement.

GETTING HERE, GETTING AROUND

If any road feels like the gateway to Madison it has to be John Nolen Drive. There is nothing that equals the impact of that first view of the Capitol rising out of the downtown skyline and reflecting off the waters of Lake Monona. The Capitol dome, especially when lit up at night, captures the eye. It seems to draw visitors over the causeway across Monona Bay and along John Nolen Drive's gentle lakeside curve across the isthmus where the Frank Lloyd Wright-inspired Monona Terrace Community and Convention Center seemingly rests on the surface of the lake.

At the center of the city, the Capitol sits atop a glacial hill on the narrow isthmus between Lakes Mendota and Monona and is visible for miles in all directions. The street plan around the Capitol, laid out even before Wisconsin became a state, was based on a European Baroque design similar to the layout for the nation's capital. Streets leave the Capitol Square in eight directions like the points on a compass. The streets that make up the Capitol Square go one-way counter-clockwise around the Capitol itself. The Capitol Loop streets do the same but one block off the Square, like a box around a box.

But for all the beauty and harmony of the city's street plan, the one-way roads, the angled avenues off the corners of the square, and the constrictions of the isthmus can make driving downtown a little tricky for the newly arrived. Throw some road construction in the mix and the real fun begins.

Knowing the general plan is helpful. Washington Avenue is a four-lane divided street leading to the Capitol Loop and Square from east and west. The main thoroughfares through the heart of downtown, bypassing the one-way loops around the Capitol, are Johnson Street and University Avenue/Gorham Street. Johnson is one-way heading east through the University of Wisconsin campus and downtown, while Gorham/University is one-way heading west on a parallel course one block to the north. The streets reconnect and become two-way roads several blocks out of the downtown area in either direction. To the east, Gorham is reabsorbed into Johnson at Baldwin Street. To the west, University and Johnson meet and become Campus Drive which heads past the west end of campus and University Hospital before becoming University Avenue once again. ("Old" University Avenue also continues west off the intersection where Johnson and University become Campus Drive. Confused yet?)

Getting *to* Madison is not nearly as complicated. Madison conveniently sits central to Milwaukee, Minneapolis, and Chicago and is connected to these metropolises by Interstates. The regional airport is an easy way to get in and offers a dozen direct flights and connections into the hubs of the major airlines. Though on a bad day some locals may disagree, the traffic in Madison is nothing like that of major metropolitan areas. Madison enjoys a reputation of being an outdoors city. With over 100 miles of trails, it is definitely a bike-friendly town, and you will even see commuters some winter mornings on mountain bikes pedaling through the previous night's snowfall. The university campus area shows the most pedestrian traffic, and the bus system gets a decent amount of use, but otherwise the automobile dominates. Downtown sees a lot of scooter traffic, so be careful of college students buzzing around between classes.

When it comes to getting around, Madisonians can be a little careless. Offenders represent all categories of travel from four wheels to two feet: inattentive and impatient drivers and transplants who grew up in places that have never seen snow; bicyclists who ride two abreast, hold up traffic, and consider red lights merely a matter of motorized vehicular concern; and pedestrians completely oblivious to Don't Walk signs. And don't forget the three lanes of drivers that may be more concerned with jockeying for rush-hour position through downtown than checking for random college students stepping off the curb somewhere midblock without even checking to see if the way is clear. My advice: Use turn signals. Look both ways. Be patient. Wear a helmet. That goes for bicyclists as well.

BY CAR

Getting to Madison by car is a cinch. Three Interstates converge just at the edge of the city: I-94 east connects Madison to Milwaukee in just over an hour, I-90 heads three hours southeast to Chicago, and both Interstates join and head west to Minneapolis/St. Paul for about a five- to six-hour drive. I-39 follows US 51 and goes straight up the center of the state. Various state highways lead out from Madison in all directions including US 151, which bears northeast toward Oshkosh, the Fox River Valley, and Green Bay, and southwest toward Iowa and the Quad Cities.

> **i** Locals will refer to US 12/14/18/151 as the Beltline from where they begin interweaving from I-90/94 in the east across the belly of Madison and turning northward toward Middleton.

Traffic congestion can be an annoyance on the **Beltline Highway** especially when weather or even a fender bender can lock up one side or the other. Because the isthmus is already a natural bottleneck, the thoroughfares that traverse it—University Avenue, Gorham Street, and Johnson Street—can go slowly around peak hours. Commuters may use one of three Park and Ride lots at Dutch Mill (at US 12/18 and US 51),

North Transfer Point Park and Ride Lot (at Huxley Street and Aberg Avenue), and Sherman Plaza (at Sherman Avenue and Northport Drive). Madison Metro buses serve these.

If there is any branch of law enforcement trying to outdo the others, it has to be the parking police. Parking meters take only quarters and charge a hefty $1.50 (only $1 outside the downtown area) per hour with a limit of two hours. Before 8 a.m. and after 6 p.m. from Monday through Saturday you don't need to feed the meters. Sunday grants you parking amnesty. Two-hour zones are clearly marked and *some* may be exempt on Saturdays, but most are only unenforced on Sunday and city holidays (not always including *federal* holidays). Read the fine print on the signs. Parking is not allowed within 4 feet of a driveway or 15 feet of a painted crosswalk, never mind if the curb is not painted yellow. If you are around for the snow season November 15 to March 15, find out about alternate side parking for plowing purposes. Information about this and all other parking headaches can be found in meticulous detail on the City of Madison Web site at www.cityofmadison.com/parking. Ticket payments can be made online or mailed to the City Treasurer's Office address on the ticket.

Right turns are allowed on red lights unless posted otherwise. Certain sides of the streets, especially on Williamson, Gorham, Johnson, and Regent Streets, are off limits for parking during rush hours depending on the direction of rush-hour traffic. The tow truck is always on time and leaves cars around the corner with sizeable fines.

For the most up-to-date information on road conditions and construction season headaches, contact the Wisconsin Department of Transportation by calling 511 or going to their Web site at www.dot.wisconsin.gov. Madison is no slouch when it comes to tearing up roads, so also check The City of Madison Web site at www.cityofmadison.com/transportation/roadworks.

BY PLANE

Just over 10 minutes from downtown, Madison's highly user-friendly **Dane County Regional Air-**

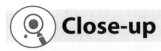

Close-up

Parking Downtown

Residents in the downtown area—often students—must acquire neighborhood stickers from the City of Madison to park on the streets beyond the posted two-hour limits. Visitors can try their luck with meters and two-hour parking or use one of several parking ramps in the area. The Capitol Loop is served well by public parking ramps at the four corners where each of the four streets of the "loop" connect to the next segment. These are prime locations for the Capitol Square as is the Overture Center ramp just over 2 blocks off the square on West Mifflin Street. Twin ramps at the campus end of State Street can be entered from Lake and Frances Streets and are best for State Street and campus visits. During special events some of these Capitol and State Street ramps may charge a single entry fee rather than issue a timed ticket. The Buckeye Lot has metered parking between Gorham and Gilman Streets next to Pizzeria Uno and a few steps north of State Street on Gorham. Campus ramps and lots open to the general public include Southeast Campus Parking Ramp at Johnson and Lake Streets, a small lot next to the Memorial Union, and underground parking at Helen C. White Hall at the end of North Park Street. All of these show parking meters. There are no change machines so be sure to bring quarters.

port, abbreviated MSN, is served by six commercial airlines—American Eagle, Continental Express, Delta Connection, Midwest Connect, Northwest, and United Express—and offers direct, non-stop flights to Atlanta, Chicago–O'Hare, Cincinnati, Cleveland, Dallas–Fort Worth, Denver, Detroit, Memphis, Milwaukee, Minneapolis, New York–LaGuardia, Newark, St. Louis, and Washington, D.C. The single terminal has gates numbered 1 through 13, all with enclosed jetways, except gate 11. Airport services include gift shops, seven restaurants and drink establishments (including a branch of the local brewpub The Great Dane), massage and shoe shine services, an interfaith chapel, and eight car rental agencies. The gift shops have a plethora of quirky Wisconsin souvenirs including cheese curds and University of Wisconsin–Madison apparel.

Long-term parking is available for a low daily fee and is a five- to 10-minute unsheltered walk. A parking ramp is directly across from the terminal for hourly or daily parking. The taxi stand is located at the end of the terminal/drop-off area outside the last door from the baggage claim, past the car rental counters. A Madison Metro bus operates hourly during the weekdays connecting to the North Transfer Station. The bus stop is across from the baggage claim exit on a median island alongside the bus lane. If someone is not at the information booth in baggage claim, the bus schedule should at least be posted there on the counter alongside some area brochures and information.

Chartering a plane might seem like a luxury but depending on needs it can actually be affordable and at the very least, convenient. Wisconsin Aviation has been operating out of Madison since 1994. Their fleet consists of 24 aircraft ranging from single-engine to executive twin-engine jets. They pick up at Dane County Regional Airport but also a variety of other lesser known local airfields. For weekend trips to, say, a Badger game or a girls' getaway, the group rate may actually compare to commercial fares. If you're more of a do-it-yourself person, they also offer flying lessons. Call (800) 594-5359 or visit www .wisconsinaviation.com for quotes.

The closest of the small local fields is Middleton Municipal Airport–Morey Field. Used for civilian purposes, Morey Field sees an average of just over 100 aircraft operations per day. The airport has plane storage and two runways and is located about 5 miles northwest of Middleton.

Flight Delay Advice

Not only do winter storms occasionally delay or cancel flights, but rainstorms or even fog off the lakes may affect flight times. Just because O'Hare, a common connection, is operating without delays does not mean that MSN, a mere 25-minute stretch of airtime away, is not without problems. On occasions when you are stuck in O'Hare and a rescheduled flight looks unlikely, consider the **Van Galder/Coach USA** bus from the airport to Madison. Often airlines will gladly print you a voucher for the three-hour ride, and it may actually be quicker than waiting for the plane.

TAXIS, LIMOUSINES, AND CAR RENTALS

Taxis and Limos

Taxis are about $3.50 for the first 1/8 mile and 30 cents for each additional 1/8 mile, plus 30 cents per 30 seconds when stopped in traffic. At the airport, drivers are not supposed to solicit you, and you do not have to take the first taxi in line. A toll of about $1 applies to taxis picking up or dropping off at the airport.

Union Cab of Madison is a taxi cooperative with over 200 owner-operators. Call (608) 242-2000; www.unioncab.com.

Badger Cab uses a zone system and shared rides. You can actually call or check the Web site for the fixed fare. So it's good for a fair price no matter the route the driver takes, but the shared aspect of pick ups and drop offs along the way might bother some. Call (608) 256-5566; www.badgercab.com.

Madison Taxi is the third alternative. There have been reports by visitors of drivers taking the long way around and trying to rack up a hefty fare. (Yours truly once had this experience.) These are likely not regular occurrences but should be reported. (608) 255-8294; www.madtaxi.com.

If you prefer to arrive in style, rent a limo from one of these services:

AJ Prestige Services, (608) 338-5800; www.ajprestige.com

Gallant Knight Limousine, (608) 242-7000 or (800) 725-5655; www.gallantknightusa.com

Mad City Limo, (608) 235-6196; www.madcitylimo.com

Presidential Limousine Service Ltd., Cambridge, (608) 423-2300; www.preslimousa.com

Sunlife Limousine, (608) 288-1111 or (877) 546-6487; www.sunlifelimo.com

Sunset Limousine Service, Stoughton, (608) 279-5466; www.sunsetlimollc.com

Car Rentals

All major car rental agencies operate in Madison out of the airport. Some have offices in the city as well.

Alamo, (608) 249-1449 or (800) 462-5266

AVIS, (608) 242-2442 or (800) 831-2847

Budget, (608) 249-5544 or (800) 527-0700

Dollar, (608) 661-4941 or (800) 800-4000

Enterprise, (608) 661-4900 or (800) 325-8007

Hertz, (608) 241-3803 or (800) 654-3131

National, (608) 249-1614 or (800) 227-7368

Thrifty, (608) 661-4940 or (800) 847-4389

Community Car

Community Car is an option for residents who prefer not to own a vehicle. Some do go car-less in the Mad City, and this is essentially a car you pay for by the hour and miles. Call (608) 204-0000 or go to www.communitycar.com for fee and membership details.

BY BUS OR TRAIN

Intercity Buses

Despite Greyhound's diminished routes over the years, Madison remains well connected to the outside world with a few other intercity bus lines. The **Madison Bus Depot** is located at 2 South Bedford St., but not all lines stop there. The **Dutch Mill Park and Ride** is a common stop for intercity buses as it is just off the Interstate highways on Madison's east side. Find it on East Broadway one block east of Stoughton Road (US 51) just north of the Beltline (US 12/18). Likewise bypass the depot and start or stop near the bike rack in front of the Memorial Union at the University of Wisconsin at 800 Langdon St. Both non-depot stops are billed as "unsheltered" but you can duck inside the Memorial Union, and Dutch Mill has a small glass bus shelter plus a convenience store just 200 feet away with a clear view of the stop.

Badger Bus runs six round trips daily between Madison and Milwaukee and Milwaukee's Mitchell Airport. All trips depart from the Madison Bus Depot but some start first at the Memorial Union. Call (608) 255-6771 or go to www.badgerbusonline.com.

Coach USA/Van Galder connects Madison with Janesville, WI; South Beloit, IL; and Chicago at O'Hare or Midway Airports or downtown. Tickets can be purchased on the bus. University students should check with student services about student tickets. The terminal stop in Madison is at the Memorial Union, but the bus also stops at the Dutch Mill Park and Ride. Call (608) 752-5407 or (800) 747-0994 or go to www.coachusa.com.

Greyhound Buses connect Madison into their nationwide system primarily via Milwaukee, Chicago, and Minneapolis. There are a variety of routes that may stop in various other Wisconsin cities but they are not always the shortest distance between two points. Consider Wausau, WI, in the north by way of Milwaukee and Green Bay. Still it is good to know that if you need to get to, say, Wisconsin Dells, Tomah, or Eau Claire, you may have an option. Greyhound departs from the Madison Bus Depot only. Call (608) 257-3050 or go to www.greyhound.com.

Jefferson Lines, based out of Minneapolis, MN, serves a variety of smaller communities in Wisconsin, Minnesota, Iowa, and other western states. They no longer depart from Madison but they may connect with Greyhound to reach smaller communities. Visit them at www.jefferson lines.com.

MegaBus runs to Minneapolis and Chicago, but sometimes arrivals are in the wee hours. The farther in advance you order tickets, the cheaper the price. For information call (877) 462-6342 or go to www.megabus.com.

Trains

Madison has no direct train service. The closest **Amtrak** stop (800-872-7245, www.amtrak.com) is in Columbus, WI, 28 miles northwest of Madison. **Amtrak Thruway** bus service connects to the bus stop in front of the Memorial Union and the Dutch Mill Park and Ride. The Union Pacific Northwest Line of **Metra** (815-943-5244; www.metrarail.com) heading into Chicago can be met just over the Wisconsin border in Harvard, IL, a 74-mile drive from Madison. This is a good park and ride alternative for day trips to the Windy City.

Madison Metro Buses

For a city of just over 200,000, Madison's public bus system isn't too bad, but is most effective during commute times. Destinations far from the city center often require a transfer at one of four transfer stations (north, east, south, or west). A majority of the lines pass through the Capitol Square except during special events such as a street festival or a marathon. In these cases, they usually follow the square one street farther out from the Capitol. Buses run from 6 a.m. to midnight on weekdays and from 7 a.m. to 11 p.m. on weekends and holidays.

Bus frequency can be an issue. Buses often pass just once an hour except on certain routes in peak hours, but they do generally run on time and will not depart a stop before the scheduled time. Be aware that weekday schedules change on weekends and holidays, and a few routes don't even run on those days.

Have the exact fare ready because drivers do not make change. Buses numbered in the 80s are free and run routes most useful for the university campus. Multiride, monthly, student, and other passes are available online or at sales outlets. One-day unlimited passes can be purchased on the bus where you will also find route maps and schedules. If you are commuting and don't want to drive downtown, Metro buses serve area Park-and-Ride lots at the edges of the city (see "By Car" above).

Buses can "kneel" for special-needs passengers and all are equipped with front-end bike carriers (video instructions are on the Web site). Call (608) 266-4466 or go to www.cityofmadison .com/metro for more information.

BY BICYCLE

Several city streets have designated bike lanes, especially in the campus and downtown area. Several nicely paved bike paths serve commuters. The **Capital City Trail** on the east side and the **Southwest Path** are two of the most popular and useful (and plowed in the winter). Designated off-road bike paths are shared public spaces, so be on the alert for other users. For more information about bicycling, consult the Recreation chapter on page 139.

BY CANOE OR KAYAK

Really? Since 1997, the June public-awareness program **Take a Stake in the Lakes Days** has sponsored Paddle to Work Day. Find out more about this at www.takeastakeinthelakes.com and in the Recreation chapter on page 139.

ACCOMMODATIONS

Madison is a funny place when it comes to lodging. At first look it seems to offer a whole world of accommodations from budget hotels to luxury properties with a hostel and several excellent bed-and-breakfast options as well. How could all these places ever fill up at once? Yet they do. On Badger football game weekends, during the various conventions, expos, and other special events, as well as on parents' weekends or during student arrival/departure periods at the University of Wisconsin, the city can book solid. Special annual events such as the Ironman Triathlon or Art Fair on the Square often fill up the hotels closest to downtown. Hotel rates may also spike during these special events.

The University of Wisconsin provides some housing. Much of it is reserved for visiting academicians or other guests of the university, but a couple options are available for alumni and parents or even the general public. Madison also has its own hostel in a prime location right off the Capitol Square and an RV park at the end of the chapter.

For a hometown sort of feel to your stay in Madison, definitely consider the bed-and-breakfast option. All of those listed here really have great charm and character and offer high quality. Business travelers are also welcome.

This chapter first lists the hostel, the University of Wisconsin options, and the bed-and-breakfast properties. After those listings, the hotels are arranged by location: Downtown/Campus, East Side (which includes Monona), South Side (which includes Fitchburg), and West Side (which includes Middleton). Travelers visiting the university will probably want to stay downtown, though to be honest nothing is more than about 15 minutes from the center of the city in any direction. Parking can be an issue downtown so be sure what your hotel's options are. The west and east sides of Madison show the bulk of all the big chains and the extended stay hotels. Many of the eastside hotels often bill themselves as "airport" but really aren't any more convenient to that location than downtown. The areas around both east and west side locations are often filled with shopping centers and franchise restaurants most travelers know by name, and only hotels lacking nearby restaurant options are noted.

The south side hotels near the **Alliant Energy Center** are a short drive from downtown and offer easy access to the Beltline and thus the east and west sides of the city. Though this may be perfect for concerts and expos, there is little else in the way of attractions, and without a car, visitors who stay here will rely on a hotel's shuttle, if there is one, or taxis. Farther south a couple more miles along Fish Hatchery Road is neighboring Fitchburg with some properties as well as local dining. These remain less than 15 minutes from the Capitol.

Many hotels have airport shuttles, but be clear on where they go and at what times during the day. Some shuttles advertise for a 7 a.m. start, for example, while the earliest flights out of Madison are before that time. Other shuttles serve more than just the airport. Don't get the runaround: when taking a taxi from the airport, the drive to downtown should not involve any kind of major highway and is about 10–15 minutes. Even to the far west side, the fare should come in around $35 for a ride of less than 25 minutes.

As of July 10, 2010, all hotel rooms are non-smoking in the state of Wisconsin.

Locals refer to the intertwining US 12, 14, 18, and 151 as the Beltline. From I-90 in the east it crosses along Madison's south side before curving north and heading up to Middleton. The various numbered highways join and depart the four-lane divided highway throughout its length starting with 12 and 18 in the east and finishing with 12 and 14 in the west.

Price Code

The following price codes are based on a regular room with double occupancy and reflect basic room rates ("rack rates") during the peak season. Prices here do not include local sales and room taxes, tips, service charges, or other additional fees.

$	Under $70
$$	$70 to $99
$$$	$100 to $149
$$$$	$150 to $199
$$$$$	more than $199

HOSTELS

MADISON HOSTEL $
141 South Butler St.
(608) 441-0144
www.madisonhostel.org
An old Victorian house has been converted to the city's only hostel. Affiliated with Hostelling International, the property enjoys a prime location just a couple blocks off the Capitol Square and under a 10-minute walk to State Street. The interiors are painted with vibrant assorted colors. Eight rooms hold 29 beds. Three of the rooms are dormitory-style with six beds each. One private room has four twins, two rooms have a full-size bed and a twin, and two more rooms have just one full-size bed. There are five bathrooms in the hostel: one private male bathroom, one dorm-style female bathroom, a unisex toilet, and private baths in rooms three and four. The hostel is a shoes-off environment and guests leave their shoes at the door. Slippers or flip-flops are a good idea to bring along. A common room offers a TV and VCR with a selection of videos, a computer with Internet connection, and some very small individual

lockers for valuables. A modest library of mostly guidebooks is in the back corner along with brochures about other Hostelling International locations and various area maps. Wireless Internet is free and available throughout the house. A shared kitchen on the 2nd floor contains a stove, refrigerator, microwave, and a dining table. Dishes and cooking equipment are all stocked. Guests are required to wash their own dishes. Towels and bedding are included in the rate and there is coin-op laundry on site.

The front door is locked after 9 p.m., and hostel guests must use a numbered code, which changes daily, to enter. Quiet hours are enforced from 11 p.m. to 7 a.m. No alcohol is allowed on the premises. Some parking is available for a daily fee, and the office also has a map of the neighborhood indicating where the cheap or free parking areas are. **Café Costa Rica** is located in the lower level and sometimes offers breakfast deals for hostel guests. Guests do not have to be members of Hostelling International to stay here but will pay a nominal daily fee of about $3. Stays are limited to up to 10 nights per month, but in off-season (winter) long-term stays might be arranged. This is not wheelchair accessible and pets are not allowed. The hostel fills quickly during major Madison events such as the Ironman Triathlon.

THE UNIVERSITY OF WISCONSIN

THE LOWELL CENTER $$
610 Langdon St.
(608) 256-2621
http://conferencing.uwex.edu/lodging.cfm
The center provides lodging for guests in town for business with the university such as conferences or presentations. But University of Wisconsin alumni and parents of students can also stay here. Guest rooms total 81 and are furnished with either two European double beds or one queen-size bed. Amenities include coffeemakers, hair dryers, irons and ironing boards, TVs, telephones, work areas, and high-speed Internet access as well as WiFi signal. The rooms are in nice shape, and the facilities include an indoor swimming

pool, sauna, and fitness room. Continental breakfast and parking (one car per room) are included in the rates. The rates may go up during special events such as football weekends or commencement. This is a very short walk to State Street and to the Memorial Union and other campus buildings. Wheelchair accessible.

WISCONSIN UNION GUEST ROOMS $$
Memorial Union
800 Langdon St.
(608) 265-3000
www.union.wisc.edu

It's not exactly five-star luxury, but the beloved Memorial Union is both a convenient place to be and perhaps a thrill for those who are fascinated with the historical building. On the 4th floor are six guest rooms: two standards, three lake view rooms, and one suite. The standards have a double or single bed and a sleeper sofa, while the lake view rooms offer two double beds. The suite has two rooms, one with a queen-size bed and another with two doubles. All rooms have private baths with showers and hair dryers. Rooms have phones and TVs, and guests receive a parking permit.

These rooms book up fast for football games or other special events, and the environment here can be loud and busy, especially in the summer when there are weddings and the Terrace hosts live music. Check-in is on the 1st floor at the Essentials desk. Union members and current UW students can book at a discounted rate. No pets are allowed. There is wheelchair accessibility. Checks are not accepted. Make reservations by phone.

i The University's New Union South at 227 North Randall Ave. will have many more hotel rooms and more formal service when it opens in 2011.

BED-AND-BREAKFASTS

ANNIE'S GARDEN BED
AND BREAKFAST $$$$$
2117 Sheridan Dr.
(608) 244-2224
www.anniesinmadison.com

The "garden" part of the name is not just affectation. This rustic Craftsman-style house built in the 1960s is surrounded by lovely flowers, herbs, and trees and features a gazebo, a stone terrace, and a pond full of lilies and goldfish. Annie and Larry Stuart have been in this business since 1985 and have perfected the B&B experience. This is about as private as it can get. Accommodations consist of one full suite on the 3rd floor. The master bedroom offers a queen-size bed and there is a second, smaller room which can be used as an additional bedroom for families, with a double bed and its own full bath. Room amenities include a TV, VCR, private phone, radio and alarm clock, bathrobes, refrigerator, iron and ironing board, and hair dryer. The large library connected by balcony to the suite is loaded with books and music. Although the building is air-conditioned, the entire house, with its abundant large windows, opens up in the summer for great cross breezes. A two-person whirlpool and stone fireplace are on the lower level, as is a DVD surround-sound theater with its own refrigerator and microwave, as well as a selection of about 300 DVDs. The dining room ceiling is two stories up, and the balcony overlooks the space and its crystal chandelier.

A full breakfast is included and guests choose the time between 7 and 10 a.m. These meals are tailor-made according to a previsit interview and so vegetarians and others with special meal requests are accommodated. Snacks are available on request often in the form of Wisconsin cheese and crackers. Fresh coffee and a wide variety of teas are also on demand, and in summer lemonade and iced tea are the norm.

Just behind the property lies the 225-acre Warner Park with its half mile of public lakeshore and walking/biking paths. The inn is not far from Governor's Mansion or Governor's Island or the urban garden at Troy Gardens. July's Olbrich Home Garden Tour includes a stop at Annie's. A shed on site is perfect for storage for guests with bicycles, and in winter snowshoeing and cross-country skiing can be enjoyed at nearby Warner Park. Small weddings (think about 20 or fewer people) can be hosted. Children over

10 are allowed if well behaved. There is a two-night minimum stay but there are also deals on extended stays. No pets are allowed. The owners have a cat and a dog but they are not allowed into guest rooms. This property is Certified Green for Travel Wisconsin and is also on the National Wildlife Federation Habitat list. Birders can enjoy the terrace and the visitors to the many hand-made feeders and houses. Annie's is a 10-minute drive to both the airport and the Capitol Square. Parking is off street and lighted. This is not wheelchair accessible. Bookings are by telephone only and though there is an answering machine, it is best to call around dinnertime.

ARBOR HOUSE, AN
ENVIRONMENTAL INN $$$–$$$$
3402 Monroe St.
(608) 238-2981
www.arbor-house.com

Old meets new in this historic building with its eco-designed annex. Originally the Plough Inn, this was a tavern and stagecoach stop as far back as 1853 when it would have been a good distance from the residential area of Madison. In 1996 the innkeepers built an annex using everything from organic and recycled building materials to energy efficient appliances garnering the inn notoriety for its sustainability and eco-savvy in a wide variety of publications. An arbor connects the two structures passing through a small garden with a small goldfish-filled pond and fountain. The original inn structure is on the National Register of Historic Homes, and nothing of the rowdy rough and tumble tavern atmosphere remains. Accommodations total seven rooms and a two-room studio popular with families. All rooms have their own unique character and features vary with claw-foot tubs for two, stone showers, stone fireplaces, whirlpool tubs, balconies, antiques, and queen- or king-size beds. Hair dryers, irons and ironing boards, and phones with voice mail are in all rooms and most have TVs. All rooms have private baths and one guest room is wheelchair accessible.

A common-area service kitchen has a refrigerator for keeping farmers' market goodies and a microwave for leftovers or perhaps popcorn. The library holds books and movies, and a fireplace makes the sitting room cozy in winter. Full breakfast is served on the weekend, often incorporating ingredients from the inn's on-site gardens, and a continental breakfast is served during weekdays. Organic and fairly traded and locally roasted coffee is served, and the varying menu can include anything from poached eggs Florentine to zucchini-potato pancakes. Hot and herbal iced tea is on the house. A special evening beverage hour serves drinks and appetizers.

A computer and fax machine are available for guests. Wireless signal is complimentary and available throughout the property. Corporate rates are offered during the week and meeting space is also on hand. A dry sauna is on-site. Guests have free use of the inn's mountain bikes and receive a coupon for one free hour of canoe or kayak rental at the nearby Wingra Park on Lake Wingra. The small northern section of the University of Wisconsin Arboretum is right across the street offering nice strolls through woods and marsh right in the heart of the city. Arbor House is certified by Travel Green Wisconsin. The inn is less than 10 minutes from Camp Randall Stadium and the university campus and half that from Edgewood College. The Beltline (US 12/14/18/151) is just five minutes away. No pets are allowed and children are accepted under special consideration. A staff sitter gives the adult guests a break from the kids. Cash or checks are preferred but major credit cards are accepted. The owners take the environmental mission seriously, but the hospitality is also tops. E-mail inquiries are fine, but bookings are by phone only as this is a highly personalized experience and even the menu is adapted to guest preferences and needs.

GILMAN STREET RAG BED
AND BREAKFAST $$–$$$
125 East Gilman St.
(608) 257-6560
www.hawkhill.com/gilmanbb.html

This lovely 1885 Queen Anne Victorian home is another Mansion Hill beauty and has been an inn since 1997, operated by Jane Denny. Two rooms and a full apartment are available as accommo-dations. The two rooms share a bathroom and at just around $100 each per night, they make a nice family option. One room has a double bed and the other has two twins and either of them can be rented for a bit extra to make the bath-room private. (The other room remains empty.) The rooms have an assortment of books and artwork, tables with chairs, and flat-screen TVs. A continental breakfast is included in the room rate.

The 3rd-floor unit is a complete apartment, windows on four sides of the house. The bed-room has a queen bed and a balcony with a table, chairs and umbrella, and a nice view of the Capitol. A turret room features a small library. The kitchen has all supplies needed to fend for oneself including a stove and full-size refrigera-tor, so breakfast is not included. A futon couch in the living room folds out into an extra bed. The dining room has a table and four chairs and there are two flat-screen TVs in the apartment. WiFi is complimentary to all guests and bicycles are available as well. The wraparound porch is a perch any time of day. The apartment rents for about $600 for a weekend plus $100 for each additional night. The minimum stay for that unit is four nights. Pets are welcome as are children. Free off-street parking is a blessing in such a downtown location. Not wheelchair accessible.

HOTEL RUBY MARIE BED
AND BREAKFAST $$$
524 East Wilson St.
(608) 327-7829 or (877) 690-7829
www.rubymarie.com
Originally a railroad hotel in the early-1870s, this 15-room hotel located just a few blocks from the Capitol is part of a treasured little histori-cal neighborhood that includes Essen House, a German restaurant. The interiors have preserved the original woodwork. An elevator takes guests up to the 2nd-floor lobby from the parking lot behind the building. Up North Saloon shares the 1st floor with a German-themed gift shop and The Lakeview Bakery which is open weekdays. Rooms are decorated with a Victorian theme and come in three categories, all of which have

private baths. The best are the Premiums with king beds, Jacuzzis, and fireplaces. All rooms have coffeemakers, TVs, refrigerators, CD clock radios, and include complimentary sodas, juices, beer, and snacks as well as free parking. Wire-less high-speed Internet connection reaches all the rooms. Street noise might bother some but a few of those same rooms offer a view of the lake beyond the busy intersection. A small inner courtyard deck makes a secluded sitting area. The hotel location is just four blocks from the Capitol Square and all the restaurants and bars that area has to offer. Lake Monona and its lakeshore path are across the street. Willy (Williamson) Street begins here heading east as well. Corporate rates are available. Weekends included a bigger break-fast at the Essen Haus or Come Back In next door. Pets are not allowed, but guests can take bikes in the room. Some wheelchair accessibility.

MANSION HILL INN $$$$$
424 North Pinckney St.
(608) 255-0172 or (800) 798-9070
www.mansionhillinn.com
Mansion Hill is where Madison's wealthiest lived in the late 19th century, and though many of the houses here have been converted to student housing, the exteriors still show much of the grace and grandeur of what was known as Big Bug Hill. This Four-Diamond boutique hotel was the first residence there, built in 1857 by Alexan-der McDonnell, the contractor who was building the second Capitol at the same time. Built of Prairie du Chien sandstone, the German Roman-esque Revival house still shows much of the fine detail in the stone and wrought-iron balcony rail-ing. From the turn of the century until the 1930s it was run as a high-class boarding house by Carrie Pierce and then just apartments during the decades that followed. From 1983 it has been a reputable hotel, and in 2008 it was purchased by Trek Bicycles and Trek Hospitality and given more restoration and amenity upgrades.

Guests have their pick of 10 rooms in the four-story structure, each in its own distinct style but all showing period antique furniture with king- or queen-size beds and large flat-screen

TVs. Kohler products give the bathroom modern elegance with rainshower heads (some double) or whirlpool tubs. Turndown service includes some Gail Ambrosius chocolates (see Shopping page 98). A mahogany spiral staircase leads up to a belvedere with a view of the Capitol. The two downstairs parlors are classy without being stuffy and each has a fireplace. One of them also has a small bar with a nice wine list and four local beers on tap plus a few snack plates. Continental breakfast is served with pastries from Marigold Kitchen (see Restaurants–Breakfast Joints page 47). No pets are allowed and children must be at least 13 to stay here. Complimentary WiFi is available as are Trek bikes for exploring downtown Madison. The building is security locked and a staff person is on site 24 hours a day. Staff is not just accommodating but also extremely knowledgeable about area attractions and events and can arrange reservations and tickets for guests. Valet parking and a couple of on-site spots serve guests with cars and the inn has no airport shuttle. This is not wheelchair accessible due to rules regarding modification of historical sites, but ground-floor rooms are certainly doable with a little help.

SPECKLED HEN INN $$$–$$$$
5525 Portage Rd.
(608) 244-9368 or (877) 670-4844
www.speckledheninn.com

Innkeepers Patricia and Robert Fischbeck opened their home to guests in 2000. The house has an English country style to it with elegant interiors but not a stuffy atmosphere. The 50-acre property lies just outside the city but close to the airport and features pastures with sheep and llamas, wetland and grassland areas with walking trails, streams, evergreen plantations, orchards, and gardens. It is not uncommon to see deer, turkeys, and pheasants in the yard, and the birdfeeders, gazebo, and the surrounding hillside oak and hickory woods make this a great birding site. Three rooms feature king-size beds and one has a queen. All rooms have private baths with tubs and separate showers and include amenities such as TVs with DVD players, cotton sheets

and down comforters, an iron and ironing board, bathrobes, and hair dryers. Three rooms have their own fireplaces. The large gathering room houses a piano, wood-burning stove, a home theater, and a library. Wireless Internet signal is available throughout.

A multi-course breakfast with a creative menu is served in the dining room often by candlelight. Many of the ingredients come from the property itself including the eggs and organic fruits and vegetables. The scones should not be missed. Special food requests are taken before guest arrival and a guest pantry has snacks such as popcorn. Snacks and beverages are served in the afternoon and coffee, tea, soft drinks, and hot chocolate are complimentary. Over a dozen wines on hand are available by the bottle or the glass. The airport is just a 10-minute drive away and downtown is about 15 minutes. This property is not wheelchair accessible and kids must be over 12 years old. The inn is certified by Travel Green Wisconsin. Parking is on-site. Reservations are taken by phone or on the Web site.

HOTELS

Downtown/Campus

BEST WESTERN INN ON THE PARK $$$$
22 South Carroll St.
(608) 285-8000
www.innonthepark.net

If not for this hotel building, the state capital may have moved elsewhere. Opened in 1871 to keep Madison as the star on the map when others suggested moving it to Milwaukee, this structure has undergone its share of upgrades. Located right on the Capitol Square, walking distance to State Street and the University of Wisconsin, this 215-room hotel is a safe but ordinary bet, and its status as the only hotel on the square is its justification for the steep pricing. Suites and standard rooms come with king, queen, or twin beds, as well as coffeemakers, irons and ironing boards, blackout curtains, alarm clocks, phones, and large TVs. Suites add a minifridge and a seating area. Extra occupants incur a nominal charge.

Continental breakfast is lacking but a restaurant and bar serve food all day. Service is solid but the interiors are just ordinary. Shuttles connect to the airport and, based on availability and sign up, to the university campus. Free wireless Internet is available throughout the building and DSL can be had in the rooms. Guests without laptops can use the small computer room. Valet parking is included for one car for each room. A swimming pool, whirlpool, and small fitness room are on-site. Several rooms are wheelchair accessible, but pets are not allowed. Guests on the 9th floor need to take the elevator to the 8th floor and then switch to another as the 9th floor was previously a more exclusive arrangement. Ask for rooms with a Capitol view.

BEST WESTERN INNTOWNER $$$$
2424 University Ave.
(608) 233-8778 or (800) 258-8321
www.inntowner.com

Located just minutes from Camp Randall Stadium (about an 8-block walk) near the west end of the university campus, this hotel is long established with campus and University Hospital visitors and football weekenders. Occupying four floors, these 176 rooms are divided into traditional rooms, suites, and 46 luxury rooms on the Highland Club level. Rooms are spacious and clean but nothing fancy. The prices reflect the prime location, though downtown properties are better for walking to local attractions. Beds are kings or two queens and room amenities include coffeemakers, irons and ironing boards, hair dryers, telephones with voice mail and free local calls up to 30 minutes, alarm clock radios, and free wireless Internet. Suites add a sitting room, another TV, dining table and chairs, a sleeper-sofa and a kitchenette with a microwave and a full-size refrigerator. Highland Club rooms are even more comfortable with pillow-top mattresses, duvets, 32" LCD TVs, stereo CD clock radios with MP3 capability, and in-room refrigerators. Highland Club guests also get fresh-baked cookies with turndown service, and have access to a private lounge with complimentary continental breakfast, evening cocktails, and hors d'oeuvres as well as concierge service. All

guests have access to free airport and downtown area shuttles. A small fitness center is on-site as is a standard indoor swimming pool and hot tub. A restaurant and lounge are inside the hotel, but options west toward Hilldale Mall, south along Monroe Street, or downtown to the east are much better. No pets allowed. Children under 12 stay free with one paying adult and no extra bed. Free off-street parking. From downtown heading west, University Avenue splits to the left at the west end of the university campus where Campus Drive splits right. The hotel is about one mile down University Avenue from this point. Wheelchair accessible rooms are available.

DAHLMANN CAMPUS INN AND
CHANCELLOR'S CLUB $$$$
601 Langdon St.
(800) 589-6285
www.thecampusinn.com

This hotel was built in the 1960s and operated at Madison Inn until 1999 when the current owners took over and set about upgrading the entire production. What used to be a motel drive-through arrival now is a swanky lobby showing marble, woodwork, and oriental rugs. These rooms are the most luxurious you can find right next to campus and arguably in the entire city. The seven-floor tower provides 74 rooms from standards to suites. Dahlmann Hotels has two other upscale boutique hotels in Ann Arbor, MI. Standards come with two queens or a king bed, desks, 27" TVs, two two-line speaker phones, clothing steamers, and cozy bathrooms with marble surfaces, hair dryers, and combination baths with massage showerheads. Daily newspapers (*USA Today* or others on request) are delivered to rooms each morning.

Parlor suites are more spacious with larger sitting areas and also add DVD players with complimentary movies. Regent suites take another step up with granite-topped wet bars with refrigerators, full-size sofas, and dining tables. The presidential and governor's suites outdo them all with separate bedrooms and whirlpool tubs, nicer furnishings, full-size refrigerators, and an extra bathroom with a separate vanity area.

Guests can request local gourmet chocolates, a cheese basket, champagne, or a bottle of Wisconsin's Wollersheim Winery Prairie Fumé when booking rooms online. Internet is complimentary and offered via WiFi and DSL throughout the property.

The Chancellor's Club, which is open to all guests, serves complimentary continental breakfast and hosts an evening reception with complimentary hors d'oeuvres, delicious desserts, and coffee or tea. Cocktails, soups, and panini sandwiches and breakfast sandwiches are available for purchase. There is no pool but the fitness center has a treadmill, weight machine, free weights, stationary bike, a TV, and water cooler. Parlor suites on the north side of the hotel and corner kings have the best views of Lake Mendota. Rooms 4th floor or above and facing east see the Capitol. Kids stay free and cribs are available. Extra guests incur extra charges. Complimentary taxi transportation to and from the airport can be arranged for all guests. Parking is free in an underground garage with a few outside spaces as well. Pets are not allowed, and wheelchair accessible rooms are offered. This is just a stone's throw from the campus Memorial Union and State Street, and about a 10-minute walk from the Capitol.

DOUBLETREE HOTEL $$$$$
525 West Johnson St.
(608) 251-5511
http://doubletree1.hilton.com

Located right at the curve on Johnson Street as it passes through the heart of downtown, this hotel is a reliable choice both for quality and proximity to the university campus and downtown. Everything is walkable and the Kohl Center is just a couple blocks away. Rooms are spacious and come with one king, two double, or two queen beds as well as 27" flat-screen TVs, work desks, irons and ironing boards, hair dryers, lighted vanity mirrors, in-room safes, and Wolfgang Puck coffeemakers. High-speed wireless Internet is complimentary as are printing services, a plus for the business traveler. Suites add turndown service and large sitting rooms separated from bedrooms by double doors and furnished with sofas,

tables, small refrigerators, microwaves, complimentary bottled water, and snacks. A heated indoor pool and whirlpool are standard, and the fitness center is medium-size with the usual exercise and weight machines, a TV, and water cooler. Business center provides computer and Internet access as well as free printing services. Copies and faxes can be made at a charge. The casual Badgerland Bar and Grill serves breakfast, lunch, and dinner daily as well as drinks from a full bar. Room service is also available, but a huge variety of restaurants is just a few blocks away on State Street or up around the Capitol Square. A free shuttle service serves the airport, the university campus, Alliant Energy Center, and downtown hospitals. Wheelchair accessible rooms are available. No pets are allowed. A warm chocolate-chip cookie at check-in is a nice touch. Prices are a bit high but better deals can be had with advance purchase online.

THE EDGEWATER HOTEL $$$
666 Wisconsin Ave.
(608) 256-9071
www.theedgewater.com

With all the lakes Madison has, it is hard to believe this is the only place to stay lakeside. With views across Lake Mendota toward the University, they couldn't have picked a better spot. Right down Wisconsin Avenue from the Capitol, the Edgewater opened in 1948 and added its east wing in 1973 bringing its room total to 107. Despite the reputation with big-name guests, the rooms—though comfortable, clean, and orderly—are not overly stylish. These range from singles and doubles with lake views to two-bedroom suites. DSL Internet is available in the rooms, while WiFi can be had in the lobby area. Rooms have iPod ports with speakers, coffeemakers, very small tube TVs, irons with ironing boards, and desks and armchairs. Junior suites add sitting areas and some of those add minifridges and microwaves in kitchenettes. Beds are kings or queens. Bathrooms are basic and rather small, but come with hair dryers. Turndown service comes with bottled spring water, an ice refill, and the next day's weather forecast and events.

Free coffee is served in the lobby and *USA Today* is delivered to rooms on weekdays. Free parking is on the 4th floor though the garage is actually down the sloping driveway from Wisconsin Avenue. This is one of the few hotels where the 7th floor is actually the lowest one in the building as the 5th, 6th, and 7th floors descend to the waterline and the rooms here have the lake views. The elevator serving rooms on the 1st through 3rd floors in the cream-brick east wing is located to the right of the reception desk.

An outdoor pier allows boaters to stop in for a meal or a drink but does not allow overnight mooring without special permission. The pier makes a great place for a sunset cocktail. The Cove bar and lounge is indoors and serves the fine-dining restaurant, the Admiralty Room. All three locations have their own menus and room service is available. Along the Cove's walls are photos of the many famous guests who have stayed at the Edgewater. The impressive litany of names includes Elvis Presley and Mahatma Gandhi. Live piano music is featured on Fri and Sat evenings and during Sun brunch. A band plays on the pier on Thurs nights in the summer.

A business center has a computer connected to the Internet and a printer, while the fitness center includes a rowing machine, Stairmaster, treadmills, bikes, and a TV. Five function rooms are on site and the Oasis Day Spa pampers guests and non-guests alike. There is no pool or sauna. Complimentary airport transfers are provided either by van or limousine. Pets are allowed and in fact, a pet bed or feeding dish can be provided as well as a welcome gift bag—for your pet. Ten rooms are wheelchair accessible.

HILTON MADISON
MONONA TERRACE $$$$
9 East Wilson St.
(608) 255-5100
www1.hilton.com

Boasting arguably one of the finest hotel views in town, the Hilton is just two blocks from the Capitol Square and connected by a skywalk to the Frank Lloyd Wright-inspired Monona Terrace Community and Convention Center. The AAA Three-Diamond hotel offers 240 rooms with Hilton Serenity Beds: one king bed or two doubles. Suites have separate sitting areas and come with one king bed. The interiors are contemporary wood furnishings and all rooms come with work desks, coffeemakers, alarm clock radios, 27" TVs, irons and ironing boards, and hair dryers. The views are either of the Capitol or Lake Monona. The best lake views over the neighboring Monona Terrace Convention Center are on the 4th floor or above. High-speed Internet is available but for a daily charge. A step up are the Executive rooms which add bathrobes, high-speed Internet, additional bath amenities, and a continental breakfast served in a lounge on the 14th floor. Wheelchair accessible rooms come with one king or two double beds.

The Capitol ChopHouse serves lunch and dinner daily and specializes in 28-day aged beef and locally grown ingredients. Vegetarian options are also available and an outdoor terrace opens in warm seasons. Dress is business casual and the restaurant is closed on Sun. The Breakfast by Hilton buffet is available daily in the Olive lounge and the coffee is from Starbucks. The lounge opens after 4 p.m., serves a dinner menu, and offers a full bar. The wine list has consistently garnered awards from *Wine Spectator*. Room service runs round the clock. Several nice restaurants around the Capitol Square are just a short walk away. The indoor pool is heated and a whirlpool adjoins it. The fitness center offers Precor equipment. The business center has two computers connected to the Internet and a printer. There is complimentary valet parking available in the evenings but parking has a daily fee with in-and-out privileges. The parking ramp is a tight squeeze for its two-way traffic; drive carefully. Complimentary airport transportation runs to and from the airport. Pets are allowed.

THE MADISON CONCOURSE HOTEL $$$$
1 West Dayton St.
(800) 356 8293
www.concoursehotel.com

It says something of the spirit of Madison that what is perhaps the city's finest hotel is not affiliated with a franchise. Located just off the Capitol Square and a 10-minute walk from the University of Wisconsin, the 13-floor, 356-room luxury hotel has been around since the 1970s. Some floors may be in the midst of upgrades. Beds are kings or two queens and feature Comfort Collection bedding with 300-thread-count sheets. Room amenities include coffeemakers, alarm clocks, irons with ironing boards, and complimentary wireless Internet. Large, interactive flat-screen TVs provide DIRECTV sports, digital music, movies, games, and video check-out. Most bathrooms are shower only (some have tubs as well) and come with hair dryers. Rooms on the upper floors of the street side of the hotel offer views of Lake Mendota, while the back side of the hotel looks up to the Capitol dome. Standard rooms are on a rotation for upgrades, however, the unrenovated floors remain comparable with other properties. The 100 upscale Governor's Club rooms, completely renovated in 2009, have sharp contemporary appeal with 42" flat-screen TVs, granite-top furniture, refrigerators, and spacious bathrooms with walk-in showers. They also add whirlpool tubs or Jacuzzis and include a continental breakfast in the private lounge.

The view of the Capitol from the club lounge is priceless and the full bar offers hors d'oeuvres in the evening. The hotel restaurant, Dayton Street Grille, serves all meals and is run by Charles Lazzareschi, a celebrated local chef. A full bar serves drinks daily, and its lounge features live music, typically jazz, on weekends and often once during the week. On-site facilities include an indoor swimming pool, Jacuzzi, and sauna. The fitness center looks through glass to the pool and offers the latest exercise equipment with personal TVs as well as free weights. There's no spa on-site but the hotel offers packages for Cameo Day Spa and Salon nearby (608-284-1956; www.cameospasalon.com). The business center in the lobby has two computers, three printers, and Internet access. Wireless Internet and remote printing are available throughout the property. A free shuttle whisks guests to and from the airport and a kiosk in the lobby allows guests to print boarding passes. Rooms with wheelchair acces-

sibility are available. Parking is under the hotel for a nightly fee. Pets are not allowed.

THE UNIVERSITY INN $–$$
441 North Francis St.
(608) 285-8040
www.universityinnmadison.com

The big draw for this 45-room hotel is its location directly on State Street, just a few minutes' walk from either the University of Wisconsin campus, the Kohl Center, or the Capitol Square. The current owners took over in the late 1970s and at one time this was a Best Western. Though it has been upgraded since that decade, the decor is dated and drab. The aging carpeted rooms are furnished with minifridges a bit larger than normal, as well as tube TVs, phones, alarm clocks, irons with ironing boards, and either double or king-size beds. Some rooms connect. The bathrooms are very small and come with hair dryers. Corner rooms are a bit bigger. State Street–side rooms may suffer from some street noise especially around bar closing time, and guests concerned about that sort of thing should request the parking lot side. Complimentary fresh coffee is available in the lobby which opens out to the parking lot and the end of Francis Street, which is a couple dozen steps from State Street. Visiting professors and conventiongoers often use this for convenience sake, and during sports weekends it is nearly always filled to capacity. Some guests make reservations six months in advance according to Big Ten football or basketball schedules. Parking is free as is WiFi throughout the hotel, and a computer in the lobby serves those who don't travel with laptops. Don't expect any frills here, but for a place to crash at the end of a great day in Madison, this does the trick. Not wheelchair accessible and no pets allowed.

East Side

BAYMONT INN AND SUITES
MADISON EAST $
4202 East Towne Blvd.
(608) 241-3861
www.baymontmadison.com

Located just in front of East Towne Mall right off of East Washington Avenue, Baymont represents an economical option just a short drive from downtown and a couple minutes from I-90/94. Rooms have one or two double beds or a queen or king bed. All rooms have cable TVs, telephones with free local calls, coffeemakers, clocks, irons and ironing boards, and hair dryers. Some rooms also have microwaves and refrigerators or whirlpools. A guest Laundromat is on-site as is a small fitness center, but there is no pool. Complimentary wireless Internet is available throughout the property. The continental breakfast is complimentary and for something more substantial a Denny's Restaurant is next door. Other franchise restaurants are nearby as well. The hotel accepts pets up to 25 pounds, but previously that was only in smoking rooms. With the statewide smoking ban in effect, it would be wise to double-check. Parking is ample. There is no elevator.

BEST WESTERN EAST TOWNE SUITES $$
4801 Annamark Dr.
(608) 244-2020
www.madisoneasthotel.com

This is a basic economical motel with a heated indoor swimming pool and a small fitness center located just off East Washington Avenue/US 151 just southwest of the juncture with I-90/94. Rooms come with king- or queen-size beds, TVs, work desks, microwaves, refrigerators, coffeemakers, telephones with free local calls, irons and ironing boards, complimentary bottled water, and hair dryers. Wireless and wired Internet are complimentary. A breakfast buffet with a few hot items is also included. A business center is on-site as is a 24-hour convenience store. Pets are allowed for a fee. The complimentary airport shuttle requires a booking at least 24 hours in advance. Wheelchair accessible rooms are available.

CAMBRIA SUITES $$$
5045 Eastpark Blvd.
(608) 241-7070
www.cambriasuites.com

Opened in 2009, this 121-suite hotel is located northeast of the city center off US 151 at the American Parkway exit just beyond the I-39/90/94 interchange, about a 15-minute drive from both the airport or the Capitol. Lounge seating in the lobby atrium makes for a good casual meeting space and a large flat-screen TV pipes in the latest news and weather. The levels of suites are generally based on bed size: king suites, two-queen-bed suites. Tower suites are corner room king suites that offer floor-to-ceiling windows with better light and views. There are also four double-king suites that are the most spacious. All beds have pillow-top mattresses.

Standard room amenities include two flat-screen LCD TVs, a plug-and-play MediaHub, MP3 players, game consoles and digital cameras, microwaves, refrigerators, coffeemakers with Wolfgang Puck coffee, and an iron and ironing board. DVD players are available at the front desk for complimentary use. Bathrooms are stylish with European sinks and vanities, Bath and Body Works amenities, hair dryers, and combination baths with adjustable showerheads. Speaker phones include voice mail and free local calls. Cribs can be requested at no cost while rollaway beds incur a small daily fee. The *Wall Street Journal* is delivered to rooms in the morning and *USA Today* is also available. Guests can use coin-op laundry facilities or dry-cleaning service can be arranged.

The casual Reflect Dining Area serves a nice breakfast buffet plus an a la carte menu, and then reopens for dinner with a standard American menu of soups, sandwiches, salads, pasta dishes, and pizzas. During breakfast coffee is free. No staff is on hand for the lunch hour, but an assortment of grab-and-go items from frozen entries to organic snacks are for sale. A bar opens in the evenings and a barista bar is open 24 hours for caffeine fixes (Wolfgang Puck coffee) and other light snacks. A sundry shop is open 24 hours a day, seven days a week. The indoor heated pool and whirlpool are open 24 hours as is the fitness center which features state-of-the-art equipment including treadmills, elliptical machines, free weights, exercise bikes, yoga mats, core training, and a TV and water cooler. A business center has two computers with Internet, fax, copy, and printing capabilities. A plus for the business traveler: free printing and faxing. The free wireless high-speed Internet and remote printing are usable throughout the hotel. No pets are allowed. Free airport transfers are available throughout the day. Parking is free in a lighted lot on the property. Wheelchair accessible rooms are available.

COMFORT INN AND SUITES $$$
4822 East Washington Ave.
(608) 244-6265
www.comfortinn.com

Located just off the junction of I-90/94 and East Washington Avenue/US 151, Comfort Inn offers a convenient location at a reasonable price with quality service. Beds are one king, one queen, or two doubles. Amenities include TVs with pay-per-view movies, telephones with free local calls, coffeemakers, irons and ironing boards, and hair dryers. Some rooms offer whirlpools. There is an adequate heated indoor swimming pool and whirlpool as well as a small fitness center. High-speed wireless Internet is complimentary as is a continental breakfast. A free shuttle runs to the airport. Guest laundry is on-site and wheelchair accessible rooms are available. Pets are not allowed. Management is accommodating and service-oriented.

COUNTRY INN & SUITES MONONA $$
400 River Plaza, Monona
(608) 221-0055
www.countryinns.com

Right off the Beltline Highway at the Monona Drive exit, this hotel could just as easily pass as "south side." Rooms come with king or queen beds and include cable TVs, telephones with free local calls, coffeemakers, irons and ironing boards, and hair dryers. A small swimming pool, whirlpool, exercise room, and business center are on-site. Breakfast and Internet service are included in the rates. Pets are allowed. Wheelchair accessible rooms are offered.

COURTYARD BY MARRIOTT $$$
2502 Crossroads Dr.
(608) 661-8100
www.marriott.com

Situated to the east of I-90/94 in a somewhat tricky location, the Courtyard offers fine Marriott quality for a mid-range price. Staff is polite and helpful while furnishings are stylish. Room amenities include a large work desk, flat-screen TVs with premium channels, pay-per-view movies and video games, minirefrigerators, coffeemakers, two phones with voice mail and speaker phone options, irons with ironing boards, and hair dryers. Wired and wireless high-speed Internet is included in the rates. Suites add microwaves. Beds are kings or two queens, and some rooms add whirlpools or sofa beds. Bathrooms are spacious. Courtyard Café serves a breakfast buffet and the lobby lounge serves drinks in the evening. The hotel has a business center as well as fitness center, an indoor pool, and a whirlpool. Wheelchair accessible rooms are available. Pets are not allowed. The location requires a car as there are no other attractions, shopping, or restaurants nearby, but otherwise this is a well maintained property with good service.

CROWNE PLAZA EAST TOWNE $$$
4402 East Washington Ave.
(608) 244-4703
www.ichotelsgroup.com

This six-floor, 226-room hotel is clearly visible from East Washington Avenue, right across from East Towne Mall. Thus it is a stone's throw from the I-90/94 ramps and about a 15-minute straight shot from downtown. The hotel, renovated in 2009, has a solid reputation for good service and clean comfortable rooms. Beds are one king or two doubles. Room amenities include TVs with video games, CD players, two telephones with voice mail, coffeemakers, morning papers delivered to the room, irons and ironing boards, and hair dryers. Executive rooms and suites come with refrigerators and suites add microwaves. Wireless Internet is included but the Web browser for the TV incurs a fee. A pleasant heated indoor swimming pool and whirlpool offer recreation options. Guests can use the 24-hour fitness center or obtain a pass to a nearby gym for a small fee. The Prairie Café just off the lobby serves a breakfast buffet. Growlers Bar and Grille serves dinner with local beers on tap, a decent wine list, and a surprise of organic menu items. Kids eat for free. Starbucks coffee is served in the lobby each morning. A business center and guest laundry services are also on-site. A free shuttle heads to the airport. Wheelchair accessible rooms are offered. Pets are allowed for a fee and receive a check-in treat. They are not, however, allowed in suites or Concierge level rooms.

DAYS INN $–$$
4402 East Broadway Service Rd.
(608) 223-1800
www.daysinn.com

The 64 rooms in this economical hotel are on three floors with an elevator. Rooms come with one king or one or two queen beds. Suites are also available. Amenities include cable TVs with HBO, telephones, coffeemakers, irons and ironing boards, and hair dryers. Some rooms have microwaves and refrigerators or two-person whirlpools, and business rooms add laptop-size safes. Internet connection and continental breakfast are both complimentary. A business center, a small indoor pool, a whirlpool, and a small fitness center are all on-site. Pets allowed for a fee. Wheelchair accessible rooms are offered. This hotel is 2.5 miles east on the Beltline Highway from the Alliant Energy Center and just off US 51/ Stoughton Road.

ECONO LODGE $–$$
4726 East Washington Ave.
(608) 241-4171
www.econolodge.com

Renovated in 2008, this facility remains a low-cost, no-frills option with unexciting decor in a convenient location among higher priced options. Ninety-nine rooms are spread throughout two floors with indoor halls. The location is on the north side of East Washington Avenue on the frontage road portion of East Washington just before the I-39/90/94 interchange and

across from the East Towne Mall area. Rooms are moderate in size and of the basic hotel/motel variety. Beds are kings or two doubles. Kids under 12 stay for free and extra guests are $10 and can get rollaway beds. Cribs are also available. Free wireless and DSL Internet is offered in the rooms and copy and fax services are available at the front desk. Coffeemakers, alarm clock radios, telephones with free local calls, hair dryers, large TVs, refrigerators, and microwaves are standard. Some rooms have irons and ironing boards or they are available on request. The in-room safes incur a daily charge. There's a nominal charge for up to two pets. Continental breakfast is complimentary, coffee is served around the clock, and a variety of franchise restaurants are nearby for other meals. A computer in the lobby can get guests online. Wheelchair accessible rooms are available on the 1st floor. There is no elevator to the 2nd floor. Downtown is less than a 15-minute drive straight down East Washington Avenue to the Capitol. Parking is free on-site.

FAIRFIELD INN & SUITES
BY MARRIOTT $$$
2702 Crossroads Dr.
(608) 661-2700
www.fairfieldinnmadisoneast.com

Opened in 2009, this is Fairfield's east side option. The hotel's 99 rooms and 31 suites are on four floors. Beds are kings or two queens and some rooms offer sofa beds. Room amenities include TVs with premium channels, pay-per view movies and video game consoles for rent, telephones with free local calls, coffeemakers, irons and ironing boards, and hair dryers. A heated indoor pool, whirlpool, and fitness center are on-site. Breakfast is complimentary and coffee is served in the lobby all day. A business center is here and wireless Internet is free and available throughout the property. Free parking is plentiful on-site and a complimentary shuttle runs to the airport. Wheelchair accessible rooms are available. Pets are not allowed. The location on the east side of I-90/94 can be slightly tricky to find and also offers little within walking distance.

GRANDSTAY RESIDENTIAL SUITES $$
5317 High Crossing Blvd.
(608) 241-2500
www.grandstaymadison.com

Located just off I-90/94 and US 151/East Washington Avenue, the three-floor, 53-suite hotel is convenient to downtown. This is a reasonably priced option for long (or short) stays that won't offer the luxury of the bigger places, but a realistic option for families or business travelers who don't need too many frills. The suites come in studios, one- and two-bedroom options, and all have fully equipped kitchenettes with full-size refrigerators, stovetops, microwaves, and dishwashers. Amenities include flat-screen TVs with cable, DVD players, free wired and wireless Internet, telephones with two lines, voice mail and free local calls, irons and ironing boards, and hair dryers. An outdoor grill area is a nice plus. The recreational facilities are modest with a kiddie-size swimming pool, whirlpool, and small fitness center, but there is also an outdoor sporting area with basketball court, putting green, and a swing set. A complimentary continental breakfast is served in the lobby area where there is also a small convenience store. Wheelchair accessible rooms are available. Pets are allowed.

HAMPTON INN MADISON EAST $$$
4820 Hayes Rd.
(608) 244-9400
www.madisoneast.hamptoninn.com

This 115-room inn, located off East Washington Avenue on the northside frontage road right before the I-39/90/94 interchange, is popular with business travelers. Its last renovation in 2007 gives it some nice modern appeal. Sleeping comfort is premium and the hotel offers its own line of beds: Cloud Nine–The Hampton Bed Experience with a choice of feather or foam pillows. Beds are kings or two double beds and rollaway beds can be requested for no extra charge. Rooms show dark wood furnishings, white duvets in the beds, and work desks. Lap-desks are included for those who take work to bed with them. Basic cable on flat-screen TVs includes HBO channels. All rooms come with alarm clock radios, coffeemakers, irons and ironing boards, and hair dryers. The bathrooms show tubs with WaterPik showerheads and curved shower rods for more room and light. *USA Today* is delivered free to rooms on weekdays. WiFi Internet is free throughout the property. One double-bed room is wheelchair accessible.

There is no restaurant on-site, but Pizzeria Uno is available for room delivery. Hot breakfast is included in the room rate and typically includes sausage patties, scrambled eggs, French toast sticks, and endless coffee as well as fruit and juice. Complimentary coffee and fruit is out all day and on most weekdays there are also cookies. An "On the run breakfast bag," available on weekday mornings, caters to those in a rush with bottled water, a muffin, an apple, mints, and a breakfast bar. The unstaffed business center offers two computers with Internet and a printer, and copy and fax services can be had at the front desk. A small fitness center and an indoor pool and whirlpool are also on-site. Cribs and high chairs are available for families. This hotel has no airport shuttle. Service is sharp and accommodating. The location is just under 15 minutes to the airport or Capitol and downtown, and a quick hop onto the Interstate. No pets are allowed. Parking is free in the surrounding lighted lot.

ℹ From hotels on Hayes Road it is only possible to turn right (west) on East Washington Avenue from the first entry from the frontage road. Better to continue on the frontage road to the next intersection with traffic lights if you want to go left (east) to get back on I-90/94 or US 151.

HOLIDAY INN MADISON AT
THE AMERICAN CENTER $$$
5109 West Terrace Dr.
(608) 249-4220
www.holidayinn.com

Located north of East Washington Avenue/US 151 just beyond the I-39/90/94 interchange, about a 15-minute drive from both the airport or the Capitol, this a shining example of how nice a Holiday Inn can be while maintaining a reasonable price. Four floors count 139 rooms only four of which are suites. Accommodations are clean and spacious, beds are comfortable, and double-glazed windows keep the noise out. All rooms come with work desks, coffeemakers, safes, irons and ironing boards, hair dryers, and 32" flat-screen HD TVs with in-room movies and video games on demand. Video check-out is also possible. Each room has two phones with voice mail and free local calls, and complimentary high-speed Internet comes via DSL and WiFi. Executive club level rooms add a minifridge, while the suites add that plus a microwave and a sofa bed in the sitting room. Free morning papers are delivered to rooms.

The hotel restaurant, Geier's Grill, serves breakfast and dinner from an American cuisine menu, while Chief's Lounge opens nightly for cocktails. Kids under 12 eat free breakfast. There is no lunch venue. The fitness center is up-to-date with elliptical, stationary bikes, treadmills, some free weights, and a core ball, and each station has its own TV. The free-form, island-themed indoor pool is kid-friendly and a hot tub with a waterfall is nearby. A convenience store and newsstand are also on-site. Complimentary WiFi is available throughout the property. An unstaffed business center provides two computers with Internet connection, a printer, and photocopy and fax services. Same day dry-cleaning is available as are coin-op laundry facilities. Cribs and connecting rooms can be requested. No pets allowed and guests must be at least 21 for check-in. The adjacent parking lot is free and lighted at night. Eight rooms are wheelchair accessible. A complimentary 24-hour shuttle runs to destinations within a 5-mile radius and the airport. Service gets high marks here, and its location at the edge of town offers quick highway access to the other side of Madison and a short, direct drive to the city center.

HOWARD JOHNSON PLAZA $$
3841 East Washington Ave.
(608) 244-2481
www.hojo.com
Just about 10 minutes from the airport and the same to downtown along Washington Avenue,

the hotel has a better location than some might figure from a map. This is a budget option and offers the basics for an overnight stay. Service and housekeeping are inconsistent. Rooms come with one or two double beds as well as cable TVs, desks, clock radios, two telephones, arm chairs, coffeemakers, irons and ironing boards, safes, and hair dryers. There is a heated indoor swimming pool, a small exercise room, and a large game room on-site. A free shuttle runs to the airport. Pets are allowed for a small fee. A parking lot is adjacent. Wheelchair accessible rooms are available.

LA QUINTA INN AND SUITES MADISON AMERICAN CENTER $$
5217 East Terrace Dr.
(608) 245-0123
www.lq.com
The 120 units in this reliable chain hotel are all suites. The location, just off US 151 at the American Parkway interchange and not far from I-90/94, is not close to much of anything but just a 15-minute drive from downtown. All rooms come with cable TVs, microwaves, telephones with voice mail and free local calls, coffeemakers, irons with ironing boards, alarm clocks, and hair dryers. Free wireless Internet is available throughout the property. The heated indoor swimming pool is nice and there's a small fitness center. A continental breakfast is included and guest laundry facilities are on-site. Wheelchair accessible rooms are available. Pets are accepted.

MAGNUSON GRAND HOTEL MADISON $$
3510 Millpond Rd.
(608) 224-1500
www.magnusonhotels.com
Formerly the Wingate Inn, this hotel had a declining reputation. Initial reports since the name change suggest a change of direction. The inn is right next to Yahara Hill Golf Course and just a few miles north of Dejope Gaming. The location is outside the city, east of I-90 and just off US 12/18 so to get anywhere at all will require driving. All rooms come with sofa beds, TVs with premium channels, telephones with free local

calls, coffeemakers, irons and ironing boards, hair dryers, microwaves, and small refrigerators. Some rooms offer whirlpools. Breakfast and wireless Internet are complimentary. On-site are a heated indoor swimming pool, whirlpool, and small fitness center as well as a business center. A weekday happy hour offers free drinks and popcorn. Pets allowed for a fee. Wheelchair accessible rooms are offered.

MICROTEL INN & SUITES $
2139 East Springs Dr.
(608) 242-9000
www.microtelinn.com

Another budget option, the Microtel offers a good value for short stays. Rooms come with one or two queen beds. Amenities include TVs with expanded cable and pay-per-view movies, telephones with free local and long distance calls, coffeemakers, irons with ironing boards, clock radios, and hair dryers. Jacuzzi suites are available as are rooms with refrigerators. Wireless Internet service is complimentary. Guests received a free continental breakfast, and there is a small business center in the lobby. Wheelchair accessible rooms are offered. Pets are allowed. The location is tucked in behind East Towne Mall, and so the property may be slightly hard to find the first time but close to the Interstate and only 15 minutes to downtown.

RED ROOF INN $–$$
4830 Hayes Rd.
(608) 241-1787
www.redroof.com

This motel franchise is a consistent bet for economical prices and basic, comfortable lodging. The location here is close to the Interstate—both for access and potential highway noise—and about 15 minutes from the Capitol and the university beyond. The 108 rooms are on two floors and there is no elevator. Rooms offer two full-size beds or one king. Free coffee and newspapers are in the lobby. All rooms come with telephones with voice mail and free local calls, work desks, clock radios, hair dryers, and cable TV with in-room movies and video games (for a fee). Wire-

less Internet service is included in some rates. Other room amenities can vary with the rate and bed size so it is important to clarify what you are getting when you book. Wheelchair accessible rooms are available. Pets are allowed.

RESIDENCE INN BY MARRIOTT EAST $$$
4862 Hayes Rd.
(608) 244-5047
www.marriott.com

Studio versions of these 66 suites start at 500 square feet and get bigger with one- and two-bedroom options. The inn has three floors with an elevator. Each room has a fully equipped kitchen with stovetop, microwave, refrigerator, and dishwasher, and a grocery shopping service is offered. Some rooms have fireplaces. Other amenities include flat-screen TVs with premium channels, two telephones with two-lines, free local calls, voice mail and a speaker phone option, irons and ironing boards, and hair dryers. Beds are kings or queens and sofa beds are also included. Complimentary breakfast is included, and a manager's reception serves a few light food items evenings from Tues through Thurs. High-speed Internet access is also free and a full-service business center is on-site. The property has a heated indoor pool, whirlpool, and a small fitness center as well as a 24-hour convenience shop. Wheelchair accessible rooms are offered. Pets are allowed for a fee. The hotel is located via a frontage road off East Washington Avenue/US 151 not far from the juncture with I-90/94.

RODEWAY INN SOUTH $
4916 East Broadway
(608) 222-5501
www.rodewayinn.com

Consider this a sort of last resort. Rooms are basic and in need of updates/maintenance. On Badger game weekends this may be an option. Beds are one king or two doubles and room amenities include coffeemakers, irons and ironing boards, telephones, TVs, and hair dryers. Some rooms add refrigerators, microwaves, and sofa beds. Breakfast is free as is Internet connection. There is a heated indoor pool, hot tub, and a small fitness center. Pets allowed for a fee. Wheelchair accessible rooms are available. The location is just east of US 51/Stoughton Road just a quick hop off of the Beltline Highway so less than 3 miles from the Alliant Energy Center and about 20 minutes from downtown.

SELECT INN $
4845 Hayes Rd.
(608) 249-1815
www.vistarez.com

This budget hotel is part of the Hayes Road neighborhood of lodging and has standard, clean rooms without frills. Rooms come with large cable TVs, refrigerators, microwaves, coffee pots, clock radios, and hair dryers. Family Suites add futons while one-bedroom apartments provide full kitchens and a separate living room and are aimed at long-stay guests. Wireless Internet is included, and guests without a computer can use one with Internet connection in the lobby. A hot tub is open around the clock, and some exercise equipment is there as well. Continental breakfast is included in the rates. Complimentary tea and coffee are available at all times in the lobby. Pets are allowed for a fee. One room is fully wheelchair accessible while others have some accessible features. Perkins Restaurant is right next door for those looking for a bigger breakfast.

SLEEP INN AND SUITES $$
4802 Tradewinds Pkwy.
(608) 221-8100
www.sleepinn.com

Located south of the Beltline Highway at the Stoughton Road/US 51 exit, this hotel is reached from the first intersection south toward McFarland. Beds offered are one king or two queens. Rooms come with TVs with pay-per-view movies, telephones with voice mail and free local calls, microwaves, refrigerators, coffeemakers, irons with ironing boards, and hair dryers. Some rooms offer two-person sofa beds and suites come with whirlpools. Breakfast and wireless Internet are included in the rates. On the property are an indoor heated pool, a whirlpool, an exercise room, and a video arcade. A small business center has a computer with an Internet connection. Pets are allowed for a fee. Wheelchair accessible rooms are offered.

STAYBRIDGE SUITES–
MADISON EAST $$–$$$
3301 City View Dr.
(608) 241-2300
www.staybridge.com

Located just east of I-90/94, Staybridge offers 90 suites with the comforts of a small apartment. Rooms are quiet with double-glazed windows that can be opened. Beds are either kings or queens in studios or one- or two-bedroom suites. Amenities include a kitchenette with microwave and dishwasher, TVs with premium channels, two telephones with two lines, voice mail and free local calls, iron and ironing board, and a hair dryer. An expanded continental breakfast is included, and an evening reception Tues through Thurs serves free drinks and appetizers. A heated indoor swimming pool, whirlpool, and a 24-hour fitness center are all on-site. Other facilities include a library with books and board games, an outdoor basketball hoop, and a barbecue area by the pool. A small business center is unstaffed. A free airport shuttle is offered but with at least 24 hours notice. Pets allowed for a hefty fee. Wheelchair accessible rooms are available. There isn't much to do in the neighborhood but East Towne Mall, restaurants, and shopping are on the other side of the Interstate, and downtown is about a 15-minute drive straight down Washington Avenue.

SUPER 8 MOTEL EAST $
4765 Hayes Rd.
(608) 249-5300
www.super8madisoneast.com

Expect an economical motel experience: cheap, nothing too fancy, and clean. Some rooms open to the outdoors in true motel fashion while others can be reached by interior halls. Rooms come with a king, a queen, or two double beds and amenities include cable TVs with premium channels and pay-per-view options, telephones with free local and long-distance calls, coffeemakers, irons and ironing boards, hair dryers, and work spaces. Microwaves and refrigerators are in some rooms at an extra charge. Internet connection is complimentary and a small business center is on-site. A free, simple breakfast buffet is included. There is a heated outdoor pool and guest laundry facilities. Passes are available to use the indoor pool, sauna, and exercise equipment at nearby Princeton Health Club. A shuttle to the airport is by request only and incurs a fee. Wheelchair accessible rooms are available. Ample parking is on the property. Pets are allowed with manager approval.

South Side

AMERICINN LODGE AND SUITES
OF MADISON SOUTH $$
101 West Broadway, Monona
(608) 222-8601 or (800) 396-5007
www.americinn.com

The location, just off the Beltline Highway near Monona Drive, puts the hotel outside the downtown and Alliant Energy Center areas, but the proximity to the highway grants quick access to both. The John Nolen Drive exit for the center and a five-minute drive to downtown is only about 2 miles west and the far west side is only about another 10-minute drive (depending on traffic of course). The property itself is clean and modern, a good economical choice with 61 rooms and four suites (three of those are two-bedroom). Beds are a king or two queens. Room amenities include two-line telephones with free local calls and voice mail, clock radios, coffeemakers, hair dryers, irons and ironing boards, microwaves, mini-refrigerators, easy chairs, and work desks. DVD players are available from the front desk. Cable and wireless Internet are included and newspapers are delivered to the rooms. Suites offer fireplaces or whirlpools. Breakfast offers cereals, pastries, bagels, biscuits and gravy, waffles, juice, and coffee and is included in the rates. A heated indoor pool and sauna are on property as is a business center. Guest laundry and an ATM are also here. Children under 12 stay free. Wheelchair accessible rooms are offered.

Restaurants up Monona Drive are close by and downtown is only 15 minutes away.

CANDLEWOOD SUITES $$–$$$
5421 Caddis Bend, Fitchburg
(608) 271-3400
www.candlewoodsuites.com

This extended-stay hotel offers studio or one-bedroom suites with fully equipped kitchens. Rooms come with one king or two queen beds, TVs with in-room movies, DVD players, irons and ironing boards, two speaker phones with voice mail and free local calls, and hair dryers. Facilities on-site include a swimming pool, hot tub, fitness center, business center, and guest laundry. Pets are allowed for a fee. Wheelchair accessible rooms are available. A complimentary shuttle serves the airport and any other destination within a 5-mile radius. Some underground parking is available otherwise the lighted lot is ample. Located a few minutes south of the Beltline Highway along Fish Hatchery Road, the suites are walking distance to a couple of good restaurants including Liliana's and the Great Dane Brewpub.

CLARION SUITES CENTRAL $$$
2110 Rimrock Rd.
(608) 284-1234
www.clarionhotel.com

Right next to the Exhibition Hall at the Alliant Energy Center this is a perfect location for those in town for events there. Downtown and the Monona Terrace Community and Convention Center are less than 10 minutes away along John Nolen Drive by car, and the on-ramp for the Beltline Highway US 12/18 is just a couple blocks the other direction. The 140 suites operate as a comfortable home base and all provide kitchenettes. They come in three levels: studio suites, one-bedroom suites, and executive suites. All suites include microwaves, refrigerators, desks, phones with voice mail, DVD players, coffeemakers, irons and ironing boards, and hair dryers. Beds are one or two queens. Two-room suites add two-person sofa beds. Heat registers and air-conditioning are attached to the walls beneath the windows. Rooms are blandly decorated but clean and comfortable, and all the little complimentary extras make a big difference. A complimentary hot breakfast buffet is served daily, including Belgian waffles. A manager's reception is free each evening. Wireless and wired Internet is free and available throughout the property. Newspapers are delivered to the rooms on weekdays and in-room telephones offer free local calls. Airport transfer is complimentary, and free parking is in the adjacent lighted lot. A heated indoor pool and hot tub are on-site and there are a business center and fitness room. Coin-op laundry facilities are available. Up to two pets are allowed per room with a somewhat hefty nightly fee.

HOLIDAY INN EXPRESS $$$
722 John Nolen Dr.
(608) 255-7400 or (800) 345-8082
www.hiexpress.com

Another reliable option on the south side, this four-floor hotel offers 92 rooms. For guests with cars, the location is convenient, just off the Beltline Highway at the John Nolen Drive exit and minutes from the Capitol and downtown. The Alliant Energy Center is just across the road and the more upscale Sheraton is next door but arguably not as nice a deal. Beds are kings or two queens. Rooms come with satellite TV, work desks, coffeemakers, microwaves, refrigerators, two phones with voice mail and free local calls, irons and ironing boards, and hair dryers. Cribs can be requested. The continental breakfast is complimentary, but there are no restaurants on site and few nearby. A heated indoor swimming pool and hot tub are here as well as a small exercise room. Wireless Internet is included and available throughout and a business center offers a computer and Internet connection. Fax and copy services are also offered. Ample free lighted parking. An airport shuttle is available at a charge. Wheelchair accessible rooms are available. One pet up to 25 pounds is allowed for a fee.

QUALITY INN & SUITES $$$
2969 Cahill Main, Fitchburg
(608) 274-7200
www.qualityinn.com

Located south of the Beltline Highway off of Fish Hatchery Road, the hotel has a fine reputation for quality and service. Rooms come with one king or two queen beds, cable TV, telephones with free local calls, clock radios, irons and ironing boards, coffeemakers, and hair dryers. Some rooms also offer sofa beds, microwaves, refrigerators, and whirlpools. Some bathrooms are shower-only. Breakfast is included as is high-speed Internet. Tuscany Mediterranean Grille restaurant and lounge opens for lunch and dinner. Facilities include a game room, business center, heated indoor pool, whirlpool, and an exercise room. A free shuttle runs to and from the airport. Pets are allowed for a fee.

SHERATON HOTEL $$$–$$$$
706 John Nolen Dr.
(608) 251-2300
www.sheratonmadison.com

The location of this 239-room hotel is ideal for the Alliant Energy Center right across the street, plus downtown is mere minutes away on John Nolen Drive if you have a car. Otherwise there is not much in the neighborhood other than a nice park and the city bike/walking path. Beltline Highway access is within sight and so access to the east and west sides of Madison is also a cinch. Rooms are spacious and come with Sheraton Sweet Sleeper beds. Amenities include phones, large flat-screen TVs, irons and ironing boards, hair dryers, single-cup coffeemakers with Starbucks coffee, and work spaces, but there are no refrigerators. Internet is available for a fee but is free in the lobby. The on-site fitness center also requires a fee. Club Level rooms offer some freebies including fitness center and Club lounge access. The indoor heated pool is nice for kids. Heartland Grill opens for all meals daily with an American menu. Harvest Lounge is open for lunch and dinner on weekends and from the afternoon until late on weekdays serving sandwiches, entrees, and drinks with a big-screen TV setting. Level 1 Coffee Bar opens early and offers Danishes, muffins, and fruits besides coffee to stay or to go. Wheelchair accessible rooms are available and an elevator serves the eight floors. Pets allowed for a fee. A free shuttle takes guests to several places around town. Watch for Internet offers which bring this hotel price way down among the economical properties in slower seasons.

SUPER 8 MOTEL $
1602 West Beltline Hwy. 12/18
(608) 258-8882
www.super8madison.com

This 88-room Super 8 offers the expected economical motel experience: cheap, nothing too fancy, and clean. The southside location is right off the Beltline Highway making the east and west sides of Madison easy to get to by highway. Also not far away is Fish Hatchery Road which heads north a couple miles to Park Street which connects into downtown and the University of Wisconsin. The Alliant Energy Center is only 2 miles away as well at the Rimrock Road exit off the Beltline. Rooms come with a king or one or two queen beds and amenities include cable TVs with premium channels and pay-per-view options, coffeemakers, refrigerators, irons and ironing boards, hair dryers, and work spaces. Internet connection is complimentary and a business center is on-site. A free, simple breakfast buffet is included. There is a heated indoor pool and hot tub, and also a fitness center and guest laundry facilities. Kids 17 and under stay for free with adults. A shuttle to the airport has a fee. Wheelchair accessible rooms are available. Ample parking is on the property.

West Side

AMERICINN OF MADISON WEST $$
516 Grand Canyon Dr.
(608) 662-1990
www.americinn.com

A few minutes from the West Beltline Highway at Gammon Road, this former Hampton Inn is a good westside location and now part of a reliable franchise for a clean, up-to-date, economical choice. Rooms total 121 and beds are kings or two queens with pillow-top mattresses. Room amenities include two-line telephones with free local calls and voice mail, clock radios, coffee-

makers, hair dryers, irons and ironing boards, microwaves, mini-refrigerators, and work desks. Cable and wireless Internet are included and newspapers are delivered to the rooms. The complimentary breakfast offers hot and cold choices, from eggs and waffles to cereals, pastries, and bagels, plus juice and coffee. The reception from 5 to 7 p.m. each day offers Wisconsin's own Spotted Cow beer, wine, popcorn, and other snacks. A heated indoor pool and a hot tub with a nice patio area are on property as is a small business center. Children under 16 stay free. Wheelchair accessible rooms are offered. West Towne Mall and several strip malls and restaurants are nearby. Getting downtown takes about 15 minutes via the Beltline to Park Street or John Nolen Drive or just following Odana Road east to Monroe Street. Pets are allowed for a fee. A complimentary shuttle to companies within a 5-mile radius serves business travelers.

BAYMONT INN AND SUITES $–$$
8102 Excelsior Dr.
(608) 831-7711
www.baymontinns.com

Not far off the Beltline Highway at the Old Sauk Road exit and just south of Middleton, this 128-room hotel offers a great value for budget travelers. Some rooms have a pool view. Beds are a king or two doubles with options for a standard room or suite. Amenities include cable TV with premium channels, telephone with free local calls, coffeemaker with coffee, iron and ironing board, and hair dryer. *USA Today* is delivered to rooms weekday mornings and high-speed wireless Internet is included in the rates. The complimentary morning breakfast includes waffles, eggs, and French toast as well as the typical continental items. In the evening the Old Sauk Lounge opens and offers a complimentary drink for overnight guests. A heated indoor pool, whirlpool, sauna, exercise room, and game room are all on-site, and the business center consists of a computer in the lobby area with a printer. Laundry facilities are available. Guests who want to avoid steps should book a 1st-floor room as there is no elevator. Customer service is excellent.

A free airport shuttle operates from 7:30 a.m. to 9:30 p.m. A variety of chain restaurants are nearby as are several shopping areas. Children under 18 stay free with parents. Pets are allowed. Wheelchair accessible rooms are available.

COMFORT SUITES $$$
1253 John Q. Hammons Dr.
(608) 836-3033
www.comfortsuites.com

Just west of the Beltline Highway at the Greenway Cross exit just before Middleton, this AAA 3 Diamond hotel offers 95 suites on three floors. The hotel is quiet and clean, and management and staff are very attentive to guest needs. Beds are kings or two doubles, and in the larger suites, two kings. Room amenities include TVs with premium channels, microwaves, refrigerators, telephones with free local calls, irons with ironing boards, and hair dryers. Internet service is also included. Some suites have whirlpools. Facilities include a heated indoor pool and hot tub, a small fitness center, and a game room. The on-site Duffy's Pub and Wine Bar serves a free cocktail hour Mon through Sat and some hot snacks. The free continental breakfast includes some hot items as well. Copy and fax services are available, and pets are allowed. A free shuttle runs to and from the airport daily. Greenway Station is a short walk away with several chain restaurants and shopping. From the next exit north on the Beltline Highway, take University Avenue east to get downtown in about 15 minutes. Wheelchair accessible rooms are offered.

COUNTRY INN & SUITES MADISON $$
6275 Nesbitt Rd.
(608) 270-1900
www.countryinns.com

Located a few miles south of the Beltline Highway off Verona Road near County Road PD, the hotel is really on the southwest part of the city and close to Verona. Rooms are spacious, with king or queen beds, and offer cable TV, telephones, microwave ovens, refrigerators, coffeemakers, irons and ironing boards, and hair dryers. Breakfast and Internet service are included. Suites

are available. Facilities include a heated indoor swimming pool with basketball hoops and a children's play area, a large whirlpool, an exercise room, and a business center. Nothing much is in the area, so driving to downtown or other locations will be necessary and takes around 15 minutes. Wheelchair accessible rooms are available.

COURTYARD BY MARRIOTT
MADISON WEST–MIDDLETON $$$
2266 Deming Way, Middleton
(608) 203-0100
www.marriott.com

Located just north of US 14/University Avenue on the west side of the Beltline Highway where it enters Middleton, this four-floor hotel offers 129 rooms and seven suites and offers a good mid-range value. Room amenities include a large work desk, flat-screen TVs with premium channels, mini-refrigerators, coffeemakers, two phones with voice mail and speaker phone options, irons with ironing boards, and hair dryers. Wired and wireless high-speed Internet are included in the rates. Suites add microwaves. Beds are kings or two queens and some rooms add whirlpools or sofa beds. Courtyard Café serves a breakfast buffet with eggs made to order and other options and the Courtyard Lounge in the lobby serves drinks in the evening. Chain restaurants are nearby and some local options are a short drive away into Middleton. The hotel has a full business center as well as fitness center, an indoor pool with a zero-depth entry and some toys (great for kids), and a whirlpool. Wheelchair accessible rooms are available with roll-in showers. Pets are not allowed.

EXTENDED STAY AMERICA
MADISON WEST $–$$
55 Junction Ct.
(608) 833-1400
www.extendedstayamerica.com

Located to the west of the Beltline Highway at the Old Sauk Road exit, the 104 no-frill suites are well suited for long visits and come at a very economical price. All suites offer fully equipped kitchens with refrigerators, microwaves, and stovetops.

Rooms show TVs, telephones provide free local calls and personalized voice mail, coffeemakers, irons and ironing boards, and hair dryers. Internet connection comes with a small on-time fee per visit, and laundry facilities are on-site. Pets are allowed for a fee. Wheelchair accessible rooms are offered. Office hours are from 7 a.m. to 11 p.m.

FAIRFIELD INN & SUITES BY MARRIOTT–MADISON WEST $$$
8212 Greenway Blvd., Middleton
(608) 831-1400
www.marriott.com

The inn was renovated in 2009 giving the interiors a nice boost in quality. The hotel's 93 rooms and 10 suites are on three floors and though nothing extraordinary, the property is a reliable choice for a good stay. Compared to nearby Courtyard, Fairfield is just slightly less inclined toward families. Beds are kings or two doubles and some rooms offer sofa beds. Room amenities include TVs with premium channels, pay-per-view movies and video game consoles for rent, telephones with free local calls, coffeemakers, irons and ironing boards, and hair dryers. A heated indoor pool, whirlpool, and fitness center are on-site. Breakfast is complimentary and coffee is served in the lobby all day. A business center is here and wireless Internet is free and available throughout the property. Free parking is plentiful on-site. A taxi from the airport can be reserved for a set rate from the hotel. Wheelchair accessible rooms are available. Pets are not allowed.

HILTON GARDEN INN $$$
1801 Deming Way, Middleton
(608) 831-2220
www.madisonwestmiddleton.stayhgi.com

The hotel is located in the Greenway Station area of Middleton, 7 miles from downtown Madison and 8 miles from the University of Wisconsin. All rooms include one king-size or two queen-size beds, sleeper sofas or chairs with ottomans, large work desks with ergonomic chairs, two speakerphones with two lines and voice mail, complimentary high-speed Internet access, refrigerators, microwaves and coffeemakers, irons with ironing boards, and hair dryers. The indoor pool and accompanying Jacuzzi are open until midnight, and a fitness center is also on-site. A lounge offers a full bar and breakfast is served in the American Grill. Many other restaurants are located in the shopping areas nearby. Pets are not allowed. Wheelchair accessible rooms are offered.

HOLIDAY INN HOTEL AND SUITES WEST $$$
1109 Fourier Dr.
(608) 826-0500
www.wiscohotels.com

The four-floor, 158-room Holiday Inn shows a bit of elegance and a variety of services making it a competitive value in the west side market. Catering to the business traveler, the hotel offers complimentary wireless Internet, a 24-hour business center, and large work desks as well as executive level rooms and an accompanying lounge. But families are not neglected as the indoor S. S. Crawdaddy Water Park is also on-site. Pool access rooms on the 1st floor open right out into the water park. Rooms are spacious with two queens or a king bed and there are 69 suites available, some with two-person whirlpools. Amenities include TVs, telephones, irons and ironing boards, coffeemakers, in-room safes, and hair dryers. Every room has a microwave and refrigerator. Complimentary happy hour drinks and munchies are served in the lobby piano bar from Mon through Thurs with free membership in the Priority Club. Members also get a few free drinks on the weekends. George's Chop House serves breakfast and dinner. On the property are a heated indoor swimming pool, fitness center, and a convenience store and gift shop off the lobby. A free shuttle runs to and from the airport. Wheelchair accessible rooms are available and pets are not allowed.

HOMEWOOD SUITES BY HILTON–MADISON WEST $$$
479 Commerce Dr.
(608) 271-0600
www.madisonwest.homewoodsuites.com

Opened in Oct 2008, the hotel offers 122 suites varying from simpler studios to one- and two-bedroom units. All come with fully equipped kitchens with full-size refrigerators, stovetops, microwaves, dishwashers, sofa beds, large flat-panel TVs with premium channels, free wireless and wired high-speed Internet access, DVD players, irons and ironing boards, hair dryers, and coffeemakers. Grocery shopping service is provided. A business center is available around the clock as is free coffee, and breakfast is complimentary. A pool, whirlpool, and fitness center are on-site, and a couple of outdoor grills and a putting green are offered as well. A happy hour reception Mon through Thurs offers free drinks and light appetizers. Pets are allowed for a fee. Wheelchair accessible rooms are available. The hotel is located just west of the Beltline Highway but a few minutes south of the nearest on-ramp at Mineral Point Road.

MADISON MARRIOTT WEST $$$
1313 John Q. Hammons Dr., Middleton
(608) 831-2000
www.marriott.com
Just off the Beltline to the west at the Greenway Boulevard exit, this 10-floor hotel with its 238 rooms and 54 suites shows the fine visual appeal of a Marriott. Rooms are quite spacious starting at 420 square feet. Beds are kings or two doubles and offer feather pillows as an option. Televisions come with premium channels, pay-per-view movies, and an Internet browser. Other room amenities include two-line telephones with free local calls and voice mail, coffeemakers, irons with ironing boards, and hair dryers. Some rooms add sofa beds or microwave ovens and wet bars. Internet comes with a fee as does in-room bottled water. Concierge level rooms offer upgrades in amenities and service. Recreation at the hotel consists of an indoor heated pool, whirlpool, sundeck, and fitness center. Falling Water Café and Falling Water Lounge are both open for all three meals serving from an American menu. During Badger games there is a first-come, first-served shuttle for a small fee, otherwise from the airport a taxi is required for about $35 one-way. Guest laundry is on-site. Wheelchair accessible rooms

are available and parking is free and plentiful. Pets are allowed for a hefty fee.

RADISSON HOTEL $$
517 Grand Canyon Dr.
(608) 833-0100
www.radisson.com
This hotel has been around a while and this may be apparent in some of the interiors. Rooms come with adjustable Sleep Number beds plus cable TVs, telephones with voice mail, work desks with lights, clock radios, coffeemakers, irons and ironing boards, and hair dryers. Some have refrigerators and microwaves. Internet connection is available in all rooms. A heated pool, whirlpool, and fitness center are on-site as is a business center. Breakfast is included only with specified rates and a restaurant is on-site. Pets are not allowed. Wheelchair accessible rooms are available. This is located just off the Beltline Highway east of the Gammon Road exit on Odana Road.

RESIDENCE INN BY MARRIOTT–MADISON WEST MIDDLETON $$$
8400 Market St., Middleton
(608) 662-1100
www.marriott.com
Roomy with modern designs, the Residence Inn offers a home away from home. Each room has a fully equipped kitchen with stovetop, microwave, refrigerator, and dishwasher, and a grocery shopping service is offered. Some rooms have fireplaces. Other amenities include flat-screen TVs with premium channels, two telephones with two lines, free local calls, voice mail and a speaker phone option, irons and ironing boards, and hair dryers. Beds are kings or queens and sofa beds are also included. Complimentary breakfast is included. A heated indoor pool and whirlpool are on-site. High-speed Internet access is also free and a full-service business center is on-site. The inn is within walking distance of the Greenway Station shopping and restaurant area. Wheelchair accessible rooms are offered. Pets are allowed for a hefty fee.

**STAYBRIDGE SUITES MIDDLETON/
MADISON–WEST** $$$
7790 Elmwood Ave., Middleton
(888) 299-2208
www.ichotelsgroup.com

The location is just off the Beltline Highway at the University Avenue exit in Middleton making a trip downtown about a 15-minute drive. Rooms are quiet with double-glazed windows which can be opened. Beds are either kings or queens in studio, one-, or two-bedroom suites. Amenities include a kitchenette with microwave and dishwasher, TVs with premium channels, two telephones with two lines, voice mail and free local calls, iron and ironing board, and a hair dryer. A buffet breakfast with a couple of hot items is included in the rates. The heated indoor pool, whirlpool, and the fitness center are open 24 hours. The staffed business center is also open round the clock. A library has a book exchange and board games and outside is a basketball court. Restaurants in Middleton are within walking distance. A free airport shuttle must be scheduled at least 24 hours in advance. Free underground parking is heated. Guest laundry facilities are on the property. Wheelchair accessible rooms are offered. Pets allowed for a fee.

RV PARKS

LAKE FARM PARK
3113 Lake Farm Rd.
(608) 242-4576
www.co.dane.wi.us/lwrd/parks/lake_farm.
aspx

Lake Farm has the atmosphere of a quiet country site, yet the city is just a minute down the road and around the bend. Part of the Capital Springs Centennial State Park, this 328-acre park has three shelters, a playground, an accessible boat launch, a fish-cleaning facility, hiking and cross-country ski trails, and a Native American Archaeological Trail. Thirty-nine of the reserveable 54 sites have electrical hook ups for RVs (50 amp). The park roads are paved and sites are wide with a gravel surface. Facilities include nice showers, picnic tables, steel fire rings at each site, several water wells throughout, a sanitary dumping station, and even wireless Internet. The Capital City Trail passes right along the park edge.

RESTAURANTS

Madison often boasts of having the most restaurants per capita. If that claim isn't always exactly true in the topsy turvy world of the restaurant business, it is always reliably somewhere very close to the top of that list.

For a small Midwestern city—some would say "town"—Madison has an impressive variety of restaurants. Ethnic fare crosses a broader spectrum than you might see in a much larger city let alone in one of around 200,000 people. How many cities have one Nepali restaurant let alone *three?*

Madison is fortunate to be surrounded by farmland. Vegetables, meats, and dairy products are in abundance, making it easy for restaurants to build their menus around local and often organic ingredients. From the fine dining at Harvest to a tavern hamburger at the Caribou, the buy-local ethic has really taken hold. For those being strict about it, a change in season means a change in menu as the tomatoes don't do well under a foot of snow.

Check out the Best Burgers category for truly the finest hamburgers you'll ever find. The eateries listed there range from bar and grills to more eclectic dining and are likely to even have some vegetarian specialties on their menu.

There is little in the way of a dress code and restaurants might seat university students in shorts and flip flops just one table over from a couple dressed sharply for an evening at the Overture Center for the Arts. Fish fries are a long-standing Wisconsin tradition, and a variety of restaurants offers them from fine dining and supper clubs to the neighborhood tavern or even a church basement. See the Close-up at the end of the chapter about this cultural phenomenon.

The City of Madison banned smoking in restaurants and other workplaces, and soon after the state followed suit with a ban taking effect as of July 5, 2010, so all dining experiences are now smoke-free. Some establishments may offer outdoor seating smoking areas.

What may come as a shock to some is that the typical restaurant may stop serving around 8:30 or 9 p.m. Late-night meals can be limited to bars, and even then you might find grills closing by 11 p.m. Unless otherwise indicated, restaurants take major credit cards, and by "major" you can be guaranteed it means at least MasterCard and Visa. Other cards can be hit or miss such as Discover cards and especially the high-fee American Express card.

Establishments are arranged by cuisine but it is worth paging through to see the categories as Brazilian and Peruvian fall under South American, for example, and Contemporary Fine Dining covers some rather diverse menus. Notable bakeries are also worked into the restaurant list. Food carts are popular around campus and the Capitol Square, and a couple good take-out-only shops were musts to mention (see the corresponding Close-ups). Madison is not your ordinary town so expect a few odd arrangements such as Greek food served at a gas station, Thai in a convenience store, or first-rate sushi in a landlocked state. Anything can happen.

Many of the local publications such as *Isthmus, 77 Square, Madison Magazine*, and the A. V. Club section of the *Onion* publish restaurant reviews in print and online, and a great local Web site/blog is Eating in Madison A to Z (www.madisonatoz .com) which chronicles an alphabetically-ordered attempt by Nichole and J. M. to try every eatery in town.

Price Code

The price code for this chapter is based on one lunch or dinner entree.

$.................... **Under $10**
$$ .... **$10 to $20**
$$$ .... **$21 to $30**
$$$$ .... **more than $30**

AFRICAN

BURAKA $–$$
543 State St.
(608) 255-3646
www.ethiopianrestaurant.com/wisconsin/
buraka.html

Ethiopian cuisine commonly consists of meat and vegetarian stews (spicy or mild) scooped up on torn pieces of a sort of sourdough-crepe bread called *injera*. The injera in this basement restaurant is quite nice but Buraka sets the tables with silverware anyway. A good option is the beef *tibs*, both tender and flavorful, or their unusual take on the traditional chicken stew (*dorowot*), which is easy on the hot spices (*berbere*) and doesn't incorporate the hard-boiled egg. Meals, which can also come with rice, are served with a simple vinaigrette salad or lentil salad. For a more traditional experience, request your meal on a platter for all at your table to share. Open for lunch and dinner but closed Sun. The closest parking ramp is at Lake Street/Frances Street just off State Street. Not wheelchair accessible but there is sidewalk seating.

i Buraka started as a food cart on Library Mall at the campus end of State Street. That cart still operates during lunch on weekdays.

BAKERIES

CLASEN'S EUROPEAN BAKERY $
7610 Donna Dr., Middleton
(608) 831-2032
www.clasensbakery.com

This is an Old World treat that has been around since 1959 when a couple of brothers from Cologne, Germany, settled in Middleton. The next generation, daughter Michelle, carried on the tradition of goodness and acquired her pastry degree. Business has grown and the products are made by a staff of German Master Bakers. Patrons can have a free cup of coffee and some samples as they shop for hearty breads and delectable pastries. Breads are the heavy European variety with a nice crust on the outside, and a variety of ryes and some sourdough are among the styles. Other goodies include chocolates, cookies, tortes, tarts, and even wedding cakes. Various Madison-area grocers and restaurants sell Clasen's products and a list is on the Web site. Some soft music is piped in and just a couple of tables are available for customers. Juices and bottled water are also for sale. The service is as warm and personal as the bread. Closed Sun.

GREENBUSH BAKERY, INC. $
1305 Regent St.
(608) 257-1151

This kosher-certified bakery is a donut lover's heaven. Demand is high and sometimes orders of 15 or 20 dozen head out the door. The old-fashioned cake donuts are popular and late-night drunks seem to gravitate toward the "Oreo," a donut topped with that famous cookie and filled with vanilla crème. If you want one of their phenomenal apple fritters, you better get there early in the morning. The bar crowd rolls in at night with serious cravings, while business people come here before work. This is not a sit-down place though there are a couple benches on the sidewalk. Coffee is served as are milk, soda, juice, and water from a cooler. Occasionally, cookies and muffins are sold. The bakery closes Sun afternoon and opens again Mon afternoon. Other than that little quirk, hours are daily. On Fri and Sat it stays open past midnight.

NATURE'S BAKERY COOPERATIVE $
1019 Williamson St.
(608) 257-3649
www.naturesbakery.coop

Since 1970, this worker's collective bakery has been producing some of the finest bread you'll ever find. A vegetarian bakery, it is committed to using organic whole grains. Nine sliced sandwich breads, one unleavened sourdough, and a whole grain pita bread make up the bread selections. Sweeteners are unprocessed and include pure honey, barley malt, maple syrup, and blackstrap molasses in the bread and granola. Eight granola blends are on offer including almond raisin, molasses almond raisin, cashew raisin, peanut butter, and six grain. Two of the blends are oil-free and many are vegan. Essene bread is unleavened and made from sprouting wheat berries. The breads are available in area grocery stores such as Willy Street Co-op and Regent Street Co-op, but for the freshest loaves stop in at their 2nd-floor location on Mon, Wed, or Fri afternoons when all the baking just finishes. Some (very few) of the outdated loaves come back from the stores and are discounted by the front door. Cash or check only. Open Sat from 10 a.m. to 2 p.m., and weekdays in the morning and afternoons (except Wed which is afternoon only.)

BARBECUE

FAT JACKS BARBECUE $–$$
6207 Monona Dr., Monona
(608) 221-4220
www.fatjacksbbq.biz
Hickory-smoked barbecue is the main attraction and the back ribs come highly recommended. Like most barbecue joints the atmosphere is casual. The decor at Fat Jacks is old Wisconsin and the beer selection also remains loyal to the home state. Watch for all-you-can-eat ribs and chicken specials. Barbecue sauce, often served on the side rather than on the meat, comes in hot and mild options. Burgers and sandwiches are also on the menu and a simple salad bar offers something beyond the meat. A good ole Wisconsin fish fry is hosted on Fri. Closed on Mon. Otherwise open for lunch and dinner on weekdays, closing briefly between meals, and open for dinner only on weekends. Wheelchair accessible.

PAPA BEAR'S BBQ $–$$
4527 Cottage Grove Rd.
(608) 222-2374
www.papabearsbbqmadison.com

Papa Bear is Jeff Norwood and his barbecue is no nonsense. Many come for carry out but there is a small dining room as well with minimal atmosphere—think plastic utensils. Whatever effort was spared on decor seems to have been put to the food. The meat is smoked slowly over hickory wood and the mild sauce is made in-house. Ribs are a staple but rib tips are also on offer, a seeming rarity at some places. Rib dinners come with two sides. Pulled pork, beef brisket, and burgers are served. The menu also offers a portobello sandwich for the vegetarian caught in a meat zone. Combos are also available and family packs serve larger groups quite well. Open for lunch and dinner, and closed Sun. Wheelchair accessible.

SMOKY JON'S #1 BBQ $
2310 Packers Ave.
(608) 249-7427
www.smokyjons.com
Smoky Jon's isn't just boasting to be the best in town, but best in the universe. His superlative claim, however, has numerous national and even international awards to wipe the grin off your face along with that barbecue sauce. Marinated barbecue chicken, finger-licking good ribs, pork and beef sandwiches with a wonderful smokiness to them—this place is indeed a barbecue champion. The unassuming exterior with a few barnyard animals painted on it might be why some people barely notice it, but the interior is like a Tennessee cabin with pine-log walls and rough-cut ceiling planks and food smells that will make your mouth water. Plates come with a choice of two sides and tables have rolls of paper towels on them. The restaurant's barbecue sauce is available for purchase. Parking is best done down the side street off Packers Avenue. Wheelchair accessible.

BEST BURGERS

ALCHEMY $
1980 Atwood Ave.
(608) 204-7644
www.alchemycafe.net

Any place that pre-packs the bacon into the burger itself is on the right track for burger notoriety. Formerly Wonders Pub, a beloved neighborhood tavern with a connoisseur's rotating tap list, Alchemy seems to have picked up where Wonders left off. The fish fry is fantastic on Fri. Vegetarian and vegan items are also clearly marked and include an excellent grilled portobello sandwich as well as stuffed grape leaves (*dolmades*) and sweet potato fries. The soups, made from scratch, are quite notable too. And yes, that tap list at the bar still shows several notable microbrews. Limited sidewalk seating is available in summer and a game is usually on at the bar. Live music sets up in a tiny corner regularly. Open daily, serving food until late. Wheelchair accessible.

THE CARIBOU TAVERN $
703 East Johnson St.
(608) 257-5993

Not everyone finds their way over to the 'Bou, and when university classes are in session, this is a common watering hole for study avoidance. You'll find nothing of pretension here: it is a tavern about as long as the bar and twice as wide as the bar is deep. The posted daily specials never change and all are reasonably priced and hearty eating, but the star of the show is the burger. Fresh ground beef is brought in daily from Jenifer Street Market and the hand patties are cooked to order. Get it with grilled onions. The fries are pretty stellar too. No credit cards accepted but an ATM is on-site. Not wheelchair accessible.

DEXTER'S PUB $
301 North St.
(608) 244-3535
www.dexterspubmadison.com

Once known as The Sandlot (for the sand volleyball pit out back) this neighborhood pub just off East Washington Avenue has more class than its drab collection of booths and tables might suggest. To call this bar food would be an insult. The menu is prepared with care and concern and sandwiches such as the ahi tuna steak are superb. Burgers are cooked to order. The burger known as The Defibrillator will require one and is

piled high with ham, bacon, fried onions, cheddar and pepper jack cheeses, and an over-easy fried egg. Fried sides include cheese curds, pub fries, and onions, as well as the stellar garlic/chili fries which you won't find elsewhere. The pizzas are good and the salads are not an afterthought to the menu. Sunday's breakfast is famous for the Puppy Pile: American potatoes buried with bacon, onions, mushrooms, two eggs to order, and several ounces of prime rib. (The larger Dog Pile is offered as a challenge.) Thirteen tap lines serve a rotating list of top-notch microbrews from around the state and country. During Badger football season, the weekend breakfast menu expands and the bar runs a shuttle to Camp Randall for the game.

DOTTY DUMPLING'S DOWRY $
317 North Frances St.
(608) 259-0000
www.dottydumplingsdowry.com

Dotty's is a bit of a legend and the build-your-own burgers are part of any serious conversation about the city's best burgers. Its original location was razed to make room for the Overture Center for the Arts and there are some who question that decision. Burgers are cooked to order and if you say rare, you'll get it. Hand-patties made fresh daily weigh in at a third of a pound and the options are numerous and potentially messy in a finger-licking sort of way. The Melting Pot burger comes with three cheeses, English garlic sauce, and bacon. Ostrich, bison, turkey, and veggie patties are also available as are some non-burger items such as tuna, salmon, and portobello mushrooms. Salads are decent and two soups are served daily. A full bar looks tavern and the good beers are numerous, but the booths and atmosphere are still family friendly. The interiors which are a bit on the dim side now make this look like a legitimate restaurant unlike the lovably homely previous location. However, the charm of the eclectic collection of sports and Wisconsin memorabilia and some large-scale airplane models from the previous incarnation are still alive and strong. Wheelchair accessible. Open daily for lunch and dinner.

HARMONY BAR & GRILL $
2201 Atwood Ave.
(608) 249-4333
www.myspace.com/theharmonybar

This is bar food at its glorious best. The burgers are made with fresh ground beef from the Jenifer Street Market just a few blocks away and are always made to order. Vegetarians should not be shy because the menu has a veggie burger that could convert a carnivore, and the portobello sandwich is great as well. Though not exactly a sports bar, any Badger, Brewer, or Packer games are bound to be on the various TVs. The Reuben contends to be the best in town, a credible claim. Fried cheese curds are great and the house-made deep-fried potato chips with bleu cheese dressing are a specialty. The pizza is as reputable as the burgers and great for late-night group outings with a few pitchers of beer. Nine beers are on tap at the full bar and most of them hail from Wisconsin.

The establishment gives a lot of support to the Goodman Community Center and is itself a sort of social center in the neighborhood. The owner has 100 of his own CDs in the jukebox leaning heavily toward blues and jazz. Live music is hosted every Sat night and some Fri and Sun, and the bands tend toward rhythm and blues with a bit of bluegrass on occasion. Cash only but there is an ATM on-site. Open daily from 11 a.m. until bar closing. Food is served late, especially on weeknights until just about midnight. For the last two weeks before Labor Day, the Harmony Bar closes to give the great staff a little bit of a break. The bar is wheelchair accessible and there's a ramp in back with a bell to push if assistance is needed. Parking is on the street or in a small lot behind the bar.

THE OLD FASHIONED $–$$
23 North Pinckney St.
(608) 310-4545
www.theoldfashioned.com

Much like the drink that this eatery is named for, this is quintessential Wisconsin fare. Have you ever had a hamburger with a fried egg on top? Deep-fried cheese curds, beer cheese soup, liverwurst,

and some cheese plates are obvious homeland items, and the salads and sandwiches are great. Roughly two dozen different beers are on tap, all of them Wisconsin brews. Order a Lazy Susan tray of pre-meal munchables, a Badger State supper club norm that includes such items as sausage samplers, deviled eggs, smoked trout, pickled beets, sweet gherkins, and rye bread. Nightly specials range from mac & cheese to local grilled trout. The place fills up for lunch and the after-work crowd from around the Capitol; expect a certain esprit de vie and lively conversations but not intimate date ambience. Open daily with happy-hour specials on weekdays. Watch for two-for-one burgers on Mon. Wheelchair accessible.

THE PLAZA TAVERN $
319 North Henry St.
(608) 255-6592
www.theplazatavern.com

This is not your gourmet, cooked-to-order variety burger, but it is a Madison institution. The bar is, shall we say, homey? Walls show paneling and some booths along the wall opposite the full bar. Two pool tables, a hockey-themed plastic-bubble-covered equivalent of foosball, a jukebox, and sometimes a few of the customers are the entertainment, and there might be a game on the big screen TV. Often a popular haunt for college students at night or lunch for the Capitol crowd, this tavern offers a great bar burger at a pocket-change price. You don't often see a thin patty like this with a bit of pink to it, but they somehow pull it off. The burger's "secret sauce" is something on the order of ranch dressing. The french fries are perfectly done and the beer comes cheap as well. This is wheelchair accessible. Does not accept credit cards but there is an ATM on-site.

WEARY TRAVELER FREEHOUSE $–$$
1201 Williamson St.
(608) 442-6207

This eastside neighborhood eatery is extremely popular and tables fill fast during meal times. There's not a lot of elbow room and the atmosphere is more akin to jovial hangout than quiet conversation nook. The menu includes Hungarian goulash, Wisconsin cheese and sausage platters, and sides like garlic-fried potatoes, but the Bad Breath Burger is legendary. It's made with local organic beef with garlic and mustard worked into it, adds Jamaican pickapeppa sauce, cream cheese, caramelized red onions, mayo-based dressing with fresh herbs, tamarind, tarragon, chives, parsley, and is served on a house-made briochelike roll. Cooked to order. Eight beers are on tap at the full bar. A small corner stage area hosts live music, often local Americana singer/guitarist Catfish Stephenson. Food is served until 1 a.m. which is a big plus in a city of early restaurant closing times. Open daily for dinner and serves lunch all days but Mon. No checks. Twitter for dinner specials @WearyChef-Joey. Wheelchair accessible.

BREAKFAST JOINTS

THE CURVE $
653 South Park St.
(608) 251-0311

This is the epitome of a greasy spoon breakfast nook located at the curve of Park Street before it meets Fish Hatchery Road going south. The walls are lined with mirrors for surreptitious people watching and no one's coming here for elegance. Sit at the counter or one of the handful of tables. The prices are low and the food has that homemade quality to it. Odds are good that you and your companions will all be named "hon" while you're here. The Curve special omelet comes with veggies and ham. A bottomless cup of coffee is a nice bonus. While not on the menu, the "homewrecker sandwich," consists of a large serving of ham, topped with fried eggs and melted American cheese between two thick cut pieces of toast. Open daily for breakfast until about 1 p.m. Cash only. Parking on the street.

HUBBARD AVENUE DINER $
7445 Hubbard Ave., Middleton
(608) 831-6800
www.foodfightinc.com/hubbard.htm

Many locals nevertheless refer to this as Hubbard *Street* Diner, but don't worry, you're in the right

place. A modern construction of a throwback diner, this downtown Middleton eatery is getting raves for its pies. Multigrain pancakes, potato/zucchini pancakes, and good quiches. The good eats go way beyond breakfast, and not many restaurants have a gluten-free menu at all, let alone a good one like this diner's. Beer and wine are served. Open daily for all meals with an extended brunch on weekends. Wheelchair accessible.

LAZY JANE'S CAFE & BAKERY $
1358 Williamson St.
(608) 257-5263

Bring a book or some good conversationalists because everyone's waiting to get in—and for good reason. This quaint shop with the name spelled out with giant Scrabble letters outside is a Willy Street breakfast magnet. Organic and vegetarian options are many. One of which is a hash with potatoes, roasted red peppers, broccoli, and seitan chunks. Eggs with scallions and cream cheese are great. Don't leave without trying one of the fresh-baked scones. Sandwiches, salads, and soups make up the lunch menu. What makes Jane's "lazy" is that orders are placed at the counter and names are called as the food is ready. An ATM is in-house. Wheelchair accessible. Open daily for breakfast and lunch, but breakfast only on weekends.

MARIGOLD KITCHEN $
118 South Pinckney St.
(608) 661-5559
www.marigoldkitchen.com

Though it also does for a very nice lunch, Marigold Kitchen is best known for breakfast, and especially for brunch for the Sat morning farmers' market crowd on the Capitol Square. The menu does not aim for the standard breakfast items like at a greasy spoon; choices are a bit more creative and higher quality and prices reflect that. The chile poached eggs with toasted French rosemary bread, prosciutto, and manchego shouldn't be missed. The transition from breakfast to lunch is a half hour gap in the service hours and can catch some customers coming in for the wrong menu on weekdays. And the place can fill up pretty fast. Vegetarians have good options and a kids' menu serves the under eight crowd. Alcohol is served so a mimosa or Bloody Mary is possible if it's just one of those mornings. Open weekdays for breakfast and lunch, and on Sat for brunch. Wheelchair accessible.

MICKIES DAIRY BAR $
1511 Monroe St.
(608) 256-9476
If you are looking for gourmet, this is probably not it. But for a big appetite the plates here come heaping and cheap. The Scrambler is a mountain of eggs on a bed of hash browns, sprinkled with meat and cheese and smothered with sausage gravy. The pancakes are large and often just one does the trick. The milkshakes and malts here are the stuff of legend and don't be surprised to see diners washing down breakfast with them. The counter occupies the center of the small restaurant and booths can fill up fast. Weekday specials and soups are worth a look too. On Badger football days and even many weekends, the wait will be long. Street parking only. Open for breakfast and lunch, but closed Mon. Does not accept credit cards.

MONTY'S BLUE PLATE DINER $
2089 Atwood Ave.
(608) 244-8505
www.foodfightinc.com/montys.htm
Opened in 1990, this was the first creation by local restaurant group Food Fight Inc. A bright and friendly diner with counter seating and booths, Monty's is commonly known for its breakfasts (served all day) as well as the vegetarian and vegan menu items. One fine choice (of many) is the Mediterranean Sunrise: two poached eggs covered with tomatoes, artichokes, mushrooms, black olives, capers, basil, onions, and garlic, served over a toasted English muffin with Mornay sauce on the side. Parking in the lot can get tight on busy days, especially during breakfast. Beer and wine are served and the property is accessible for wheelchairs. Open daily for all meals.

THE ORIGINAL PANCAKE HOUSE $
5518 University Ave.
(608) 231-3666

516 River Plaza, Monona
(608) 222-1137
www.originalpancakehouse.com
This national chain nevertheless has a serious local appeal here in Madison. The apple pancake is quite popular and the Dutch Baby, an oven-baked puffy pancake with lemon, whipped butter, and powdered sugar, is another signature dish. Waffles, crepes, and the usual egg and meat options are also on order. Open daily serving breakfast only (but through the lunch hour). On weekends you may have to wait up to a half hour for a table when it's busy. Only cash and checks are accepted and an ATM is on-site. Off-street parking in back. Wheelchair accessible.

BREWPUBS & BREWERIES

ALE ASYLUM $
3698 Kinsman Blvd.
(608) 663-3926
www.aleasylum.com
Brewer Dean Coffey made a name for himself when he was at the now defunct Angelic Brewing Company off State Street. Not long after he left in 2005 he and his crew opened Ale Asylum on the northeast side in a nondescript brick commercial building on Stoughton Road. This is the only brewery with a bottling line in town. Hopalicious, an American Pale Ale, was an immediate hit and now accounts for half their production. With views through the glass to the brewing operation, the bar has a relaxed lounge atmosphere to it, but the staff makes you feel like a house guest knocking out any sort of pretension. A small beer garden opens in nice weather. There's also a pool table. "Fermented in Sanity" is their motto, as they stick to very pure ingredients and methods of brewing. A few seasonals come and go through the year. The menu is limited but good with a few hot sandwiches and a thin-crust pizza handmade in Columbus, WI. Wheelchair accessible. Open daily with limited hours on Sun.

CAPITAL BREWERY AND BIER GARTEN $
7734 Terrace Ave., Middleton
(608) 836-7100
www.capital-brewery.com

Capital Brewery was once named the #1 Brewery in America at the Beverage Tasting Institute's World Beer Championships. Its first beer was released in 1986 and the climb to success has been steady. Capital brews 16 beers per year. Wisconsin Amber is a regular on taps around town. Island Wheat, made from grain grown on Washington Island in Door County, WI, is extremely popular around the state. Seasonal releases such as Autumnal Fire and limited specialty brews are waited for with great anticipation. The brewery offers scheduled tours for about $3 per person on Fri and Sat. A major attraction for the brewery is its Bier Garten with the brewery's own beers, several wines, and soda on offer along with an assortment of snacks like chips and pretzels. The Bier Garten is open Tues through Sat from May through Sept. After Sept everything moves indoors to the cozy and classy Bier Stube until May again (except for Dec when it's closed for holiday parties). Live music plays on Fri from Memorial Day Weekend to Labor Day Weekend. The brewery is popular with the after-work crowd and is family friendly. Though there's no menu here, many patrons will order out from nearby eateries such as Roman Candle Pizza (see Pizza page 67). A gift shop is on site selling brewery paraphernalia and carry-out beer. Wheelchair accessible. Watch for special events such as February's Bockfest (see Annual Events–February page 163).

GRAY'S TIED HOUSE $–$$
950 Kimball Lane, Verona
(608) 845-2337
www.graystiedhouse.com

Fred Gray represents the 5th generation of brewers in his family-run Janesville brewery. In 2006, Gray made the move into the brewpub business in Verona just 20 minutes southwest of Madison. A tied-house was a term for a tavern back in the day when it was obliged to sell a single brewer's beer. In the same spirit, Gray's beers are on tap including the popular Honey Ale, Rathskeller Amber,

and Oatmeal Stout. The menu includes brick-oven pizzas, sandwiches, and burgers, and various items with a beer twist to the recipe such as beer-battered fresh cheese curds, beer cheese soup, and a pulled pork sandwich with hot honey ale barbecue sauce. On weekends the 13 TVs make this 450-seat restaurant a good place to watch some sports. Outdoor seating lasts well into fall thanks to space heaters, and live music is usually a weekly event. Open daily and wheelchair accessible.

Fauerbach Brewery

In 1848, the same year that Wisconsin became a state, Adam Sprecher opened Madison's first commercial brewery. Twenty years later, Peter Fauerbach moved in and renamed it Fauerbach Brewery. The beer stayed in the family for generations, and except for a temporary shutdown during Prohibition, was brewed until 1966 when like so many other breweries, Fauerbach closed its doors. **Middleton's Capital Brewery** opened in 1986, bringing local beer back in fashion, and **The Great Dane Pub & Restaurant** brought hometown brew officially into the city limits in 1994. But Fauerbach lives on: **Janesville's Gray's Brewing** produces various beers from the old recipes for the Fauerbach family.

THE GREAT DANE PUB &
BREWING CO. $–$$
123 East Doty St.
(608) 284-0000

357 Price Place
(608) 661-9400

2980 Cahill Main, Fitchburg
(608) 442-9000
www.greatdanepub.com

When Fauerbach Brewery closed its doors in 1966, beer ceased to be commercially brewed in Madison. That is, until 1994 when the Great Dane opened its doors in what was originally The Fess Hotel, a historic property dating back to the mid-19th century. The Dane has become a success of major proportions. At one time there might be 17 draft beers on offer from a classic Peck's Pilsner to an Emerald Isle Stout and every shade, style, and nuance in between. Showing a bit of brass, the place is expansive with one bar in the King Street side being more of a jukebox ringing pool hall, and the Doty side being the heart of the restaurant, also with its own bar. The basement, with its stone walls, has yet another bar, and in seasonable weather a beer garden opens in back of the building. The pub menu is as expansive as the property and offers several items incorporating the beers into the recipe.

Two other Dane properties brew beer on-site in the Madison area and another non-brewing restaurant, located inside the airport, serves beer from the downtown location.

i Great microbrews hail from places close to town. Furthermore Beer is based out of Spring Green, Lake Louie calls Arena home, Tyranena is to the east in Lake Mills, and New Glarus Brewery is in the Swiss-style town of the same name. Their beers are regularly on tap around town and any liquor store should carry them.

CAJUN & CREOLE

THE BAYOU RESTAURANT $-$$
117 South Butler St.
(608) 294-9404
www.thebayoumadison.com
Jambalaya, étouffée, and gumbo are on the menu, and all are good, but if you are looking for good po'boy sandwiches, this is the spot. Spices here can range from blistering to a mild blush, but the friendly waitstaff can guide you. The Bourbon Street Po'boy has fried shrimp and crawfish, sweet potato fries, and remoulade sauce on the side. Fresh fish specials come and

go and tend to be a bit pricier than the rest of the menu. A varied dessert menu includes changing flavored crème brûlée, and the sweet potato bread pudding with bourbon caramel sauce is amazing. It's a casual, convivial joint especially on Tues nights with regular live music. Wheelchair accessible. Open for lunch, dinner, and Sat breakfast, but closed Sun.

LILIANA'S RESTAURANT $$
2951 Triverton Pike, Fitchburg
(608) 442-4444
www.lilianasrestaurant.com
For a New Orleans-style restaurant there is a lot that is actually quite local about Liliana's. Chef/owner Dave Heide, who studied at Le Cordon Bleu, insists on patronizing local purveyors and producers which means the menu is seasonal and changes often. The wickedly good jambalaya is a signature dish, but the selections often go beyond Creole and Cajun classics such as étouffée and filé gumbo to some international specials such as the periodically appearing seared sea scallops. Bread and beignets are baked on-site and even the meats and sausages are ground in house. You'll also find a fresh oyster menu and over 300 wines all available by the glass. A weekly tasting menu offers a three-course meal every Tues. Live music, tending toward jazz, plays in the bar area adding atmosphere most evenings and for Sun brunch. The stylish decor channels some details of Bourbon Street with local wrought-iron work simulating balconies and Dave's father's Big Easy photography adorning the walls. Outdoor seating is on three patios, one of them nonsmoking. This is a great place for a business lunch or dinner with friends or sweethearts and the food will bring you back. Open daily.

LOUISIANNE'S ETC. $$$
7464 Hubbard Ave., Middleton
(608) 831-1929
www.louisiannes.com
This upscale New Orleans-style restaurant set in a cozy basement with exposed brick walls has received raves for years. Start off with Oysters Louisianne baked in a smoked mushroom, bacon,

and crawfish sauce, topped with Parmigiana Reggiano cheese. Whether you enjoy surf or turf the menu has some delectable choices such as several styles of catfish, seafood fricassee, a stuffed tenderloin, classic jambalaya or étouffée, or even maple-cured duck and coffee-roasted chicken. You'll find a full bar with the standard beers and a few local brews, and the wine list shows over 75 wines. Hear live jazz piano most nights during dinner. Open daily for dinner except Sun.

CARIBBEAN & CENTRAL AMERICAN

CAFÉ COSTA RICA $
141 South Butler St.
(608) 256-9830
www.mangomancooks.com

It's not the first time a good Madison food cart found a permanent address. Thony "Mango Man" Clarke took his successful Costa Rican fare to this little lower-level cafe just a couple blocks off the Capitol Square. Seating is rather limited both inside and on the small patio outside, but this can be passed off as cozy. Tacos and burritos come with chicken, beef, pork, or tilapia and some Tico staples such as plantains and gallo pinto (beans and rice). Beans might sound boring to some, but Thony's spices make them stand out. Curried chicken or tilapia sautéed in garlic are fine choices as well. Alcohol, rum in particular, is served and the caipirinhas and mojitos rock while the spectacular mango margarita is made with real mangos. Weekdays the cafe opens about 6 a.m. for pastries and coffee, plus gallo pinto, scrambled eggs, and more thereafter. On weekends they open a couple hours later. On any day they are a good bet for a later dinner when other places have already closed. Not wheelchair accessible though outdoor seating is manageable. The patio stays open into fall thanks to a portable heater. Look for that food cart on Library Mall on campus.

DAVID'S JAMAICAN CUISINE $
5734 Monona Dr.
(608) 222-8109

Built into a former Taco Bell now painted up in green and yellow, this Jamaican delight is easy on the wallet and spicy on the tongue. The jerk chicken and pork are the most popular dishes and jerk steak is an excellent choice as well. Ackee codfish, a truly Jamaican dish, occasionally graces the menu and is flown in fresh and not to be missed. A Fri-night and lunch-hour buffet allows customers to explore the cuisine a bit. Jerk tofu is on the menu for vegetarians. Don't miss the banana cake. There is outdoor seating and beer and wine are served. The jerk sauce is so good they sell it in bottles. Wheelchair accessible. Parking on-site. Carry-out available. Open daily but Sun hours change with the seasons.

JAMERICA CARIBBEAN RESTAURANT $$
1236 Williamson St.
(608) 251-6234
www.jamericarestaurant.com

Port Antonio native Martin Deacon opened a Jamaican grocery and take-out store in 1965 and based on his success added the small restaurant area. The menu has all the Jamaican standards from jerk meats and fried plantains to callaloo soup. The mango tofu curry is a good vegetarian option. Locals have voted it Best Caribbean Restaurant in a local people's choice survey. Look for the Jamerica food cart down on Library Mall on the University of Wisconsin campus weekdays during lunch. Beer is served in bottles and jerk is available for carry-out. Parking is on the street. Open daily for lunch and dinner (but a little late for lunch on Sun).

JOLLY BOB'S JERK JOINT $$
1210 Williamson St.
(608) 251-3902

This is a long-standing Jamaican restaurant with a reputation for great drinks. Walk in past the bar and into a colorful, fun dining room with a large aquarium in the center. The menu is heavy on grilled meats or seafood and of course features spicy jerk recipes usually served with rice. Entrees are a bit pricey but feasting on appetizers is a good alternative. Tropical drinks from the full

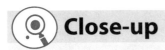 # Close-up

Take Out: Two Madison Classics

NEW ORLEANS TAKEOUT $

East
1920 Fordem Ave.
(608) 241-6655

West
1517 Monroe St.
(608) 280-8000
www.eatmobettah.com

Since 1985 Madison has been fortunate to have some really good and affordable take-away in the Big Easy style. Owner John Roussos' two locations serve the classics: po' boy sandwiches, filé gumbo, étouffée, and jambalaya. Deb's Barbeque shrimp with spicy dirty rice is incredible, dripping with lemon and butter and a bit of rosemary, and the fried catfish is lightly breaded, just right. Most meals come in two sizes. Bread pudding and sweet potato pecan pie are delectable dessert offerings. Open for lunch and dinner. Closed Sun.

MYLES TEDDYWEDGERS CORNISH PASTY $

101 State St.
(608) 257-2383

Wisconsin's nickname of the Badger State didn't come from the ornery little animals but from the lead miners who settled here in the 19th century and burrowed in the ground for their fortunes. Many of them hailed from Cornwall in England and carried with them the traditional Cornish pasty. Teddywedgers offers the hearty meat and potatoes meal in half or whole portions plus a veggie alternative and some chicken, cheese, and even pizza versions. Purists may pine for the rutabaga pieces lacking in these pasties, but the rest of us might be grateful. Breakfast versions with Canadian bacon, eggs, and cheese are a hit as well. Open from early morning into the dinner hour. Closed Sun.

---

bar are nice and lean on the strong side, and in summer the courtyard out back is a nice place to dine. On some weekend evenings the indoor tables get moved back to make room for a bit of dancing. Not wheelchair accessible. Parking is on the street. Credit cards are not accepted.

i The weekly newspaper *Isthmus* releases its *Annual Manual* in Aug every year where you can find the results of the readers' poll of citywide favorites, including restaurants.

CHINESE

HONG KONG CAFÉ $–$$
2 South Mills St.
(608) 259-1668
www.hkcafemadison.com

In an old brick building at the corner of Mills and Regent, Hong Kong Café is a long-time favorite for Chinese. Close to Meriter and St. Mary's Hospitals and not far from the UW campus they do a steady business. The menu has the usual massive list of dishes one might expect from a Chinese restaurant, but the food actually tends toward authentic Chinese fare not the Americanized version. Portions are large and service is sharp. The dishes use vegetable oil sparingly and "special diet" items are all steamed. Most of the dishes don't use MSG. Vegetarians will find a lot of options here. Dim sum is served on weekends during lunch time. Open daily for lunch and dinner. Takeout and delivery also available. Wheelchair accessible.

WAH KEE WONTON
NOODLE RESTAURANT $
600 Williamson St.
(608) 255-5580

Perhaps the name gives away the specialty. The noodles were once made by hand on-site but now, though still made fresh and in Madison, are made with a special machine and off-site. There is a predictably large menu of the expected Chinese dishes such as sweet and sour chicken and even a few Thai and Vietnamese items or Korean kimchee, but the draw here is still the noodle menu. The angel-hair egg noodles come in two ways: tong mein (noodles in broth) and lo mein (broth on the side) have varied accompanying ingredients including vegetable or meat, plus hot and sour soup. Rice noodles and soba noodles are also available as are rice dishes. Daily specials are easy on the wallet. Beer and wine are served. Open daily for lunch and dinner with two-hour service gaps between the meals on weekdays. Carry-out and delivery are also available. Wheelchair accessible.

CONTEMPORARY FINE DINING

HARVEST $$–$$$$
21 North Pinckney St.
(608) 255-6075
www.harvest-restaurant.com

The trend toward locally sourced and organic foods continues to grow, but Harvest reigns supreme with its farm-to-table approach. Given Chef Derek Rowe's commitment to a seasonal local menu in a land of four seasons, the challenge can be great. But the results always speak for themselves with delicious gourmet dishes even in January using winter vegetables. Recipe influences may include French, Spanish, and

Italian cuisine, but the real heart and soul of Harvest's food is Wisconsin. Though the menu changes, expect Wisconsin grass-fed beef and other local meats, vegetables, and herbs as well as seasonal mushrooms and house-made pastas. Seafood Service is top-notch and staff know the menu well enough to explain the occasional ingredients only a hardcore foodie might know by name. This is a unique gourmet dining experience. Harvest is open Mon through Sat for dinner only and serves a themed dinner once a month on Sun. Reservations are not required, but appreciated. Outdoor seating is available seasonally. Wheelchair accessible.

L'ETOILE RESTAURANT $$$$
CAFÉ SOLEIL $
25 North Pinckney St.
(608) 251-0500
www.letoile-restaurant.com

Since opening its doors in the 1970s, L'Etoile has supported community-based, sustainable agriculture and created a unparalleled gourmet dining experience. Chef Tory Miller's menus showcase fresh and local ingredients grown by small farmers often organically. Favorite ingredients include Wisconsin artisanal cheeses, beef, pork, and locally farmed fruits and vegetables. Though menus are seasonal and vary, options always include beef, seafood, and vegetarian selections. The fine-dining L'Etoile operates on the 2nd floor, while the breakfast and lunchtime Café Soleil is at street level. Café Soleil serves create-your-own croissant sandwiches at breakfast and a variety of specialized sandwiches, salads, and personal pizzas at lunch. Both dining rooms show exposed brick, and the front windows look out on the Capitol grounds across the street. The cafe has an espresso bar and bakery that serves sweet and savory pastries, outstanding croissants, cookies, and breads. Reservations for L'Etoile are strongly recommended. Wheelchair accessible dining is available when prearranged, and dietary restrictions can be accommodated with prior notice. A prix-fixe menu is offered every Tues evening. L'Etoile occasionally offers cooking classes that include a three-course meal with wine, instruc-

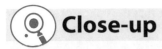 **Close-up**

Coffee Culture and Tea Revival

Coffee and tea are all the rage in Madison and it is a bit of mystery how so many coffeehouses can survive in such close proximity to one another. In the six blocks of State Street there is at least one dedicated coffeehouse per block and a few other cafes or restaurants that offer the same but with a fuller menu. Three companies roast coffee in the city and all support fair-trade commerce with growers: **Johnson Brothers**; **Ancora Coffee Roasters**, which serves many indie shops but also runs five outlets of its own in Madison alone; and **Just Coffee Co-op**, which partners with small grower cooperatives abroad. Milwaukee's **Alterra Coffee Roasters** does well here also. Two dedicated teahouses are listed below. However, the coffeehouses (which typically serve tea as well) are too numerous, and rather than list them out here, they can be found in the Nightlife/Entertainment section, if they are notable for live music, or the Art section, if they have rotating galleries by local artists. Free wireless Internet for customers is nearly universal, but for a few cases and even then it is probably part of a no-cell-phone zone philosophy.

DOBRÁ TEA

449 State St.
(608) 258-0488
www.dobratea.com

This is the second location in the United States for this Czech-based tea house franchise. *Dobrá* means "good" in Czech, and the tea houses' mission is to serve the best teas sourced from growers around the world in a fair-trade manner. Over 70 varieties of loose-leaf teas are on the menu. Servers attempt the Japanese matcha tea service and while they may not have gone through the years of requisite training, they do make a good effort. Gongfu, a Chinese traditional service, is also offered. In keeping with the conversational and personal atmosphere, WiFi is absent and management requests that cell phones be turned off. A variety of world music and eclectic decorations give Dobrá a Bohemian atmosphere, right in line with State Street. Small snack items are served, such as a hummus plate. Some sidewalk seating is available and hookah service is offered there. Open daily. Wheelchair accessible.

MACHA TEAHOUSE AND GALLERY

1934 Monroe St.
(608) 442-0500

An art gallery-cum-teahouse set in an old house just a few minutes west of Camp Randall Stadium, Macha is peaceful space for conversation and a spot of tea. The four tea rooms are works of art in themselves, tastefully decorated and richly painted, they offer either comfortable lounge furniture or traditional floor mats or cushions. Over 60 loose-leaf teas are sold by the ounce or brewed to order. Matcha, the traditional Japanese powdered green tea is served. Some sweets and light menu items go well with a pot. Closed Mon and the first Sun of every month.

tion, and recipes to take home. Watch the Web site or sign up for e-mail announcements. L'Etoile is open for dinner only and closed Sun and Mon. Café Soleil is closed on Sun and is wheelchair accessible. Local art adorns the walls.

OTTO'S RESTAURANT & BAR $$$
6405 Mineral Point Rd.
(608) 274-4044
www.ottosrestaurant.com

Set in a restored 1870s farmhouse, Otto's is that sort of place to take a date if you want to make an impression. The dining room has class while remaining relaxed. Service is professional and attentive, and the menu offers a number of Mediterranean and continental specialties favoring steaks and seafood. The sea bass and a grape-leaf wrapped salmon are a couple of the most popular dishes. Generally this enters the realm of pricey but the four-course tasting menus are excellent deals offered weekly after the summer jazz season. A full bar offers a wine list of more than 30 choices, including several by the glass. Jazz and blues on the deck is a summer treat on weekdays and reservations for this are strongly recommended. Watch for happy hour specials. Ample parking on-site. Closed on Sun and Mon but serving dinner and early appetizers all other days. A few steps to the door means this is not wheelchair accessible.

RESTAURANT MAGNUS   **$$–$$$**
120 East Wilson St.
(608) 258-8787
www.restaurantmagnus.com
Since it opened in 1998, Restaurant Magnus has made quite a name for itself. The menu has been constantly evolving but a few items gave it the reputation of a South American restaurant. In 2009 management announced it was focusing on Scandinavian cuisine. Chef Nicholas Johnson is committed to using local, organic, and seasonal foods whenever possible. This can be tricky in Wisconsin in winter, but the challenge is met. Preserving, curing, and canning contribute to the menu's depth, and the chef's creativity is apparent with dishes such as cubed raw tuna on Himalayan salt brick with cured tuna, pickled cucumbers, quail eggs, and a horseradish-dill dressing; or gravlax salmon and caviar with red onion, sour-cream custard, and a shot of dill-infused aquavit; or cinnamon-smoked lamb chops. The menu changes every three months and might include duck, venison, quail, wild boar, and much more. Vegetarian choices are numerous and 65–75% of the menu is gluten-free. Desserts are extraordinary and incorporate berries and fruits of the North such as the Veiled Norwegian Farm Girls, cinnamon-toasted bread

crumbs layered with apple compote, blackberries, and vanilla bean cream. A small plate menu complements the full bar with selections easier on the wallet. Live jazz is featured nightly and often demands a cover charge on weekends. Open daily for dinner with the last diners being seated by 10 p.m. Wheelchair accessible.

SARDINE   **$$$**
617 Williamson St.
(608) 441-1600
www.sardinemadison.com
When John Gadau and Phillip Hurley, the fellows responsible for Marigold Kitchen, opened this fine bistro in 2006 it was an immediate success, garnering Madison Magazine's Best New Restaurant Award. Located in the Machinery Row building where Willy Street meets John Nolen Drive, the sophisticated but unpretentious eatery is a relaxed fine-dining experience and offers a nice view of Lake Monona. Grilled scallops make an excellent appetizer, and for something a bit more regional check out the fried smelt with pickled cabbage and tartar sauce. The warm duck confit salad is popular. Entree options include pasta, seafood, meat, and poultry. Look for goat cheese-stuffed chicken breast with lima bean, corn, and bacon lardon ragout; or the pan-seared skate wing. Steamed mussels and frites is a reliable option. The brunch menu includes omelets, Belgian waffles, grilled salmon, and a German sausage platter. The restaurant has a full bar and parking is conveniently off-street and behind the building along the shore of Lake Monona. Open for dinner daily except Mon and for brunch on the weekends. Wheelchair accessible.

DELIS AND SANDWICHES

ELLA'S DELI AND ICE CREAM PARLOR   **$**
2902 East Washington Ave.
(608) 241-5291
www.ellas-deli.com
Ella Hirschfeld opened Ella's on State Street as a small kosher style deli/grocery/restaurant in the early 1960s. The current owners took over a few years later, dropped the grocery element,

and expanded the menu. The current location opened in 1976 and its collection of animated displays, designed and built on-site, keep kids—OK, and adults—entranced and intrigued. Baking is done in-house. The menu is long and includes Reubens, grilled chicken, lox, Matzo ball noodle soup, bagels, chopped liver, as well as the usual burgers and franks. Kids have an expanded menu to choose from with numerous healthy side-order alternatives to fries. For the sweet tooth, Ella's serves shakes, malts, sundaes, splits, fresh-baked pies, and vanilla custard ice cream with nearly 30 different toppings, plus a variety of hot fudge concoctions and other original creations. Open daily, ample parking onsite.

FRABONI'S ITALIAN SPECIALTIES
AND DELICATESSEN $
822 Regent St.
(608) 256-0546
www.frabonisdeli.com

For all things Italian this deli/specialty shop lies in the old Greenbush neighborhood where the Italian immigrants first put down roots in Madison. Dominic and Palmina Fraboni came to the United States in the early 1900's and opened a deli in Minnesota. Their son Angelo settled in Madison and in 1971 opened this store with his wife. Two of the couple's sons continue to run the deli and opened a second location in Monona in 1986 (108 Owen Rd., 608-222-6632). The sub sandwich menu is competitive with Subway pricing but of so much higher quality. Try the Muffuletta with ham, salami, mortadella, provolone, mozzarella, and Fraboni's homemade olive salad mix. Hot sandwiches with seasoned roast pork or meatballs are also available, and the house-made Italian sausage, which is only served on Thurs, is excellent. Soups and salads (lettuce or pasta) are for sale, and just about anything needed for cooking real Italian recipes can be found on the grocery shelves. Orders can be faxed or called in ahead of time. Seating is limited to a picnic table out back in summer. The store is wheelchair accessible.

GINO'S ITALIAN DELI $
4606 Verona Rd.
(608) 273-1981

This family-owned deli opened in the 1970s and has a solid reputation among the locals. Service is fast especially for lunch, and for customers who don't want to wait even just a little for a freshly made sandwich there are a few prewrapped items. Some salads are also prepackaged for customers on the go, otherwise the house-made salads are sold by weight. The veggie sandwich puts olives and artichoke hearts with vinaigrette dressing on wheat bread. The lasagna is a very hot item and also available in frozen form to reheat at home, and the meatball and hot Italian beef sandwiches are also popular. The Italian grocery part is a little small but not a bad place to pick up some good authentic ingredients. Wheelchair accessible. The Verona Road location only has two tables and some outside seating, but there are more places to sit down in the Middleton deli (6509 Century Ave., 608-827-0999).

GOTHAM NEW YORK BAGELS AND EATS $
112 East Mifflin St.
(608) 467-7642

702 South Park St.
(608) 467-7833
www.gothambagels.com

Locally owned, but New York-themed, this is more than just a bagel shop. The bagels themselves are hand-rolled and made fresh each morning. Eggs for breakfast bagels are local and organic, and the sausage comes from Milwaukee. Soups and salads incorporate fresh local produce and are made on-site. The build-your-own sandwich comes with bread options of sour dough, whole wheat, rye, multi-grain, and hero, or the varied list of bagels.

Lox and pastrami are from the Big Apple and the cream cheese is artisan-made in California. Some of the favorites are the Long-Guy-Land which has house-roasted turkey breast with fontina cheese, arugula, tomato, and mayo. There's the Spanish Harlem featuring shredded, roasted pork shoulder, capocollo ham, melted baby

Swiss, pickles, and Dijon mustard. The Williamsburg showcases the pastrami with a generous portion served on toasted rye with deli mustard. For vegetarians/vegans the "V" is a bagel with scallion tofu, roasted poblano peppers, tomato, arugula, and avocado. The Manhasset is made with hummus, roasted red peppers, sprouts, cucumbers, and black olive puree. Illy and local Kickapoo coffee are served. Wheelchair accessible. Metered parking on the street out front. Gotham has a second location in St. Mary's Hospital. Open daily from breakfast through lunch at both locations, but open an hour or two later at the Park Street location.

WILLY STREET CO-OP $
1221 Williamson St.
(608) 251-6776
www.willystreet.coop
The co-op is an eastside institution and the place to shop for local and organic groceries. The delicatessen is one of the best in town and the most expansive. The hot case offers far more than the typical salads and meat and potato options of a standard grocery store, and the menu changes daily. Examples are spicy Indian curries, vegan versions of Stroganoff, a vegan pot pie with tofu, and steelhead trout and leek fried rice. The hot case opens just before lunch while the cold case and salad bar are open all day. Made-to-order sandwiches are available most of the day as well, starting after the breakfast hour. The sushi is fresh; the California roll uses real crab meat, and the vegetarian rolls have avocado, broccolini, burdock root, sprouts, cucumber, and asparagus. Fresh organic and fair-trade coffee and a variety of teas, juices, and smoothies are also available. Wheelchair accessible. Customers who are not members of the co-op pay a 10% mark-up.

FRENCH/BISTRO

BRASSERIE V $–$$
1923 Monroe St.
(608) 255-8500
www.brasseriev.com

With the atmosphere of a casual Euro pub with a bit of class, Brasserie V has some great food to pair with great beer. In-house made linguine is a hit, and the sandwiches are under $10 and made on fresh Madison sourdough bread. Vegetarians have some good options in the apple and provolone, or cucumber and cream cheese sandwiches, as well as grilled portobello mushroom. A signature appetizer is moules frites—mussels cooked in garlic, wine, and butter, or some other sauce du jour, and accompanied by frites (that's fries, not French, but Belgian as they should be). Over 40 bottled Belgian imports and another 40-plus quality beers are available as well as two dozen wines by the glass. The centerpiece of the full bar are the 13 taps which lean toward Belgian, or at least Belgian-style, beers. This is a relaxed place to hang and savor fine flavors, and a nice spot for a casual date. Open daily, lunch and dinner most days, but brunch only on Sun. Some simple live music is offered most Sat nights. Parking is on the street, metered until 6 p.m. Wheelchair accessible. Does not accept reservations.

GERMAN

THE ESSEN HAUS $$
514 East Wilson St.
(608) 255-4674
www.essen-haus.com
Looking for a bit of sauerkraut with your wiener schnitzel? This restaurant, with its dark wood interior, could be right out of Bavaria. Staff dress in dirndls and lederhosen, and polka bands entertain diners and late-night lager drinkers. The wood back bar is from Madison's old Fauerbach Brewery. Sixteen German beers are on tap and served in authentic steins, and well over 200 other bottled varieties hail from around the world. For a communal drink order the giant glass boot of beer and learn the traditional rules of passing it around the table. Sauerbraten—beef marinated in red wine vinegar and topped with sweet and sour gravy—is served with red cabbage and bread dumplings. Apple strudel is on the dessert menu, and big bready pretzels satisfy happy-hour munchies. For a quick change of

scene and menu step through the door connecting to Come Back In Tavern (see Fish Fry page 65). Open for dinner all days but Mon. A parking lot is out back.

INDIAN

MAHARAJA $–$$
6713 Odana Rd.
(608) 833-1824

1707 Thierer Rd.
(608) 246-8525
www.maharajarestaurants.com

Consistently rated the top Indian restaurant in town, the two locations satisfy both eastsiders and westsiders. Recipes are from both northern and southern regions of India. The chicken tikka masala and rogan josh—lamb in a yogurt-based sauce—are a couple of the more popular dishes and of course there are many other curries, meats, and vegetarian options. A variety of fruit-based drinks are available, such as the classic mango lassi, and a full bar complements the menu. Kids under five eat free. Parking is in the lot out front. Open daily for lunch and dinner. Wheelchair accessible.

TAJ INDIAN RESTAURANT $–$$
1256 South Park St.
(608) 268-0772
www.thetajindianrestaurant.com

Another contender for best Indian food in town, Taj stakes its claim on the south side of town and is just minutes from downtown. Taj is located in a sort of mini-strip mall with a parking lot between it and Park Street. The menu offers a variety of curries paired with lamb, beef, chicken, vegetables, or seafood. Tandoori is also on the menu of course. The spiciness of dishes is adjusted to client wishes. Vegetarian options are numerous but the vegetable biryani (a basmati rice dish similar to paella) might be the king of the lot. Wine and domestic and Indian beers are served. The lunch buffet is great for the indecisive types who like to try everything. Open daily for lunch and dinner. Wheelchair accessible.

INDONESIAN

**BANDUNG INDONESIAN
RESTAURANT** $–$$
600 Williamson St.
(608) 255-6910
www.bandungrestaurant.com

This Indonesian restaurant is just another example of Madison's broad spectrum of ethnic cuisines. Family-owned and operated, it consistently wins local praises for its food. With the abundance of Chinese and Thai food, there is always a call for something a little different. The catfish curry is quite popular as is the Indonesian fried-rice standard, nasi goreng. Fried noodle dishes, soups, and stir-fries come with a variety of meats or vegetable versions. The menu already lists a good number of vegetarian dishes, but the kitchen can also modify recipes for vegans and other special food requests. Takeout and delivery are also available. Open daily for dinner and only weekdays for lunch. Wheelchair accessible.

ITALIAN

CAFÉ LA BELLITALIA $
1026 North Sherman Ave.
(608) 243-1200
www.cafelabellitalia.com

This small, family-owned establishment brings the owner's Sicilian birthplace to Madison. The marinara is as sweet as it would be in Sicily itself. Portions are generous while prices are moderate. Ravioli options include a variety stuffed with lobster which receives raves. Eggplant parmigiana is authentic and the fried eggplant strip appetizers are cooked perfectly. This is the best place in town for spaghetti and meatballs. Pizza is also on the menu and available for delivery. Tiramisu is a good dessert choice and beer and wine are served. The management is friendly and accommodating and this makes for a great family dining experience. Family specials are very reasonably priced and serve dishes such as spaghetti or baked ravioli for three to four people with three loaves of garlic bread. Some coupons on the Web site can be printed. There is off-street parking but the lot is small and can get cramped. Open for lunch on weekdays and dinner daily. Wheelchair accessible.

LOMBARDINO'S ITALIAN
RESTAURANT & BAR $$–$$$
2500 University Ave.
(608) 238-1922
www.lombardinos.com

This is widely regarded as Madison's best Italian restaurant and a good choice for a fancier meal or romantic date. Matt Lombardino gave his name to it when he opened it in 1954. New owners took over in 2000 and left the rustic appeal of the dining room. The chef tries to use locally produced and organic foods whenever possible and travels to Italy periodically to maintain relationships with vendors and the cuisine itself. The menu has a great selection of antipastos and entrees, and the pastas are prepared perfectly—sad rarity in many American Italian eateries. Food is consistently good. Superbly prepared pizza is also on the menu and is brick-oven baked Napoletana style. The menu is seasonal and changes every couple months. The restaurant makes its own limoncello and offers a fine assortment of grappa at the full bar. Reservations recommended. Open for dinner all days but Mon. Located close to University Hospital on the near west side.

> **i** Some of the pizzerias are recommended for Italian dishes beyond a pizza pie. Look under Pizza below.

VIN SANTO TRATTORIA $$–$$$
7462 Hubbard Ave., Middleton
(608) 836-1880
www.vinsanto.us

This is the kind of unassuming little place one might find in an Italian neighborhood. Pasta is fresh and ingredients are wholesome and simple. Nothing is overdone or overpriced. The dining room is small and cozy making this a nice casual dinner date destination or perhaps a night out with old friends. Pasta dishes are well under $20 and vegetarian options are numerous. Try the eggplant torte (melanzane) for a delicious vegetarian option. There is a full bar and the

restaurant is wheelchair accessible. Open daily for dinner. Call for reservations.

JAPANESE

RESTAURANT MURAMOTO $$
225 King St.
(608) 259-1040
www.muramoto.biz

Since owner/chef Shinji Muramoto opened his restaurant in 2004 it has become the ideal of Asian fusion fine dining. A long curving bar and a classy modern interior go well with photogenic minimalist plates. The miso-marinated black cod is quite popular, and dishes such as lamb curry might alter conceptions of what is Asian fusion. At dinner, a small bite menu (sakizuke) allows diners to sample various items for a gradually decreasing price. Expertly prepared sushi is also on the menu. Sunday evenings often offer set-price chef's tasting menus. The full bar offers some unusual and slightly pricey cocktails. Consider Hendrick's Pepito gin muddled with cucumber and lime. Open daily for lunch and dinner during the week, and dinner only on the weekends. Wheelchair accessible.

SUSHI MURAMOTO $$
546 North Midvale Blvd.
(608) 441-1090
www.muramoto.biz

On the near west side at Hilldale Mall is the second restaurant of owner/chef Shinji Muramoto. A full-blown sushi bar serves some painstakingly prepared rolls that should satisfy the most fastidious of sushi fans. A few other meals are on the menu including the miso black cod so popular at the other Muramoto location. Open daily for lunch and dinner. Wheelchair accessible.

WASABI JAPANESE RESTAURANT AND
SUSHI BAR $–$$
449 State St., 2nd floor
(608) 255-5020
www.wasabi-madison.com

Probably the most affordable sushi in town and done well at that. The setting, in a two-story

State Street fast-food looking building, doesn't do much for ambience, but the food speaks for itself. Expect soba noodle and tempura and the lacquered boxes in which lunches are often served in Japan. The sushi and sashimi menu is ample and Sapporo Beer and sake are served. Open for lunch and dinner, with breaks between the two meals, but closed on Mon. They don't split checks. Wheelchair accessible (there is an elevator).

KOREAN

NEW SEOUL KOREAN RESTAURANT $–$$
2503 University Ave.
(608) 238-3331

Get your kimchee fix at Madison's only Korean restaurant. Be sure to try the bibimbap—rice with veggies, a raw egg (it cooks as you mix ingredients), and a choice of meat or tofu served in a hot stone pot. Korean barbecue is also served. Vegetarian items are available on request. Beer is served and carry-out is available. The setting is nothing special, but the service is friendly and the recipes authentic. Not wheelchair accessible. Closed Sun. Open for lunch and dinner with a short closing in between the two meals.

MEDITERRANEAN

ATHENS GYROS $
5420 Willow Rd., Waunakee
(608) 249-6720
www.tradergus.com

Located inside a Shell Station off County M just west of WI 113/Northport Road, this little Greek eatery has one of the best gyros in town. It may be in a gas station but it is not the usual microwaved schlock from the freezer. This is the homestyle cooking of Gus and Angela Kyriakopoulos. For a long time, Gus managed Parthenon Gyros on State Street. In addition to gyros, the menu offers chicken and pork (*souvlaki*) and a spinach/feta option (*spanakopita*), as well as salads and desserts such as baklava. American alternatives such as burgers, grilled cheese, and chicken tenders should satisfy members of the dinner party

not partial to Greek fare. Don't expect ambience; most business is carry-out, and decor includes racks of junk food and coolers of drinks and convenience items. If you are fishing the Yahara River nearby or on the way to Governor Nelson State Park, this is a good place for picnic food. Alcohol is served. Wheelchair accessible. Open daily.

THE DARDANELLES RESTAURANT $–$$
1851 Monroe St.
(608) 256-8804
www.thedardanellesonmonroe.com

Though it bills itself as Mediterranean, many fans think of it as a Turkish restaurant—which is still Mediterranean, no? Grilled marinated lamb is one of the house specialties and the couscous salad is a good opener. Vegetarians may prefer the Atlas Casserole made with lentils, squash, carrots, spinach, rosemary, and thyme and served with a dill-yogurt sauce. The lunch menu differs from the dinner options and options include falafel, spinach, and feta pastries (Turkish *borek*), and lamb meatballs (*kofta*). Baklava is on the dessert menu with a few other sweet options. Turkish coffee is available after the meal, and the owner and executive chef Barbara Wright can read fortunes in the grounds. Parking is on the street. Open daily, but for brunch only on Sun. Wheelchair accessible.

PARTHENON GYROS RESTAURANT $
316 State St.
(608) 251-6311
www.parthenongyros.com

A gyro here is a piece of Wisconsin history. When Parthenon opened its doors in 1972, this was the first place to serve them in the state. In the front window, the vertical spit of that blend of lamb and beef that only comes in a gyro slowly rotates across the burner. The tzatziki, a yogurt-based cucumber sauce, is fabulous and no gyro is whole without it. Chicken is available as well. Pitzsas are pita pizzas with various toppings including a veggie version. A phyllo-dough spinach pie with feta is another great meatless option and baklava is on for dessert. The french fries here are some of the best. The rooftop terrace is great in fair weather. Open daily for lunch, dinner, and some late-night fare until 11.

PLAKA TAVERNA $-$$
410 East Wilson St.
(608) 251-4455
www.plakamadison.com
The old Cleveland Diner, a long-time breakfast standard, went Greek in 2008. Plaka still serves the popular American breakfast with a few Greek twists (gyros omelet, for example). Lunch offers an assortment of gyros and salads, and a few other nice alternatives including several vegetarian dishes. Dinner goes a bit nicer adding a good selection of appetizers (*meze*) as well as finer meals beyond gyros such as *moussaka* (a traditional eggplant-based casserole) and kabobs. But the atmosphere remains casual and social as the taverna label implies. A full bar serves some local beers as well as Greek brews and wines and a fine selection of ouzos. Watch for backgammon nights. Open very early for breakfast and then serving lunch and dinner. Closed Mon, and Sun is breakfast only. Wheelchair accessible.

MEXICAN

What qualifies as a good Mexican restaurant depends on one's criteria. The philosophy used here is that it is a simple operation, often family-run, with menus that may include some items that don't appear on the typical North American menu (tripe or beef tongue, for instance). These places do not aim for the Chi Chi's or the Taco Bell crowd. Not listed here are Madison's Pedro's, Laredo's, or even La Hacienda, which, however popular, have more of an air-brushed, crossover appeal. The restaurants below probably won't have a single sombrero on the walls and may even lack decoration entirely. What they won't be short on is quality, fresh ingredients, and authenticity, and odds are good a Mexican soccer match or soap opera will be on the TV. This is by no means an exhaustive list and new places pop up in unlikely neighborhoods offering a sort of Mexican food treasure hunt.

ANTOJITOS EL TORIL $
515 Cottage Grove Rd.
(608) 358-7718
This cozy little place is like eating at your Mexican friend's parent's house. Friendly service complements good hearty Mexican fare for an economical price. Handmade tortillas and fresh chips with two nice salsas are standard, and all the usual items—tacos, gorditas, enchiladas—are served with shredded queso blanco and authentic Mexican cream. Avocado enchiladas are a nice vegetarian choice, and menudo is served on the weekends. Many local fans swear by the horchata here. Beer and wine are served and there is outside seating and a small parking lot. Wheelchair accessible. Open daily for lunch and dinner.

LA MESTIZA MEXICAN CUISINE $-$$
6644 Odana Rd.
(608) 826-0178
www.lamestiza.net
Located on Madison's west side in the Market Square strip mall, the interiors here are much nicer than hole-in-the-wall with booths and tables and colorful artwork on the walls. The chips and salsa are fresh and good and tortillas are handmade. Look for the *cochinita pibil*. A specialty of the Yucatan, it is citrus-marinated pork with the reddish color of annatto added and cooked slowly. Beer, wine, and real margaritas are served as are horchata and tamarindo. The weekend brunch has good breakfast options such as huevos rancheros. Coupons can be printed off the Web site. Wheelchair accessible. Open for lunch and dinner daily and brunch on weekends.

TAQUERIA EL PASTOR $
2010 South Park St.
(608) 280-8898
This may be the only place in town to find *huitlacoche*, a mushroomlike blight on corn sometimes called corn smut but considered a delicacy in Mexico. Even here it may not always be on the menu. The *carne asada* is fantastic and lamb barbacoa is an unusual find. Seafood lovers should not miss the shrimp cocktail. Alcohol is served.

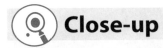 **Close-up**

Food Carts

Around the Capitol Square and along the entrance into Library Mall at the campus end of State Street, the carts come out during the day. Some of the area restaurants such as Buraka or Café Costa Rica got their start finding a fan base with their cart-based meals. Menus range from Mexican (from Santa Fe) and various Asian cuisines (Thai, Indian, Vietnamese, Japanese, Indonesian) to fantastic smoothies and fresh juices. Some carts also come out on Sat mornings around the Capitol during the farmers' market. **Dandelion** food cart serves vegetarian/vegan specialties on Martin Luther King Jr. Boulevard off the Capitol Square. Carts receive assigned sites each year and this is based on a panel of judges scoring each cart on the variety of its menu and the cart's appearance. Don't worry about food safety out there—city inspectors are active and strict.

Open daily from breakfast to late night for all meals. Wheelchair accessible.

TAQUERIA GUADALAJARA $
1033 South Park St.
(608) 250-1824
www.lataqueriaguadalajara.com

You know this is not a trendy Americanized version when you see beef tongue and cheeks and tripe on the menu. Built into a house, this family-operated taqueria is cozy with a few spots at the counter and some tables in the back room. Odds are a *fútbol* game is on the TV. A deck outside with a few tables and umbrellas feels like a cookout with the neighbors. Selections include tacos, tortas, and gorditas, as well as huaraches and sopes, homemade thick corn tortillas topped with beans, sour cream, lettuce, tomatoes, meat, and cheese. Huaraches add green sauce and avocado. Vegetarian options are also available and specials come and go. The prices are as delicious as the food and the tamales should not be missed. It's street parking only but there is usually enough space on Park or around the corner on Emerson Street. If you don't want to wait for a seat, they do carry-out and delivery. Open daily. Not wheelchair accessible.

MIDDLE EASTERN

KABUL AFGHANISTAN RESTAURANT $$
541 State St.
(608) 256-6322

Kabul has been around a good long time on State Street, and reviews over the years have been consistently good. The menu includes Middle Eastern/Mediterranean options beyond the Afghani tradition as well. Meals start with flatbread and then salad or some good soup. Baked artichoke hearts with Parmesan is an excellent appetizer choice. There are some vegetarian choices on the menu, and the couscous is especially good. Outdoor seating is nice and there is a full bar. This is wheelchair accessible. A great spot for lunch on a State Street sort of day.

LULU'S DELI AND RESTAURANT $-$$
2524 University Ave.
(608) 233-2172

This was Madison's first Middle Eastern restaurant and its longevity is testament to its quality and reputation. Expect the traditional Arabic lamb, chicken, and beef dishes and healthy and flavorful appetizers such as hummus and baba ghanoush. Entrees include vegetarian options and grilled selections along with classics shawarma and kibbe. Sandwiches with falafel, shawarma, or other options make great affordable lunches. A few wines and beers are served. Wheelchair accessible. Open for lunch and dinner all days but Sun, and closed for a break between the two meals from Mon through Thurs.

MEDITERRANEAN CAFÉ $
625 State St.
(608) 251-8510

"Cheap and delicious" is a killer combination. Add this cafe's proximity to the university and you've got a serious draw for students. Falafel for the vegetarians, lamb shawarma for the carnivores. The lentil soup is superb. Closed Sun; otherwise open from mid-morning to late afternoon. Does not accept credit cards but there are ATMs not far up State Street. Wheelchair accessible.

SHISH CAFÉ INC. $$
5510 University Ave.
(608) 236-9006

Syrian chef Rabeh Bnyat owned a restaurant in Damascus before he moved to the United States. He and his staff blend spices by hand and work from his own recipes. An extensive menu does well for vegetarians and in fact all but two appetizers are meat-free. The seafood is superb as is the variety of lamb dishes. The kebab platter serves two and is a great choice. Unlimited house-made pita comes with every meal and beer and wine are served. Don't forget baklava for dessert. The lunch menu is smaller but adds sandwiches. Service is relaxed creating a great atmosphere for the slow enjoyment of a meal as is more customary in the Middle Eastern cultures. A belly dancer entertains on the first and third Sat of every month. Wheelchair accessible. Open for lunch and dinner with a service break between the two meals. Closed Mon. The cafe offers catering and private parties and carryout is available.

NEPALESE

One may be impressed to encounter even one Nepalese restaurant in a city, but Madison has three. It's not coincidence, but rather the growing success of a family business that began with Himal Chuli on State Street.

CHAUTARA RESTAURANT $$
334 State St.
(608) 251-3626

Building on the Himal Chuli (see below) experience, Chautara's menu shares a few basic items but ventures into its own identity with higher-end plates and a bit more meat and fish (though vegetarians can still be happy here.) The tofu wrap on the lunch menu is popular. Beer and wine are served. Wheelchair accessible. Open daily for lunch and dinner.

DOBHAN $$
2110 Atwood Ave.
(608) 242-4448

The newest of the three, Dobhan is also the most spacious and finely decorated. Located on the east side it has a bigger draw for dinner and a more adventurous menu that dabbles a bit into Indian cuisine bordering on fusion. Reservations are a good idea. Serves alcohol. Wheelchair accessible. Open daily for lunch and dinner.

HIMAL CHULI $$
318 State St.
(608) 251-9225

Decorated with Nepali tapestries, statues, and photographs, and accompanied by Indian music, the small restaurant features a six-page menu filled with exotic dishes followed by detailed descriptions. Himal Chuli has a plethora of vegetarian and vegan selections. This is a good place to escape State Street's bustle and to relax and take in a slow meal. Beer and wine are served. Momocha, the vegetable dumplings are recommended, as are the flat bread roti and the lentil soup *dal*. Cash only. Wheelchair accessible.

PIZZA

CAFÉ PORTA ALBA $–$$
558 North Midvale Blvd.
(608) 441-0202
www.cafeportaalba.com

In Italy it took national legislation to define what is truly a traditional Neapolitan pizza. A pizzeria must pass inspection in order to use

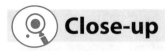 **Close-up**

The Fish Fry

It's Friday and that means time for a fish fry. This Wisconsin institution can be traced back to at least the 1920s but has its roots in Catholic tradition.

From the early days of Christianity, Fridays were considered days of abstinence out of respect toward the crucifixion of Christ. In the 9th century, Pope Nicholas I made it specifically a meat issue. Fish, who may be offended they don't rate as flesh, were still allowed as they were not the meat of a warm-blooded animal. Ergo, they became a protein source of choice. When Catholics such as many of the Irish, Polish, German, and other immigrants settled in Wisconsin, this practice came with them. In the 19th and early 20th centuries, fish was still abundant in Wisconsin lakes. During Prohibition, taverns—which had lost the primary source of their business—began serving fish meals to stay afloat (and in some cases to draw clients to sell beer under the table). Frying is a great way to prepare an abundance of it and make it taste good, even if it didn't otherwise.

The meal often is an all-you-can-eat serving of cod, walleye, lake perch, if you're lucky, or even bluegill. Battered and deep-fried it comes with coleslaw and perhaps french fries or another form of potato.

Now many restaurants, taverns, and supper clubs serve a Friday night fish fry. In some cases, public halls host them for fund-raisers or just nice social events for the family at the end of the work week. Watch for them at church halls. The family-friendly, social event is officially served on a Friday, and more often during the Lent season, the 40 days leading up to Easter. Though some eateries will offer it at other times in the week, it somehow loses that charm of "everybody-all-together."

See a list below of some of the best places to enjoy a fish fry in the Madison area.

ST. PETER CATHOLIC SCHOOL

7129 County Hwy. K, Middleton
(608) 831-4846
www.stpetermiddleton.org

This tiny little country church outside Middleton (actually Ashton, WI) is arguably *the* place to go for a traditional fish fry. Held only once or twice a month, the all-you-can-eat fish fries

the label Verace Pizza Napoletana. By assuring the proper ingredients (from the Naples area), dough preparation and thickness, and the high baking temperature in a wood-fired brick oven, Porta Alba has passed inspection and holds the label. The cafe name has historical significance: Porta Alba was the first pizzeria in Naples with table seating; prior to that street vendors sold it. Owner Vincenzo Pugliese's first pizza memories are of his mother baking the simple pies in the family's wood-fired oven in a small town not far from Naples. Vincenzo adheres to the principles of these simple and healthy pizzas. Other items on the menu include some pasta dishes (for dinner only, but as the business grows these will likely be offered for lunch as well), some salads and panini, as well as desserts such as tiramisu. Rotating specials offer some other Neapolitan originals like *impepata* of mussels, which uses San Marzano tomatoes and a spicy pepper sauce. The aim is authenticity, from Lavazza coffee and an oven built by a third-generation artisan in Italy, to the plates and tableware. The marble tabletops are even imported. Beer and wine are served

draw upwards of 1,700 people to the school basement. Deep-fried cod with baked potato or fries, veggies, coleslaw, homemade bread, dessert, and milk and coffee. Beer and soda are available out of a big cow tank. Get there early or late, as the wait in line has been reported up to an hour at its busiest. Served on scheduled Fridays from about 5 to 8 p.m. Check the Web site for dates and prices. No credit cards accepted.

POPULAR FISH FRIES

Alchemy
1980 Atwood Ave.
(608) 204-7644
www.alchemycafe.net

The Avenue Bar
1128 East Washington Ave.
(608) 257-6877
www.avenuebarmadison.com

Come Back In
508 East Wilson St.
(608) 258-8619
www.essen-haus.com

Dexter's Pub
301 North St.
(608) 244-3535
www.dexterspubmadison.com

The Esquire Club
1025 North Sherman Ave.
(608) 249-0193
www.esquireclubmadison.com

The Essen Haus
514 East Wilson St.
(608) 255-4674
www.essen-haus.com

The Old Fashioned
23 North Pinckney St.
(608) 310-4545
www.theoldfashioned.com

Quivey's Grove
6261 Nesbitt Rd.
(608) 273-4900
www.quiveysgrove.com

Stamm House
6625 Century Ave., Middleton
(608) 831-5835
www.stammhouserestaurant.com

Toby's Supper Club
3717 South Dutch Mill Rd.
(608) 222-6913

Village Green
7508 Hubbard Ave., Middleton
(608) 831-9962

and takeout is available. The entrance faces the Hilldale Mall entrance near Sundance Cinemas. Open daily for lunch and dinner. Parking is in Hilldale's free ramp right behind the restaurant. Wheelchair accessible.

GLASS NICKEL PIZZA CO. $$
2916 Atwood Ave.
(608) 245-0880
www.glassnickelpizza.com
This is one of Madison's favorite pizzas and alternative-fuel delivery cars can be seen buzzing them around town from multiple locations. The dine-in restaurant on the east side has a full bar with a tap list of 16 microbrews and imports and a wine list of about a dozen. The menu goes far beyond pizza with a wide variety of sandwiches, salads, and pasta dishes. This is a casual dining room as much a bar as a restaurant. Glass Nickel has locations at 5003 University Ave. as well as in Fitchburg and Sun Prairie. Parking is behind the restaurant off Fair Oaks Avenue. Open daily, the restaurant offers a 5% discount when customers pay in cash.

GREENBUSH BAR $
914 Regent St.
(608) 257-2874
www.madisonsbestpizza.net

Not much remains of Madison's early Italian neighborhood, Greenbush, other than the name and memories. But this bar, located in the basement of the old brick Italian Workman's Club building, lives on. Much is homemade from the soups and peasant bread to the Italian sausage, and all meat and eggs are acquired locally. The crackerlike, thin-crust pizza is the highlight, though they also do a thick-crust variety, and the sandwiches and pastas aren't bad either. The decor is unpretentious to say the least, with colored lights strung along the ceiling like perpetual Christmas. Tall clientele may have to duck their heads as they descend into the basement from the street. Out of the way and quiet, this is a good place for conversation or an off-the-beaten path casual date. A full bar has a small but nice selection of wines and good beers. The homemade cannoli are recommended for dessert. Parking is on the side streets. Greenbush is closed on Sun but otherwise open for dinner and serving a bit later than most places. Not wheelchair accessible.

IAN'S PIZZA BY THE SLICE $
319 North Frances St.
(608) 257-0597

115 State St.
(608) 257-9248
www.ianspizza.com

Ian Gurfield came to Madison in 2001 on a mission to open a good late-night pizza-by-the-slice shop for the hungry college students. He picked the perfect town. So successful was he that he opened another location on State Street, Ian's Pizza and Salad. By the pie or by the slice, it's a decent and affordable hunger stopper, and though traditional toppings are offered, the slightly unusual blends are what get some double takes from first time clientele. You won't often see grilled chicken mashed potatoes or chili cheese fritos pizza on a menu. Fans swear by the steak and fries pizza, but the mac 'n cheese slice is historically the best seller. Vegetarians have good options here. Open Mon through Sat from 11 a.m. to bar closing. The State Street location delivers and is open daily.

LA ROCCA'S RESTAURANT
AND PIZZERIA $-$$
940 Williamson St.
(608) 204-9100
www.laroccaspizzeria.com

Vito and Caterina La Rocca hail from Marsala in Sicily and opened this Willy Street restaurant in 2006 in a former appliance store. The menu has five combination pizzas, including the La Rocca, a four-cheese pizza with ham, sausage, mushrooms, and black olives. Topping options are quite numerous and include *bresaola*, a thinly sliced cured beef not commonly available. The pies come in four sizes from 10" to 16" and styles: thin, thick, pan, and stuffed. Entrees are a variety of solid pasta plates from cheese tortellini to lasagna and fettuccine Alfredo. The homemade cannoli, a Sicilian contribution to Italian cuisine, are sure to please. Pizza is available by the slice during lunch. Soda comes in bottles, and beer and wine are also served. The dining space is a bit small, but friendly and casual. Open for lunch and dinner weekdays, dinner only on Sat, and closed Sun.

PAISAN'S RESTAURANT $-$$
131 West Wilson St.
(608) 257-3832
www.paisansrestaurant.biz

Paisan's has been around since the 1950s. Once located in an odd sort of strip mall in the heart of the campus area, Paisan's (and others) had to clear out for new construction. Their current location overlooking Lake Monona is a vast improvement. The patio seating is lovely in warm seasons, and the circular booth seating around the bar is nice for cocktail hour. Some interior booths are not terribly comfortable, but are rather private. Come to Paisan's for a great thin-crust pizza; the sizes range from petite (6") to large (16"). The rest of the menu shows pastas, sandwiches, and salads, but is largely forgettable with the notable exception of the Garibaldi sandwich. Underground parking is free on weekends and after 5 p.m. on weekdays. Open daily for lunch and dinner.

PIZZA BRUTTA $
1805 Monroe St.
(608) 257-2120
www.pizzabrutta.com
If you've ever been to Italy you will recognize this as an Italian pie. Baked in a wood-fired brick oven the crust comes out charred a bit on the outside and chewy on the inside. Patrons order at the counter and wait at a booth or table to be served. The pizzas are divided into two styles: *rosso* (red) and *bianco* (white). The *rosso* has a base of San Marzano tomatoes, fresh mozzarella (the soft kind, not the firmer American version), olive oil, and sea salt, while the *bianco* offers the same minus the tomatoes. For elegant simplicity, try the *Margherita,* a pizza rosso with fresh basil. Much like Neapolitan pizzas, the toppings are not overwhelming, and the pies are small enough for one person, so big-portion eaters be aware. Don't let the pie steal the show, however; the sandwiches and salads work great for lunch. Local beers are on tap. Open daily for lunch and dinner.

ROMAN CANDLE PIZZERIA $$
1054 Williamson St.
(608) 258-2000

1920 Parmenter St., Middleton
(608) 831-7777
www.theromancandle.com
This cozy and popular neighborhood pizzeria stresses using local food sources and makes for a good outing for families. The outside seating in nice weather adds to the community appeal. The menu shows a full-range of combo pizzas and notably some good vegetarian options such as the Animal Lovers Pizza with broccoli, spinach, onion, red pepper, and fresh basil. The Pestoral Pizza is their best seller topped with pesto, feta, mozzarella, artichoke hearts, roasted red pepper, kalamata olives, and roma tomatoes. Building your own pizza can get pricey, so it might be best to stick to menu combos if you're on a budget. The roasted red pepper and tomato soup is also highly regarded. Beer

and wine are served, and the place is wheelchair accessible. Open daily for lunch and dinner.

SEAFOOD

Many of the contemporary fine-dining restaurants also serve great seafood. For fish fries see the Close-up section on pages 64 and 65.

OCEAN GRILL $$$
117 Martin Luther King Jr. Blvd.
(608) 285-2582
www.foodfightinc.com/oceangrill.htm
Seafood in Wisconsin is often treated with a heavy hand so it is nice to have such a gourmet approach. The open-concept kitchen and chic interiors have a big city appeal. Fresh seafood is brought in daily. The chef's pride and joy and a customer favorite is his own creation, potato-crusted sea bass. Another signature dish is the sesame ahi tuna tacos. Small plate options are extensive and include seafood enchiladas and jumbo lump crab cakes. Steak, pork, and chicken are also on the menu. Lunch, which often caters mostly to business clientele as it is right downtown near the Capitol and Monona Terrace, has its own menu and includes From the Grill, a list of six different types of fish which can be prepared six different ways. There is a gluten-free menu available and dairy-free options as well. The full bar runs a great happy hour and has 30 martinis on its menu. The wine list approaches 100 vintages and free wine tastings on Wed. Patio seating is available in seasonable weather. Ocean Grill is great for special dining experiences. Wheelchair accessible. Closed Sun but open for dinner all other days, and lunch only on weekdays. Underground parking is in the Block 89 Building with an entrance on Doty Street. The restaurant staff validates parking tickets for dinner.

SOUTH AMERICAN

INKA HERITAGE (PERUVIAN) $–$$
602 South Park St.
(608) 310-4282
www.inkaheritagerestaurant.com

Inka Heritage opened in 2007 and immediately drew attention with its high-quality food and some recipes not familiar to the average Madisonian. Appetizers are delicious but offer a few unusual items such as fire-roasted beef heart marinated in a pepper paste, herbs, and spices and served with Creole sauce. Potatoes, of which there are over 4,000 varieties in Peru, play a large role in the menu. The signature dish is the Lomito Inka Heritage, tenderloin served with rice and beans, golden fried yucca, and topped with a fried egg. Seafood entrees total about a dozen and include unique preparations of shrimp, trout, sea bass, and much more. *Ceviche*, the classic lime-marinated fish dish of Peru, is on the menu as well. Fri nights host live music. Just a five-minute drive from downtown, Inka Heritage is open daily for lunch and dinner. Not wheelchair accessible.

SAMBA BRAZILIAN GRILL/
CABANA ROOM $$$–$$$$
240 West Gilman St.
(608) 257-1111
www.sambabraziliangrill.com
Call it carnivore heaven. Meat is served gaucho-style, meaning the meats, roasted on a spit, are brought around to the tables to be carved to order. Start out with sides from the salad bar. The all-you-can-eat meats start coming when diners change the table color-code to green. Meat options are many, often up to 10, and include sirloin, tenderloin, Parmesan-encrusted pork loin, ribs, chicken breast, and spicy Portuguese sausages. The famous Brazilian drink *caipirinha* is recommended from the bar. Open for dinner daily plus brunch on Sun. The wine list is long and touches on South American and Spanish vintages and more, and the rum list tops 40 choices. Live jazz is featured most weeknights. The downstairs restaurant is Cabana Room and is open for lunch and dinner with a full bar. The menu offers soups, stews, salads, grilled Cubanos, burgers, and wraps. Outside seating is available. An elevator takes guests up to Samba. Wheelchair accessible.

SOUTHWESTERN & TEX-MEX

ELDORADO GRILL $$
744 Williamson St. # 2
(608) 280-9378
www.foodfightinc.com/eldorado.htm
More upscale than a neighborhood taqueria, the Western-themed dining room at Eldorado brings a nice blend of Tex-Mex and Southwestern to the table. Standards are there such as massive burritos, but the choices go wider into seafood (lobster enchiladas) and alternatives such as bison meatloaf, smoked chile roasted duck, or Thai vegetable fajitas. The smokehouse menu offers Texas-style brisket, sausage, ribs, pulled pork, and chicken, but vegetarians also have a wide selection to choose from. Consider grilled spinach enchiladas. Check out the Sun brunch and try the big blue-corn griddle cake with chile butter and chile syrup. The signature dessert is pecan pie with chile flakes, chocolate chips, and a bit of tequila. The full bar has an excellent tequila selection (more than 80) and the margaritas get raves. Outdoor seating is available and parking is in a sizeable lot. Open daily for dinner and on Sun for brunch. Wheelchair accessible.

PASQUAL'S SOUTHWESTERN
RESTAURANT $
2534 Monroe St.
(608) 238-4419
www.pasquals.net
A casual Southwestern option that won't empty the wallet, Pasqual's does good burritos, tostadas, enchiladas, fajitas, and more. The shredded beef tacos are especially delicious, and the double tacos come with a soft flour tortilla wrapped around a hard corn tortilla with a layer of guacamole or refried beans sticking them together. Huevos rancheros is always a hit for breakfast, and vegetarians and vegans have good choices. The tortilla chips are fresh-made and the salsa and guacamole are some of the best. A children's menu offers hot dog and grilled cheese sandwich-style options for the timid tongue. Service is deli-style at the Monroe location but their Hilldale eatery (608-663-8226)

offers sit-down service, a full bar, and makes a good happy hour/dinner meeting place before a movie at Sundance Cinema nearby. Open daily.

SPANISH/TAPAS

ENO VINO WINE BAR AND BISTRO $$–$$$
601 Junction Rd.
(608) 664-9565
www.eno-vino.com

A great place to unwind after work, Eno Vino dims the lights and offers a convivial atmosphere with a large fireplace and comfortable lounge furniture. The bruschetta gets raves and offers six styles or a combination of any four. The "To Share" menu has a variety of nice appetizers such as portobello mushroom ravioli and crab spring rolls. There's a full bar, but the wine list is the main attraction offering a number of wines by the glass. Gourmet cheese and meat plates make for great wine pairings. Outdoor seating is available in season, and parking is in a private lot. This place qualifies as nightlife as much as it does a restaurant. Open daily from 4 p.m. Wheelchair accessible.

TAPAS RIAS $–$$
2518 Allen Blvd., Middleton
(608) 831-0528

Don't let the strip mall environs fool you; this tapas bar has a pleasant upscale ambience. The authentic and varied Spanish tapas go well with great sangria and a good looking bar. Vegetarians have some healthy options here and this is one of those rare places that serves paella. The wine list tops 80 vintages. Open daily. Wheelchair accessible.

STEAKHOUSES

JOHNNY DELMONICO'S STEAKHOUSE $$$–$$$$
130 South Pinckney St.
(608) 257-8325
www.foodfightinc.com/delmonicos.htm

This is a great place for special occasions and has been voted best steakhouse in Madison in *Isthmus'*

annual reader survey. The dining room has a touch of class expected from a fine-dining experience with white linen on the tables and smart service. The mahogany bar is a perfect perch for an aperitif. Though the aged Angus steaks are the specialty, seafood should not be overlooked and the rack of lamb is quite popular as well. The wine list is extensive. The nicely priced three-course seasonal meal is the chef's choice of appetizer, entrée, and dessert and changes frequently. Contrary to the more sizeable tab you can expect to run for dinner, the lunch is very affordable with sandwiches and smaller entrees. Open daily for dinner and weekdays for lunch. Wheelchair accessible. Parking is underground at Block 89 Building on Doty Street and requires customers to bring their parking ticket with them for validation at the restaurant. Reservations recommended.

SMOKY'S CLUB $$$
3005 University Ave.
(608) 233-2120
www.smokysclub.com

Since 1953, this steakhouse, founded by a married couple, has been the place to go for T-bones, ribeyes, and filet mignon. All are of course carefully cooked to order, seared, and served sizzling on a metal platter. It's even been named the #1 Steakhouse in the Midwest by *Midwest Living Magazine* and numerous other publications. Other menu items include seafood options—most notably an African lobster tail—and a few appetizers (cheese curds), a kids' menu, and ice cream for dessert. The martinis rise to the level of art. The decor is a collection of oddities and knickknacks but unlike the contrived suburban chain restaurant, there is a story behind most of the objects. Smoky's is an age-old Madison classic and if you're looking for that supper-club appeal, including the expected soup, salad, and relish tray sides, you'll find it here. Reservations are rarely accepted so best to just get there early and grab yourself a drink or two.

TORNADO STEAK HOUSE $$$
116 South Hamilton St.
(608) 256-3570
www.tornadosteakhouse.com

You can't miss this place with its flashing neon arrows marking the spot. What appears to be just another downtown tavern is actually one of the best steakhouses in town and serves organic grass-fed and corn-fed beef. The interior is about 50 years out of date but white linens are on the tables. But if you want to skip the supper club experience you can even eat at the bar. Besides fantastic steaks the menu offers pork, duck, rabbit, lamb, and seafood. The Caesar salad is quite nice and the Friday Fish Fry is reputable. The full bar serves an excellent Cosmopolitan. A late-night menu goes past midnight. Open for dinner daily. Parking is on the street or at Fairchild and Main Streets. Reservations are recommended. Not wheelchair accessible.

THAI/LAO

CORNER STORE $
901 Williamson St.
(608) 256-7255

This is one of those under-the-radar local sweet spots and the cheapest Thai deal in town: Corner Store is a light grocery and sub shop on Willy Street where it intersects with Paterson Street. On offer are two or three Thai curries for carry out. Yellow curried chicken is always on while the others rotate. Some other Thai dishes and sauces are in the deli display. Shopkeeper Bousou cooks the dishes himself fresh daily and serves them for lunch and dinner. You can also get tacos and burritos here, but really you'd be missing the main attraction. Closed Sun.

LAO LAAN-XANG RESTAURANT $-$$
1146 Williamson St.
(608) 280-0104

2098 Atwood Ave.
(608) 819-0140

Many patrons simply lump Thai and Lao together and honestly most Thai restaurants are Lao-owned in Madison. The differences won't matter to most. The food is delicious and portions are ample. The squash curry is one of the most popular menu items. Spiciness can be calibrated to order (4 is the blistering variety). The dining room can get loud when crowded, and at the peak of the dinner hour it may likely fill up. Beer and wine are served. Not wheelchair accessible. Closed Sun but otherwise open for lunch and dinner.

SA-BAI THONG THAI CUISINE $-$$
2840 University Ave.
(608) 238-3100
www.sabaithong.com

Lacking some of the stereotypical Thai decorations, the restaurant instead shows bright color interiors. This local favorite is open for lunch and dinner daily. Numerous traditional soups including Tom Yum and Tom Ka are on the menu and moderately spicy. The variety of curries includes red, yellow, green, and the partly peanut panang. Vegetarian options are actually vegetarian, i.e., made without fish and oyster sauce. Jungle curry is delectable, a red curry with basil, tofu, straw mushrooms, baby corn, bamboo shoots, red pepper, rhizome, green beans, broccoli, and Thai and purple eggplant. Beer and wine are served. Parking is off-street. Carry-out and delivery are available. Wheelchair accessible.

SALA THAI $-$$
36 South Fair Oaks Ave.
(608) 246-1889

6802 Odana Rd.
(608) 828-9565

The shining wood interiors go a lot farther than just some Thai decoration to invoke the Kingdom of Siam. The dining room has only about 15 tables and at peak hours may fill quickly as the place is well liked in the neighborhood. The menu offers a nice assortment from pad thai to the standard four curries (green, red, yellow, panang) which are properly spicy (though serious spice fans may still ask for more). Spring rolls with plum sauce are popular. There are six tofu-based dishes for vegetarians plus several other standard dishes with the tofu option. Beer is served, including Singha from Thailand. Service is not for someone in a hurry. Not quite wheelchair accessible. Dinner only on Sun and Mon, but open the rest of the week for lunch and dinner with a service gap of around two hours between the meal times. Carry-out is available.

VEGETARIAN/VEGAN/ GLUTEN-FREE

Many places have vegetarian items on their menus, but these are a few that seem to go out of their way to cater to vegetable fans or have a particular item on the menu that deserves mention. Thai, Nepalese, and Indian restaurants are often quite vegetarian friendly. The Madison Area Gluten Intolerance Chapter maintains a great list of area eateries that either offer specific gluten-free menu items or can alter recipes on request. See their Web site at www.glutenfreemadison.org.

ALCHEMY $
1980 Atwood Ave.
(608) 204-7644
www.alchemycafe.net
The grilled portobello mushroom sandwich is stellar. (Read more under, ironically, Best Burgers page 44.)

BUNKY'S CAFÉ $$
2827 Atwood Ave.
(608) 204-7004
www.bunkyscafe.net
Bunky's bills itself as Mediterranean/Italian. Appetizers show hummus and baba ghanoush as well as stuffed grape leaves. Lentil soup, veggie lasagna, and some salads as well as some eggplant and falafel dishes give a better range of vegetarian choices than the average restaurant, and vegans can inquire about menu items that can be cooked for them. Pasta dishes are varied. There are meat dishes as well, such as kabobs and lamb chops. Some items are gluten-free including the pizza crust from The Silly Yak Bakery. Closed Mon. Open for lunch and dinner, but dinner only on Sun. Wheelchair accessible.

DAISY CAFÉ & CUPCAKERY $
2827 Atwood Ave.
(608) 241-2200
www.daisycafeandcupcakery.com

A coffee shop, cafe, and cupcake bakery all rolled into one, Daisy Café made a big impression on Madison when it opened in 2009. The gourmet cupcakes emphasize taste and quality, not size—so some diners might debate the cost/value, though the flavors are unassailable. The handful of daily choices includes one or two vegan cupcakes as well. Breakfast options include omelets and sandwiches as well as granola, and something called stratas, an egg casserole with sweet options such as apples and cinnamon or something heartier such as crimini mushrooms and Gruyère. Open daily, serving breakfast and lunch from morning into mid-afternoon but still serving cupcakes until they sell out or 5 p.m., whichever comes first. Wheelchair accessible.

HUBBARD AVENUE DINER $
7445 Hubbard Ave., Middleton
(608) 831-6800
www.foodfightinc.com/hubbard.htm
Has a separate menu dedicated to gluten-free choices. (See Breakfast Joints page 47.)

WILLY STREET CO-OP $
1221 Williamson St.
(608) 251-6776
www.willystreet.coop
The deli here has a great number of vegetarian and vegan options. (Read more under Deli/Sandwich page 57.)

VIETNAMESE

SAIGON NOODLE $
6754 Odana Rd.
(608) 827-9120
Set in a strip mall on the west side, this family-run restaurant passes under the radar. A big bowl of pho (noodles) is the standard order (beef is the most popular) but stir-fried noodles and rice are also available. This is not Americanized—note the tripe and tendon; the kitchen uses family recipes. Spring rolls and egg rolls are good appetizers. Wheelchair accessible. Open for lunch and dinner with a service gap between. Closed Mon.

NIGHTLIFE

The Mad City occasionally gets a mention for its university/party-school reputation and per-haps for good reason. But Madison is much more diverse than the label might imply. Bars are numerous, of course, and for better or for worse are part of the Wisconsin culture. Blame it on—or credit it to—the German immigrants who brought so much beer-brewing talent and motivation with them. Local beer is in abundance at the microbreweries themselves but also on the regular tap lists at a majority of the places serving suds. Live music is in abundance and styles run the gamut. Indie rock, metal, country, bluegrass, blues, jazz, classical, Latin, Irish—on any given week the entertainment sections of *Isthmus* and *77 Square* offer an assortment with regular local acts mixed in with touring national or even international ones. DJs have their niche, and anyone looking to let it all out on the dance floor needn't go far.

Slightly more cerebral activities are abundant as well. Book readings, lectures, and gallery openings happen every week, and nights out at the movies get good representation from the independents, documentaries, and foreign films. The thriving performing arts scene is greater than such a modest population might expect.

The closest thing Madison has to a centralized entertainment area is State Street and the Capitol Square. Other neighborhoods such as Atwood–Schenck on the east side or Monroe Street on the near west might offer two or three bars or restaurants close together, but to list them as nightlife destinations by themselves would be misleading. That said, the Mad City does offer a variety of places to go, and since getting around is easy, the lack of a central entertainment zone isn't really an issue.

State Street is open only to buses, delivery vehicles, and bicycles. That should be enough to make sure you cross with care, but insignificant enough to create a pedestrian zone. Bars, restaurants, and shops line both sides of the six blocks between the Capitol Square and the Library Mall where the University of Wisconsin campus begins. Coffee shops are in abundance, and street musicians are only slightly outnumbered by panhandlers. Connecting state government and state university is a strange mix, and State Street really does show people of all walks of life. Most bars down around the Capitol Square get busy at quitting time with the state and local government crowd.

The University of Wisconsin–Madison has been a mainstay on *Playboy*'s "Best Party Schools" list since its inception. When classes are in session the city has a bit more of a, er, buzz to it,

and in the downtown area students keep the bars and restaurants full. One venue that seems to appeal to a wider audience—drawing families, business people, travelers, and of course college students—is the Terrace behind the Memorial Union on campus. Locals refer to it either as the Union or the Terrace (although the Monona Terrace might sometimes cause confusion). Der Rathskeller is the lounge area inside.

Cover charges at bars are almost always specifically for shows and can range from a nominal two or three dollars going directly to the band to a full-blown $10 for a weekend event. Weekday nights tend to be free. A few places occasionally offer all-ages shows and post that information in advertising for each event, otherwise one can expect the 21 and over crowd. Bar closing time in Madison is 2:30 a.m. on Fri and Sat evenings and 2 a.m. on weekday nights. Most bars will make

Area Entertainment Guides

The A.V. Club
www.avclub.com/madison

The A.V. Club is a pull-out section of the *Onion,* a fake-news newspaper that was originally founded in Madison. Though often humorous or irreverent in tone, it is not satire like the *Onion* and reviews movies, books, comics, music, DVDs, and video games. The Web site is also known as The Decider.

Isthmus
www.thedailypage.com

Several good sources will tell you who's playing where and when and a whole lot more about events, arts, and entertainment. Online your best bet is *Isthmus*' Daily Page, which along with the weekly paper's reviews and articles about everything from movies and shows to book readings and social-group events, has a well-maintained searchable listing. The free newspaper, available in vestibules and stand-alone newspaper boxes almost everywhere, hits the streets on Thurs and highlights critics' picks of the upcoming weekend and following week's events.

Maximum Ink
www.maximumink.com

Published in Madison but covering the music scene of the entire state, *Max Ink* is a free newspaper that has been around since 1996. Check it for a monthly live music calendar as well as interviews, reviews, and articles on performers in all styles of music, from local to international. The Madison section is divided into Downtown, Eastside, Westside, and Southside sections and is updated monthly.

77 Square
http://host.madison.com/entertainment

This is another weekly paper and a part of the Madison.com Web site. Sections are dedicated to movies, music, theater, food, arts, TV and games, city life, and an events calendar. Like *Isthmus* the paper is free and available around town in vestibules and newspaper boxes.

WORT 89.9 FM
Insurgent Radio Kiosk
http://irkiosk.blogspot.com

WORT is community-supported radio and runs a wide variety of alternative programming from news and local issues to interviews and an eclectic range of music. Insurgent Radio Kiosk is a five-minute pre-recorded segment that airs four times a day and features a commentary, this-day-in-history, and a calendar of the day's events. The blog displays the events portion.

last call somewhere between 2 a.m. and 2:15 a.m. to make sure the patrons are all out in time. Clocks at most places are set 10 or 15 minutes ahead, in other words they are on "bar time" so you can feel like you are cutting it close. Enforcement can result in fines for the establishment, so don't resist the bartenders and bouncers.

You can't buy beer in Madison from the local grocery or liquor store after 9 p.m. Open intoxicants in city streets are not allowed, but a few public parks do permit it. Always remember: don't drink and drive. It's just common sense and respectful of the lives and well being of others. With the exception of establishments that make at least 10% of their business from the sale of tobacco products other than cigarettes, a no smoking ban is in effect for all Madison businesses. Cigar bars, for example, are exempted as are casinos which are technically governed by Federal law. The ban is statewide as of July 2010.

Sources for information and listings of what's going on are numerous and a compilation of the best of them is listed below. Tickets for big events can often be found at Ticketmaster (www.ticketmaster.com), but many shows advertise a list of local businesses which are acting as box offices for general admission. Sections for live music venues, clubs, and concert venues have some crossover so it is worth familiarizing yourself with all of them. The Majestic Theater, for example, often has live shows featuring national or even international acts, but is well known for DJ parties, film showings, and even an occasional cabaret, while High Noon Saloon is a great bar but arguably one of the best concert venues in town.

CONCERT VENUES

ALLIANT ENERGY CENTER
Veteran Memorial Coliseum and Willow Island
1919 Alliant Energy Center Way
(608) 267-4142
www.alliantenergycenter.com
Previously known as the Dane County Coliseum, the Veteran Memorial Coliseum is part of the Alliant Energy Center complex and hosts big-name concerts and other shows such as monster truck rallies. The capacity of the coliseum is 10,321 people, and the fixed seats are padded and upholstered. A 29-acre grassy area also on the grounds is known as Willow Island. The "island" is actually a 7-acre strip of land bordered by two ponds, but the whole area is a venue for outdoor festivals featuring live music as well. Watch for Classic Rock station WJJO's Band Camp to be hosted here in Aug of each year with over 30 rock bands, as well as Madison Roots Festival. The center has its own parking which typically incurs a fee and all the facilities are wheelchair accessible. Beverages including beer are commonly served.

BARRYMORE THEATRE
2090 Atwood Ave.
(608) 241-2345
www.barrymorelive.com
Built in 1929 as The Eastwood, the third of Madison's cinemas, the theater survived showing movies—at one point, adult films—into the 1970s. After some renovation and a name change it opened again in 1987 but as a live music venue. The theater seating remains though for most shows part of the crowd gathers on their feet in the space between the seats and the edge of the stage. Most of the 100 or so shows are live music with the occasional comic, movie, or play. Acoustics are good and musicians the likes of Richard Thompson, The Subdudes, and Luther Allison have all made live recordings here while Bob Dylan used the space for rehearsal. Most shows are general admission and all ages. Ticket prices vary but acts are something worth spending a little extra money on and often national names in varying genres of music. Tickets can be bought online, by phone, at area ticket outlets (see the list on the Web site), or in the case of shows that don't sell out, at the door for a few dollars more.

CRYSTAL GRAND MUSIC THEATRE
430 Munroe St., Lake Delton
(608) 254-4545
www.crystalgrand.com
This 2,000-seat music hall features performances by comedians, country stars, oldies favorites, and

classic pop and rock musicians in a beautiful building. Lake Delton borders Wisconsin Dells and is about a 45-minute drive from Madison.

KOHL CENTER
601 West Dayton St.
(608) 263-5645

The home of Badger basketball and hockey, the Kohl Center also hosts some big name concerts. Since 1998 names everyone knows—including Sting, Elton John, Britney Spears, and Dave Matthews—have performed here. The seating arrangement varies for the different events the center can handle, but for concerts room is for just over 16,000 people. Concerts here are somewhat random and just a handful are scheduled throughout the year. Upcoming shows are likely to receive a lot of publicity on radio and in print. Parking for the Kohl Center is in parking ramps a couple blocks away and along the west end of State Street or by chance on the streets.

MAJESTIC THEATRE
115 King St.
(608) 255-0901
www.majesticmadison.com

As far as big names that have graced the stage at this 1906 theater, how does Harry Houdini rate? Like the other theaters, the Majestic is a survivor from the Vaudeville and silent movie era on through a couple of resurrections and a period of triple X marks the spot. Most recently it was a nightclub before a musician and an agent, both disillusioned by bad behavior in the venue management world, decided they could do it right. In 2007 the Majestic returned to its original stage performance roots and now is a pretty sweet place to see a show. In addition to the genre-jumping concerts, the Majestic hosts other stage shows such as comedy acts, and DJ-driven theme parties. Brew 'n View events pair some suds with a one-night-only film showing. Shows are general admission and in many cases the ground floor is just standing room. Balcony seating is first-come, first-served. Reserved box seats are often available. There's not a bad seat (or place to stand) in the house. Doors open one hour before

posted concert times. Most shows are cheaper if tickets are purchased in advance. Tickets can be purchased off the Web site and printed out. A bar serves alcohol but this is an all-ages venue. Bring an ID if you expect to drink. The closest parking ramp is on the corner of Pinckney and Doty Streets and there is street parking which is metered until 6 p.m.

> **i** Wisconsin was the second state (after Michigan) to ratify the 21st Amendment thus repealing Prohibition, on April 25, 1933. But the city of Madison had already voted to allow the sale of beer with 3.2 percent alcohol as far as the edge of the University of Wisconsin campus. The Regents didn't stand for this long and on October 11, 1933, authorized its sale in the Memorial Union.

THE MEMORIAL UNION TERRACE AND DER RATHSKELLER
University of Wisconsin
800 Langdon St.
(608) 262-7395
www.union.wisc.edu/music

The combination of a lakeside setting, the youthful vigor of a bustling university, and an impressive lineup of free live music that ranges from local favorites to international legends is what makes "The Terrace" the quintessential Madison night out especially in the summer. The characteristic design of the brightly colored metal chairs reminds anyone in the know of the one place that might best capture Madison's laid-back vibe and natural beauty. The sun sets over Lake Mendota and people of all ages and walks of life gather around tables and picnic tables on the lakeside terrace to watch it. Buy some university-made ice cream inside, perhaps grab something from the terrace grill, order a soda or one of a dozen or so tap beers, and if you get there early enough, get a table and hold onto it for the show. At 5 p.m. on Fri the Behind the Beat series features a mellow performer, often jazz, to unwind the work-week woes. Every Fri and Sat evening the terrace's outdoor stage hosts musicians from near and far, classic and up-and-coming, often with an opening act or two. The evening shows start around 8:30 p.m. and are done around midnight. In inclement weather and throughout the winter, the concerts move into Der Rathskeller, the German-themed dining and drinking hall. Local bluegrass is featured on many Thurs and an open mic night is often a weekly event during the school year. Admission is always free and the property is wheelchair accessible.

ℹ️ In the past only those with Union memberships could purchase beer at the Memorial Union. Now nonmembers can receive a temporary card when they purchase their first beer.

MONONA TERRACE ROOFTOP
Monona Terrace Community and Convention Center
One John Nolen Dr.
(608) 276-9782
www.mononaterrace.com
Though when a local says "the Terrace" they generally mean the one behind the University's Memorial Union, there is a second terrace with a capital T. The Monona Terrace Community and Convention Center hosts events throughout the summer on the rooftop. "Concerts on the Rooftop" and "Dane Dances!" are weekly free events from June through Aug. Seasonally other events are hosted indoors. Food and drinks, including alcohol, are typically served. The view of Lake Monona on one side and the lighted dome of the Capitol on the other make for a pretty special evening.

ORPHEUM THEATRE
216 State St.
(608) 255-6005
www.orpheumtheatre.net
Its marquee and its vertical ORPHEUM sign can be seen from all the way up or down State Street. Known generally as a cinema with a hankering for independent films, the venerable downtown icon is also a concert venue. Once the competition of the Capitol Theatre across the street, the Orpheum, built in 1926, attracted some of the best and brightest stars. The likes of Frank Sinatra, Louis Armstrong, Bob Marley, and Johnny Cash have all graced the stage, and the opulent interiors were as much a part of going to the movies as the film itself. In 1999 new ownership saved the Orpheum from other ideas for "development" that would have ruined the historical site. Now the theater is being preserved for future generations while offering live shows and films. The lobby's grand staircase, chandeliers, and statue of Orpheus remain and really the only change over the years is the second theater, the StageDoor, which was added in the 1960s. The venue offers 1,700 seats including a large balcony. Since its rebirth salsa legend Ruben Blades has played here, Ben Folds has been through several times, as have The Decemberists, Bela Fleck, and many others. A full bar serves drinks and a restaurant occupies the lobby. Parking is available at various State Street ramps.

STOUGHTON OPERA HOUSE
381 East Main St., Stoughton
(608) 873-6677
www.stoughtonoperahouse.com
The opera house opened in 1901 as a city auditorium on the 2nd floor of the city hall building. The venue played host to a variety of events and activities from Vaudeville acts to temperance meetings, and for a short time hosted graduation ceremonies for local schools. By the 1950s, however, the building was falling apart and it wasn't until the 1980s that interest in restoration finally found action. Today the clock in the previously empty clock tower has been replaced, and the redone interiors are spectacular. Look for year-round concert events of all styles and open to all age groups.

LIVE MUSIC VENUES

A wide variety of restaurants and lounges may have occasional performers or background music. But the places listed here—typically bars—are really focused on the music and are thus concert venues but not in the sense of having concert-style seating.

THE ANNEX AT THE REGENT STREET RETREAT
1206 Regent St.
(608) 256-7750
www.regentstreetretreat.com
Since 1984, this sports bar and grill has been a good place to go during Badger game days when it is wall-to-wall sports fans. Expect a fun bar staff and good drink specials. The menu is bar fare with decent wings and the Regent Street Retreat burger. In the fall, the cook features his own "Pat roast," a pot roast served with mashed potatoes and steamed carrots. An addition to the space in the mid-90s, the Annex is a 450-person concert venue adjoining the bar. Generally this place is for those of legal drinking age (21). However, the Annex does sometimes host 18+ shows. Tickets range from $5 to $20 and the music favors rock of all varieties with the occasional reggae or hip hop act. Being close to the university, the joint is favored by students, but the crowd does vary.

i Pat McCurdy, a bit of a music/comedy staple here in Madison, plays weekly at Regent Street Retreat from his extensive repertoire of clever original songs, 80s medleys, and more. He does a good job of involving the crowd and his cult following often sings along with his classics. (www .patmccurdy.com)

AREA 51 BAR AND GRILL
2513 Seiferth Rd.
(608) 222-7800
www.area51bar.com
With just a leaning toward metal, Area 51 books local and national acts for Fri and Sat night shows. The building has a warehouse look to it from the outside and inside the venue is on the small side in a good way. DJs and karaoke fill in on other nights and large-screen TVs show sporting events. Darts, foosball, and pool are the remaining entertainment options. The bar took on its live music focus in 2009. Closed Mon.

CRYSTAL CORNER BAR
1302 Williamson St.
(608) 256-2953
www.thecrystalcornerbar.com
Built in 1917 as a grocery store with apartments on the 2nd floor, this popular neighborhood bar first became Coughlin's Tavern in 1935. When co-owner Florence Coughlin's husband died, she was refused a liquor license on account of being a woman. Her father-in-law did her the favor of holding it to keep the doors open and when he too passed in 1944, Florence successfully petitioned the city to become the first woman to hold a liquor license in Madison. She remodeled, adding the glass block around the doors and windows from which the Crystal Corner got its new name. Several owners later, this workers' tavern hasn't lost its everyman appeal, but has also built a reputation for some great live music, often of the blues, rock, or country variety. Cover charges occasionally apply.

THE DRY BEAN
5264 Verona Rd., Fitchburg
(608) 274-2326
www.thedrybean.com
The Bean was often labeled as a country bar, but the range of music here is not so specific. There's karaoke on a couple nights, a bluegrass jam on another. Throw in a range of bands on the weekends playing Top 40, classic rock, country, and some acoustic tunes and it's really got a much wider appeal. The outside patio features some music in the summer. An extended happy hour shows good drink and appetizer specials. A brunch goes over well for the football crowd on Sun. The entrance to the parking lot is reached via Anton Drive despite the Verona Road/US 151 address. Go west at the controlled intersection at Williamsburg Way and Anton Drive is the first left (south). Nominal cover charges may apply.

HARMONY BAR & GRILL
2201 Atwood Ave.
(608) 249-4333
www.myspace.com/theharmonybar

Madison loves its neighborhood taverns and this is a popular one on the east side. The food is good, the beer selection is notable, and a few TVs make for a nice collective sports experience. On the weekends, however, this is also a great place to hear some live music, primarily blues. The back room has a small stage. Cover charges can be in the $5–10 range. Parking is mostly on the street with a few spots in the lot out back.

THE HIGH NOON SALOON
701 E. Washington Ave. # 101
(608) 268-1122
www.high-noon.com

One of the hottest venues in town for live music, High Noon is the after-the-fire incarnation of O'Cayz Corral. It was an untimely demise of the charming hole-in-the-wall bar, once *the* place to play for all upcoming bands of rock, grunge, punk, and more (consider Nirvana, The Replacements, and Elliot Smith, just to name a few). In 2004 owner/manager Cathy Dethmers brought the spirit of O'Cayz back in a much expanded venue in the renovated Buy and Sell Shop building on the corner of East Washington Avenue and Blount Street. Open seven days a week, the bar serves pizza from Glass Nickel by the slice at night. A second bar opens on the opposite side of the hall when crowds are big. Beer taps rotate and include a few Wisconsin beers and other microbrews. There is typically a cover for live music in the $5–10 range with potentially higher ticket prices for more nationally recognized acts. Generally there are three bands on the bill. A sort of mezzanine with several small tables overlooks the rest of the exposed industrial interior with Wild West accents.

> **i** During the summer watch for Concerts on the Square, free Wed evening performances on the Capitol steps by the Wisconsin Chamber Orchestra, and Jazz at Five, free Thurs quitting-time gigs at the top of State Street.

THE LOFT
149 Waubesa St.
www.myspace.com/theloftwi

All-ages venues are often in short supply so The Loft fills an important role in the live music scene. Look for up and coming acts from here all the way to national level. Madison area bands generally fill the opener spots with a chance for some good exposure. Look for The Loft on MySpace. This is not a bar, and the focus is totally on the music. Drunken patrons are really frowned upon.

MR. ROBERT'S BAR & GRILL
2116 Atwood Ave.
(608) 249-1660
www.mrroberts.net

While "bar and grill" isn't exactly a misnomer, the name does leave out the very heart of this little hole-in-the-wall neighborhood tavern's spirit: live music. Every night but Sun and Mon Mr. Robert's is thumping to some kind of band's beat. Generally this is rock of some sort, a bit of Americana, blues, and maybe some funk and a few others in the mix. There's some parking in back otherwise find it on the street. Typical bar food is served, such as burgers, pizzas, and fries. No cover charge for shows. Wed host open jam sessions.

Bars and Restaurants with Live Music

BADGER BOWL
506 East Badger Rd.
(608) 274-6662
www.badgerbowl.com

Where else would a person go to hear a good rock and roll band but a bowling alley? This 30-lane alley hosts live bands on Fri and Sat primarily playing classic rock, alternative rock, country, and blues. Big-screen TVs keep the sports fans happy and poker nights are a good draw. Pool tables and video games are here as well as wireless Internet. One night a week hosts West Coast Swing dancing and another night is devoted to karaoke. A full bar also serves appetizers. The establishment runs a shuttle to Badger football home games. Open daily.

THE BRINK LOUNGE
701 East Washington Ave.
(608) 661-8599
www.thebrinklounge.com

Located in the basement of the same building as High Noon Saloon, the operative word here is "lounge." Music is set up in the bar or back room and offers a nice intimate experience, while the furniture is akin to a hotel lobby with some couches and comfortable chairs along with the usual tables as well as a four-sided bar. Music styles vary but include rock, jazz, and acoustic shows. This is not a bad place to start the night and can be nice for slipping back and forth between acts at the High Noon. Tip: try the Wisconsin cheese and meat plate. Typically there's no cover charge, and open mic nights and dance nights are common. The bar sometimes hosts private parties. A good selection of wines is on hand, and during the week there are good specials on bottled wine and other drinks. The menu includes an assortment of pizzas and appetizers and a list of martini options. Open from 4 p.m. but closed on Sun and Mon.

i Support your local composers: Madison Songwriters Group (www.madisonsongwriters.com) hosts Songwriters in the Round on the fourth Wed of every month except Nov and Dec at The Brink Lounge. See and hear some artists working on their craft. A small cover charge applies.

CAPITAL BREWERY AND BIER GARTEN
7734 Terrace Ave., Middleton
(608) 836-7100
www.capital-brewery.com
This is a popular after work destination especially on Fri nights from May through Sept. Live music, Capital beer, and wine are featured in the Bier Garten, along with an assortment of snacks like chips and pretzels. Live music plays on Fri from Memorial Day Weekend to Labor Day Weekend. Soda is also served and the crowd is family-friendly. Though there's no menu here, many patrons will order out from nearby eateries such as Roman Candle Pizza.

i For other brewpubs and microbreweries check out the Restaurants chapter.

CLUB TAVERN
1915 Branch St., Middleton
(608) 836-3773
www.clubtavern.com
Built in the late 19th century, this former boarding house became a tavern in 1880 and specifically the Club Tavern in 1921. It survived Prohibition with a locally famous chicken dinner. The restaurant and bar area are separate though you can dine in both places. The bar features a raised stage for acts heavy on (but not limited to) the blues. Most Sat and some other nights offer live music. Often there is a cover charge. The bar also offers dartboards, pool tables, and foosball and runs a sandpit volleyball league, and fans come out to watch sporting events on the various TVs. James Werner, one of the owners, is known by all as "Moose." The Moose burger on the menu is one of the best in town, and there are nightly dinner specials including a Fri night fish fry. Parking is on-site.

THE ESSEN HAUS
514 East Wilson St.
(608) 255-4674
www.essen-haus.com
This German restaurant is noted not just for wiener schnitzel and big pretzels, but also the giant glass boots and the superb selection of beers from around the world. That German tradition carries over into the entertainment. This is the place to go for a bit of live polka music. Servers wear the expected Oktoberfest-looking apparel and lederhosen is not unheard of. This is a decent restaurant with its own unique atmosphere in Madison, and a good place to roll out the barrel in more ways than one. Parking is in a lot out back. Come Back In, another great bar with great beer selections and hearty bar food, is next door and reachable through a doorway in the restaurant.

THE FREQUENCY
121 West Main St.
(608) 819-8777
www.madisonfrequency.com
This small, intimate venue—the capacity is only 99 people—offers seven nights a week of live

music with a good variety of local, regional, national, and even international acts.

Weekly features include an open blues jam on Tues, and every other Fri a variety show with local favorites The Gomers. Funky Mondays feature a Madison legend, Clyde Stubblefield. If you haven't heard of him, you've at least heard his work. As drummer for James Brown from 1965–70 he played on hits such as "I Feel Good." Drink specials run during Freqy Hour (6–8 p.m.) and after 10 p.m. each night. Food is limited to frozen pizzas and snack food. With the exception of special ticketed events, there is no cover charge for the front bar, though the band is audible but not visible there. This is a 21+ venue.

i Check out The Gomers (www.beeftone .com/gomers-home.htm), a group of very talented musicians who mix live karaoke and clever twists on popular music for humor's sake without sacrificing musical integrity.

THE IVORY ROOM PIANO BAR
116 West Mifflin St.
(608) 467-2404
www.ivoryroompianobar.com
Stop in for the great Happiest Hours drink specials and a few old standards from the piano player later in the evening. Makes for a classy night out with cool lounge ambience, and several musicians work the weekly schedule for some good variety. Closed Sun and Mon. Typically there's no cover charge.

MOTHER FOOL'S COFFEEHOUSE
1101 Williamson St.
(608) 259-1301
www.motherfools.com
It doesn't get much more intimate than this little quirky corner coffee shop which has a few tables and some couches for patrons. Organic coffee, vegan pastries, and performers set up practically in the front window by the door. Folksters and acoustic music do well here. Shows are every Fri and Sat night. Cover charges generally apply. Free wireless Internet for customers. Parking is on the street.

TRICIA'S COUNTRY CORNERS
3737 County Rd. AB, McFarland
Corner of Buckeye Road and Femrite Drive
(608) 222-2077
www.triciascountrycorners.com
Though the names have changed, the place remains the same: a popular country and western nightclub. Set in a 1928 building, the bar also serves lunch from a menu of burgers and hot and cold sandwiches with deep-fried sides all at slightly cheaper outside-of-Madison prices. Live country bands typically play on Thurs, Fri, or Sat and often there's no cover charge. On Sun stop in for breakfast featuring biscuits and gravy and a Bloody Mary bar. Located a few minutes east of Madison just north off of US 12/18. Open daily.

i Restaurants such as Liliana's or Jolly Bob's Jerk Joint bring in regular jazz performers or DJs every week. Check the Restaurants chapter listings to find a great dinner venue with some tunes on the side.

CLUBS

THE CARDINAL BAR
418 East Wilson St.
(608) 257-BIRD (2473)
www.cardinalbar.com
The Cardinal is a landmark in Madison. Cuban–American Ricardo Gonzalez opened the bar in 1974 in the ground floor of the 1908 Cardinal Hotel building. The mosaic-tile floor and dark woodwork have survived, and the stained glass and mirror of the back bar have an old-school charm to them, while the music combines Latin varieties and modern dance classics. This was a cool place to get a martini long before the recent martini craze. Ricardo stepped out of the business in 2004 but took it back over in 2009 when he didn't like the direction the bar was taking. Renovations in 2009 expanded the dance area, adding a natural wood dance floor and sprucing up the entire bar quite nicely. The mojitos and daiquiris are exceptional as is the signature drink, the Havana Cooler, made with dark rum, mint, and ginger ale. Of the eight tap

lines seven are Wisconsin microbeers and one is a rotating import. Happy hour is from 5 to 7 p.m. On Fri some appetizers are available during that time and some live Latin jazz sets the mood. Sun nights host local Latin jazz great Tony Castañeda and his band. Thurs and Sat nights host Latin dancing, sometimes with lessons beforehand. Cover charges of around $5 are common and students are sometimes offered a discount.

INFERNO
1718 Commercial Ave.
(608) 245-9583
www.clubinferno.com
Goth, retro, punk, metal, industrial—the list of genres goes on and on at this dance bar and the Web site offers a click-the-genre feature to see when the next event of that style is coming up. With multiple bars it is not hard to get a drink. The club is on the small side so it's somewhat intimate, but on some nights there is a lot of elbow room. The statewide smoking ban, however, might bring bigger crowds as the poor air quality was a frequent complaint in the past. Head here on Wed through Sat nights and watch for the Leather and Lace and fetish nights. DJs primarily serve the music, but the occasional live band is also on the calendar.

SCATZ SPORTS BAR AND NIGHT CLUB
2248 Deming Way, Middleton
(608) 203-8252
Billed as Dane County's largest nightclub, Scatz also caters to the sports bar scene with a variety of flat-screen TVs and several pool tables. Live music is common with cover bands, hard-rock bands, and dance oriented groups. DJs host nights as well and such is the variety at this place that even a polka band has been seen on its calendar. A stage is upstairs and a dance floor is on the main floor. Food is served. The crowds that gather around Scatz have gotten a rowdy reputation and police calls are common. Occasional tribute bands are on the bill. A cover charge applies to some acts.

BARS AND TAVERNS

Downtown

BROCACH IRISH PUB AND RESTAURANT
7 West Main St.
(608) 255-2015
www.brocach.com
The name is Gaelic for "badger den." Two old brick buildings are joined together for this popular and heavily Irish-stylized tavern. Guinness, Bass, Smithwick's, Newcastle, and the like are on tap, Irish and Scotch whiskeys are abundant, and wine is available by the glass. The lunch, brunch, and dinner menus have typical Emerald Isle fare such as shepherd's pie, stew, fish and chips, but plenty of other options including meze plates, salads, vegetarian options, and burgers. The upstairs has some big lounge furniture made apparently for people without elbows, but the room looks out on the Capitol. Live Irish music is common, and a bagpipe player sets up out front during Sat morning farmers' market. Sidewalk seating is available in summer. Open daily.

GENNA'S COCKTAIL LOUNGE
105 West Main St.
(608) 255-4770
www.gennaslounge.com
The original location of Genna's, founded in 1964, was on University Avenue. During the 1960s war protesting and activism, it was a popular hangout for radicals. Having trouble with the landlord, the family-owned tavern made its move to the Capitol Square in 1993. When the business day is done, there's a footrace to this happy-hour haven that might find state workers, lawyers, and college students rubbing elbows. The triangle-shaped tavern with its copper-top bar is a cozy conversation setting until tables fill up fast, and it's standing room only for a good portion of the night. Drinks are reasonable, the staff is personable, and the atmosphere is festive. Happy hour offers free munchies and drink specials and not just on the cheap stuff. Thurs nights a DJ sets up upstairs. Summer sees an abundance of sidewalk seating and the views of the Capitol from there—

or even from inside—only add to the cool factor. The ground floor is wheelchair accessible.

NATT SPIL
211 King St.
Word of mouth or some tables on the walk are what might bring patrons to this spot. No phone, no Web site, no neon sign outside—it almost passes under the radar yet it is often quite busy. The room is deep and narrow and dimly lit by red Chinese lanterns and candles on the tables. There are no TVs or games. Nightly DJs set the mood and the full bar has a nice selection of microbrews and serves skillfully made cocktails. This makes a cool gathering place for drinks, eats, and a night out. The wood-fired oven makes the food here quite special, and pizzas are notable including a brie and apple pizza. A portion of the menu is dim sum, and the most popular dish is the Three Cup Chicken, a popular Chinese bar food. A tofu version is also available. The cherry-wood smoked pulled-pork sandwich is simply extraordinary. Nothing is deep-fried. This is a great place for a late-night meal and in summer there is patio seating. Open daily from 5 p.m. Wheelchair accessible. No credit cards accepted but there is an ATM on-site.

East Side

DEXTER'S PUB
301 North St.
(608) 244-3535
www.dexterspubmadison.com
A great assortment of microbrews and after-happy-hour drink specials are on offer. TVs show important sporting events, and trivia nights are free and always a blast.

JADE MONKEY COCKTAIL LOUNGE
109 Cottage Grove Rd.
(608) 819-8501
www.jademonkeylounge.com
For an east-side bar with some class without pretension, head to the Jade Monkey. The comfy horseshoe-shaped booths fill up fast on weekend nights. Drink prices are reasonable, the beer list is long, and the selection of scotches isn't bad. They

don't have much in the line of food, just some frozen pizzas later in the evening. The outdoor patio with its waterfall-fountain gives some more space as this bar fills up as the evening goes on. Pool, shuffleboard, and darts provide some entertainment and the crowd loves the jukebox. Retro B-movies are shown on the TVs and a DJ plays on Sun nights. Credit cards not accepted but there's an ATM on-site. Open daily.

THE MALT HOUSE
2609 East Washington Ave.
(608) 204-6258
Union soldiers on their way to Camp Randall used to stop at this site when it was the Union Hotel. The bar got a lot of business on paycheck day (as did some of the hotel rooms, let's say, at an hourly rate). All that remains of the hotel is the bar and back bar which are housed in what became The Malt House in 2008. The creation of Bill Rogers, the concept of this small tavern is social gathering over simply top-notch drinks. There's no food (though order-in is allowed), no TV, and no dartboard. A screen door opens to the parking lot and some outside seating. The 18 taps are split between primarily Belgian imports and Wisconsin microbrews (plus the occasional out-of-stater). Another 150 beers are in bottles. The full bar offers over 30 selections each of either bourbons or Scotch whiskeys. Open in the afternoon until the wee hours, this bar is a connoisseur's dream, free of distractions from drink and conversation. Wheelchair accessible. Closed Sun.

MICKEY'S TAVERN
1524 Williamson St.
(608) 251-9964
This east-side neighborhood pub draws an eclectic and funky crowd, what some like to call old hippies and new hipsters. Take that with a grain of salt—everyone is welcome and can feel at home. In a converted house, the tavern has a pool table in one room, some comfy lounge furniture here and there, and a long bar in the front room. Don't be surprised to see an Irish music jam/rehearsal.

The Bloody Marys are wicked good, and the tap beer selection is notable. The food menu is a recent development and initial reviews are positive. Breakfast is a good idea with a tomato-based beverage. Not wheelchair accessible. This is just off the Capital City bike path and near the path that crosses the isthmus from Tenney Park.

West Side

BLUE MOON BAR & GRILL
2535 University Ave.
(608) 233-0441
www.bluemoonbar.com

Sports are on the TVs and a sociable crowd fills the space up at night in this neighborhood pub with a mezzanine floor overlooking the bar. Several local beers are on tap along with the usual big name brews. Some locals swear by the burgers here and fried foods are abundant. The three dart boards and two pool tables are in frequent use. The lot fills fast but there is parking on the street right out front. Open daily from lunch until close.

BRASSERIE V
1923 Monroe St.
(608) 255-8500
www.brasseriev.com

A very relaxed bistro environment with a killer list of Belgian beers on tap. (Read more under Restaurants – French/Bistro page 57.)

SPORTS BARS

BABES AMERICAN GRILL
5614 Schroeder Rd.
(608) 274-7300
www.babesmadison.com

This has long been a staple of the sports bar scene. Located on the west side just south off the Beltline Highway at Whitney Way, Babes is a spacious place to watch the big game on a big-screen TV and eat decent food—hand-pattied burgers, fried appetizers, ribs, salads, and whatnot. Open from lunch until close.

BIG TEN PUB
1330 Regent St.
(608) 251-6375
www.jordansbig10pub.com

Just a short two blocks from Camp Randall this is a good, if crowded, place for Badger games if tickets are not available and you still want to remain part of the collective vibe. A good collection of TVs, great drink specials, and some pretty darn good deep-fried battered cheese curds. Open daily. It has a parking lot but finding a space is an issue during Badger home games.

> **i** When it's home game day in Madison, check your local bar and grill for shuttles to Badger games.

POOLEY'S
5441 High Crossing Blvd.
(608) 242-1888
www.pooleysmadison.com

All the special satellite sports packages and a load of TVs makes this the best spot to catch a game on the far-east side. Sports memorabilia adorns the walls and an indoor volleyball pit hosts leagues. Open daily.

THE STADIUM SPORTS BAR AND EATERY
1419 Monroe St.
(608) 256-2544
www.stadiumbar.com

Right across the street from Camp Randall Stadium, the bar has a lot of room, a fair number of huge TVs, and an outdoor beer garden with grilled food on game day. Perfect to stay and watch or eat and run to the game. Open daily.

STATE STREET BRATS
603 State St.
(608) 255-5544
www.statestreetbrats.com

Having a bratwurst is another Wisconsin rite of passage. If there's a Badger game going on, this is a happening place downtown to watch and check the brat off your list of life accomplishments. The outdoor seating is the largest on State Street and has a small Statue of Liberty to watch over things. Two floors of seating offer TVs in every direction, the usual bar menu, good tap selection, and frequent specials. An ATM is right out front. Open daily from lunch to close.

SMOKING BARS

MADURO CIGAR BAR
117 East Main St.
(608) 294-9371
www.madurocigarbar.com
Step into the Frank Sinatra world in this lounge just off the Capitol Square. Couches keep clients comfy as they sip a variety of wines and fine microbrews as well as a list of whiskeys, brandies, rums, and grappa. Good DJs and the occasional lounge act set a great mood for the evening. A rotating selection of cigars can be found in the humidor. Due to its cigar focus, the bar was allowed to keep its smoking permission, but only for cigars and pipes. Cigarette smokers must take to the street. Street parking is metered until 6 p.m. and a parking ramp is a block and a half away on Doty Street.

MEDITERRANEAN HOOKAH LOUNGE & CAFÉ
77 Sirloin Strip
(608) 251-7733
www.medhookahcafe.com
Bringing a bit of the Middle East to Madison, the lounge rents the region's characteristic water-filled smoking device and sells various flavors of tobacco. Even for nonsmokers it is a mild and interesting experience. The menu offers appetizers or dinners and patrons can eat at the bar or relax in a lounge area with a collection of cushy couches and arm chairs. The smoky baba ghanoush and falafel are quite nice. Belly dancers of both genders entertain periodically. A separate bar area has foosball and a pool table.

Best Campus Bars

Just turning 21? There are some Madison traditions for the birthday. **The Nitty Gritty** offers a mug and a free beer on the actual day (I.D required of course). Kiss the moose at **State Street Brats**. Get a "fishbowl" from **Wando's**. Make your friends pay for that fishbowl—it's pricey. And beware: it's potent.

The Nitty Gritty
223 North Frances St.
(608) 251-2521
www.nittygrittybirthdayplace.com
Jefferson Airplane once had a jam session here and none other than Muddy Waters played here as well. This place has been around since the days of tear gas and tire burning, and it is said the notorious bombing of Sterling Hall was planned here over beers. It's decidedly less radical these days, and the bar and grill now touts a birthday tradition and a great burger with its own special "Gritty sauce." Sports are on the TVs and UW students often fill the place. A second location loses the student crowd (1021 North Gammon Rd., Middleton; 608-833-6489). Open daily.

Wando's Bar
602 University Ave.
(608) 256-5204
www.wandosbar.com
Heavily frequented by students in the academic year, the bar is legendary for a free bacon night. Drink specials charge amounts you might be able to pay by collecting change off the sidewalk on your walk to the place. Check out a "Fishbowl": exactly what the name says, only filled with alcohol. Karaoke as well. You were warned. Open daily.

WINE BARS AND COCKTAIL LOUNGES

BARRIQUES
1831 Monroe St.
(608) 284-9463

127 West Washington Ave.
(608) 268-6264

5957 McKee Rd., Fitchburg
(608) 277-9463

8410 Old Sauk Rd., Middleton
(608) 828-9502

1901 Cayuga St., Middleton
(608) 824-9463
www.barriquesmarket.com
With five locations each with its own vibe and style, you are never too far from Barriques—and that's a good thing. In the morning expect fresh baked goods, espresso, and brewed coffee. Some locations serve sandwiches and other eats. The wine selection is extensive and several locations feature the Wall of 100. Buy a bottle with a friend or two or sample some by the glass. Beer is served on tap or by the bottle, and scotch by the glass is also dependent on location. Wine tastings are generally held on Fri and Sat at the various locations. Check the Web Site for an updated schedule.

ENO VINO WINE BAR AND BISTRO
601 Junction Rd.
(608) 664-9565
www.eno-vino.com
A west-side after-work sort of place, Eno Vino has over 150 different vintages and more than 40 wines by the glass. Appetizer options are great for sharing. This is a nice place to meet old friends and quite good for making new ones (nudge, nudge, wink, wink).

LILIANA'S RESTAURANT
2951 Triverton Pike, Fitchburg
(608) 442-4444
www.lilianasrestaurant.com

Liliana's serves a huge selection of wines by the glass in the restaurant bar while live music is a given. (Read more under Restaurants – Cajun & Creole page 50.)

THE OPUS LOUNGE
116 King St. #1
(608) 441-6787
www.opuslounge.com
The cocktail menu at this place requires careful study because unless you are an expert, you haven't heard of these or even considered the possibilities. Mix masters provide some heavenly concoctions, and the atmosphere is classy and sophisticated without stuffiness. You won't be finding any $1 PBR beers here, so expect to put down a bit of cash. The menu features some elegant light appetizers, a bit of sushi, and a few desserts. Watch for half-price glasses and bottles of wine specials. Sidewalk seating happens in pleasant seasons. Open daily.

GAY NIGHTLIFE

Madison ranks as one of the top places in the country for gays and lesbians to live. So generally speaking Madison bars and clubs are very open to the LGBT community. There are, however, a few places that are either billed as such, have special events oriented to that crowd, or simply seem to have an ample gay/lesbian clientele. All of these places, of course, are open to people of all persuasions.

CLUB 5
5 Applegate Ct.
(608) 277-9700
www.club-5.com
Club 5 brings out members of all social groups of Madison's gay community: men and women, students and professionals. This is one of the top dance floors in town. DJs regularly pump up the crowd and special events such as country line dancing or Latin dancing are scheduled from time to time. There are three bar areas including The G. Bar which caters to women, and the Bar-

racks which serves the men. An outdoor patio is open in season. Theme parties and happy hour specials abound and 18- to 20-year-olds are allowed into designated special events. Certain events exact a cover charge. Open daily from 4 p.m. Located just south of the Beltline Highway off Fish Hatchery Road.

PLAN B
924 Williamson St.
(608) 257-5262
www.planbmadison.com

Looking to give Club 5 a run for its money, Plan B hit the LGBT scene in 2009. The location in the old Star Photo building on Willy Street is convenient to downtown and offers a parking lot in a street parking neighborhood. DJs keep the dance floor moving and drink specials are good. A light menu serves salads, paninis, wraps, and appetizers such as hummus and pita plates. Roman Candle pizza slices are also on offer. Cover charges apply at night.

> **i** A Room of One's Own bookstore (307 West Johnson St.; 608-257-7888; www.roomofonesown.com) offers an up-to-date collection of works on gay and lesbian studies as well as works of LGBT fiction. This is a good place to connect and find information of particular interest to the LGBT community. Room hosts frequent book readings/signings.

SHAMROCK BAR
117 West Main St.
(608) 255-5029
www.shamrockbar.com

The Shamrock dates back to 1985 and draws a mostly male crowd of all ages from students to longtime regulars. A menu of standard bar and grill fare is offered. The bar has a relaxed, neighborly atmosphere and makes a good place to hang out and grab a few evening drinks. Dart tournaments and karaoke are common as are drag queen shows. The location is just off the Capitol Square and in the midst of some good restaurants. Open daily.

THE TORNADO ROOM (THE CORRAL ROOM)
116 South Hamilton St.
(608) 256-3570
www.tornadosteakhouse.com

Known for some fabulous steaks, the Tornado Steakhouse is a star on the culinary map. The Corral Room is a dimly lit retro lounge in the restaurant's basement. Some members of the Shamrock crowd also frequent this place which is good for late-night cocktails. Marked by neon, The Tornado is just half a block off the Capitol Square. Open daily.

WOOF'S
114 King St.
(608) 204-6222
www.woofsmadison.com

Just a half block off the Capitol Square, which seems to be a required characteristic for what makes a gay bar in Madison, Woof's takes the angle not of a dance club but a sports bar. Dart, pool, and bowling leagues meet regularly and a good pool table is on-site. The important sporting games are on, and the bar opens a bit earlier on Sun for the Packer games. But this is not to say Woof's is without dancing. DJs and a jukebox work up the disco beat on weekend evenings and karaoke nights are common. Pretzels and popcorn are free and affordable pizzas are served. No cover charges.

> **i** Mediterranean Hookah Lounge & Café has a gay friendly environment, serves good food and a variety of flavored tobaccos for the water pipe, and often hosts belly dancers of both genders.

CASINOS

DEJOPE GAMING
4002 Evan Acres Rd.
(888) 248-1777
www.dejope.com

Originally opened as a bingo hall in 1999, DeJope is operated by the Native American Ho-Chunk Nation. The 60,000 square-foot facility contains over 1,000 electronic bingo and slot machines.

DeJope is open daily and closes for just three hours in the early morning. Gamers Grille features theme nights and remains open with the casino serving a long breakfast menu and a variety of salads, wraps, soups, sandwiches, and burgers. Casino patrons must be at least 18 years old. To get there drive a half-mile east of I-90 on US 12/18 (The Beltline) and go right (south) on Millpond Road following it to the casino.

HO-CHUNK CASINO, HOTEL AND CONVENTION CENTER
S3214 US Hwy. 12, Baraboo
(608) 356-6210 or (800) 746-2486
www.ho-chunk.com

For something more than DeJope's gaming machines drive north from Madison about 45 minutes to visit the fifth largest Native American casino in the country. Ho-Chunk offers blackjack (regular and high-stakes), poker, craps, off-track betting, 2,400 slot machines, and video poker. A bingo hall seats 600. The gambling is possible around the clock. The casino offers a resort experience with four restaurants, including a steakhouse, buffet, bar and grill, a cafe, a swimming pool, fitness center, and a place for the kids and child care services. The hotel has 315 rooms and suites. Special events such as live music or other entertainers are common, but guests must be 21 years old or older to attend shows.

DANCING

Tango, tap, line dancing, Latin salsa, clogging, Italian folk dance… the list goes on. A certain segment of the Madison population likes to move their feet, and in any given week there might be half a dozen or so places where you can drop in for some lessons, and about as often as there is a fee, it might also be gratis. The Cardinal Bar and Pachuco's, under Clubs above, have weekly Latin dance nights, and the latter offers some country dancing as well. Check *Isthmus* or www.thedailypage.com and search under dancing for events.

THE BRINK LOUNGE
701 East Washington Ave.
(608) 661-8599
www.thebrinklounge.com

The bar hosts tango, Latin dance, Lindy Hop, and swing dance on various nights typically without cover charge. (Read more under Nightlife – Live Music page 78.)

INTERNATIONAL FOLK DANCING
(608) 241-3655
www.plantpath.wisc.edu/~tdd/mfdu.htm

Emphasizing dances from Eastern Europe and Turkey, this group offers free instruction and dance. They can often be seen on Wed and Sun evenings at Library Mall on the University of Wisconsin campus between Memorial Library and the fountain or indoors at The Crossing at 1127 University Ave. See the Web site for specific details.

MADISON WEST COAST SWING CLUB
(608) 222-7750
www.madisonwestcoastswing.org

For some this was a brief fad, but many haven't lost the urge to get out and swing dance. This group meets at Badger Bowl and offers monthly workshops at The Right Step. Lessons are available.

THE RIGHT STEP
1004 East Broadway, Monona
(608) 221-1921
www.windancerstherightstep.com

This dance studio, run by a couple of professional instructors, offers classes, workshops, and open dances for varying prices. Styles are many including ballroom, Latin dances, country dancing, and much more.

TANGO BASICO
www.tangobasico.net

Founded in 2006, the group gives lessons in Argentine Tango and hosts dances. Watch the Web site for upcoming events and locations.

COMEDY CLUBS

ATLAS IMPROV COMPANY
Electric Earth Café
546 West Washington Ave.
(608) 259-9999
Stop in on Sat nights for one of two scheduled but unplanned performances at the Electric Earth Café. Tickets are at the door or available by phone for about $6. The improv group also offers workshops for anyone trying to be funny. Traveling comedy groups sometimes join the local troop. The cafe serves light food, coffee, smoothies, and bottled beer.

THE COMEDY CLUB ON STATE
202 State St.
(608) 256-0099
www.madisoncomedy.com
Though it has changed location a few times, the Comedy Club has been around since the mid-1980s and continues to bring national and touring comics to Madison. The venue has a capacity of 250 people and reservations are recommended, especially for bigger acts. Thurs through Sat evenings bring the headliners plus a couple of opening acts. On Thurs nights those openers are upcoming comedians from the Madison, Milwaukee, and Chicago areas. There is a two-drink minimum on top of the cover charge which hovers around $8 to $10 except for special events which may cost a bit more. Wed evening is known as the Big Deuce, an open mic night for locals to try their own jokes on a live and willing audience. The cover charge is just a few dollars, and the drink minimum is suspended. Admission to all shows is restricted to patrons 18 years or older. Discounts apply to members of the armed forces and on Thurs to students with an I.D.

MONKEY BUSINESS INSTITUTE
at Glass Nickel Pizza
2916 Atwood Ave.
(608) 658-5153
www.monkeybusinessinstitute.com
This popular local improv group won the *Isthmus* Readers' Poll for its comedy while their venue frequently wins honors for pizza. Every Fri night at Glass Nickel Pizza the institute is up to, well, you know, monkey business. Some of these faces should be familiar to anyone who has seen the YouTube hit series about Darth Vader's middle-management younger brother, *Chad Vader*. Another Madison original. Tickets are around $5. Watch for Sun evening shows as well.

BOOK READINGS & AUTHOR EVENTS

The bookstores listed here all host readings and book signings. Additional details are written for those that do so most frequently. (See also the Distinguished Lecture Series at the University of Wisconsin.) Look under bars for Genna's, which occasionally hosts spoken word events. Again, all events of this nature will be listed in the local entertainment guides in *77 Square* and *Isthmus* under "Words."

BARNES AND NOBLE BOOKSELLERS EAST
1 East Towne Mall
(608) 241-4695
www.bn.com (search on Madison, WI)

BARNES AND NOBLE BOOKSELLERS WEST
7433 Mineral Point Rd.
(608) 827-0809
www.bn.com (search on Madison, WI)

BOOKED FOR MURDER
2701 University Ave.
(608) 238-2701
www.bookedformurder.com
This genre bookstore brings in mystery writers regularly for readings.

BORDERS BOOKSTORE EAST
2173 Zeier Rd.
(608) 240-0080
www.borders.com

BORDERS BOOKSTORE WEST
3750 University Ave.
(608) 232-2600
www.borders.com

Of the two Borders locations, this one hosts the biggest and most frequent events, setting up on the 2nd floor. Some of the biggest names in publishing come through here.

THE DISTINGUISHED LECTURE SERIES
Wisconsin Union Theater
800 Langdon St.
www.union.wisc.edu/DLS

Seven to 10 prominent speakers from a list of audience nominations from the previous season are selected and invited to the university by the DLS committee. Subjects are wide ranging from current politics, human rights, and sub-atomic physics to the satire of the *Onion* and *The Daily Show*. Past speakers have included Isabel Allende, Kurt Vonnegut, Richard Dawkins, and Brian Greene. Tickets are free and available at the Union Theater Box Office in the Memorial Union at designated dates. UW students, staff, and faculty have first dibs one week in advance. Remaining tickets are available to the general public the Thurs before each lecture. Events start at 7:30 p.m. and tickets are valid only until 7:20 p.m. After that point, the doors open to anyone with or without a ticket. On the occasions when the theater fills, a video simulcast is set up in another venue. Each speaker lasts around 45 minutes to an hour and then the audience may ask questions.

RAINBOW BOOKSTORE COOPERATIVE
426 West Gilman St.
(608) 257-6050
www.rainbowbookstore.org

The bookstore with the progressive and leftist bent occasionally hosts authors of like mind.

A ROOM OF ONE'S OWN
307 West Johnson St.
(608) 257-7888
www.roomofonesown.com

This bookstore frequently hosts events most often in line with social justice, LGBT, and women's issues.

THE UNIVERSITY BOOKSTORE
Campus Location:
On the State Street Mall
(across from the Memorial Library)
(608) 257-3784

Hilldale Shopping Center location:
702 North Midvale Blvd.
(608) 238-8455
www.uwbookstore.com

The campus location hosts occasional readings which tend to get crowded fast. The Hilldale location does events more frequently, setting up signings on the main floor and readings and pre-sentations in the much roomier basement level.

CINEMAS

EAST GATE CINEMAS
5202 High Crossing Blvd.
(608) 242-2117
www.marcustheatres.com

The east side's only cinema features 14 screens and the latest digital technology with stadium seating and White Castle hamburgers.

MAJESTIC THEATRE
115 King St.
(608) 255-0901
www.majesticmadison.com

Though really more of a music venue (see Concert Venues page 75), the Majestic will show films from time to time. Typically, these are movies that have passed under the radar, certain independent films, or cult classics such as *Rocky Horror Picture Show*.

MARKET SQUARE THEATRES
6604 Odana Rd.
(608) 833-1500
www.marketsquareodanaroad.com

On the west side this five-screen Cineplex is nothing fancy but all movies are second-run. This means ticket prices are less than half of normal. And because this is Madison, the "cheap seats" often offer more than just the usual recycled blockbusters, venturing into independent, docu-mentary, and foreign films.

ORPHEUM THEATRE
216 State St.
(608) 255-8755
www.orpheumtheatre.net

The 1926 theater has two cinemas. The main screen has the grand old decoration of the classic cinema days with the velvet curtain, ornate decorations, and a mezzanine. The acoustics in this large room, however, can be a little tricky for some ears. The StageDoor cinema located in back is smaller and narrower. Don't miss the lobby which retains the style and grace of yesteryear and houses a restaurant and full bar. See more under Concert Venues, page 76.

POINT ULTRASCREEN CINEMA
7825 Big Sky Dr.
(608) 833-3980
www.marcustheatres.com

Madison's west side is served by this 16-screen Cineplex with stadium seating and a 75-foot wide, three-story high UltraScreen and a RealD digital 3-D auditorium.

i Eat dinner at nearby Pizzeria Uno (7601 Mineral Point Rd.; 608-833-7200) and buy your Point Cinema tickets at a discount at the restaurant.

STAR 18 AND IMAX CINEMAS
6091 Mckee Rd., Fitchburg
(608) 270-1414
www.kerasotes.com

Situated on the south side of Madison, this is the city's only IMAX theater. Along with the monster screen are 18 other screens with stadium seating in a modern building. This is arguably the nicest of the mainstream cinemas in town.

SUNDANCE 608 CINEMAS
Hilldale Mall
430 North Midvale Blvd.
(608) 316-6900
www.sundancecinemas.net

The first to open of Robert Redford's Sundance Cinemas, this six-screen cinema offers comfortable stadium seating and serves food and beer along with the usual popcorn, soda, and snack options. Ticket prices include an extra $2–3 "facilities fee" which allegedly allows the cinema to show films without non-preview advertising beforehand. Though originally an independent-only cinema, it now often shows the usual assortment of Hollywood new releases as well. A Sundance gift shop, cafe, and the popular seasonal rooftop bar are also on-site. Free WiFi on-site.

PERFORMING ARTS

For decades, members of the Madison community had talked about—and fought about—building a proper center that would support a culture of art and performance, something that would enrich the community. The Overture Center for the Arts is a crown jewel that satisfied the city's craving when it opened in 2004. Set in the heart of downtown, a portion of it occupies the space of an original theater from 1928. The creation of the Overture Center, however, required a whole city block, and now it is home to several resident performance groups and art galleries.

While the Overture Center is indeed grand, Madison has a fine collection of humbler settings where highly entertaining and varied performances are taking place, from the boundless Broom Street Theater to the Young Shakespeare Players Playhouse. Going beyond the city limits opens up even more options including the Tony Award-nominated American Players Theatre and the high-class Fireside Dinner Theater. From ballet to opera, from traveling Broadway musicals to locally written plays, the performing arts scene shows good taste, good talent, and good humor.

DANCE

CYCROPIA AERIAL DANCE
www.cycropia.org
This local dance troop gets a bit more hang time by creatively using trapezes, hoops, bungees, and more for their productions to create works that capture breath and imagination. The group typically gives a free performance every year under a large oak tree at the Orton Park Festival.

JAZZWORKS
Madison Professional Dance Center
3214 Syene Rd., Suite 4
(608) 273-3453
www.madisonprofessionaldancecenter.com
The center offers professional dance training from three years old on up. The resident dance company Jazzworks performs at home and abroad featuring a critically acclaimed selection of works including contemporary ballet and modern jazz. Local venues vary but include the Overture Center on occasion.

KANOPY DANCE COMPANY
341 State St.
(608) 255-2211
(608) 258-4141 (Overture Box Office)
www.kanopydance.org
Founded in 1976, this modern dance performance group brings resident and guest artists not just to Madison audiences but indeed around the country. Their home performance venue is Promenade Hall in the Overture Center and their office is nearby. For show schedules or community outreach performances outside Overture, check the Web site or call the office directly. Ticket prices are often around $24.

MADISON BALLET
160 Westgate Mall
(608) 278-7990
www.madisonballet.org
The ballet started out in 1981 as the Wisconsin Dance Ensemble before changing its name in 1999. The group made its initial reputation off its well regarded seasonal performances of *The Nutcracker*. Now in addition to the holiday classic,

Madison Ballet puts on two other annual productions. Performances take place at the Overture Center for the Arts and the Wisconsin Union Theatre on the University of Wisconsin campus. Since 2005 the organization has also operated the School of Madison Ballet for dancers of all ages. Tickets, which can be purchased by phone or at the Overture Center box office, range from $13 to $60 with discounts for children and seniors. Season tickets are also sold.

ℹ️ For strictly music performances or comedy clubs, be sure to check out the venues in the Nightlife chapter page 72.

MUSIC

CAPITOL CITY BAND
(608) 835-9861
www.madison.com/communities/ctyband
This community band got its start in 1969. Conducted by Jim Latimer since 1981, the 24-player band performs free concerts every Thurs night from mid-June through Aug. Show time is 7 p.m. and the venue is Rennebohm Park at 115 North Eau Claire Ave. just off Regent Street. Music is crowd pleasing, heavy on the marches and polkas, as well as some jazz and vocal selections.

FESTIVAL CHOIR OF MADISON
(608) 274-7089
www.festivalchoir.org
Founded in 1973 as the Diocesan Choir by Vernon Sell, the reputable 40-voice choir performs throughout the year in area venues and has traveled as far as Austria. Tickets are in the $12 to $15 range with discounts for multiple shows. The venues vary and often include area churches.

MADISON OPERA
(608) 238-8085
www.madisonopera.org
www.madisonopera.blogspot.com
The Madison Symphony Orchestra commonly is hired to provide the instrumentation for the Madison Opera Chorus as well as performances by the Madison Youth Choirs. Performances are part of the annual lineups at the Overture Center for the Arts and can be seen both in Overture Hall and The Playhouse. Traditionally, the company also does an outdoor performance in July called *Opera in the Park* at Garner Park. This event is free and encourages greater interest in the art. This annual event began in 2002. As many famous operas are in other languages—French, German, and Italian, for example—the performances feature projected translations above the stage. Wisconsin Public Radio sometimes broadcasts performances as well.

MADISON SAVOYARDS
(608) 231-9005
www.madisonsavoyards.org
If you love Gilbert and Sullivan, this is your gig. Since its founding in 1963, the Savoyards have done every one of the pair's works. Each summer they stage another production with full orchestra. Ticket prices range from $20 to $40. Venues vary as well but have included the Bartell, Wisconsin Union Theater, and the First Unitarian Society's auditorium.

MADISON SYMPHONY ORCHESTRA
(608) 258-4141
www.madisonsymphony.org
The MSO is made up of about 90 contracted musicians and directed by John DeMain. Performances that include the Overture Hall's organ are rather special events; watch for them. The Madison Symphony Chorus, currently directed by Beverly Taylor, first performed in 1927. Since that time the chorus, made up of volunteer vocalists, has regularly collaborated with the orchestra. The home venue is Overture Hall in the Overture Center. Tickets cost $15 to $75.

WISCONSIN CHAMBER ORCHESTRA
(608) 258-4141
www.wcoconcerts.org
A chamber orchestra is a smaller group than a symphony orchestra made up of about 25 to 40 musicians generally of soloist skill level. This orchestra, directed by Andrew Sewell, may be best known for its extremely popular Concerts on

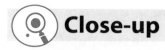 **Close-up**

Children's Theater of Madison

When Madison public schools cut creative drama in 1965, a group of four women, members of Zeta Phi Eta speech sorority, came up with the idea for CTM. With the backing of the Madison Junior Women's Club and the American Association of University Women, they were able to round up the funding for a production. Edgewood College also got involved and provided the theater space. Over the years a variety of impressive talents have taken the stage including internationally recognized vocalists, Metropolitan Opera performers, and popular actors the likes of George Wendt (Norm from *Cheers*). Today performances take place at the Overture Center for the Arts in either The Playhouse or the Capitol Theater. The stories of these productions revolve around children and often involve child actors. The organization also offers acting courses for children. Read more about it in the Kidstuff chapter, page 148. Check the Web site for upcoming auditions. Productions are generally scheduled on the weekends and include matinee performances on Sat and Sun. Children's Theater of Madison, 228 State St.; (608) 255-2080; www.ctmtheater.org.

the Square, when they set up on the steps of the Capitol on Wed evenings in the summer for a free public performance. The home venue is the Capitol Theater at the Overture Center, but the group performs at various other venues as well throughout the year. Before Overture performances, a buffet dinner is hosted in the center's Wisconsin Studio. The director and featured soloist attend and discuss the night's upcoming performance. Call for reservations (608) 257-0638.

THEATERS AND PERFORMING ARTS CENTERS

AMERICAN PLAYERS THEATRE
5950 Golf Course Rd., Spring Green
(608) 588-2361
www.playinthewoods.org
Shakespeare in the Park? Try Shakespeare in the *Woods*. In 1978, a group of theater nuts had the idea to put together an outdoor performance venue. Not far from Spring Green, just a 40-mile drive west of Madison, they found the perfect location. Appropriately, the first production, staged in July 1980 was Shakespeare's *A Midsummer Night's Dream*. APT has been a success ever since, even garnering a Tony nomination. The season begins in late spring and continues to

the fall. Productions emphasize the classics with a special nod toward the Bard. Just over 1,100 seats are available "up the hill" and tickets may go fast for certain performances, especially on weekends. In 2009, APT opened the **Touchstone Theatre,** a 200-seat indoor venue which offers productions with a more intimate focus. Traditionally, playgoers arrive early for a picnic just outside the gate. Complimentary mosquito spray is available inside for when the bugs are biting. A day in advance theatergoers can order food via the APT Web site from Hubbard Avenue Diner in Middleton. These prepared meals are delivered to the theater. Spring Green's Furthermore Brewing serves Proper, a beer specially brewed for APT. The facility is wheelchair accessible but with a hill to climb.

BARTELL COMMUNITY THEATRE
113 East Mifflin St.
(608) 294-0740
www.madstage.com
First operated as a dance school, this 1906 building spent some years as first a premier cinema and finally a budget cinema called The Esquire. In 1998, several years after the cinema closed its doors, Bartell reopened them. Performances

by several local acting companies can be seen here including works from Encore Studio for the Performing Arts, Madison Theater Guild, Strollers Theatre, StageQ, Mercury Players, and the Laboratory Theatre. Community is an operative word here: actors are indeed paid professionals but the talent is hired locally. Often the playwrights and designers are locals as well. In fact, this is the only theater in the country controlled by a sort of cooperative by the resident theater companies. The building houses two intimate performance areas: The Drury and The Evjue Theatres which have seats for 196 and 99 people, respectively. The building is wheelchair accessible. The average ticket price hovers around $15.

BROOM STREET THEATER
1119 Williamson St.
(608) 244-8338
www.broomstreet.org

"No censorship, no restrictions, no limits." This mantra for the city's experimental theater should be warning enough for the easily offended and an invitation for theatergoers looking to go beyond the usual. Founded in 1969, Broom Street is the longest operating all-original work theater in the country, and their seven annual productions touch on diverse topics, from the politically controversial to the delightfully absurd. Two hundred volunteers keep this project running. Playwrights hail from as far away as Australia and each play runs for six weekends. Be there on time because reserved seats will be given up 10 minutes before the production. Performances are on Fri and Sat evenings with a matinee show on Sun and the ticket prices are quite reasonable. Wheelchair accessible.

FIRESIDE DINNER THEATRE
1131 Janesville Ave.
Business Hwy 26 South, Fort Atkinson
(800) 477-9505
www.firesidetheatre.com

Since 1978 when the popular family restaurant added a theater, the Fireside has built a fantastic reputation for itself as a fine-dining and fine theater destination. Guests come for dinner and stay

Theater Bus

For members of the 55 and older population Dane County has a nifty way to get to various theatrical, cultural, and social events not just in Madison, but farther afield in Milwaukee and Chicago. The Theater Bus is a nonprofit organization offering escorted transportation to places such as the Crystal Grand Music Theatre at the Ho-Chunk Casino in Baraboo or the Fireside Dinner Theatre in Fort Atkinson. They even make museum and festival visits. Three pickup locations include the west side, east side, and downtown Madison. Contact them or go to their Web site and check the calendar events to see where they are going next. Theater Bus, 517 North Segoe Rd., #200A; (608) 257-0003; www .theaterbus.org.

for a Broadway-style show in a nearly 600-seat theater-in-the-round. Each year sees six productions lasting about two months each. Auditions are done in New York. Dinner is required for all shows. Business casual or nicer dress is required. The facility is wheelchair accessible. Tickets are for sale on the Web site or by phone. Fort Atkinson is about a 45-minute drive east of Madison.

MIDDLETON PERFORMING ARTS CENTER
Middleton High School
2100 Bristol St., Middleton
(608) 829-9853

When Middleton received a couple of accolades as the best place to live in the United States, one of the supports for that claim surely was this outstanding arts center. The center is part of the high school campus but has its own separate entrance and an impressive lobby with a glass atrium. The 891-seat theater hosts a variety of cultural and performance events and is home to Middleton Players Theatre, a community theater group, which puts on Broadway-style musicals and some smaller or original productions as well.

THE MITBY THEATER
Madison Area Technical College
3550 Anderson St.
(608) 243-4000
http://matcmadison.edu/plus/mitby-theater
This 975-seat theater was intended for the local orchestra so special attention was paid to acoustics in its design and construction. The college puts on theatrical productions by the Performing Arts Department and concerts by the Music Department throughout the year. Tickets for concerts are often free while theater productions carry a nominal ticket fee.

i A good Internet source for up-to-date openings and closings at Madison area theaters is www.madstage.com.

THE OVERTURE CENTER FOR THE ARTS
201 State St.
(608) 258-4141
www.overturecenter.com
Paul Sauglin, a student-activist-leader-turned-mayor, started the push for a performing arts center in 1974 and by 1980 the city had the Madison Civic Center with the Oscar Mayer Theater at its heart. For 23 years the Civic Center brought in first-class entertainment—concerts, touring shows—and served as the prime venue for several local performance groups. But in the end, the performing arts scene was still cramped and needed something a bit more substantial with more rehearsal space as well as multiple venues and modernized facilities. The big jump forward came with an astounding pledge of $205 million from local businessman W. Jerome Frautschi. Argentine-born American architect César Pelli, who designed Kuala Lumpur's Petronas Twin Towers, was given the job to design the building, and ground was broken in 2001. The first phase of the project opened in 2004, the second phase just over a year later.

A lighted glass dome shifts colors at one end of the block on State Street, and at the other a stairwell rises up through what looks like a ship's prow made of glass. Façades from two of the early 20th century buildings originally on this site were worked into the modern additions, and the lobby rises four-stories enclosed in more glass. The center is home to the Madison Museum of Contemporary Art, the James Watrous Gallery, the rooftop restaurant and bar Fresco, and a museum gift shop. Additionally, the 75-foot high glass lobby hosts a variety of events and performances including occasional happy-hour live music.

Overture Hall is the granddaddy of the performance venues with 2,251 seats. The design and lighting with gold and sky blue highlights is a sight in itself. Seats occupy four levels.

The hall houses a German-made organ. Big national acts often perform here as do the Madison Symphony Orchestra, Madison Opera, and Madison Ballet. The Capitol Theater was the name of the 1928 venue originally on this site. Starting with Vaudeville acts and cinema, the theater lasted into the 1970s. In 1980 it was restored and rededicated as the Oscar Mayer Theatre, hosting performances for 23 years. In the construction of the Overture Center it received a serious makeover and actually a reduction in size. The original ornate façade facing State Street, however, was preserved as were the Grand Barton Organ, the ornate ceiling, various wall niches and chandeliers, and the proscenium arch. The capacity is for 400 on the main floor and 600 in the balcony. The Wisconsin Chamber Orchestra plays here and the theater also hosts productions by other groups and Overture center events as well. The Playhouse, with room for 347, is a smaller theater for more intimate performances and until 2009 was occupied by the Madison Repertory Theater. Since that company's unfortunate demise, other smaller groups have found opportunities to use it.

Promenade Hall features retractable bleachers that can be drawn out to create other performance venues. Its resident company is Kanopy Dance. The Rotunda Stage is located in the lower level and opens up into the atrium above. Seats are of a fixed bleacher variety, and Kids in the

Rotunda performances are held here. This venue is always open to the public during business hours. The closest off-street parking is available in the Overture Center parking ramp on East Mifflin Street and the State Street Capitol ramp on North Carroll Street. The Fairchild Street entrance to the Overture Hall lobby is best for dropping off patrons or for performances in other venues, use the main entrance on State Street or the back entrance on Henry Street. The entire facility is wheelchair accessible.

REGINA THEATRE
Edgewood College
1000 Edgewood College Dr.
(608) 663-6710
http://theatre.edgewood.edu
Students from the college perform in four main-stage productions throughout each academic year, ranging from classics such as Shakespeare or Greek drama to modern comedies and musicals. Other student projects and one-act plays fill the calendar in between. Tickets are in the $10 range with discounts for students and seniors.

RIVER ARTS INC.
105 Ninth St., Prairie Du Sac
(608) 643-5634
www.riverartscenter.org
Just 20 minutes north of Madison across the Wisconsin River, River Arts Center serves as a high quality performance venue for Sauk City and Prairie du Sac. Throughout the year a variety of shows is presented in the 492-seat theater as are several exhibitions in the gallery space. Works by the high school drama department and the community-based **Sauk Prairie Theatre Guild** are part of the lineup mixed in with visiting productions and musical and dance performances. Tickets range from $10 to $25 with discounts for students and advanced purchase.

STOUGHTON CENTER FOR
THE PERFORMING ARTS
515 East Main St., Stoughton
(608) 873-0717
www.stoughtonperformingarts.com

Set in a restored tobacco warehouse with exposed brick and an open-beam ceiling, the center seats over 100 and provides space for receptions and workshops. Three music studios are also inside. The facility is wheelchair accessible.

THE UNIVERSITY OF WISCONSIN–
MUSIC HALL
925 Bascom Mall
(608) 263-9485
www.music.wisc.edu
In an 1878 building at the foot of the famed Bascom Hill of campus, this hall hosts the University Opera as well as recitals and concerts from the music department. The building's Carol Rennebohm Auditorium holds 385.

THE UNIVERSITY OF WISCONSIN–
UNIVERSITY THEATRE
Vilas Hall
821 University Ave.
(608) 265-2787
www.utmadison.com
The university's Department of Theatre and Drama puts on four productions during the academic year. The Hemsley Theater is a 125-seat black box theater and usually hosts two productions. The Mitchell Theater holds a modified thrust stage and seats 321 people and also produces two shows. Both are located in Vilas Hall on University Avenue. Tickets cost around $20 with discounts available for students, children, and seniors.

THE UNIVERSITY OF WISCONSIN–
THE WISCONSIN MEMORIAL UNION
800 Langdon St.
(608) 265-ARTS
www.uniontheater.wisc.edu
The main auditorium at the Union is the Wisconsin Union Theater, a 1,300-seat hall with a large stage for performing arts events, seminars, films, and lectures. The Fredric March Play Circle is more intimate and frequently hosts films and simpler live performances with a seating capacity of 168.

VERONA AREA PERFORMING ARTS SERIES
(608) 848-2787
www.vapas.org
Verona's arts center, part of the Verona Area High School campus, stages productions by the Verona Area Community Theater and the high school but also a few national acts from time to time. Tickets can be ordered by mail or via a link on the Web site.

YOUNG SHAKESPEARE PLAYERS
1806 West Lawn Ave.
(608) 258-0015
www.ysp.org
This not-for-profit organization gives kids 7 to 18 the chance to study and rehearse full-length Shakespeare plays with the end goal being a public performance. There are no auditions—anyone can take part. Larger enrollments of kids mean multiple casts for the play, so everyone gets a speaking part and takes part in technical aspects as well. In addition to Shakespeare, dramatic readings are also produced. This is a unique organization and mission, and the results consistently impress audiences and critics. The Web site posts upcoming performances throughout the year.

SHOPPING

The Madison shopping scene has always had some eclectic offerings. Although the malls and a few other shopping areas have most of the major name brands represented, the locally owned businesses have survived a long time on their faithful fans and a community ethic of supporting the home team.

On the east side, just about where the passing Interstate crosses East Washington Avenue/US 151, is East Towne Mall and its surrounding neighborhood of big box stores such as Best Buy, The Home Depot, as well as Wisconsin-based Shopko, Kohl's, and Menards. The anchor stores at East Towne Mall are JCPenney, Sears, Boston Store, and Dick's Sporting Goods. There is a midsize Barnes and Noble next to the food court. On the west side is West Towne Mall at the Gammon Road exit of the Beltline Highway. A bit busier than the eastside mall, West Towne is anchored by the same big name stores. To the west of the mall is a row of big box Best Buy, Kohl's, Shopko, Cub Foods, and a large Barnes and Noble Bookstore. A scattering of strip malls and big stores sits just west of the westside Beltline starting from Mineral Point Road exit and continuing north to Middleton's Greenway Plaza, another popular shopping destination. More central is Hilldale Mall at Midvale Boulevard and University Avenue. It's smaller and more boutique feeling than the two larger malls and its Sundance Cinema and its surrounding restaurants including The Great Dane brewpub make it an evening destination as well.

But for the boutique and unique, look elsewhere. Madison is the kind of place where a random store might exist in the middle of a residential neighborhood. But there are a few good best bets throughout the city. Downtown is the biggest. With the presence of Gap, American Apparel, and Urban Outfitters, State Street has lost a little bit of its local edge, but longstanding specialty shops still carry on. The nice selection of restaurants and coffee shops with sidewalk seating in between makes for leisurely window shopping as well. Many will combine a stroll down State Street with a Sat morning trip to the farmers' market on the Capitol Square. Watch for July's Maxwell Street Days when most of the State Street shops put sale priced merchandise out on the sidewalk and street.

On the near west side Monroe Street offers two short stretches of neat little shops, galleries, and restaurants in the 1800-1900 blocks right across the street from Trader Joe's and again farther west in the 2400-2600 block area. Also on the west side, the length of University Avenue west past the University Hospital shows various small strip-mall shopping centers.

On the near east side is Williamson (Willy) Street, the length of which offers a scattering of neighborhood shops and eateries and a residential setting (although the street itself is rather busy). Farther east from there on the same road is the Atwood/Schenck neighborhood which has a similar feel to Willy Street. North Sherman Avenue has a couple little strip malls and is trying to breathe some life back into the northside neighborhood with a few specialized food stores, a bookstore, resale shops, and restaurants. There is ample parking at both of them.

ANTIQUES

ANTIQUES MALL OF MADISON
4748 Cottage Grove Rd.
(608) 222-2049
www.antiquesmadison.com

Don't let the bleak strip mall location discourage you. Over 120 dealers contribute to this antique collection offering thousands of items, many of which are priced quite reasonably. Since 1982 the mall has offered a wide variety of collectibles including jewelry, vintage clothing, advertising memorabilia, tin toys, Steiff silver, Red Wing pottery, baseball cards, fine china, and furniture. Open daily.

J TAYLOR'S GALLERIES
18 1/2 North Carroll St.
(608) 255-6277
www.jtaylorsgalleries.net
To peer into the window of this Capitol Square shop is to look into a mystical storybook. The statues surely must come alive at night. As much a museum as an antiques shop, this gallery tickles the imagination and offers an eclectic collection of items one might expect to find in the home of an old explorer. Rare books and maps are a specialty. Resist all temptation to look with your hands. Remember these are rare and expensive items and you may not want to accidentally damage and subsequently pay for what appears to be "just a book" but is in fact a first edition worth thousands. The hours are inconsistent. Open Tues through Sat or by chance or appointment.

JANET'S ANTIQUE GALLERY
3800 University Ave.
(608) 238-3300
www.janetsantiques.com
This mother-daughter team of Janet Hoopes and Elizabeth Jane Barber owns a 6,000-square foot gallery at the intersection of University Avenue and Midvale Boulevard. The collection includes abundant furniture from the last three centuries, from Victorian and Rococo to Art Deco and Retro, as well as antique glass and fine art. Elizabeth Jane is a member of The American Society of Appraisers and The American Cut Glass Association. If you are looking for something specific that they don't have, let them know and they will alert you when it turns up.

KAPPEL'S CLOCK SHOP
2250 Sherman Ave.
(608) 244-6165
Since 1970 Karl Kappel has been fixing clocks in this old corner store at the intersection of Sherman and Fordem Avenues. Kappel buys and sells antique timepieces but nothing electric. If you are looking for a mantle clock or grandfather, this is the place to go. Hours are around midday. Closed Sun.

BOOKSTORES

FRUGAL MUSE BOOKS
Prairie Town Center
235 Junction Rd.
(608) 833-8668

North Gate Shopping Center
1193 North Sherman Ave.
(608) 242-0000
www.frugalmuse.com
Arguably Madison's most ambitious used bookstore, it started in a previous westside location in 1994 and grew rapidly into surrounding shop space before moving farther west. An eastside location was also added. The collection of books turns over frequently and prices are quite fair. An ample selection of music, videos, and games is also on hand. Items bought or traded from customers are part of the stock, and the store offers good trade rates. Some new releases are also on hand with usually at least a 25% discount off the cover price. The staff are knowledgeable and friendly. The eastside location is in a strip mall set back from Sherman Avenue. Open daily at both locations.

HALF PRICE BOOKS
Essex Square
4250 East Towne Blvd.
(608) 244-1189
www.halfpricebooks.com
Part of a chain of used bookstores, Half Price Books now only has one location in Madison. The selection is good and well organized and includes music and videos. Many overstock items

from other stores end up here as well. The store buys more of what it sells as well and pays a fair price. Open daily.

PAUL'S BOOK STORE
670 State St.
(608) 257-2968
This bookstore is perfect for anyone who grew up loving old books. The smell of it from the street is enough to stop a book person. The history collection is especially large and browsing always turns up something delightfully unexpected. Music plays in the background. New releases aren't likely to be here, but for browsing and lingering with a spine across your hand, this place is classic. Open daily.

RAINBOW BOOKSTORE COOPERATIVE
426 West Gilman St.
(608) 257-6050
www.rainbowbookstore.org
Since its opening by volunteers in 1989 this independent bookstore has been serving the book needs of progressives and left-leaning political minds. The store hosts readings and political and social events. In addition to its book collection, it has a variety of magazines, underground publications, and textbooks for progressive classes at the UW or Edgewood. Located just off of State Street, the store is open daily.

> **i** Many of the branches of the Madison Public Library host weekend book sales. Some of them even do so on a monthly basis. Watch the Web site (www.madisonpubliclibrary.org/calendar/booksales.html) or check local listings in *Isthmus* newspaper for the next sale. The selections are donated books and proof that Madison reads good stuff.

A ROOM OF ONE'S OWN
307 West Johnson St.
(608) 257-7888
www.roomofonesown.com
Bright and nicely organized, this indie bookstore has been serving the Madison community since 1975 offering a thorough collection of women's literature, magazines, music, T-shirts, and posters. Sizeable collections of gay and lesbian studies and works of LGBT fiction are also on hand. The bookstore also acts as a good hub for information on housing, jobs, support, special events, and workshops of interest to women and the LGBT community. Though the collection of specialized books is sizeable, Room also gives space to a variety of local authors. Room hosts frequent book readings/signings and has an e-mail list for upcoming events. Open daily.

> **i** Notable novelist and short-story writer Lorrie Moore is a Madison resident and professor of English at the University of Wisconsin. Another Wisconsin resident author and humorist Michael Perry makes frequent appearances in Madison and should not be missed.

THE UNIVERSITY BOOKSTORE
Campus Location:
On the State Street Mall
(across from the Memorial Library)
711 State St.
(608) 257-3784

Hilldale Mall Location:
702 North Midvale Blvd.
(608) 238-8455
www.uwbookstore.com
This independent bookstore has been around since 1894. The campus location is the primary provider of textbooks to the University of Wisconsin and carries both new and used copies. A wide variety of school and art supplies are also for sale as well as a selection of magazines, mass-market books, and Wisconsin Badger apparel. The campus location hosts occasional author readings. The Hilldale location, across the hall from Sundance Cinemas and with easy parking in back, does not have the textbooks, but has more frequent author events in an area near the children's book section downstairs. Open daily.

BOUTIQUES & SPECIALTY SHOPS

BURNIE'S ROCK SHOP
901 East Johnson St.
(608) 251-2601
www.burniesrockshop.com
Stop in to see some beautiful gems and rocks of all kinds as well as jewelry and lapidary equipment. They also repair jewelry. Just around the corner is **Burnie's Design Annex** at 221 North Paterson St. where you can discuss your design ideas with a professional. Closed on Mon.

ORANGE TREE IMPORTS
1721 Monroe St.
(608) 255-8211
www.orangetreeimports.com
Located in a mismatched pair of buildings—one short and one tall—Orange Tree Imports gets awards for its window displays which draw the curious inside just to see what's what. It is hard to sum up the assorted products for sale here: kitchen accessories, toys, gifts, jewelry, soaps, candles—the list is endless. Specialty foods and candy are also for sale and despite the suggestion of the business name a lot of it is locally produced. This family business has been a part of the Monroe Street scene for over 30 years. Even if you don't know what you are looking for, you will find it here. Looking for a Japanese tea pot or cleverly designed cheese knife? What to do with some of their kitchen tools? Sign on for one of their many cooking classes. Orange Tree keeps a wedding registry as well. Open daily.

PEGASUS GAMES
6640 Odana Rd.
(608) 833-4263
www.pegasusgames.com
For all things associated with role playing and interactive gaming, check out this shop in the Market Square strip mall on the west side. Choose from a wide selection of games, books, and miniatures. The store often hosts games and tournaments as well. Open daily.

POP DELUXE
310 State St.
(608) 256-1966
www.popdeluxe.net
This store is nothing if not fun. Shop here for gifts unique and often colorful (both literally and figuratively speaking) or decorate your home or office with a variety of creative items either functional or just quirky. Open daily.

SACRED FEATHER
417 State St.
(608) 255-2071
www.sacredfeather.com
Set in an 1884 sandstone house, the only residential structure left on State Street, Sacred Feather is a local landmark famous for its selection of high-quality hats and caps. The options are numerous, with styles for both men and women, and include fedoras, berets, pork pies, cowboy hats, straw hats, newsboy caps, fezes, and even pop-up silk top hats. Various fleece-lined caps are popular to battle the Wisconsin winter. Quality leather goods such as purses, bags, and some belts are also for sale. Closed Sun.

SHANGRI-LA COLLECTIONS
125 State St.
(608) 259 9395
www.shangrilacollections.com
Two brothers from Nepal opened this lovely little shop in what was once a horse stable for the local fire department. For sale are arts and crafts, rugs, jewelry, soaps, and clothing from the Himalayan region as well as books, DVDs, and music. The owners deal directly with artisans in Nepal and part of the store's mission is to promote and preserve the culture. Open daily.

THE SOAP OPERA
319 State St.
(608) 251-4051
www.thesoapopera.com
Before the Bath and Body Works craze swept the country, this little downtown boutique shop knew what smelled nice and it would be hard to beat the selection of soaps, essential oils, mas-

sage oils, body lotions, candles, herbal remedies, and much more. Staff can assist customers in finding the proper soap for their skin type, and custom scenting is available for several exclusive products. Scentless products are also available. Open daily.

CLOTHING STORES

Children's Clothing

CAPITOL KIDS
8 South Carroll St.
(608) 280-0744
www.capitolkids.com
Located downtown, Capitol Kids offers clothes, games, and toys for the little ones, as well as a play area to keep them busy while you shop. Read more under Kidstuff – Shopping, page 159.

WILD CHILD INC.
1813 Monroe St.
(608) 251-6445
www.wildchildclothes.com
This locally-owned store sells mix and match clothing for infants and toddlers. Quality is high and market ethics are a big part of their mission. Read more under Kidstuff – Shopping, page 159.

Men's Clothing

CONTEXT
113 King St.
(608) 250-0113
www.contextclothing.com
Young hip men rate this place highly and come here expecting to spend some serious money on high quality threads. Much of what Context carries is exclusive to the Madison market and denim is the fabric of choice. The staff is into what's being sold and can lead you through if you are a newbie. The Web site is quite useful for shopping and shipping is fast.

JAZZMAN
340 State St.
(608) 256-2062
http://jazzmanclothing.com

Far bolder and more unique than mainstream Gap across the street, Jazzman contemporary men's clothing selection offers various name brands which are harder to find in the Midwest. The staff is very helpful with finding the look that is good for the shopper. Open daily.

Outlet Shopping

If you are looking for outlet stores, a day trip out of the city is in order. About 45 minutes east on I-94 is Johnson Creek Outlet Mall with 60 different brand name stores. It takes about the same amount of time to reach Tanger Outlet Center in Wisconsin Dells which offers just over 60 stores as well. Check out a Wisconsin Dells excursion in the Day Trips chapter.

Johnson Creek Premium Outlets
575 West Linmar Lane, Johnson Creek
(920) 699-4111
www.premiumoutlets.com

Tanger Outlet Center
210 Gasser Rd., Wisconsin Dells
(608) 253-5380
www.tangeroutlet.com/wisconsindells

Women's Clothing

ATTICUS
18 North Carroll St.
(608) 204-9001
http://atticusshop.com
Located on the Capitol Square, this store sells a wide variety of designer clothing for both men and women, with some eco-friendly options in the mix. Atticus also sells accessories and Malin+Goetz bath and body products. The Web site takes orders and ships around the United States. Closed Sun. Parking is metered just off the Capitol Square, otherwise use the Overture Center Parking Ramp on Mifflin Street.

KAREN & CO. SASSAFRAS
307/309 State St.
(608) 258-5500
www.karencomadison.com

Karen & Co. and Sassafras were separate State Street businesses from the 1970s which merged and restored the old State Street storefront they occupy. Shop here for modern women's clothing from over two dozen designers and including leather, knits, coats, lingerie, and accessories. Staff stylists can help you decide what looks best on you. Watch for the picks of the week. Closed Sun.

SUZEN SEZ
2421 University Ave.
(608) 238-1331

If you are looking for something a little different, the colors, patterns, and fabrics here aim for just that. Handbags, watches, scarves, and belts are for sale as well.

TIGER LILY BOUTIQUE
128 State St.
(608) 251-1225
www.tigerlilystores.com

This locally owned boutique sells a snappy collection of dresses, tops, shoes, and jewelry at reasonable prices. They do alterations on-site as well. The Web site has a shopping section and ships anywhere with a 15-day return policy. A second location, Tiger Lily Too, is at 341 State St., and more shops are in both East Towne and West Towne Malls.

Vintage Clothing

RAGSTOCK
327 State St.
(608) 251-3419
www.ragstock.com

This used clothing store is locally owned but part of a growing midwest chain. Look here for some of the funkiest clothes around. Some will shop here for their new look, others for their Halloween costume. If you are not too excited about dropping big bucks on a prom dress, check here. The shop occupies two floors and the nearest parking is a State Street ramp. Open daily.

FARMERS' MARKETS

Madison has the largest producer-only farmers' market in the nation. Its wealth of offerings from meats, cheeses, and produce to flowers, baked goods, and preserves, surrounds the magnificent Capitol every Sat morning. But this is but one of several weekly markets in the city. Look for a market on just about every day of the week. At all of them you can expect all the produce currently in season and commonly meats (chicken, pork, beef, or even bison, ostrich, and elk), eggs, cheeses, and other dairy products, potted plants (decorative or for food gardens), flowers, preserves, baked goods, and sometimes crafts. Recycle your leftover egg cartons by giving them to a vendor and bring your own bag if you think of it.

With very few exceptions all markets only allow products produced in Wisconsin. Markets usually run from Apr or May through Oct depending on seasonal weather in those shoulder months. For an up-to-date listing and precise hours go to the city's Web site at www.cityofmadison.com/residents/farmersmarket.cfm.

A whole slew of other markets exists just outside of Madison and makes for pleasant outings throughout the week. Look for them at the Southern Wisconsin Farm Fresh Atlas Web site at www.reapfoodgroup.org/atlas.

DANE COUNTY FARMERS' MARKET
On the Capitol Square
Sat mornings, mid-Apr into Nov
www.dcfm.org
(See also Winter Markets page 105)

This is the biggie and is often celebrated by foodie magazines as the nation's best. In 1972 the then city mayor Bill Dyke was searching for a bridge between the urban and rural cultures of Madison. His solution has become an award-winning farmers' market with close to 300 vendors that is as much a social event as a shopping experience. Getting there early might beat the rush but only by a little. Booths line the walks on all four sides of the Capitol and everyone walks in a counterclockwise direction further enhancing the event's sense of ritual. On offer is just about everything imaginable: fruits and vegetables, fresh and cured meats (including ostrich, elk, or bison), fish, fresh cheese (including Wisconsin's famous cheese curds), honeys, syrups, jams and salsas, flowers for bouquets, plants for the garden, fresh-baked breads, muffins and cookies, milk, eggs, yogurt, pesto, and popcorn. At the foot of the steps at the Capitol's four corners expect to find campaigners for causes addressing anything from human rights, politics, or religion to conservation, hiking, or the local opera. Street musicians set up across the street as do other nonmarket vendors selling smoothies, gourmet coffee, popcorn, or perhaps arts and crafts. Parking hunting headaches can be avoided by using one of the four ramps just off the square on the Capitol Loop or opting to bike or hike it. Remember that much of the two-hour parking on the surrounding streets is still enforced on Sat. Read the signs carefully for exceptions.

Wed morning there is another, smaller Dane County Farmers' Market which starts just a bit later in the morning and runs just past the lunch hour. This market can be found in front of the City-County Building just a block from the Capitol in the 200 block of Martin Luther King Jr. Boulevard.

EASTSIDE FARMERS' MARKET
201 Ingersoll St.
www.willystreet.coop/ESFM
Tues from 4 to 7 p.m. from about May through Oct, this market sets up in a gravel lot next to the Capital City Bike Path where it crosses at Ingersoll Street. There are places to lock your bike and street parking nearby for easy access. The market is as relaxed and casual as its neighborhood, and two-wheeled commuters will hop off the trail for some fresh food on their way home from work.

NORTHSIDE FARMERS' MARKET
Parking lot near the corner of Sherman Avenue and Northport Drive
Sun mornings, 8:30 a.m. to 12:30 p.m.
www.northsidefarmersmarket.org
Parking is available right next to the vendors making this very convenient for those on a quick

shopping mission. However, the pace here is a lazy Sun morning variety and the market draws primarily from this neighborhood. In addition to the usual offerings, you will find a row of local arts and crafts vendors, and a fresh breakfast—eggs, pancakes, and the like—cooked to order and served at a few small plastic tables.

SOUTHSIDE FARMERS' MARKET
Labor Temple parking lot
1602 South Park St.
www.southmadisonfarmersmarket.com
This is truly a moveable feast. The market operates five days per week: Sun, Mon, Tues, Wed, Thurs. On Tues and Sun the market is on the grounds at the Labor Temple on Park Street with the hours in the afternoon on Tues and starting late morning and finishing mid-afternoon on Sun. On Mon afternoons look for the market at 2500 Rimrock Rd. On Wed the market moves to the United Church of Christ at 1501 Gilbert Rd. on the west side. On Thurs afternoons it's back to the south side at the parking lot of Villager Mall at 2300 South Park Street. These locations of course are subject to change. The organization also plans community events centered around whatever's in season to give locals an opportunity to sample and socialize. The market is affiliated with P.E.A.T. (Program for Entrepreneurial Agricultural Training) which trains area youth not just how to raise healthy food but how to become self-employed.

WESTSIDE COMMUNITY MARKET
Hill Farms Department of Transportation Parking Lot
(just south of University Avenue on Segoe Road)
Sat 7 a.m. to 1 p.m.
Apr through Nov
www.westsidecommunitymarket.org
This is another great Sat option for a market. The market is in the middle of a parking lot and shoppers can pull up right next to it. The market is a good option if you don't have the time or energy for the market on the Capitol Square. Despite the smaller size, there is still a solid variety of products.

Surrounding Community Markets

FITCHBURG FARMERS' MARKET
5511 East Cheryl Pkwy., Fitchburg
(in the Agora Pavilion)
(608) 277-2606
www.fitchburgcenter.com/farmersmarket
.htm
South of Madison in next door Fitchburg, this Thurs afternoon market is yet another south side option. Each month features a special event such as Strawberry Fest in June or Flowerama in May for Mother's Day. The Web site keeps a list of vendors as well as what's currently in season.

MIDDLETON FARMERS' MARKET
Deming Way at Greenway Station
(608) 872-2152
www.greenwayshopping.com
Look for this market on Thurs mornings in the parking lot near T.G.I. Friday's on Deming Way.

MONONA FARMERS' MARKET
Ahuska Park on East Broadway in Monona
Sun 9 a.m. to 1 p.m.
www.mononafarmersmarket.com
Parking is right next to the vendors and there is also a playground for the kids. The market is about the same size as the Eastside Market, with just over a dozen or so vendors, but the variety is good. Check the Web site for monthly events such as sustainable living exhibits.

Winter Markets

Winter doesn't mean the end of the markets. The Dane County Farmers' Market (www.dcfm .org) continues on Sat from Jan into Apr, but moves indoors at the Monona Terrace Convention Center for Nov and Dec, and the Madison Senior Center at 330 West Mifflin St. from Jan into Apr. A nice breakfast is served for just under $10 at the Senior Center market. The Northside Farmers' Market has also set up indoors in the past in an open space. Check their Web site (www.north sidefarmersmarket.org) for the current location.

i It is said fresh spinach actually tastes better in the winter—the freeze and thaw cycle sweetens it up a bit. Watch for it at the markets.

MUSIC

B-SIDE RECORDS
436 State St.
(608) 255-1977
www.b-sidemadison.com
A bit of a State Street fixture since 1982, one wondered how they would survive the demise of vinyl in the CD age. The funky little shop still keeps some select vinyl LPs and an appealing range of new and used CDs and DVDs. This is a great place for browsing, finding those elusive or collectible titles, or discovering something new. If they don't have it, they'll order it. Open daily.

STRICTLY DISCS
1900 Monroe St.
(608) 259-1991
www.strictlydiscs.com
When it opened in 1988, this was the first all-CD store in town. The selection of new and used compact discs is quite good, and whatever is not on-site can be ordered. Staff is knowledgeable and seven listening stations access 500 recent releases. Used vinyl is also on hand. This is also a good place to sell used CDs and LPs. Open daily.

OUTFITTERS & SPORTS SHOPS

FONTANA SPORTS SPECIALTIES
251 State St.
(608) 257-5043

231 Junction Rd.
(608) 833-9191
www.fontanasports.com
In such an outdoors-oriented sort of town, places like Fontana are kept quite busy. A wide variety of sports are covered from tennis, fishing, and in-line skating to scuba diving, skiing, snowboarding, and disc golf. They carry Patagonia, North Face, and Columbia apparel. Open daily.

RUTABAGA PADDLESPORTS
220 West Broadway, Monona
(608) 223-9300
www.rutabaga.com
Most famous for its incredible selection and knowledge of canoes and kayaks, Rutabaga also carries camping equipment. Situated on the water's edge near Lake Monona, the shop offers test-paddling of their boats. They host Canoecopia, the nation's largest paddling expo, in Mar. They also sell used boats and rent equipment. Open daily.

SOUVENIR SHOPS

SCONNIE NATION
521 State St.
(608) 661-4350
www.sconnie.com
A couple of University of Wisconsin students found the nickname "Sconnie," commonly used by out-of-state students to label Wisconsin residents, humorous. To celebrate the moniker they made a few T-shirts to sell around the dormitory. When these disappeared as quickly as lightning, they knew they were on to something. The line of Wisconsin-, er, *Sconnie*-themed apparel and souvenirs caught on fast, including the "We'll Never Forget You, Brent" Brett Favre T-shirt. The Web site offers purchase and shipping options and the State Street shop is convenient for downtown shoppers. Open daily.

i For University of Wisconsin Badger apparel, check out the University Bookstore.

SPECIALTY FOOD STORES

BAVARIA SAUSAGE
6317 Nesbitt Rd.
(608) 271-1295 or (800) 733-6695
www.bavariasausage.com
Fred Voll, a German immigrant from Bavaria, sold his first bratwurst in Madison in 1961. Now man-

aged by the second generation of sausage makers, this is the real deal, all mixed by hand with quality ingredients and no chemical additives. In addition to the meats, snacks, candy, chocolates, beverages, and oven-ready German meals such as Sauerbraten, Rouladen, and Fleischkase are also for sale as is a select variety of Wisconsin and imported cheeses. Fresh cheese curds are delivered here each week. Closed on Sun and only open half the day on Sat. Go west on County Highway PD off of Verona Road/US 151 to find Nesbitt Road, a sort of frontage road.

CARR VALLEY CHEESE STORE
2831 Parmenter St., Middleton
(608) 824-2277
www.carrvalleycheese.com
This is one of the company stores of the award-winning regional cheese maker. Carr Valley has been producing high-quality cheese for over 100 years. Master cheesemaker Sid Cook has won many awards for his own creations and several of his traditional cheeses as well. Samples, of course, are on hand as is the wide variety of cheeses that Carr Valley produces. Cheeses are made from cow, sheep, and goat milk and blends among the three. Along with aged and smoked cheddars, gouda, feta, Gloucester, and Colby, Carr Valley's artisanal line also includes many styles only a true connoisseur may have heard of. Closed Sun.

FROMAGINATION
12 South Carroll St.
(608) 255-2430
www.fromagination.com
This upscale specialty shop on the Capitol Square offers a variety of imported, national, and Wisconsin artisan cheeses and cheese boxes. Sandwiches and picnic meals are for sale for take-out. Other regional products including wines, beers, and preserves are also sold. The shop hosts occasional tastings and cheese-related cooking classes. Check the Web site for upcoming events. Closed Sun.

CHOCOLATE

CANDINAS CHOCOLATIER
Factory & Retail Store
2435 Old PB, Verona

Retail Boutique
Madison's Capitol Square
11 West Main St.
(608) 845-1545
www.candinas.com
Owner/chocolatier Markus Candinas completed a three-year apprentice program in Switzerland and worked among some of the finest confectioners in Europe. *USA Today* once included Candinas in a roundup of great American chocolatiers. Typically just over a dozen types of chocolates are on hand ranging from pure chocolate to fruit, nut, herb, and liqueur blended varieties. Orders are processed in Verona. Closed Sun.

GAIL AMBROSIUS CHOCOLATIER
2086 Atwood Ave.
(608) 249-3500
www.gailambrosius.com
A trip to France and a taste of dark chocolate inspired Gail to return to Paris to become a chocolatier. Dedicated as she is to sustainably farmed, fair-trade, and quality ingredients, Gail uses single-origin cacao from small producers from different parts of the world. Each day she makes small handmade batches incorporating a variety of flavors—cayenne pepper, espresso beans, vanilla, sea salt, just to name a few. Closed Sun.

i Look for Cow Pies when in Madison. No, not the fresh variety in a farmer's field, but the chocolate covered peanut and caramel treat produced by a Baraboo confectioner.

THRIFT SHOPS

BETHESDA HOUSE OF THRIFT
201 Cottage Grove Rd.
(608) 223-1228
Located on the east side in a small strip of shops set back from the road, the proceeds go toward the many projects Bethesda funds during the year. The store has a moderate selection of clothes, household items, and more. Closed Sun.

GOODWILL
Downtown
651 State St.
(608) 255-0567

East Side
2127 East Springs Dr.
(608) 246-3147

Monona
2501 Royal Ave.
(608) 224-0781

West Side
4530 Verona Rd.
(608) 271-4687
www.goodwillscwi.org/shop.php
There are four locations for this popular thrift shop, including east and west side outlets, one in Monona, and another downtown. The downtown location offers primarily clothing and accessories. Clothes are of unusually high quality and the bargains disappear fast. Open daily.

ST. VINCENT DE PAUL SOCIETY
1309 Williamson St.
(608) 257-0673
www.svdpmadison.org
Though there are actually three thrift-shop locations in Madison, the St. Vinnie's on Willy Street is the best of the outlets with an excellent selection of furniture for the new student arrival, a broad assortment of clothes including some vintage selections, plenty of kitchenware and appliances, and a used book section that has consistent turnover of very good stuff. This is a good place to drop off useable stuff you no longer need. They don't take computers and TVs. Wheelchair accessible. Closed Sun. The westside location (6301 Odana Rd.; 608-278-2924) is open daily. The southside store (1900 South Park St.; 608-250-6370), also open daily, sells clothes in bulk.

ATTRACTIONS

Most of the city's attractions—but certainly not all—are to be found downtown around the University of Wisconsin campus and the Capitol. Madison has managed to preserve a good number of historical buildings, and the University of Wisconsin offers a variety of social, historical, and educational options. The Overture Center for the Arts is a multimillion dollar facility that brings together art galleries and performing arts venues. The Capitol itself is an architectural beauty reminiscent of the nation's own capitol and rich with history. Renowned architect Frank Lloyd Wright left his mark on Madison, and some of the buildings he designed can still be visited.

The natural beauty of this area, once known simply as Four Lakes, is as much of a reason to see Madison as any other for travelers and residents alike. The attractions of a more natural sort may be found in the Parks and Recreation chapter. A cruise on the lakes provides a must-see angle on the city. See Betty Lou Cruises below or go to the Recreation chapter, page 139, to look for boating or canoeing ideas. Theaters and other performance venues can be found in the Performing Arts chapter.

The attractions are organized geographically. This chapter begins with the downtown area, starting with the Capitol and Monona Terrace, heading down State Street, and then on into the University of Wisconsin. Other attractions from around town follow.

DOWNTOWN

MONONA TERRACE COMMUNITY AND CONVENTION CENTER
1 John Nolen Dr.
(608) 261-4000
www.mononaterrace.com

One of Wisconsin architect Frank Lloyd Wright's designs that did not come to fruition in his lifetime was a community center to be built lakeside in Madison. From 1938 Wright tried to sell the city on his idea and his last design was submitted in 1959, the same year he died. But the concept didn't die with him, and in true Madison fashion furious debate and negotiation went on for years after his death before the Monona Terrace Community and Convention Center became a reality in 1997. Wright's design received some tampering—absent is the intended public marina, for example—but the attractive building sits on the shore of Lake Monona adding a key element to the city skyline, and its rooftop terrace connects to the end of Martin Luther King Jr. Boulevard via a short pedestrian mall with a fountain and a short two-block walk to the Capitol.

The views of the lake on one side and the Capitol on the other are gorgeous, and the center hosts a variety of events throughout the year from outdoor concerts on the terrace to indoor farmers' markets in the fall. A gift shop, open daily, sells a variety of Wright-designed gifts. Guided tours of the building, which include some background of the colorful Mr. Wright, are offered at 1 p.m. daily for around $3 per person. A community open house offers a free tour every Aug. The site is wheelchair accessible. Watch for Tunes at Monona Terrace and Dane County Dances in the summer. The center has its own parking ramp accessible from John Nolen Drive which passes underneath the structure. Monona Terrace has its own Facebook page communicating information about upcoming events.

Food is available at the seasonal rooftop outlet Lake Vista Café during lunch and happy hour daily except Mon, or on the fourth level at GrandView Café which serves appetizers, soups, salads, and sandwiches from Mon through Sat.

Monona Terrace offers a variety of seasonal community event series. Tunes at Monona Terrace is a free Wed-night concert series in the spring and fall featuring local and regional acts covering everything from polka and salsa to jazz and rock for a dancing good time in a family-friendly environment. In pleasant weather this is held outside, otherwise it's indoors with a wooden dance floor. Refreshments, including beer and wine, are served. Concerts on the Rooftop are also free and take place on Thurs evenings in June and July. Lake Vista Café serves food and drinks. No alcohol can be carried in, but all other outside food and drink is allowed making for a nice picnic opportunity. The event moves indoors during inclement weather. **Dane Dances** (www.danedances.org) takes over in Aug with a series of Fri evening concerts. Outside vendors serve a variety of ethnic fare and Lake Vista Café is also on hand serving from its menu and providing a full bar. The paved lakeside multi-use Capitol City Trail passes along the Monona Terrace and is a popular fishing spot for local anglers.

i Otis Redding's private plane crashed into Lake Monona on December 10, 1967, as he was arriving in Madison to perform. Three marble benches on the Monona Terrace rooftop commemorate the singer's untimely death, which occurred just three days after he had recorded his greatest hit song "Dock of the Bay."

THE STATE CAPITOL
2 East Main St.
(608) 266-0382
www.wisconsin.gov
Third time's a charm. The first Capitol was built in 1838 and for about the first decade the builder's pigs took refuge in the basement. The second Capitol was completed in 1863 by Alexander McDonnell whose former home is now Man-

sion Hill Inn (see Accommodations page 22). A devastating fire burnt it to the ground in 1904. Then from 1906 to 1917, George B. Post, who also designed the New York Stock Exchange, constructed this regal beauty. With the only granite dome in the country and marble from six different countries and eight separate states, the Capitol is as beautiful as it is historical. While not in session the various chambers of the three branches of state government are open to the public. (In fact, they are often open to the public when in session as well but in designated seating areas.) Inside the dome are four glass mosaics and, two hundred feet up to the top, a mural "Resources of Wisconsin." Throughout the Capitol are some details worth noting such as numerous murals with scenes from state history; a bust of former governor, U.S. Senator, and Progressive Party presidential candidate "Fighting Bob" LaFollette; and a statue of a badger formed of reclaimed bronze from Spanish American War cannons from the *U.S.S. Wisconsin,* just to name a few.

A guided tour is highly recommended. On the 6th floor a museum contains artifacts from the first Capitol. Passage to the outdoor observation deck at the level of the bottom of the dome is on this floor as well. The reward for the climb is a view of the surrounding city in all four directions. Both the museum and deck are open during the summer but neither is wheelchair accessible. Entry to the Capitol can be gained through revolving doors up the steps from the four corners of the Capitol Square. Wheelchair entrances are at ground level in between the wings. Tours are free and offered daily, year-round. Meet at the ground floor information desk under the Rotunda. Tours start on the hour from 9 a.m. until 3 p.m. except at 12 p.m. and on Sun mornings.

i The four wings of Madison's second Capitol were constructed around the first Capitol. The original building then was torn out to complete the new structure. Madisonians, fearing the state capital might be moved to Milwaukee, called this not a new building, but rather an "expansion."

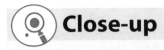

Close-up

Frank Lloyd Wright

Born in Richland Center, WI, in 1867, Frank Lloyd Wright went on to become a world-famous architect known for his organic designs and colorful personal life. He began as an apprentice to Chicago architect Louis Sullivan before venturing out on his own. His residential designs sought to harmonize with the midwestern landscape using unfinished materials, horizontal lines, low or flat roofs, and broad overhangs often referred to now as the Prairie style. His "open plan" designs encompassed wide interior spaces. From his earliest works to his last designs just before his death at the age of 91 in 1959, Wright's lifework shows a variety of notable buildings such as the spectacular Fallingwater residence in Pennsylvania, the Solomon R. Guggenheim Museum in New York City, and the former Imperial Hotel in Tokyo. He created more than thirty designs for projects in and around Madison, his final creation coming to posthumous fruition as the Monona Terrace in 1997.

He was stubborn to the last about his ideas and his disregard for what the public thought of him was plain. In his own words: "Early in life I had to choose between honest arrogance and hypocritical humility. I chose the former and have seen no reason to change." He was married three times in a time when divorce was far more controversial than it is now. But arguably the most dramatic scene of his tumultuous personal life was the murder of his mistress Mamah Cheney (a former client's wife), her two children, and four others at Wright's Spring Green estate Taliesin. All were killed by a disgruntled servant who set fire to the house and waited with an axe outside.

The stories of both the man and his work are fascinating narrations for tours out at the Taliesin Estate. Over 400 of his designs were constructed and about 300 of those still stand. Several of Wright's extant buildings in the Madison area are open to the public. The Monona Terrace Community and Convention Center—an adaptation of his last design—offers tours (see above) and also houses a permanent collection of photographs of Wright's private side and some of his works. Photographer Pedro E. Guerrero followed Wright like his shadow for much of the last 20 years of the architect's life.

At the end of Carroll Street where it meets Lake Mendota is the former site of the municipal boathouse, the design of which Wright submitted in competition in 1893. The boathouse was

State Street

Once the westerly portion of King Street off the Capitol Square, this twice-revitalized street-turned-pedestrian mall is the main artery of Madison's downtown. Closed to all traffic but city buses, bicycles, and delivery vehicles, the six blocks of shops, restaurants, bars, and coffee shops connect the Capitol Square with the University of Wisconsin campus. State Street is also home to several museums, Madison's oldest surviving cinema, and the Overture Center for the Arts. Most of the buildings along State Street date from the late 19th and early 20th century and are attractions for history and architecture buffs alike (see Walking Tours below). While there is a scat-tered assortment of chains such as Gap, Jamba Juice, and Starbucks, the street retains a reputation for its locally grown businesses.

About midway between the Capitol and campus is the diminutive Lisa Link Peace Park which is the street's only green space and, as often as not, occupied by homeless and panhandlers. Street musicians are a familiar sight and sound along State Street and many of them have become fixtures. Catfish Stephenson is known for his bluesy Americana songs (and has been featured on Garrison Keillor's *Prairie Home Companion*) and Art Paul Schlosser who doubles on guitar and kazoo plays his original State Street classics such as "Purple Bananas on the Moon." At

torn down in 1928, but a plaque at the corner of Carroll and Langdon preserves its memory. A few structures that did not meet the demolition ball are:

THE UNITARIAN MEETING HOUSE

900 University Bay Dr.
(608) 233-9774
www.fusmadison.org/mh/mhistory.shtml

Completed in 1951, Wright's innovatively designed church is now a National Historic Landmark. Design elements such as horizontal bands of windows and alternating ceiling heights are characteristically Wright and show his knack for controlling mood and movement of visitors he would never meet. Guided tours are offered according to an online schedule and the building during business hours as well. The Web site has a nice short tour of the building's features that could be printed out for a self-guided visit. Just remember that this is still an operating church and that visits during church events may mean that some areas are not available for viewing.

SETH PETERSON COTTAGE

(608) 254-6551 or (877) 466-2358
www.sethpeterson.org

While canoeing Mirror Lake back in the 1980s, Audrey Laatsch discovered an aban-doned cottage on a bluff in the woods which turned out to be one of Wright's last commissioned works. Now restored, the Seth Peterson Cottage, near Mirror Lake State Park in Lake Delton, gives guests an opportunity to spend a night in a Wright construction. An open house and tours are also offered for the public the second Sun of every month.

TALIESIN

WI 23 and County Road C, Spring Green
(608) 588-7900 or (877) 588-7900
www.taliesinpreservation.org

Less than an hour west of Madison near the town of Spring Green, Wright's estate, architectural school, and experimental home open up for several one- to four-hour in-depth guided tours from May through Oct.

(See the Day Trips chapter page 187.)

For a complete list of Wisconsin Wright sites, including some residences that are sometimes open for tours, contact **Wright in Wisconsin** (608-287-0339, www.wrightinwisconsin.org). The nonprofit organization hosts annual tours called "Wright and Like" that highlight a different area of the state each year.

night the crowd tends to center around the bar scene and, with the proximity of the university, the majority are students. But people of all walks of life and society find their way here for a stroll, window shopping, meal, or a night out.

The walks are wide and during summer and fall many of the restaurants provide sidewalk seating. There's at least one coffee shop on every block. Rollerbladers, skateboarders, and bicyclists share the road with public buses—many of which use State Street to come and go from the Capitol Square. The view up the street is tree-lined right up to the Capitol. At night the dome lights up, and around the holidays in winter, the trees are draped in lights as well.

i Don't miss the tiny Triangle Market (302 State St.), an 1899 Queen Anne building with a turret and stamped metal. The sign in the window says WORLD FAMOUS — TOURS DAILY. Stop in for a chuckle.

With the Capitol anchoring one end and the University of Wisconsin holding down the other, the five blocks of State Street (six if you count Frances Street, which doesn't actually cross) is a prime destination for a visit to Madison. A variety of attractions are located here: the 1927 Orpheum Theatre with its lighted marquee; the Overture Center for the Arts, which blends a modern performing arts design with a couple of preserved facades from the buildings removed for its construction; the Madison Museum of Contemporary Art; the Wisconsin Historical Museum; the Wisconsin Veterans Museum; and just past the end of State Street and off Library Mall on the University of Wisconsin campus is the Chazen Museum of Art. The Children's Museum was at the top of State Street until it moved to its own newly constructed location nearby on the Capitol Square. Weekenders will often combine a stroll down State Street with a visit to the Dane County Farmers' Market on Sat mornings, and everything strings right together—Capitol, State Street, campus—making the entire downtown perfectly suited for walking. State Street is also host to various annual events such as the Ironman Triathlon, Maxwell Street Days, and Freakfest, Madison's raucous Halloween street party.

i Frank Lloyd Wright fans take note of the etched pattern in the Luxfer Prism window tiles above the storefront windows of The Irish Pub at 317 State St. Wright patented 41 designs but only this flower pattern was produced.

MADISON CHILDREN'S MUSEUM
100 North Hamilton St.
(608) 256-6445
www.madisonchildrensmuseum.org
Set to open in Aug 2010, the new and improved Children's Museum has left the top of State Street and now occupies an entire city block touching on the Capitol Square. The new Leadership in Energy and Environmental Design (LEED)–certified building offers much more space for fun and educational activities aimed at children 12 and under. The rooftop terrace affords a Capitol view. A small cafe is on site for snacks and the building is wheelchair accessible. Open daily. There is an admission fee.

THE OVERTURE CENTER FOR THE ARTS
201 State St.
(608) 258-4141
www.overturecenter.com

Probably the most conspicuous of the modern constructions on State Street occupies an entire city block with a glass-enclosed stairwell like a ship's prow at one end and a 1923 French Renaissance Revival façade and modern lighted glass dome at the other. Designed by Cesar Pelli, an internationally famous architect, the impressive arts center got its biggest boost with a multi-million dollar contribution from local businessman W. Jerome Frautschi.

The Spanish/Moorish façade of the 1928 Capitol Theater still stands midblock. The Capitol, with its opulent interiors and a Grand Barton theater organ, was a smashing success and offered a then state-of-the-art moviegoing experience. But by the 1970s the best days were behind it. In 1980 the theater received a makeover and was incorporated into the new Madison Civic Center and renamed the Oscar Mayer Theatre. But the call for a larger venue for the arts continued. The answer to that call was the Overture Center, which contains the 2,255-seat Overture Hall and its 75-foot high glass lobby, the more intimate 347-seat Playhouse theater, the amphitheater-style Rotunda Stage, the Wisconsin Academy's James Watrous Gallery, the Madison Museum of Contemporary Art, and the 1,089-seat theater once again known as The Capitol Theater. The Grand Barton theater organ remains in its original state and is often fired up for concerts, demonstrations, or showings of old silent movies. Several other spaces open for performances and rehearsals. Find more information about the performance companies that operate in the Overture Center in the Performing Arts chapter.

For drop-in tour information, available year-round, call (608) 258-4157. The closest off-street parking is available in the Overture Center parking ramp on East Mifflin Street and the State Street Capitol ramp on North Carroll Street. The Fairchild Street entrance to the Overture Hall lobby is best for dropping off patrons or for performances in other venues, use the main entrance on State Street or the back entrance on Henry Street. The entire facility is wheelchair accessible.

MADISON MUSEUM OF CONTEMPORARY ART (MMOCA)
227 State St.
(608) 257-0158
www.mmoca.org

The museum, with a permanent collection totaling over 5,000 works from the 20th and 21st centuries, moved into the Overture Center for the Arts in 2006 after being housed in several locations over its 100-plus year existence. The 51,500 square feet of space includes Henry Street Gallery on the lower level, State Street Gallery, and a 230-seat lecture hall on the 1st floor. The 2nd-floor has Main Galleries, New Media Gallery, Works-on-Paper Study Center, and the rooftop Sculpture Garden. The glass prow of the building overlooks State Street and encloses the stairs up to the roof. A museum store sells crafts and jewelry, while Fresco, the museum's rooftop restaurant, offers a contemporary American menu emphasizing local, seasonal ingredients, and a full bar. The First Friday Rooftop Series combines live music, cocktails at Fresco, and an art talk or activity. These events cost about $5 for nonmembers of the museum. Check the online calendar for the museum's many special events. Closed on Mon. Admission to the museum and most events is free.

i Much as with an iceberg, what you see at the Wisconsin Historical Museum is nothing compared to the rest of the collection in storage. History buffs can request to see items from the stored collection at the Wisconsin Historical Society's headquarters at 816 State St. on the University of Wisconsin campus. Contact the curators to make an appointment.

JAMES WATROUS GALLERY
201 State St.
(608) 265-2500
www.wisconsinacademy.org

Also set in the Overture Center for the Arts is this gallery named for an artist, art historian, and longtime UW professor. Works featured here are primarily from contemporary Wisconsin artists, Wisconsin art and craft history, and works owned by Wisconsin collectors. Closed Mon. Wheelchair accessible. Free.

WISCONSIN HISTORICAL MUSEUM
30 North Carroll St.
(608) 264-6565
www.wisconsinhistory.org/museum

For a comprehensive look at Wisconsin history before and after the fur trade—the pivotal period where Native American history meets European immigration—pay a visit to the Wisconsin Historical Society's public exhibitions. New exhibits open regularly drawing on the society's vast collections. The 2nd floor is dedicated to the history of Native Americans in Wisconsin showing pottery, crafts, beadwork, and a reproduction of an Aztalan-style house. The 3rd and 4th floors chronicle the past 200 years of state history with information on the lead mining and lumber industries, stories of the immigrants that settled here, and much more. Kids can participate in workshops and art activities, while lecture series and special dinners are on offer for all. The museum is located at the top of State Street on the Capitol Square right across the street from the Wisconsin Veteran's Museum. Closed Sun and Mon. Wheelchair accessible. Entry is by a suggested donation of $4 for adults, $3 for children.

i The Wisconsin Historical Society maintains several historic sites throughout Wisconsin, many of them, such as Circus World or Old World Wisconsin, are within a one- or two-hour drive from Madison. Check the Web site for more information: www.wisconsinhistory.org/sitesmuseum.asp

WISCONSIN VETERANS MUSEUM
30 West Mifflin St.
(608) 267-1799
www.museum.dva.state.wi.us

After the Civil War, a veteran's museum was placed inside the Capitol where it stayed until 1993 when this former drugstore building took over the collection and expanded it consider-

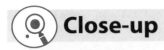

Close-up

Walking Tours

MADISON TRUST FOR HISTORIC PRESERVATION

(608) 441-8864
www.madisontrust.org

Despite the construction boom of recent decades, Madison does have a fair number of historic buildings around town. Especially of note are the Mansion Hill residences and a variety of commercial buildings in the downtown area. Throughout this book are smatterings of history in certain restaurants, hotels, or attractions, but many other stories lie in the bricks and facades of buildings along State Street or in University Heights. A walking tour is a delightful way to get the skinny on some of these places that won't show up on a list of attractions and are often overlooked even by the locals that have walked by innumerable times. Docents of the Madison Trust for Historic Preservation provide narration for walking tours during the summer, roughly from late May through Sept. Most are on Sat mornings or an occasional weekend afternoon or weekday evening. State Street, University Heights, East and West Mansion Hill, Bascom Hill on the university campus, and King Street are explored. No reservations are necessary; just check the Web site for the meeting time and location. A $5 fee is charged for nonmembers of the Madison Trust. The tours last about an hour and the ticket comes with a little freebie refreshment at a local establishment.

The King Street tour is really the most historical since this is where the first Europeans settled in Madison. But the State Street tour, beginning from in front of the House of Wisconsin Cheese on State Street, is the most popular with Sat morning farmers' market just a few steps away. The two Mansion Hill tours (East and West) tend to be about people, the movers and shakers of early Madison, while the University Heights tour, which explores the neighborhood west of Camp Randall Stadium, studies the progression of the Prairie style of architecture with notable designers Frank Lloyd Wright, Louis Sullivan, George W. Maher, and Keck and Keck. Bascom Hill is the longest of the tours and requires a bit of strenuous walking as "hill" might suggest.

The Madison Trust also hosts lectures and workshops for a nominal fee throughout the year. Check the calendar of events on the Web site. **Historic Madison, Inc.** (www.historicmadison .org) also does guided neighborhood residential tours.

DO-IT-YOURSELF

Historic Madison, Inc.
www.historicmadison.org

If you prefer to go it alone, the **Madison Landmarks Commission** offers eight neighborhood walking tour booklets, copies of which are available at the Madison Public Library. The downtown area is explored in Madison's Pioneer Buildings but there are also tours of First Settlement, Langdon Street, University Heights, Greenbush-Vilas, Third Lake Ridge (Marquette), Old Market Place, and Schenk's–Atwood neighborhoods.

ably to include not just the role of Wisconsin's veterans in the Civil War, but also the Spanish American War, World Wars I and II, the Korean and Vietnam Wars, and the most recent military campaigns in Iraq and Afghanistan. The museum is divided into the 19th-century and 20th-century galleries and also offers an area for rotating or traveling exhibits. Dioramas include realistic human figures and show scenes from the different wars. A full-size helicopter, a biplane, and a World War II Mustang are suspended from the ceiling. Be sure to check out the submarine periscope which looks out onto State Street. A 32-minute audio tour costs $2 to rent and is narrated by historian Stephen Ambrose and actor Gregory Peck. Researchers have access to a library of books, oral histories, and photos. A gift shop is also on-site. Open daily from Apr through Sept and then closed on Sun the rest of the year. The museum is located at the intersection where State Street meets the Capitol Square. Free.

ℹ Starting from the end of Park Street just before Helen C. White Hall, Observatory Drive makes a nice scenic drive up the edge of Bascom Hill and on through campus with views of Lake Mendota to the north.

THE UNIVERSITY OF WISCONSIN

This is the flagship of the state's university system with a student body of over 40,000. Founded in 1848, the same year Wisconsin became a state, the UW campus occupies the westerly half of downtown and spreads along the south shore of Lake Mendota. A member of the Big Ten Universities athletic conference, the University of Wisconsin has gained notoriety as being one of the top party schools (and more often the top) in the nation, a reputation that often excites students and frustrates the administration. But the academic reputation in a variety of fields is equally touted, so though many students play hard, a good portion of them must be working pretty darn hard as well. The UW has a strong commitment to research and sometimes spends close to $1 billion on research projects annually putting it near the top for science and engineering and number one in nonscientific fields. There are 135 majors offered for undergraduates, and master's and doctorate degree programs total 151 and 107, respectively.

WISCONSIN MEMORIAL UNION
800 Langdon St.
(608) 265-3000
www.union.wisc.edu

Campus Visitor Centers

Red Gym/Campus Information Center
716 Langdon St.
(608) 263-2400
www.visit.wisc.edu

The big red brick castle across Langdon Street from Library Mall was once an armory and gymnasium, and until the 1930 construction of the campus field house, this is where UW basketball games were held. Now this is the Campus Information Center and the place to go for campus tour information. The office is usually open daily but with limited midday hours on weekends. But on Sun later in the semester, the office closes.

Experienced guides lead 100-minute walking tours through campus familiarizing visitors with the campus life, university history, and the layout of the buildings. Tours start at 3 p.m., Mon through Fri, and at noon on the weekends with some exceptions to the schedule. Reservations are recommended. No tours are given on home football Sat, state holidays, and the day after Thanksgiving, and the schedule is reduced during semester break. All tours begin at the Red Gym. Campus Walking Tour booklets are also available as a PDF download at http://pubs.vip.wisc.edu.

Welcome Center
21 North Park St.
www.visit.wisc.edu

Another place for good campus information is a newer welcome center for walk-in and drive-through visitors. Located just north of the Park and Regent Streets intersection this is an easier stop just outside the hustle and bustle of campus and downtown.

First and foremost of all the "attractions" of the university has got to be the Memorial Union. Both students and nonstudents find the heart of the city here, and the metal chairs of the lakeside Terrace—colored yellow, green, or orange—are as much deck furniture as symbols of the University's social center, which plays such a central role in Madison's greater community. Built in 1928 to honor veterans of the First World War and then honoring veterns from World War II, it is one of the oldest student unions in the country, second only to Harvard's. A variety of spectacular murals adorn the walls in several of the rooms. Two cafeterias serve food, while coffee, light snacks, and sandwiches for those on the go, and some of the UW's very own ice cream are served from a concessionary near the front doors. Other services include a travel agency, a gift shop, a public Internet kiosk with several computers (one is wheelchair accessible), and a coffee lounge. Weddings are often held at the Union, and there are even a few rooms rented out as hotel lodging (see Accommodations page 20).

i The Union has served beer since the Regents met to decide the issue—allegedly over beers—soon after Prohibition. Up until then beer was only allowed up to the entrance to campus.

The Memorial Union houses four art galleries that are free and open to the public (www.union .wisc.edu/art). Call (608) 669-9063 from a cell phone to listen to an audio tour of the current exhibitions. The Porter Butts and Class of 1925 Galleries are open only from 10 a.m. to 8 p.m., while the Theater and Lakefront on Langdon Galleries open and close with the building itself. The Union is also the home of the Wisconsin Union Theater which hosts concerts, theatrical productions, and special speaking engagements such as the University's Distinguished Lecture Series that brings impressive speakers from a variety of backgrounds often with a high national or international profile.

Der Rathskeller has the look and feel of an old German beer hall and students gather here to study and socialize. Many of the walls are painted with historic murals. During the colder season or during rained out summer nights the live music of the Terrace moves indoors here. Adjoining it is Der Stiftskeller with a list of beers on tap that would be impressive at a good bar let alone a university campus, and popcorn and pretzels for sale. Films are shown at the Memorial Union on occasion in a small theater upstairs, in Der Rathskeller, or even outside on the Terrace in the summer.

i Wondering what conditions are like down on the Terrace? Have a look at the Terrace Webcam: www.union.wisc.edu/ webcam

The Union Terrace or just "The Terrace" (not to be confused with the Monona Terrace) is lakeside behind the Memorial Union itself and crowds gather here seasonally in the evenings to watch magnificent sunsets over Lake Mendota or to chill out with a drink or meal after the workday. A fixed grill stand serves bratwurst, burgers, hot dogs, chicken sandwiches, and the like, and offers several tap beers and soda. Two other portable beer stations set up along the Terrace during busier times. In the past, one needed to have a Memorial Union membership to purchase beer, but that rule was changed. Now a person merely fills out a temporary membership card good for that day. A few picnic tables line the concrete-step shoreline on the lowest of the three levels of the Terrace which rise up several steps at a time toward the back doors of the Union. Live music brings the real crowds on weekend nights. (Read more in the Nightlife chapter page 72). A concrete pier leads out to a roped swimming area, though the water in summer is often a bit green and not always visually appealing for a dip. That doesn't stop everyone. Other docks serve the sailing and boating crowd. The UW's outdoor recreation club Hoofers (608-262-7351) rents out sailboats, canoes, and kayaks at the Memorial Boathouse near the water's edge beneath the end of Park Street.

Metered parking is available in a Langdon Street lot between the Union and the Red Gym,

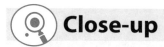

Close-up

The Wisconsin Idea

In 1904, UW–Madison President Charles Van Hise expressed his vision for the University's role in the lives of Wisconsinites in a speech: "I shall never be content until the beneficent influence of the University reaches every home in the state." The university is not bounded by the borders of a single campus but rather those of the entire state. Research is meant to benefit the lives of the state's citizens and their environment. Under Van Hise's leadership the UW extension program was developed, bringing more programs to the general population. Some cooperation between the academic world and state government resulted in such achievements as the nation's first workers' compensation legislation, and because of this the Wisconsin Idea was often associated with populist and progressive politics (much to the chagrin of Van Hise who didn't like the term "Wisconsin Idea"). However, from the UW's earliest accomplishments in bringing new technology and knowledge to the dairy industry in the late 19th century, to its modern efforts in medicine and public health and many other fields, the accomplishments of the UW have long been beneficial to the citizens of the state and even the world at large.

and additional spots are available under the Helen C. White Hall to the west along the lakeshore. The closest parking ramp is on Lake Street between State Street and University Avenue.

i The multiuse, crushed-stone Howard Temis Lakeshore Path (paved in some places) begins along the water's edge just west of the Terrace and follows Lake Mendota's shore all the way to University Bay and Picnic Point.

ALLEN CENTENNIAL GARDENS
620 Babcock Dr.
(608) 265-8502
www.horticulture.wisc.edu/allencentennial-gardens
This 2.5-acre garden is a sort of outdoor classroom for the University's Department of Horticulture. Often called the "Fred House" for a former agricultural school dean, a Victorian gothic house sits in the center and is on the National Register of Historic Places. Paths explore the colorful gardens offering benches for places to pass a quiet moment and a gazebo overlooking a pond. Open daily during daylight hours. Parking is metered in Lot 32 behind the gardens and the top level of

the ramp at Lot 36 across Observatory Drive. The Lakeshore Path passes here as do Madison Metro buses 11, 28, 38, 44, and 80. Free.

BABCOCK HALL
1605 Linden Dr.
(608) 262-3045
www.babcockhalldairystore.wisc.edu
Making ice cream might seem like a dream study program, but the UW has a highly respected dairy program. In 1890, Professor Stephen Babcock was the first to come up with a test for the butterfat content of milk and soon after started the first dairy school in the United States. Babcock Hall houses the UW's Food Science Program. The on-site dairy plant covers all its operating costs with sales of its cheese, milk, and ice cream. The Dairy Store is open to the public and a popular stop for ice cream. Cheese boxes sold here make great gifts. A sandwich bar serves daily lunch specials, and premade wraps and subs are available in the cooler. Open all days but Sun.

i For tours of the University's Dairy Barn call the Red Gym Campus Information Center at (608) 263-2400.

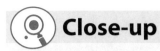

Close-up

Camp Randall

The area that is now Camp Randall Stadium was once the site of the state fairgrounds a goodly distance into the countryside from the Capitol during the mid-19th century. When the Civil War broke out in 1861, it became a training camp for Union soldiers and more than 70,000 troops trained here throughout the course of the war. The governor at that time was Alexander Randall, and in honor of his efforts to rally forces the camp took his name. In 1862, however, the camp received word that it would receive 1,300 Confederate prisoners of war to be held in confinement. The camp had nothing in the line of prison facilities, and so some basic quarters were hastily constructed before the first trainloads of prisoners arrived and were marched from the train station on the other side of the Capitol.

Initially local charity and general good prisoner behavior contributed to the success of the operation. The arrival of wounded and diseased prisoners, however, led to declining conditions. An attempted escape made easier with a bribe compelled a tougher security crackdown. Tensions rose after a young recruit shot and killed a Confederate corporal who had insulted him after the recruit had thrown a stone at his brother. The brother, suffering dysentery, had chosen to relieve himself in a place not designated for such activity. The recruit was later absolved of any wrongdoing. By the end the camp's term as a prison, 140 prisoners died of disease. Those soldiers are buried in Forest Hill Cemetery (see below).

BASCOM HILL

This was where the University of Wisconsin got its start in 1848 and as such it is the most historical area of campus. The 1857 Bascom Hall lost its dome in a 1916 fire but survived with several additions throughout its time. The hill and hall are dedicated to John Bascom, a 19th-century university president. Plaques placed throughout the Bascom Hill area tell pieces of UW history. The hill was originally intended to be a cemetery, and in fact two graves are marked with simple plaques. Abraham Lincoln, cast in bronze in 1906 and set here in 1909, looks out from the top of the hill toward the Capitol. The statue is the only copy of the original statue, which was destined for Hodgenville, Kentucky, Lincoln's birthplace.

CAMP RANDALL

1440 Monroe St.

www.uwbadgers.com

This is ground zero on football Sat when a sea of red-appareled Badger fans of all ages converges on the 80,312-seat stadium. The stadium's first football game played in 1895 put the Wiscon-sin Badgers up against the Minnesota Golden Gophers. The Badgers came out on top with a score of 6–0 and the longstanding rivalry was born. Since 1948, every time the two Big Ten teams have met, the winner of the game has gone home with the traveling trophy, Paul Bunyan's Axe. The site itself and its name figure importantly in Wisconsin state history (see Close-up). At the end of Dayton Street on the stadium's east side, check out the Memorial Arch built in 1912 to commemorate Wisconsin's soldiers in the Civil War. No walk-in tours are allowed, but to schedule a tour of Camp Randall, call the Kohl Center at (608) 263-5645 at least two weeks in advance. For more information about Badger sports see the Spectator Sports chapter, page 130.

CHAZEN MUSEUM OF ART

800 University Ave.

(608) 263-2246

www.chazen.wisc.edu

In 1970 the Elvehjem Museum of Art opened on the University of Wisconsin campus. The mission was to preserve and exhibit artwork and provide educational programming to support the mission of the university. Nearly three-quarters of the gallery space is dedicated to the permanent collection while the rest is given over to rotating exhibitions totaling about a dozen each year. The permanent collection of paintings includes European works, with an emphasis on Dutch art, dating from 1600 to 1800, some earlier European works, and 19th- and 20th-century American and European paintings. A collection of Russian works donated by former U.S. ambassador to the Soviet Union, Joseph E. Davies, is also on display. The collection of prints and photographs is quite sizeable and includes more than 4,000 Japanese woodblock prints as well as a variety of American and European creations. Ten of the sculptures date to Ancient Egypt and six to the years of the Roman Empire, while European examples include work from Auguste Rodin and into more recent times. Drawing and watercolors are also part of the collection as are coins and various decorative arts such as furniture, ceramics, and even Roman floor mosaics. Simona and Jerome Chazen donated a sizeable amount toward the doubling of the museum's size and the name of the building was changed in their honor in 2005. The expansion is expected to open in the fall of 2011. The museum shop sells a variety of art-related souvenirs from books and catalogues to posters and postcards. The store can be browsed online and takes orders there. The museum is wheelchair accessible, but check the Web site for the best entrances and closest handicapped parking. Closed on Mon. Free admission.

GEOLOGY MUSEUM
1215 West Dayton St.
(608) 262-2399
www.geology.wisc.edu
It challenges the mind to think that millions of years ago the Madison area was under a warm sea and located south of the equator. Likewise several hundred feet of ice stacked on the Capitol's hill is hard to imagine. The Geology Museum chronicles history in rock from the larger picture of the planet down to the local examples in fossil form. See a mural of Madison—ca. 10,000 B.C. Take a short

tour of fossils, rocks, and minerals, and learn about the various periods of prehistory. The most recent period of the Ice Age is called the Wisconsin Period as so many elements of glacial evidence are present in the state. Other exhibits include a re-creation of a limestone cave, a six-foot model of Earth, and a black-light display. Life-size castings and models of dinosaurs and a Wisconsin Mastodon (with the spear point found with its remains) serve as the grand finale. A cast of Stan, the best preserved Tyrannosaurus rex skull ever found, gives museum-goers something to think about. Download a copy of the self-guided tour booklet and make the most out of your visit to the museum. Geo Explorer questions in the booklet engage young visitors. Closed Sun. Admission is free.

KOHL CENTER
601 West Dayton St.
(608) 263-5645
www.uwbadgers.com/facilities
This arena and athletic center opened in 1998 and is home to the University's men's and women's basketball and hockey teams. Big-name concerts, the likes of Elton John, Bob Dylan, and Sting, are also featured here on occasion. Depending on the configuration of the seats—for concerts, basketball, or hockey—the capacity can go as high as 17,000. Call for free tours of the center. For more information about Badger sports see the Spectator Sports chapter, page 130.

L. R. INGERSOLL PHYSICS MUSEUM
2130 Chamberlin Hall
1150 University Ave.
(608) 262-3898
www.physics.wisc.edu/museum
With interactive displays, the wonders of physics come to life. A version of subatomic pinball has visitors shooting steel balls at a target to explain how scientists study the invisibly small building blocks of the universe. Photos of the Nobel Prize laureates line the walls of the long exhibit room. Scientific instruments from before the computer age offer a look at how far science has come in the last 100 or so years. One exhibit of note is the earthquake simulator. Open weekdays. Free.

LIBRARY MALL

Library Mall is the space bounded by the Wisconsin Historical Society, Langdon Street, the Memorial Library, and the wide walk that continues from the end of State Street to connect to the bottom of Bascom Hill on Park Street. A raised concrete speaking area is frequented by people with something to say or skateboarders taking advantage of the steps. A fountain sits at the center of the mall and students lounge about between classes taking in sun on the lawn. Food carts are set up on the pedestrian mall connecting State Street to Library Mall.

MEMORIAL CARILLON
1160 Observatory Dr.
(608) 263-1900
www.music.wisc.edu

This is one heavy and impressive musical instrument, in fact, the 25th largest instrument on the continent. Dedicated in 1936 this 85-foot bell tower had 25 bells. Now totaling 56, the bells, made in England and the Netherlands, weigh anything from 15 to 6,823 pounds. UW carillonneur Lyle Anderson performs public concerts on Sun at 3 p.m. during the academic year. Other concerts occur in the summer. For times and more information, contact the UW School of Music.

PICNIC POINT
Howard Temin Lakeshore Path
Lakeshore Nature Preserve
www.lakeshorepreserve.wisc.edu

One of the most popular local sites for a nature stroll and spectacular view of the lake, university, and city is at Picnic Point, a half-mile peninsula at the end of Lakeshore Path. Picnic Point juts out into Lake Mendota and has a few picnic sites with fire pits. Lakeshore Path begins from behind the Memorial Union following a well-shaded crushed rock trail along the lake and past the UW Boathouse and Lakeshore Residence Halls until University Bay. Continuing along the lake the path comes to a gate in a stone wall, the entrance to Picnic Point. From the campus to the very end of the point is about 2.5 miles. The late professor

Howard Temin, winner of a Nobel Prize in Medicine, enjoyed this walk immensely. Trails beyond Picnic Point are more rustic and secluded, and extend even farther west past Frautschi Point to Wally Bauman Woods and Eagle Heights Woods. The trail is wheelchair accessible and open to bicycles all the way to Picnic Point. The hike can be made one-way to one of two parking lots on Lake Mendota Drive, well past Picnic Point, where hikers could opt to return to campus on the #80 bus. Knowing the bus schedule from Eagle Heights (one of the University's apartment communities) is essential in this case.

THE UNIVERSITY OF WISCONSIN ARBORETUM

The Arboretum is a rich forested park in the heart of the city and abutting much of the shoreline of Lake Wingra opposite Henry Vilas Park and Zoo. At its heart is the McKay Center which offers a wealth of park information and hosts tours, lectures, and events. Within the center is also a small library of nature guides and reference books, a small gift shop, and the Steinhauer Trust Gallery, which exhibits artwork related in some way to natural subjects in Wisconsin. The 1,260-acre preserve is actually reclaimed farmland and contains miles of hiking trails amid forest, prairie, marshland, and a maintained and labeled arboretum and flower garden. (Read more in Parks page 127.)

WASHBURN OBSERVATORY
1401 Observatory Dr.
(608) 262-9274
www.astro.wisc.edu

This 1881 observatory is named in honor of the state governor who supported its construction. Located on Observatory Hill with a great view of Lake Mendota, the observatory grants public access to its 15-inch refractor (magnification about 500 times) for informal viewings. Skies must be 75% clear for the event to occur; otherwise the open house is every Wed evening from June through Sept and first and third Wed evenings through the rest of the year. Parking is on the street and the entrance to the observatory is on the opposite side of the building from the road.

ℹ️ **Make astronomy fun for the kids and pay a visit to the University of Wisconsin Space Place. Look under Kidstuff.**

ZOOLOGICAL MUSEUM
L. E. Noland Zoology Building
250 North Mills St.
(608) 262-3766
www.zoology.wisc.edu/uwzm
The zoology department of the University of Wisconsin maintains a sizeable collection of animal specimens and other research materials, a portion of which is viewable by the general public in a small exhibit area. The Ecuadorean Government has granted permission for collecting specimens from the Galápagos Islands to only three museums and this is one of them. Some old equipment such as microscopes and field instruments is also on display. Open most weekdays. Free.

AROUND TOWN

ALLIANT ENERGY CENTER
1919 Alliant Energy Center Way
(608) 267-3976
www.alliantenergycenter.com
Formerly the Dane County Coliseum, the center is composed of several buildings on 164 acres of land just north of the Beltline (US 12/18) near the John Nolen Drive exit. Veterans Coliseum, Exhibition Hall, and the Arena Building are the prime venues for conventions, expositions, consumer and trade shows, and big concerts. Willow Island, surrounded by a small lagoon, is an outdoor venue popular for summer festivals and smaller concerts. Nine modern agricultural buildings are also on the property. Check the Annual Events chapter, page 163, for upcoming festivals and expos.

FOREST HILL CEMETERY
1 Speedway Rd.
(608) 266-4720
www.cityofmadison.com/parks/foresthill.html

The names along these headstones are as familiar as street signs, for the city's founders and shapers lie within the hallowed grounds of this 140-acre cemetery, which dates back to 1858. Some of the very first of Madison's departed were first laid to rest on the east side of town in the village's first official cemetery, which is now Orton Park. All bodies but one (a poor soul taken by university students for study!) were moved by 1877 to the new cemetery with a view of city and lake. The growth of the surrounding city took away much of the view, but the abundance of trees has created a very peaceful resting place and, in fact, a lovely city park.

An effigy mound in the shape of a goose is evidence that Native Americans once used this land for the same. Unfortunately its head was removed to make way for the Illinois Central Railroad. Other effigy mounds built between 900 and 1200 A.D. can still be seen and are listed on the National Register of Historical Places. The Civil War made its contribution to the cemetery from both sides of the Mason–Dixon line. Along with the 240 Union veterans interred here are 140 Confederate soldiers who died as prisoners at Camp Randall just a mile or so down the road.

Tenney, Olin, Mills, Olbrich, Babcock—the names live on beyond these marble monuments in city parks, streets, and buildings. Several Wisconsin governors lie here, including former U.S. senator and presidential candidate "Fighting Bob" LaFollette (1855–1925) and members of his family.

Pick up a free brochure at the cemetery office on Speedway or download it from the City of Madison Parks' Web site and follow the map and self-guided walking tour. The tour begins at the 1878 Catlin Chapel and makes a 1.4-mile path past some of the more famous sites. The stories would never fit in a simple brochure so history buffs should check out the 98-page book entitled *Forest Hill Cemetery: A Biographical Guide to the Ordinary and the Famous Who Shaped Madison and the World*. The book, now in two volumes, contains history, short biographies of various characters from Madison's past, and assorted old photos and letters. It is available for sale at the cemetery office or on loan at the Madison Public Library. The cemetery is open daily and free to the public and is considered a Madison park. The office is open weekdays from 9 a.m. to 1 p.m.

i In 1885, Robert Marion LaFollette's wife, Belle Case LaFollette, became the first woman to graduate from the University of Wisconsin Law School. She is buried near her husband in Forest Hill Cemetery.

GOVERNOR'S MANSION
99 Cambridge Rd.
(608) 246-5501
www.wisgov.state.wi.us

The Executive Residence, completed in 1921, was originally the private residence of Carl A. Johnson, a Madison industrialist, but the state purchased it in 1949 and all governors and their families have resided here since. The Classical Revival-style mansion, which sits on the eastern shore of Lake Mendota in the Village of Maple Bluff, has 34 rooms, 13 bathrooms, and seven bedrooms and fireplaces. Seven gardens are on site, and the streetside wrought-iron fence once protected the grounds of the previous Capitol building. Free 30-minute public tours of the 1st floor are offered on Thurs afternoons from Apr through Aug, and during certain days in Dec when evergreen trees are decorated for the holidays. The tour schedule is subject to change each year so call to be sure. Reservations are only necessary for groups of 20 or more people. The site is wheelchair accessible.

HENRY VILAS ZOO
702 South Randall Ave.
(608) 266-4732
www.vilaszoo.org

Located in the park of the same name along the shore of Lake Wingra, the 28-acre zoo has a surprising collection of animals for a city the size of Madison. The first exhibits opened in 1911 and the zoo continues to grow. The Vilas family donated the land for both park and zoo and dedicated it to their son Henry who died young

of diabetes. One stipulation was that admission to either would always be free for everyone. The Discovery Center and Herpetarium provide interactive educational exhibits, and the tropical rain-forest aviary allows patrons to walk right through. The facilities are especially kid-friendly with a dedicated Children's Zoo where kids can feed and pet animals, a carousel, playground, and a train tour of the grounds. Concessions and a gift shop are onsite, and the adjoining park and beach area are perfect for picnics and play. Open daily with free admission and free parking. The University of Wisconsin Arboretum is right across the lake and the drive from the zoo to there is lovely.

MADISON BY BOAT
Betty Lou Cruises
(608) 246-3138
www.bettyloucruises.com

Take to the lakes to get a different perspective of the city on these powered yachts. Betty Lou and Bill von Rutenberg began in the restaurant business in 1961. The results of their years of hard work are three waterfront restaurants—Mariner's Inn, Nau-ti-gal, and Captain Bill's—and this popular lake cruise company. The captained boats have restrooms and buffet food service and run public cruises from mid-Apr through mid-Oct during lunch, brunch, dinner, or the cocktail hour. Cruises set sail from behind Machinery Row at 601 Williamson St. for Lake Monona and from Mariner's Inn at 5339 Lighthouse Bay Dr. for Lake Mendota. On Lake Monona sights include the Monona Terrace, while from Lake Mendota the university campus and Governor's Mansion are on the list. Both cruises enjoy views of the Capitol of course. Some cruises offer live music or an open bar. Ian's Pizza and Capital Brewery team up for an all-you-can-eat-and-drink cruise. Private cruises can also be booked. Advance reservations, online or by phone, are required and most cruises last two hours. The pizza and sightseeing cruises are a bit shorter at 1.5 hours. Fees range from about $20 to $50 depending on the time and food and drink services included.

OLBRICH BOTANICAL GARDENS
3330 Atwood Ave.
(608) 246-4718
www.olbrich.org

The gardens and the park across Starkweather Creek to the east are named in honor of Michael Balthasar Olbrich (1881-1929), a Progressive lawyer and politician who played a large role in the Madison Park Foundation. Sixteen acres of outdoor gardens include the Rose Garden, Sunken Garden, and Perennial Garden. Part of the visitor center is Bolz Conservatory, a glass pyramid harboring over 650 species of exotic plants and flowers—most notably many orchids—as well as a few birds and a waterfall. In the middle of winter this provides a nice illusory escape to the jungle. A horticultural library and gift shop are also on-site. The outdoor gardens are open daily and admission is free. Admission to the Bolz Conservatory is free on Wed and Sat mornings, otherwise there is a nominal $1 fee. This fee goes up a bit and free conservatory admission is suspended at the end of July and beginning of Aug when the resident butterflies are "blooming." Cross the bridge over Starkweather Creek to see the fabulous golden Thai pavilion. Olbrich Gardens is just off the Capital City Bike Trail which runs directly behind it.

STEENBOCK GALLERY
1922 Old University Ave.
(608) 263-1692

Along with the Watrous Gallery downtown inside the Overture Center for the Arts, the Wisconsin Academy of Sciences, Arts and Letters manages this gallery toward the west end of campus in a residential area. The gallery works with various other arts organizations to feature Wisconsin artists. Open weekdays.

THE WORLD FAMOUS MUSTARD MUSEUM
Middleton
(800) 438-6878
www.mustardweb.com

Opened in 1992 in Mount Horeb, WI, but relocated to Middleton in 2009, this quirky celebration of ketchup's condimental nemesis has garnered national notoriety from big newspaper coverage to appearances on the Food Network. Owner Barry Levenson has gathered 5,000 mustards and 1,500 antique mustard pots, bottles, and tins since he began collecting in 1986. Get a degree from Poupon U while visiting or watch a video in the Mustard Piece Theater. Free.

The Thai Pavilion

First built in Thailand and then disassembled and shipped in pieces to Madison, the traditional *sala* is common in Thailand as a roadside shelter. This creation, donated by the Thai Chapter of the University of Wisconsin Alumni Association and the Thai government under the approval of the Royal Family, shows intricate detail with gold-leaf etchings and lacquer finish on plantation-grown teak covered with a ceramic tile roof. No nails or screws were used in its construction. See it around sunrise or when the late afternoon sun glimmers off its gold. The garden surrounding it is made to emulate a traditional Thai garden but uses plants better suited to Wisconsin's not-quite-tropical weather. A bridge connects the pavilion and garden to the rest of the gardens. Madison's **Thai Fest**, first celebrated in 2005, is held annually at Olbrich Gardens (www.uwalumni.com/thaifest).

PARKS

In the late 1800s, taking a horse-drawn carriage ride along the lakeshore or a country lane was a common delight and there were those who had a fondness for getting out of town.

At that time, however, that could have meant any point just west of Bascom Hill. In 1892 a group of wealthy Madison residents with a love of the scenic had the idea to develop a sort of park system. Three prominent men—Edward T. Owen, Edward E. Hammersley, and John M. Olin—created the first scenic drive that year primarily using their own donated acreage and paying for the gravel road pavement themselves. They understood the importance of preserving those beautiful places not just for themselves but for the rest of Madison and its future residents as well. In 1894 they and several others officially incorporated as the Madison Parks and Pleasure Drive Association (MPPDA). From that time until the 1931 formation of a city park division, the privately funded group was responsible for a variety of recreational green space developments. Most of the parks developed by the MPPDA—Tenney Park, Olin Park, Henry Vilas Park—remain an important part of Madison's natural beauty and are frequently visited by all. In 1908, Olin rounded up local and state funding to enlist the services of nationally famous city planner and landscape architect John Nolen. Nolen's contribution to thoughtful development went beyond Madison as he also laid the foundations for the state park system.

From the very local to the national level, Madison has access to abundant public green space, nature preserves, and recreation areas. Today there are over 200 neighborhood parks in the metro area. Dane County offers several excellent parks within a 20-minute drive of the city, and the state park system is nothing short of a Wisconsin treasure. Finally, the 1,000-mile Ice Age National Scenic Trail passes close by as well.

Green space is the lifeblood of Madison. Every neighborhood has a park of some size and a look at the city map shows the spattering of green well distributed. Some parks lean more toward communing with nature, others have an emphasis on sports, and most lie somewhere in between. The following is by no means a comprehensive list, but rather a few of the best and biggest. To find others near you consult a city map or go to the City of Madison (www.cityof madison.com/parks) and Dane County (www.co.dane.wi.us/lwrd/parks) Web sites.

City parks are open from 4 a.m. to 10 p.m. and free to the public. Dogs are not allowed (even on a leash) in parks, playgrounds, and on beaches unless explicitly indicated. See the listing of dog-friendly parks below. Even those parks require either a daily or annual permit fee. No glass beverage containers or cups are allowed. No open intoxicants are allowed in park parking lots, but they may be allowed in certain parks at certain times. During special events featuring designated drinking areas (such as festivals or concerts), no alcohol is allowed outside those boundaries.

County parks are open from 5 a.m. to 10 p.m. While entry to county parks may be free, some of the parks facilities or activities have some associated fees. Users with dogs must pay either a daily fee of $5 or get an annual permit. Trail use other than for hiking (i.e., cross-country skiing, horseback riding, or biking) also exacts a daily or annual fee. Lake access fees operate similarly. However, these are good until Mar 31 of the next year. Camping has a per site fee with a stay five nights and get the sixth night free deal. Alcohol permits are required for groups larger than 10. Shelters can be reserved and rented. Disc golf courses and geocaching also require fee payments while metal detecting is free. All permits can be purchased online, and in many cases daily fees can be paid through a self-pay system at the parks.

State park hours typically run from 6 a.m. to 11 p.m. with an exception granted for overnight campers. State parks require daily vehicle fees and the annual pass is a great deal good for the calendar year at all state parks. Permit prices are slightly more for out-of-state vehicles. A state trail pass is separate and required for all trail activity other than hiking. Park visitors of legal drinking age may bring alcoholic beverages into the parks in picnic areas and campsites. Pets are allowed on leashes 8-feet long or less in most state parks with the exception of park buildings, picnic areas, and shelters, beaches not designated as "dogs allowed," playgrounds, marked nature trails (general trails are OK), groomed cross-country ski trails, and observation towers. Camping fees vary and at popular parks or during peak times such as holidays and weekends, advanced reservations are highly recommended. Make them online or call the park directly. Moving firewood from one park to another is prohibited due to the invasion of the Emerald Ash Borer which can ride deadwood on its quest to destroy a lot of trees. Please respect and protect the parks. The **Wisconsin Department of Natural Resources** (www.dnr .state.wi.us) operates an excellent Web site with an abundance of park information. Be sure to read about the Ice Age National Scenic Trail in the Close-up, page 128. The trail requires no permits or fees and is open year-round. As much of it passes along narrow easements on private property, it is important that hikers stay on the trail and carry out anything they carry in.

CITY PARKS

CHEROKEE MARSH CONSERVATION PARK
North Unit: 6098 Sherman Ave.
South Unit: 5002 School Rd.
www.cherokeemarsh.org
Along the Yahara River on the north side of Lake Mendota, the 4,000-acre Cherokee Marsh falls under multiple authorities depending on the section: the City of Madison, Dane County, and the Wisconsin Department of Natural Resources. The Cherokee Marsh Conservation Park, which is a city park, has north and south units which offer great hiking and nature watching. The south unit has a boat launch and is popular for paddlers. Dogs are prohibited in both units.

ELVER PARK
1240 McKenna Blvd.
Another park for all seasons, Elver lies right in the heart of the southwest side. Half the land is set on a prominent hill offering a nice view of the city. Here you will find the city's best sledding in the winter and some good ice-skating at the foot of the hill. Other sports include tennis, softball/ baseball, basketball, disc golf, soccer, hiking, and cross-country skiing. Dogs are allowed on leashes below the sled hill from Mar 15 to Nov 15 only.

HENRY VILAS PARK
702 South Randall Ave.
On the north side of Lake Wingra, opposite the UW Arboretum, is this 50-acre park along with the Henry Vilas Zoo (see Attractions page 122). Vilas is not far from the city center and is quite popular for picnics and reunions as well as sports requiring wide open spaces. Shore fishing is popular but for a boat launch Wingra Park is the better choice. The spring-fed lake offers a sandy beach, and a lagoon becomes an ice-skating area in winter.

JAMES MADISON PARK
614 East Gorham St.
Though merely 12 acres in size, this is surely one of the most active parks in Madison and its downtown location right on Lake Mendota makes it easily accessible. Facilities include basketball and volleyball courts, canoe and kayak rentals, and a playground. University students frequently take advantage of the grassy area for a lie in the sun or a bit of reading, and Ultimate Frisbee games are common in the open spaces. Shade trees shelter nappers. The 1863 Gates of Heaven Synagogue is the fourth oldest synagogue in the country. It was relocated to the park in 1970 and often hosts

weddings. The park also has a swimming beach with a lifeguard scheduled in the afternoons in season. Parking is on the street or in a small lot. No alcohol is allowed.

ℹ️ In 1836, James Duane Doty, the man with the dream to turn a paper city into a glorious capital, had plans to make the area that is now James Madison Park the entrance to a canal that would cross the isthmus to Lake Monona.

LAKESHORE NATURE PRESERVE AND PICNIC POINT
The University of Wisconsin
www.lakeshorepreserve.wisc.edu

Set along the south shore of Lake Mendota the preserve starts from near the Memorial Union on campus and stretches west past University Bay and Picnic Point. The multiuse Howard Temin Lakeshore trail is partly asphalt and partly crushed stone. Students commonly commute to class or use it for exercise, but it is popular with the community at large as well. Picnic Point is a peninsula, nearly a mile long, within the preserve that juts into Lake Mendota. Some fire rings are open for picnics, and the view of the Capitol and university across the water is exceptional. Areas past Picnic Point are more secluded and trails are more rustic for hiking.

ℹ️ Picnic Point was previously known as Gooseberry Point and a ferry used to run people over from the isthmus for a local dance hall.

OLBRICH PARK
3527 Atwood Ave.

Located next to Olbrich Botanical Gardens and its Thai Pavilion on the east side, the 61-acre park sits on the shore of Lake Monona and straddles Stark-weather Creek. Facilities include four basketball courts, boat launches on both sides of Atwood Avenue, (a lake-access permit is required), five lighted softball diamonds, an ice-skating rink with a warming shelter, playground equipment, a sledding hill, four sand volleyball courts, and two tennis courts. A beach is open daily in season.

OLIN PARK/TURVILLE POINT CONSERVATION PARK
1156 Olin–Turville Ct.

Another Lake Monona park with superb views of the city across the water, Olin Park offers a soccer field, baseball diamond, hiking trails, playground equipment, and a popular boat launch. On-site is also the Olin Park Pavilion, an 1884 structure once used as a dance hall among other things. Previously known as Monona Park, the park took James Olin's name in 1923 in honor of his dedication to parks and pleasure drives in Madison.

The mostly wooded Turville Point Conservation Park abuts Olin and offers rustic hiking trails and cross-country skiing in winter. They are often referred to together as Olin–Turville Park. The Capital City Trail passes along the park connecting it easily to downtown, and another paved multi-use trail follows Wingra Creek from here to Vilas Park and the UW Arboretum.

PHEASANT BRANCH CONSERVANCY
3960 Valley Ridge Rd., Middleton (Orchid Heights Park)
www.pheasantbranch.org

Much of the park's land belongs to the City of Middleton and a portion is governed by Dane County. The conservancy contains marshland, springs, prairies, meadows, lowland forest, and wooded hills perfect for nature lovers and especially birdwatchers. A large hill to the north in the county-governed portion offers a view all the way to the Capitol in Madison. Crushed-stone paths circle the park, and another path follows Pheasant Branch Creek crossing through the water but also offering stepping stones to keep shoes dry. The park is open from 7 a.m. to 10 p.m. There are several pedestrian entrances to the park area, but it is best to enter and park at Orchid Heights Park.

TENNEY PARK
1414 East Johnson St.

In 1899, Daniel K. Tenney, a Madison attorney set aside this land as a park where Lake Mendota empties into the Yahara River. The Yahara River was dredged and now seems more like a canal.

Surrounding the heart of the park like a moat is a lagoon connected by walking bridges to the rest of the park. Soccer fields, lighted tennis courts, a sand volleyball pit, a couple of small playgrounds, and a beach on Lake Mendota with a changing facility are also present. Shoreline fishing is quite popular along the river here and wheelchair access is present for both the river and the lake. There is a boat launch on the lake and on the river below the locks. In the winter, ice-skating is popular here. On windy days in the summer it is common to see kiteboarders and sailboarders gathering at the beach. A breakwater with a walkway extends into the lake and makes a great perch for fishing and watching the sunset over Mendota. Alcohol is not allowed outside designated areas. Three parking areas serve the park with room for boat trailers.

i A paved multiuse trail starts from the end of the lagoon-side parking lot at Tenney Park on the west side of the Yahara River and follows the river's edge across the isthmus until it connects with the Capital City Trail just before Williamson Street.

THE UNIVERSITY OF WISCONSIN ARBORETUM
1207 Seminole Hwy.
(608) 263-7888
www.uwarboretum.org
Set along the south shore of Lake Wingra, The Arboretum, a 1,260-acre preserve of forest, marshland, and prairie, was nothing more than clear-cut farmland in the 1930s. The reclaimed land is a treasure trove for nature lovers with a fine network of trails, a calendar of events led by naturalists, and an annual native plant sale. Birds, wildflowers, and fall colors are just a few of the draws here. The Visitor Center is open daily (excluding holidays). Trails and parking lots are also open year-round typically from dusk until dawn. Enter from the north at the intersection of McCaffery Drive, North Wingra Drive, and South Mills Street, or from the south at McCaffrey Drive and Seminole Highway, just north of the Beltline (US 12/14/18).

i A portion of the Arboretum's land is on the northwest side of Lake Wingra and offers some short hiking through marsh and forest just off of Monroe Street. Another section is south of the Beltline and has its own parking lot or can be reached via a tunnel under the highway.

WARNER PARK
1625 Northport Dr.
Named for Madison Parks and Pleasure Drive Association leader Ernest Warner and established in 1939, this park is located on Lake Mendota and Madison's north side. It is home to the Madison Mallards baseball team. The 180-acre park often hosts festivals—especially Rhythm and Booms the weekend before the Fourth of July—as well as league softball and soccer. A bike/walking path traverses the western side of the park, and there is a beach with a lifeguard at posted times in season. Facilities include three basketball courts, three soccer fields, a softball diamond, skating and hockey rink, and sand volleyball courts. The park community recreation center has a gymnasium, exercise room, game room, and craft rooms, and offers rentable spaces for private functions. Dogs are allowed on a leash in designated areas. Parking is plentiful unless large special events fill the lot.

WINGRA PARK
824 Knickerbocker St.
Like Vilas, this follows the shore of Lake Wingra but farther west. Entry is off Monroe Street. The park consists of a wide open green space, boat landing, and a recreational pavilion with concessions and restrooms. Canoes and kayaks can be rented for use on the perpetually calm and rather shallow lake. To the west of the parking area is a small patch of woodland that gives way to marsh; all of this and its trails actually fall under the auspices of the University of Wisconsin Arboretum.

COUNTY PARKS

INDIAN LAKE
8183 State Hwy. 19, Cross Plains
Indian Lake is one of the largest of the county parks with 483 acres. A hiking trail climbs a

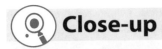

Close-up

The Ice Age National Scenic Trail

Wisconsin gave its name to the most recent period of the Ice Age. So many features of glacial activity can be found here that the state is really the perfect outdoor classroom for a geologist. So it is no surprise that the Ice Age National Scenic Trail is completely within the borders of the state. The 1,000-mile rustic hiking path offers challenges for all levels of hikers and showcases some of the most magnificent scenery in Wisconsin.

Raymond Zillmer, a Milwaukee attorney with a love of hiking, was instrumental in bringing the trail to reality. In 1926 the Izaak Walton League of Milwaukee bought land in the Northern Kettle Moraine area, a long series of the cuplike depressions of glacial deposits that runs north-south in eastern Wisconsin. With this purchase the group set aside the first portion of what would become the Kettle Moraine State Forest. Zillmer knew the trails of Kettle Moraine intimately and wanted to create a longer park that would put more people on its length and thus be more accessible than national parks far out west away from population centers.

Zillmer founded the Ice Age Park & Trail Foundation (now the Ice Age Trail Alliance) in 1958. By 1961 the Federal government was looking at the possibility of creating a national park according to Zillmer's vision. But unfortunately Zillmer died that year and the plan for the Ice Age Trail faltered. But in the early 1970s, the Ice Age Trail Council formed and began building trail segments, some of them on private land, which would connect existing trails and eventually grow to connect one end of the state with the other.

On October 3, 1980 President Jimmy Carter, with the flick of a pen, at long last signed a law that established the Ice Age National Scenic Trail. In 1987 the State of Wisconsin went further, establishing it as the only State Scenic Trail thus helping the Ice Age Trail Alliance by declaring more lands as permanently protected.

The Ice Age Trail descends from Door County, Wisconsin's peninsula jutting into Lake Michigan, down through Kettle Moraine, across southern Wisconsin to the edge of the Driftless Area where the last advance of ice stopped, and then north again bending west until it reaches the border of Wisconsin and Minnesota at the St. Croix River. That's 1,000 miles. The trail is primarily a rustic footpath with the occasional foot bridge or other modification to prevent erosion or other ecological damage. Yellow blazes on trees and trail posts mark the course with occasional blue swatches for spur trails. Volunteers and members of the alliance are to thank for the Herculean effort that went into making the trail and continues to go into maintenance and further development. Their cooperation with national and state agencies, local businesses and municipalities, and private land owners make the trail what it is—a national treasure. Eighteen million Americans live within a 100-mile drive of the Ice Age Trail. The Alliance has several local chapters for the various segments of the trail, and these chapters keep calendars of events ranging from trail maintenance or wildflower restoration to group outings such as a full-moon hike for example.

Madison is quite close to the trail and various segments of it make for great day hikes. These 2- to 18-mile stretches include, but are not limited to, the Verona, Table Bluff, Devil's Lake, Indian Lake, Brooklyn, Lodi Marsh, and Janesville Segments. Contact the **Ice Age Trail Alliance** (www.iceagetrail.org) to find more information about trails and how to purchase the *Ice Age Trail Guide* and *Ice Age Trail Atlas*. Another great resource for these segments and other area hikes is *60 Hikes Within 60 Miles: Madison*.

wooded bluff to the 1857 St. Mary of the Woods chapel built by a pioneer as a promise kept when his children were spared a diphtheria epidemic. A bench is located at a point nearby overlooking the park and lake. The park contains miles of hiking and cross-country ski trails. A log cabin warming house is open in ski season. The park also has a dog exercise area and a boat launch for the small lake (electric motors only). The Ice Age National Scenic Trail passes through the park.

PRAIRIE MORAINE PARK
1970 County Hwy. PB, Verona

Many area residents know this as a prime dog park not far from the city, but it is also home to some oak savanna and a bit of geological history. The Ice Age National Scenic Trail enters the park passing along the back of Johnstown Moraine. The park offers both off-leash and on-leash areas for dogs. The entrance is 2 miles south of US 18/151 on County Highway PB.

TOKEN CREEK
6200 US Hwy. 51, DeForest

So close to Madison and with five shelters, the 427-acre park is ideal for group picnics. The 35 campsites are reservable, and 25 of them offer electricity. Horse riding and hiking trails encircle the park and a boardwalk passes through a sedge meadow marsh and along the creek itself. The 18-hole disc golf course exacts a fee as does the dog-exercise area. The boardwalk and a fishing pier are wheelchair accessible.

STATE PARKS

GOVERNOR NELSON STATE PARK
5140 County Hwy. M, Waunakee
(608) 831-3005

On the north shore of Lake Mendota, the 422-acre park has prairie restoration, woodland, marsh, prairie hiking/cross-country ski trails, Native American mounds, and a 500-foot beach with changing rooms and solar-heated showers. Dogs have a swimming area and a concession stand is at the main beach. The four-stall boat launch has ample parking and a fish cleaning facility nearby. Interpretive signage along the woodland trails and near the beach explains Native American culture. The beach has no lifeguard. There is no camping.

LAKE KEGONSA STATE PARK
2405 Door Creek Rd., Stoughton
(608) 873-9695

Lake Kegonsa was known by pioneers as "First Lake," part of the four lakes that defined what is now the Madison area. Like the other lakes, Kegonsa was formed by a retreating glacier over 12,000 years ago. The park offers 342 acres of woodlands, restored prairie with plenty of wildflowers, and marshlands. A boardwalk passes through the wetlands and over 5 miles of trails explore the rest of the park. Cross-country skiing is possible in the winter. Campsites number 80 and there are also two playgrounds, a boat launch, a swimming beach, horseshoe pits, sand volleyball courts, a fishing pier, and a sledding hill. Dogs have their own swimming area. The lake is known for its incredible fishing; the name comes from the Ho-Chunk language and means "lake of many fishes."

DOG PARKS

Madison has been a little tough on dogs over the years. For a while many of the parks didn't allow dogs at all. However, there is an increasing number of places now to take the pup for a little running about. Dog exercise areas in local parks is posted clearly. Four parks within the city limits offer no-leash exercise areas.

Brittingham Park, 401 North Shore Dr. at Broom St. near downtown

Quann Park, 1802 Expo Dr. near the Alliant Energy Center on the south side

Sycamore Park, 4517 Sycamore Park on the east side

Warner Park, off Sheridan Dr. along the lagoon at the boat launch on the city's north side

A daily or annual permit fee applies for all off-leash parks in the city and county, and your dog must also be licensed first. Contact the City Treasurer's Office (210 Martin Luther King Jr. Blvd.; 608-266-4771). Permits are available online and at local pet stores. Daily fees are self-paid at some parks. Governor Nelson and Lake Kegonsa State Parks have dog swimming areas.

SPECTATOR SPORTS

Madison doesn't have any professional sport teams, but certainly the fan fervor of Green Bay Packer football goes far beyond its home city (less than a three-hour drive from Madison). Miller Park, the home of Milwaukee Brewers baseball, is a one-hour drive east, and Madison businesses, especially bars, have been known to occasionally organize a bus to a particular game. And finally, the NBA's Milwaukee Bucks represent Wisconsin on the basketball court.

However, that is not to say Madison is without spectator sports. Quite the contrary: The University of Wisconsin is an NCAA Division I school and a member of the Big Ten Conference, participating in a variety of sports with both men's and women's teams. With this comes the rabid fan base for the Wisconsin Badgers. Streets downtown and around Camp Randall Stadium or the Kohl Center will flood with red clothing on football and basketball game days. Visitors might be surprised how early in the morning tailgating for a Saturday football game often begins. Unless you are driving through downtown to see the game, it's best to avoid the traffic. Big games for many of the UW sports will sell out accordingly while less important opponents, and less popular sports, might make getting tickets a lot easier. In this chapter, the Wisconsin Badgers section is broken down by sport.

Madison also has baseball. It's not quite minor league, but it often feels like it. A day out at the baseball stadium is fun for the family with all the bells and whistles but without the strikeout for your wallet. For those interested in racing, the Madison International Speedway is just south of town and nearby Sun Prairie, home to Angell Park Speedway, hosts midget auto racing. For something really out of the ordinary, down and dirty, and more fun than a barrel of monkeys, check out the roller derby league. The Madison Marathon and Ford Ironman Wisconsin Triathlon draw people to the curb to watch and cheer on racers from around the country and even the world who come to challenge themselves and each other. The marathon takes place Memorial Day Weekend, while the triathlon is held each year in Sept. See the Annual Events chapter, page 163, for more information.

THE WISCONSIN BADGERS

UNIVERSITY OF WISCONSIN SPORTS
www.uwbadgers.com

The University of Wisconsin–Madison is a member of the Big Ten Conference, the oldest Division I college athletic conference in the United States. The Wisconsin Badgers compete in 25 intercollegiate sports and have won 27 national championships. Football, men's basketball, and men's hockey are the best attended, but don't miss out on the other sports that offer some of the same excitement with a little more elbow room as well as cheaper tickets. The official Web site www.uwbadgers.com has an abundance of good information about all UW sports including schedules, ticket information, seating charts, and parking maps.

The mascot name "Badgers" comes from the lead miners who flocked to southwestern Wisconsin in the 1820s and 1830s. They arrived with little more than what they could carry, but with hopes of becoming wealthy from the abundance of lead the land was offering. Until they started making enough money to provide themselves roofs over their heads, they slept in shallow dugouts in the earth, a practice that earned them the "badger" moniker. Wisconsin became known as the Badger State, and the university picked up on the name as well. Bucky Badger, the tall, lean team mascot, can be seen at any game firing up the crowd, teasing the kids, and posing for photos.

i Bucky Badger's full name is actually Buckingham U. Badger, and the costumed mascot first appeared in 1949 at the pep rally before the homecoming game. In 1973, an assistant district attorney made an effort to replace Bucky with a cow, Henrietta Holstein. Needless to say, that didn't work out.

University of Wisconsin Sport Facilities

CAMP RANDALL STADIUM
1440 Monroe St.
(608) 262-1866
www.uwbadgers.com/facilities

Camp Randall Stadium is situated on the grounds of the former Civil War training camp (and sometimes prison camp) of the same name. Named for Civil War–era State Governor Alexander Randall it was built in 1917 and is the oldest stadium in the Big Ten. It started as a simple horseshoe with stands and a circling track, but has undergone several expansions and renovations. The field has been artificial turf since 1968, one of the first stadiums in the United States to make that change. Luxury boxes were added in the last construction project completed just before the 2005 football season. The stadium seats 80,321 and is quite the roaring good time on game day.

GOODMAN SOFTBALL COMPLEX
2301 University Bay Dr.
www.uwbadgers.com/facilities

Robert and Irwin Goodman, the same Goodmans who donated graciously to the city's public swimming facility, provided the lead gift on the Goodman Diamond (a play on words as the Goodmans are jewelers). The complex was completed in 1999 and received lights for night play in 2002. The grandstands hold around 1,600 fans and face

Lake Mendota. The field is located just south of Nielsen Tennis Stadium and shares parking with that facility.

KOHL CENTER
601 West Dayton St.
(608) 263-5645
www.uwbadgers.com/facilities

Opened in 1998, the center became the home of UW basketball and UW hockey which previously played in the Wisconsin Field House and the Dane County Coliseum (Veterans Memorial Coliseum at Alliant Energy Center), respectively. The Kohl Center has a changeable center floor for the two sports and seating capacity is variable: 17,190 seats for basketball, 15,237 for hockey.

MCCLIMON SOCCER COMPLEX
702 Walnut St.
(608) 262-3256
www.uwbadgers.com/facilities

This outdoor soccer pitch with a surrounding 400-meter, eight-lane polyurethane track is the site of all Badger soccer games and outdoor track and field events. The field is lighted for night play, and general bleacher seating has room for just over 2,000 fans. Additional grass seating is available on the embankment surrounding the bleachers, and spectators may bring blankets or lawn chairs. Total capacity for the complex is 4,500. Free parking (but only on weekends and after the work day on weekdays) is available in a large lot just north of the complex.

NATATORIUM
2000 Observatory Dr.
(608) 262-3742
www.uwbadgers.com/facilities

The "Nat" is home to both men's and women's diving and swimming. The 25-yard pool has eight lanes and is equipped with a Colorado Timing System and eight-lane digital scoreboard. Divers use a separate 50' x 40' diving with three 1-meter and two 3-meter boards, as well as a 5-meter platform.

NIELSEN TENNIS STADIUM

1000 Highland Ave.

(608) 262-0410

www.uwbadgers.com/facilities

The stadium is named for the founder of the TV rating system, Arthur C. Nielsen, a Badger alum and former tennis team captain. The facility offers 12 indoor and six outdoor courts, plus five squash singles courts and one doubles court. It is located at the west end of campus behind University Hospital and has abundant parking nearby.

PORTER BOATHOUSE

680 Babcock Dr.

www.uwbadgers.com/facilities

Completed in 2005, the boathouse at the end of Babcock Drive sits on the shore of Lake Mendota. The Lakeshore Path passes between it and the lake. The 2nd floor exhibits some rowing history.

THE SHELL (CAMP RANDALL MEMORIAL SPORTS CENTER)

1430 Monroe St.

(608) 262-4756

www.uwbadgers.com/facilities

Located next door to Camp Randall Stadium, the Shell hosts the Badgers indoor track and field competitions.

THE WISCONSIN FIELD HOUSE

1440 Monroe St.

(608) 262-3354

www.uwbadgers.com/facilities

This was once the home of UW basketball until the Kohl Center opened in 1998. Now volleyball and wrestling have the run of the place. Located at the corners of Regent and Monroe Streets, the field house sits at the southern end of Camp Randall Stadium.

i If you don't have tickets, a couple of great places to watch the football game right down around the stadium are The Stadium Bar (1419 Monroe St., 608-256-2544) and Jordan's Big Ten Pub (1330 Regent St., 608-251-6375).

Athletic Ticket Office

Tickets for football, basketball, and hockey can be purchased in advance and in many cases sell out long before the games. Students should consider getting the Red Card, which provides admission to all home regular-season women's basketball, volleyball, men's and women's soccer, wrestling, softball, and women's hockey events—something on the order of 80 sporting events—at an absurdly low price of $25.

Kellner Hall
1440 Monroe St.
(608) 262-1440 or (800) GO-BADGERS
www.uwbadgers.com

Badger Sports Teams

FOOTBALL

The football team played its first game in 1889—and lost. Redemption came the following year with a 109–0 victory over University of Wisconsin–Whitewater. When the Big Ten conference was formed in 1896, Wisconsin was its first champion. After several solid years, including two undefeated seasons in 1901 and 1912, the Badgers suffered through a long dry spell. In 1952 the Associated Press rated the Badgers #1 in the nation for the first time, and with this they went on to the Rose Bowl for what was to be the first of three defeats there over the next 10 years. Then followed nearly three decades of disappointment including a couple of winless seasons, but also three bowl trips in the 1980s (Garden State, Independence, and Hall of Fame).

But then in 1990, Barry Alvarez took the head coach position and the Badgers were about to become a football powerhouse. The first three seasons weren't exactly earth shattering, and, in fact, the first of them ended in a 1–10 record. But the success of the 1993 season left Badger

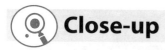

Close-up

Pat Richter: Badger Sports Superstar

Pat Richter was a nine-time Badger letterman with three in each of the sports of football, basketball, and baseball. He was also twice distinguished as an All-American tight end. With 11 catches for 163 yards, he set a Rose Bowl record in 1963 and went to the Washington Redskins on a first-round draft pick, playing for them for eight seasons. While Barry Alvarez was the coach behind the Badger's return to the Rose Bowl and football greatness, Richter was the athletic director behind the rebirth of an athletic program that would support such a possibility. Richter was hired in 1989 and faced outdated facilities and a $2.1 million deficit. Lackluster team performances weren't helping. Under his leadership the Kohl Center was built and Camp Randall Stadium received serious renovations. He also hired Barry Alvarez, then an assistant coach at Notre Dame, and the rest is Rose Bowl history. Richter holds places in the College Football Hall of Fame, the Academic All-America Hall of Fame, the Rose Bowl Hall of Fame, and the Wisconsin Athletic Hall of Fame. *Sports Illustrated* placed him on the magazine's NCAA Football All-Century Team. In 2006, two years after stepping down as athletic director, his number 88 was retired and a bronze statue of him was placed outside Camp Randall Stadium next to a similar one of Alvarez.

fans breathless (and hoarse), and Big Red went on to claim their first ever Rose Bowl victory by a score of 21–16 over UCLA. During the 16 years of Alvarez's Badger coaching career, the Badgers went 8–3 in 11 bowl games including two more Rose Bowl victories during running back Ron Dayne's UW years. Thus the Wisconsin Badgers became the first Big Ten team in history to win three Rose Bowl championships in one decade. Former defensive coordinator Bret Bielema took over as head coach in 2006 after Alvarez became the university's athletic director and had three consecutive bowl appearances. A statue of Alvarez stands outside the Camp Randall Stadium ticket office.

Say what you will about each year's team or prospects, but whatever the season promises one can bet on having a good time at a Badger football game. The students in the designated student section (Section P) are on their feet throughout most of the game leading the Wave and a variety of chants (some perhaps not exactly er, polite). The students and others traditionally flex the stadium concrete a bit when the song "Jump Around" by House of Pain blares through Camp Randall. The UW band also keeps the crowd fired up and may perform field antics or

halftime shows and classic songs such as "You've Said It All" (a variation on the former Budweiser beer jingle) or "On Wisconsin."

> **i** Don't miss The Fifth Quarter when the Badger Band entertains a crowd of about 40,000 lingering fans with interactive songs and antics that will typically include "You've Said It All" and "Varsity" as well as some polka dancing, chicken dancing, and a bit of Tequila (dancing, that is).

The season starts Labor Day weekend and ends the third or fourth week of Nov. The Big Ten Conference works with TV networks to decide on start times for football games and these schedules are announced two Mondays before game day. Tickets are available on the athletic department's official Web site and it should be known that all the home games easily sell out before the season even starts. The home football season always features four Big Ten games and generally three nonconference match ups. Big Ten games are almost exclusively on Sat.

Street parking on game day, like traffic down around the stadium, is hit or miss. Closer to the stadium private homes and parking lots sell spots

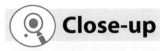

Close-up

Badger Heisman Winners

In 1954 Lino Dante "Alan" Ameche became the first Badger to win the Heisman trophy. In that same year Ameche, known as "The Horse," won All-American honors as well. In those days defense and offense were not separate platoons, and he actually played as both fullback and linebacker. His four years rushing totaled 3,212 yards, which at that time set the NCAA record. In 1955 he was named NFL Rookie of the Year for his first of six years playing for the Baltimore Colts. (He was the second first-round pick in the 1955 draft.) He helped the Colts win the 1958 NFL Championship in "The Greatest Game Ever Played," when he rushed for two touchdowns including the game-ending score in overtime, which finished off the New York Giants 23–17 in Yankee Stadium. Ameche's number 35 has been retired and his name is displayed on the Camp Randall Stadium façade.

Badger running back Ron Dayne won the Heisman trophy in 1999, the same year he became the NCAA's all-time regular-season rushing leader with a total of 6,397 yards. His career rushing total including bowl games was the first to top 7,000, and at 7,125 yards, he still holds that record. He had twelve 200-yard rushing games, a record he shares with Marcus Allen and Ricky Williams, and is one of five NCAA players in history to have 4,000-yard-plus seasons. His 71 touchdowns hold the Big Ten records for rushing and total touchdowns. During his four years at Wisconsin, the Badgers won the Big Ten Conference title twice and won three of the four bowl games they attended, including back-to-back victories at the Rose Bowl over UCLA and Stanford in 1999 and 2000, respectively. Dayne was honored as the MVP for both of those Rose Bowl victories plus the Copper Bowl defeat of Utah. He was drafted by the New York Giants in 2000. In 2007, his #33 jersey became one of six that have been retired by the Wisconsin Badgers, and his name joined Alan Ameche's on the stadium's façade.

for about $20. A great option is to find a local bar that offers a free shuttle to the game and get there beforehand for breakfast, beer, or a Bloody Mary pre-party or the like.

i Too much traffic? Bike to the game. The Southwest Commuter Path, an asphalt-paved, off-road, multiuse trail passes directly in front of Camp Randall and comes from the east and west sides of Madison.

BASKETBALL (MEN'S)

The men's basketball team played its first game in January 1899. The Badgers won their share of Big Ten Championships over the years, particularly during the coaching years of Walter Meanwell from 1911 to 1934 when they bagged eight of them (plus another under an interim coach). In 1941, coach Harold "Bud" Foster, a former All-

American Badger player, led the men's team to its first NCAA tournament invitation and its only NCAA championship to date. The team received another invitation a few years later and then went decades without similar success—that is, until the arrival of coach Dick Bennett. In 2000, with Bennett at the helm the Badgers entered the NCAA tournament ranked #8 in the West bracket. They made it to the Final Four before being eliminated by Michigan State which ultimately won the tournament that year. Since 2000 the men have consistently gotten into the NCAA tournament and continue to seek a second championship title. Games, previously played at the UW Fieldhouse, have been played at the Kohl Center since 1998. The Badgers have an amazing home court advantage and under current coach Bo Ryan have put together a very lopsided victory record of over 100 home wins and single-digit losses. The student section, known as the Grateful Red, might have something to do with that. It is located behind one of the baskets and holds 2,100 screaming students who fill the seats from the edge of the court up three decks to the ceiling. The Big Ten Conference works with the television networks that will broadcast the games to decide on game times. These are announced in late Aug.

> **i** The Wisconsin Badgers hold the national attendance record with 13,194 fans in attendance during the 1998 NCAA Championship match in the Kohl Center. In fact, the University of Wisconsin has four of the top seven listings on the collegiate sports attendance record books.

BASKETBALL (WOMEN'S)

The women's team's first season was in 1974 and their best record, 19–8, came in the 1982–83 season. Coach Mary Murphy, who coached from 1986 to 1994, was chosen Big Ten Coach of the Year in 1992 and led the women's team to their first NCAA tournament in the same year. But that was just the beginning. During her stint as coach from 1994 to 2003, Coach Jane Albright earned a record of 161–107 leading the Badgers to five NCAA tournament appearances and two Women's National Invitational Tournament (WNIT) appearances. They won the WNIT in 2000

after being runners-up the year before. Coach Albright was the Big Ten Conference Coach of the Year in 1995. Current coach Lisa Stone started with the Badgers in 2003, and in the 2006–07 season her team posted 23 wins, a team record, before making it all the way to the WNIT championship. The women's team made it to the WNIT tournament the following year as well. The season starts in Nov and ends with the Big Ten Tournament in Mar.

> **i** The University of Wisconsin Band regularly performs at football games, men's and women's basketball games, men's hockey games, and at women's volleyball matches.

HOCKEY (MEN'S AND WOMEN'S)

Drop. The. Puck! The Badger hockey team played its first game on January 14, 1922, against the Milwaukee Athletic Club, losing 4–1. This may be an ironic anecdote for a team that has gone on to become a hockey powerhouse in the NCAA. The men's team holds six NCAA National Championship titles. The biggest rivalries are with the Golden Gophers of the University of Minnesota and the Fighting Sioux of the University of North Dakota. All games during these series are typically sellouts. Otherwise, since this is the largest

 **Close-up**

Varsity Song

So you are from out of town and you are at a big Badger game and suddenly the raucous crowd is on its feet waxing nostalgic for the alma mater. And everyone begins singing with heart like it was "Danny Boy" and closing time at an Irish Pub. But you graduated from someplace else. Here's the school song so you can at least move your lips and blend in:

Varsity! Varsity!
U-rah-rah! Wisconsin!
Praise to thee we sing
Praise to thee our Alma Mater
U-rah-rah, Wisconsin!
(Trumpets blare)
Our Team is RED HOT!
(Two drum beats and repeat until you are hoarse.)

hockey arena in the NCAA, some tickets still remain for most games. Games are typically Fri and Sat nights. Parking options are on-street, in nearby parking ramps, or in a few UW parking lots that charge a nominal fee. On occasion an outdoor game is hosted at Camp Randall, and in the past the Badgers have even played at Lambeau Field, the revered home of the Green Bay Packers.

i Converting the Kohl Center from a basketball court to an ice-hockey arena is an incredible feat that takes about 120 worker hours. That means with a team of 40 (mostly paid students and a few permanent staff) it takes just three hours.

The student section is active, organized, and loud, leading a variety of chants that can be clever or off-color. Expect a taunting "Sieve! Sieve!" after every Badger goal, and for the last two minutes of the game, "Stand up, old people! Stand up, old people!" as the students all rise to their feet and bid the rest of the "older" folks to join them.

Women's games do not draw the same crowds, but it is not for lack of excitement and competition. The women's team has won three of the last four NCAA Women's National Hockey Championships. They won their first in 2006, the same year the men's team last won the championship, a tandem accomplishment never before achieved by another university. Women's team coach Mark Johnson has coached the Women's U.S. Olympic Team which has had its share of Badger players. Attendance for the Badger women hockey games is only a few thousand per game compared to an average of 15,000 or more per game for the men. Seating is general admission and costs only around $5—a steal to see a very talented team. Discounts for season tickets—all 18 home games—make that price even cheaper.

i The Kohl Center records the highest attendance in the NCAA for hockey.

ROWING

Rowing began as an intramural sport at the UW in 1874. By 1900, UW–Madison had its first national title, earned by the men's freshman eight team. Since that time another 48 Intercollegiate Rowing Association championships have been awarded to the Badgers. They went undefeated in 2008. The women's team got a later start in the 1970s, but they have also won national championships including four consecutive awards from 1975 to 1978, and their first National Collegiate Championship (first presented in 1981) in 1986. The women's lightweight eight only missed one championship title from 2004 to 2008. Races are held on Lake Wingra.

SOCCER (MEN'S AND WOMEN'S)

The men's team took the NCAA championship in 1995. Both Wisconsin men's and women's soccer are played at the McClimon Memorial Track and Soccer Complex. The seasons start for both teams in Aug and end in Nov. Soccer matches are on Sun during the day or weekday evenings. Check the schedule online for exact times and dates. All tickets are general admission and sold at the event only. There are no advanced single game sales. Tickets go on-sale starting one hour prior to the event and are available at the ticket booth located right outside the entrance. Ticket prices are $5 for adults, and $2 for students and seniors.

SOFTBALL

The Badger Women's softball team plays all home games at the Goodman Softball Complex. Tickets cannot be purchased in advance and they are general admission. Starting an hour before the game, tickets go on sale at the booth right outside the entrance to Goodman Diamond. Prices are around $5 for adults, and $2 for students and seniors.

TENNIS

Both men's and women's tennis seasons last from Aug into May when the Big Ten tournaments begin. Home matches are played at the Nielsen Tennis Stadium.

TRACK AND FIELD

The track and field season begins in Jan and continues into May and June for the various national championships. Events in winter are held at the Shell but move outdoors to the McClimon Memorial Track Complex in spring.

VOLLEYBALL

The women's volleyball team plays 13 home games each year at the Wisconsin Field House starting in Aug and ending in Nov. Season tickets offer reserved sideline seats at a deep discount. Single game general admission tickets cost $5 for adults and $2 for students and seniors and can either be purchased in advance or starting one hour before the event at Gate 1 at Camp Randall Stadium or Gate C at the field house.

WRESTLING

Wrestling duals and meets take place at the Wisconsin Field House. There are no advance single event ticket sales. All tickets are general admission, go on-sale one hour prior to the event, and are available at the ticket windows inside the Gates B and C entrances. Prices are about $5 for adults and $2 for students and seniors. Wrestling Championship tickets may have different pricing and availability.

AUTO RACING

ANGELL PARK SPEEDWAY
300 Park St., Sun Prairie
(608) 837-5252
www.angellpark.com
Named for Colonel William Angell, a Sun Prairie resident and Civil War veteran, Angell Park has been host to a variety of community events and recreational activities. Since 1946, the park has been home to a third-mile clay oval racetrack and host to midget auto racing. Don't let the size fool you: even NASCAR legends such as Jeff Gordon and Tony Stewart have raced here, and it was once considered a place to earn a reputation by racers vying for a spot in Indianapolis. Located in downtown Sun Prairie, Angell Park Speedway runs races every Sun evening from the middle of

May through Labor Day weekend. This is also the home of the National Midget Auto Racing Hall of Fame, and the speedway features the cars and racers from the Badger Midget Auto Racing Association. Take US 151 northwest from Madison until the County Road N exit. Turn left (north) and the speedway is on the right. Tickets cost from $12 to $20 with discounts for students. Kids 12 and under enter for free.

MADISON INTERNATIONAL SPEEDWAY
1122 Sunrise Rd., Oregon
(608) 835-9700
www.madisoninternationalspeedway.com
Located just off WI 138, between Oregon and Stoughton, the speedway calls itself the "Track of Champions" with racing giants such as Dick Trickle, Johnny Ziegler, and Matt Kenseth on the list of those to be named winners here. Built in 1969, the half-mile asphalt track is sanctioned by the American Speed Association and hosts weekly divisions of Super Late Models, ASA Late Models, Limited Late Models, and Area Sportsman. Grandstands seat over 10,000. Every Fri night from May through Sept gates open at 4:30 p.m., qualifying runs are at 6:30 p.m., and the racing begins at 7:30 p.m. No carry-in food is allowed but plenty of grilled food and carnival classics (funnel cakes!) are available along with soda and beer. Parking is free. Tickets are around $8–10. Children 11 and under get in free.

BASEBALL

MADISON MALLARDS BASEBALL
2920 North Sherman Ave.
(608) 246-4277
www.mallardsbaseball.com
There's really nothing like a day or evening out at the ballpark. Minor league baseball made a go of it here in the Mad City, but it was only since Steve Schmitt (of Black Earth's The Shoe Box shoe store fame) took over that baseball seems to be here to stay. This is summer collegiate baseball, which gives college players the opportunity to play as if in the minor leagues, with wooden bats and traveling overnight for games. The Mallards play 68 games each summer season in the Northwoods

League. Games here at the "Duck Pond" are entertaining both during and in between innings. Maynard G. Mallard, the mascot, often involves the fans in games and cheers, and promotional gifts are sometimes part of the fun. Kids who retrieve a foul ball get a hot dog for their efforts. A beer garden in right field, the Duck Blind, features suds and food brought in by the local brewpub, The Great Dane. Tickets are for all you can eat and drink. Suites and private deck options are also available for large groups. The front rows of the grandstands have seatbacks and armrests while the upper seats are strictly bleachers. The park is wheelchair accessible and there are picnic tables and play areas for families. The stadium is located at Warner Park at the corner of Northport Drive and Sherman Avenue. The park offers plenty of parking, as well as tailgating opportunities, adjacent to the field. Tickets range from $5 to $12. The season starts at the end of May and ends in Aug.

ROLLER DERBY

THE MAD ROLLIN' DOLLS ROLLER DERBY LEAGUE
www.madrollindolls.com
It's "hurt in a skirt." What started as a skating endurance competition on a banked, circular track eventually became a contact sport before devolving into a melodramatic production akin to "professional" wrestling on skates by the 1970s. But starting in Austin, TX, in 2001, a revival of this '50s and '60s spectacle is short on cheesy and long on some fierce rough and tumble competition. The bouts are skated on a flat track not a banked one. Founded in 2004, the Mad Rollin' Dolls Roller Derby League is made up of the Dairyland Dolls, Quad Squad, Reservoir Dolls, Unholy Rollers, and Vaudeville Vixens. All teams play each other each month. The Dairyland Dolls and Team Unicorn also compete around the country (and in Canada) in interleague play. Each event hosts two bouts. Bouts are divided into two 20-minute periods. Most bouts are held at the Alliant Energy Center and fans can count on an outrageously good time. Check the Web site for tickets and other information.

RECREATION

For the active and the outdoors enthusiasts there is much to do in Madison. The city has been listed at the top of American communities at various times for walking, biking, and simply the outdoor life. *Outside Magazine* has rated it one of the nation's best outdoors towns and tops for road biking, and even *National Geographic Adventure* chimed in with a Best Adventure Towns listing.

Just an aerial view of Madison should make water sports enthusiasts delight. Lakes Mendota and Monona offer 34 miles of shoreline. Add to that the sheltered, spring-fed Lake Wingra, plus Lakes Waubesa and Kegonsa and the Yahara River that passes through Cherokee Marsh and on down through all of the lakes. The Wisconsin River and a whole slew of lakes, ponds, and streams are not far away either. For paddling, fishing, swimming, sailing, or just a cruise across the water, Madison is heavenly. Bikers will enjoy the miles of paths throughout the city, including some lanes on major roads as well. Rollerbladers take advantage of many of those same paved trails as do pedestrians, so be careful to share the way. Hikers never need look far to find a place to disappear into forest, marsh, or meadow, and winter opens up snowshoeing possibilities and abundant skiing options. From kayaking and yoga to kiteboarding and disc golf, Madisonians are active folk. If you don't want to go it alone, look for events in the newspapers and their Web sites. Also, check out social networking sites such as www.meetup.com if you are looking to connect with fellow enthusiasts of just about any sport or activity you can think of.

BOATING AND FISHING

There are 25 boat launches and several marinas/boat storage sites on the Yahara River and the lakes it connects. These range from full-blown marinas to something more akin to the road ending in the lake. Most parks with access also have dedicated parking areas. (Never park on the grass or you can be fined!) Other street-end launches may only have on-street parking. Lake Access Permits (formerly Boat Launch Permits) are required year-round for all boats (except canoes and kayaks) at any Dane County or City of Madison sites and cost $8 per day or $30 for the year (slightly more for out-of-state residents). They can be purchased via the **Dane County** Web site (www.reservedane.com/permits) or at select area businesses. A variety of parks around the lakes have boat launches including Olin Park, Olbrich Park, Tenney Park, Governor Nelson State Park, Warner Park, Wingra Park, and Cherokee Marsh South. Lake Wingra allows electric motors only. Be sure to clean off your boat before going to another lake to help fight the spread of devastating invasive species of plants and animals.

Lakes Mendota and Monona are connected across the isthmus by a straightened, no-wake portion of the Yahara River, and Tenney Lock (608-266-4364), which is open May through Oct, negotiates the roughly five-foot difference between the two bodies of water. The lock fee is $5 daily or an annual fee of $20. A self-registration station is located below the lock. Each end of the Yahara of course is a no-wake zone.

U.S. Coast Guard approved life jackets for each person on board are required by law, and whenever the sun is not up, boat lights must be on. If you are using your own boat, be sure it is properly registered and that the registration is visible. The hours vary but generally the lock opens at noon on weekdays and a bit earlier on weekends. Closing hours are just after sunset, gradually getting later toward the peak of summer. For lock access outside opening hours contact Dane County Parks at (608) 224-3730 and expect to pay an extra fee.

Whether by boat or from shore, fishing is popular in Madison and the shores along Monona Bay or the river at Tenney Park, for example, always show anglers. Specific season dates, fees, catch limits, and such can be found at the **Department of Natural Resources** Web site (www.dnr.state.wi.us/fish). Anyone 16 years or older (or younger than 65) must have a license. Licenses are issued from Apr 1st of each year and are valid for one year. Licenses can be purchased from the DNR office (101 South Webster St.; 608-264-6012) or various local businesses including Dicks Sporting Goods, Dorn True Value Hardware, and Fontana Sports. There are different fees for state residents and non-residents.

> **i** Fish for free! On the first full weekend in June, residents and nonresidents of all ages throughout the state of Wisconsin do not need a fishing license for that Sat or Sun.

CLIMBING

BOULDERS CLIMBING GYM
3964 Commercial Ave.
(608) 244-8100
www.bouldersgym.com
Madison's only dedicated climbing gym, Boulders has over 8,000 square feet of climbing surfaces including 1,500 square feet of bouldering, 42 top ropes, and 24 lead lines. Climbing classes for adults and kids are offered. Rates are by the day and range from about $12 to $16. Gear is available for rent. Open daily.

VERTICAL ILLUSIONS
933 US Hwy. 12, Wisconsin Dells
(608) 253-2500
www.verticalillusions.com
This outfitter offers a variety of adventure sports and is one of the few places to get some outdoor rock-climbing guidance. They go to Devil's Lake

State Park, which features some rocky bluffs and cliffs, as well as Petenwell and Chimney Rock Wisconsin. They offer top rope certification and belay courses as well.

CYCLING

With miles and miles of paved off-road multi-use paths—some with connections to state trails—and dedicated bike lanes, Madison has great appeal for pedalers. In the downtown and campus area, especially University Avenue and the Capitol Square, lanes are painted for bicycles. The rolling hills of the surrounding countryside, especially around the town of Paoli, also make for some great road riding. Madisonians love their bikes and many residents are committed to commuting to work on them so that even in rain or blowing snow you might see two-wheeled transit.

Bike Path Maps

The City of Madison produces a detailed map of bike paths and roads with bike lanes that is available at public libraries and local bicycle stores or downloadable on the city Web site (www.cityofmadison.com). **Travel Wisconsin**, the official state tourism Web site (www.travelwisconsin.com) has a downloadable booklet for the entire state system. You can also request that it be mailed. **The Wisconsin Department of Transportation** (www.dot.wisconsin.gov/travel/bike-foot/bikemaps.htm) has a collection of eight maps that covers the entire state and show routes for on-road biking as well as bike trails and mountain biking areas. The Web site also offers downloadable maps for each of the state's 72 counties.

In 2007 Wisconsin dedicated its trails to one of the state's most famous conservationists. The **Aldo Leopold Legacy Trail System** includes 42 trails totaling more than 1,700 miles. Rails-to-trails projects throughout the state have created a vast network of low-grade bike paths, and Madison has a few of those former train corridors among its trail list. The Southwest Commuter Path starts at Brittingham Park along Lake Monona and passes all the way through downtown crossing Park Street on a bridge and passing Camp Randall Stadium. From there it continues through residential neighborhoods lush with private gardens and partly shaded by old trees before crossing the Beltline Highway on a bridge and coming to an end where the Capital City Trail ends. The Badger State Trail will soon be connected to the Southwest Commuter Path where it meets the Capital City Trail, and the 40-mile Military Ridge State Trail is a mile away near the corner of Verona Road and County Highway PD.

The Badger State Trail, soon connecting into the city, temporarily starts 7.1 miles south of Madison at Purcell Road near Fitchburg. From there it is a relatively straight shot to the border of Illinois with an exciting pass through the 1,600-foot Stewart Tunnel. A state trail pass is required. The Southwest Commuter Trail is actually part of the developing Badger State Trail, but even when it gets connected in the future it will not require a state trail pass inside the city. The Capital City State Trail also does not require the pass on its in-city segment, but does require it from where it enters the Centennial State Park just south of the Beltline Highway at Industrial Road on until its end at Verona Road. There are self-pay stations at those end points.

In town, the Capital City starts from Dempsey Road on the east side following along the edge of the railroad tracks, passing behind Olbrich Gardens and then all the shops along Williamson Street on a short on-road section before crossing Willy Street to Lake Monona's edge. From here the trail follows John Nolen Drive along Lake Monona passing along the Frank Lloyd Wright-inspired Monona Terrace where a bicycle elevator takes cyclists up four stories to be level with the Capitol and the streets around it. The Capital City trail, however, continues along the lake until it crosses over the Beltline Highway. Then the trail heads west still on asphalt until it ends at Verona Road with the Southwest Commuter Path. The old rail bridge it passes under near the end will one day be a paved portion of the Badger State Trail. The east end of the Capital City Trail will eventually be connected to the Glacial Drumlin State Trail which now starts in Cottage Grove and heads all the way to Waukesha where it connects into the Milwaukee area trails. Two spur trails extend from the portion of the Cap City trail along Lake Monona known as the John Nolen Path: Wingra Creek Path follows the waterway of the same name all the way to Lake Wingra, Vilas Park, and the Arboretum; Monona Trail heads east along the south shore of the lake and into residential back roads for those who want to circle the lake.

Be aware: all these paths are shared-use. This is especially important to remember when riding within the city where pedestrians, some with strollers, or even Rollerbladers may suddenly appear in your path.

Renting a bicycle is easy as there are many shops in Madison. Everyone has a preferred bike shop but there really isn't a bad one in the bunch. Most include helmets and locks with rentals. Trek is an ever-present brand in Madison in no small part because the head office is in Waterloo, WI.

> ℹ Mountain-biking enthusiasts should check out Blue Mounds State Park, southwest of the city, and John Muir and Emma Carlin State Trails, to the southeast of the city. The courses there are superb.

BUDGET BICYCLE CENTER
930 Regent St.
(608) 251-1663
www.budgetbicyclectr.com
Budget Bikes is located right downtown with four distinct shops within a four-block radius and a block off the Southwest Commuter Path. They have a wide selection of new and used bicycles, rentals of all types, and perform reliable and fast repairs.

Need to borrow a bike for the year? Madison has you covered. Each year Budget Bicycle Center Used Bikes at 930 Regent St. takes the first 300 or so people who sign up to borrow one of the Red Bikes, used rides painted completely in a Badger color. (www.budgetbicyclectr.org)

MACHINERY ROW BICYCLES
601 Williamson St.
(608) 442-5974
www.machineryrowbicycles.com
This shop, situated right on the Capital City Trail and the shore of Lake Monona at the Willy Street and John Nolen Drive intersection, has a large selection of new bikes as well as parts and accessories. Daily rental rates start at around $20 with discounts for a weekly rental. Helmets and cable locks are included. Child trailers are available as well. Open daily.

WILLIAMSON BIKES AND FITNESS
3729 East Washington Ave.
(608) 244-2453

640 West Washington Ave.
in Madison Train Depot
(608) 255.5292
http://willybikes.com
The shop has two locations with a large selection of new bicycles for sale plus accessories and parts. The downtown location on West Washington is right off the Southwest Commuter Path. Open daily.

YELLOW JERSEY
419 State St.
(608) 257-4737
www.yellowjersey.org
The shop only rents out mountain bikes and tandems and has a great four-day (long weekend) rate of $38 on the mountain bike. One business day and overnight through the next business day are around $10 and $18, respectively. A full week is about $55. Rentals include a Kryptonite lock and helmet. Reservations are not accepted

and the best availability is Fri morning. Bikes for sale, parts and accessories, and repairs are also on-site. Tip: By the back door of the store, which must be reached from Johnson Street, there is an air pump with a built-in gauge free for public use. Very kind.

DISC GOLF AND ULTIMATE FRISBEE

Nothing sounds more like a toy than the word "Frisbee." But the competitive sports of disc golf and Ultimate Frisbee have grown much over the last two decades and demand some respect. Whether you're a member of the PDGA (Professional Disc Golfer Association), a regular player, or just disc-curious, Madison has some great disc-golf courses—most of which are free—and Ultimate leagues and pickup games. For all things disc-related, including disc-golf leagues and tournaments, contact the Madison Area Disc Club at www.madcitydisc.org. MUFA, the Madison Ultimate Frisbee Association (www.mufa.org) is the local resource for everything related to the game, and they keep a Web site with information on locations and times for Ultimate pick-up games as well as leagues.

ELVER PARK
1250 McKenna Blvd.
This is Madison's beloved original course and offers 18 holes up and over a steep hill and through some challenging woods in a west-side park. Expect concrete tees for both pro and amateur lengths and don't miss the pro tee on 18—a great view and a long shot off the top of the hill. Go south of the Beltline at Gammon Road for one mile and the park is on the right.

HIESTAND PARK
4302 Milwaukee St.
Not quite as challenging perhaps as Elver, this east-side park also has concrete pro and amateur tees for 18 holes through woods nestled atop a hill. Hole #1 is on Wittwer Road just north of Milwaukee Street.

VALLARTA-ALT DISC GOLF COURSE
at Token Creek County Park
6200 US Hwy. 51, DeForest
(608) 246-3896

Just minutes north of Madison near DeForest, this is a pay-to-play course offering concrete tees on 18 well-maintained fairways with less brush than Elver or Heistand. The fee is around $5 or there is a seasonal pass. Camping is available on-site. Go north of Madison on I-90/94 to exit 132 (US 51). Go north 0.25 mile (just past the truck stop) and turn right into Token Creek Park. The park road passes the group camp, and you'll see the course kiosks and Hole #1 on the right.

GOLF COURSES

Links are not hard to come by in Madison and there are several courses open to the public both inside and just outside the city limits. On municipal courses nine holes will set you back just over $15, while a full round of 18 is just under $30. Arguably the best course is the University of Wisconsin's University Ridge.

THE BRIDGES GOLF COURSE
2702 Shopko Dr.
(608) 244-1822
www.golfthebridges.com

This privately owned course is open to the public and located on Madison's north side right at the edge of the airport. The 18-hole course has a par of 72 and five sets of tees for varying levels of skill. Greens fees change with the day and time and in some cases are cheaper than the municipal courses. Expect a few low-flying planes.

GLENWAY GOLF COURSE
3747 Speedway Rd.
(608) 266-4737
www.cityofmadison.com/golf

This municipal course on the near west side close to Forest Hill Cemetery is short and good for beginners or casual golfers with par being 32 for nine holes. The scenery is quite nice with lots of old trees along the fairways.

MONONA GOLF COURSE
111 East Dean Ave.
(608) 266-4736
www.cityofmadison.com/golf

Located on Madison's east side in the town of Monona, this nine-hole municipal course is a decent municipal course worth hitting if you are close by.

NINE SPRINGS GOLF COURSE
2201 Traceway Dr., Fitchburg
(608) 271-5877
www.ninespringsgolfcourse.com

This nine-hole par-34 course is nice for beginners. Located south of the Beltline Highway along Fish Hatchery Road.

ODANA HILLS GOLF COURSE
4635 Odana Rd.
(608) 266-4724
www.cityofmadison.com/golf

This 18-hole city course has a par of 72 and is one of the most popular in town hosting tournaments from time to time. It is located on the west side just off the Beltline. A putting green and driving range are on-site as is a clubhouse with decent food service.

PLEASANT VIEW GOLF COURSE
1322 Pleasant View Rd., Middleton
(608) 831-6666
www.golfpleasantview.com

With views of Madison and Lake Mendota, the name makes sense. The course features 27 holes with a nice par 3 course, which is great for beginners or irons work. The driving range, putting green, and pitching area are nice.

UNIVERSITY RIDGE GOLF COURSE
9002 County Rd. PD
(608) 845-7700
www.uwbadgers.com/facilities/ridge

University Ridge is the official course for the University of Wisconsin campus, and hosts the UW golf team's events. Set on 225 acres of rolling hills with meadows and deep woods, it is a par-72, 18-hole course. Publications such as *Golf Digest* and *Golfweek* have listed it as one of the country's best public-access courses.

VITENSE GOLFLAND
5501 Schroeder Rd.
(608) 271-1411
www.vitense.com
Not your typical course, Vitense offers a variety of other entertainment, from minigolf to batting cages, much of it aimed at kids. But the 9-hole, par-3 course is lighted for night play and has artificial tees. The driving range is superb and even in cold weather, some tee areas are heated.

YAHARA HILLS GOLF COURSE
6701 East Broadway
(608) 838-3126
www.cityofmadison.com/golf
This is the city's largest course with two 18-hole championship courses. The course is wide open and good for the golfer who tends to shoot for the woods.

HIKING

Many of the city parks have hiking trails that can seem a long way from the city if you can ignore distant traffic noise. The Arboretum has great variety and abundant wildlife and plant life right in the heart of the city. The north and south units of Cherokee Marsh on the north side are quite underused and Governor Nelson State Park is just across Lake Mendota. Pheasant Branch Conservancy in Middleton is another goldmine. Often considered a hiking mecca, Devil's Lake State Park just over a half an hour north near Baraboo shouldn't be missed. The towering rocky bluffs make a good challenge, and the areas away from those obvious points are often overlooked. The University of Wisconsin Arboretum often hosts naturalist-guided hikes. Another good resource is the locally authored *60 Hikes Within 60 Miles of Madison* by Kevin Revolinski that offers an abundance of hikes in and out of the city limits. The most ambitious of the hiking trails in the Madison area, however, is the 1,000-mile Ice Age National Scenic Trail (see the Close-up at the end of the Parks Chapter page

128). There are several excellent segments ranging from 1 to 18 miles within an hour's drive of the city and some just minutes out of town.

WISCONSIN HOOFERS OUTING CLUB
800 Langdon St.
(608) 262-1630
www.hooferouting.org
One must be a member to participate in Hoofer events, but need not be a UW student or staff person. Formed in 1931 Hoofers is an outdoors program of the University of Wisconsin–Madison. Within the organization are separate clubs for horse riding, scuba diving, outing, mountaineering, sailing, skiing, and snowboarding. Events are scheduled regularly. Members must be students, faculty, or staff of the university or Wisconsin Union members. To learn about becoming a member and membership benefits, contact the membership office at the Memorial Union (800 Langdon St.; 608-262-2263; www.union.wisc.edu).

ICE-SKATING

In winter, the city or groups of volunteers maintain eight ice-skating rinks at Tenney, Vilas, Elver, Olbrich, Warner, Westmorland, Garner, and Goodman Parks. Indoor public skating is offered year-round as well.

CAPITOL ICE ARENA
2616 Pleasant View Rd., Middleton
(608) 836-0202
www.madisoncapitols.com
The arena offers a varying schedule of open skating and hockey playing throughout the year. Fees are around $4 to $5 with some special all-day affairs for about double that which include longer hours, free refreshments, music, and lights.

MADISON ICE, INC.
Hartmeyer Ice Arena
1834 Commercial Ave.
(608) 442-0071

Madison Ice Arena
725 Forward Dr.
(608) 204-7606
www.madisonicearena.com

Open skating is commonly scheduled for two hours at a time at varying days during the week at both Madison Ice locations. Fees for entry are around $2 to $4 and skate rental about $2. Open freestyle figure skating incurs a fee of $10. Check the Web site or call for the schedule. This is not for hockey playing.

KAYAKING & CANOEING

RUTABAGA PADDLESPORTS, LLC
220 West Broadway, Monona
(608) 223-9300 or (800) I-PADDLE
www.rutabaga.com
In business since the 1970s, Rutabaga takes its unlikely name from a building it once occupied. Their waterside location allows you to test paddle the canoe or kayak you're considering. Staff is extremely knowledgeable about the sport and equipment, not to mention, places to go. *Canoe & Kayak Magazine* granted Rutabaga the Paddlesports Retailer of the Year Award several times. Rutabaga Outdoor Programs is the largest flatwater paddling school in the country. It offers a variety of courses and certifications for all ages. The shop rents canoes and kayaks for half- and full days for around $25 and $40 respectively. Tip: All day Sunday is counted as a half-day. Rentals must leave and return from the shop's dock. Call about off-site exceptions. Open daily.

SUPREME WATER SPORTS
James Madison Park
(608) 212-1568
www.supremewatersports.com
Built into the hill at this park on Lake Mendota, the shop rents canoes, kayaks, sailboats, sailboards, and paddleboats. Hourly, half- and full-day rental rates are available. Open daily.

i For a great paddling day trip consider a day or overnight trip down the nearby Wisconsin River. Check out the Day Trips chapter and Sauk City, page 186.

WINGRA CANOE & SAILING
824 Knickerbocker St.
(608) 233-5332
www.wingraboats.com
The location is ideal, of course, inside Wingra Park with its toes in the water of the city's most sheltered water space. The outfitter rents canoes, kayaks, paddle boats, rowboats, sailboards, and sailboats by the hour, half-day, or full day. Seasonal memberships and slips for private boats are available. The launch here is public and parking is nearby. Open daily.

SKATE PARKS

MADISON 4 SEASONS SKATE PARK
3226 Progress Rd.
(608) 222-7275
www.madison.4seasonssk8park.com
This indoor skate park is open year-round and run by skateboarders. The owner once traveled around the country as a sponsored skateboarder participating in competitions. He opened the skate park in 2001. The progressive ramp designs serve all skill levels, from beginner to professional. The daily fee is good even if you leave and come back. Skaters under 18 must have their parent or guardian sign a waiver, which is downloadable online. 4 Seasons also hosts skate camps in the summer and private lessons. Helmets are required and can be rented along with other safety equipment. The gear shop sells a variety of brands and parts for the skateboarding enthusiast. Open daily with discount rates on certain weekdays. In summer hours are expanded and a discount is offered on Tues.

QUARRY SKATE PARK
7701 Terrace Ave., Middleton
(608) 827-1044
www.ci.middleton.wi.us
Rollerbladers and skateboarders alike enjoy this 10,000-square-foot skate facility across the street from Capital Brewery. The park is seasonal, open during daylight hours from Mar 15 to Dec 15. There is no supervision on-site and proper safety equipment is highly recommended. BMX bikes

are not allowed. A portable toilet is on-site and off-street parking is available. Admission is free.

SKIING & SNOWBOARDING

When the fluff falls, typically starting in Dec—but sometimes even earlier—the skis come out. Local, county, and state parks offer some excellent groomed and ungroomed trails for cross-country skiers. Once the lakes have frozen to a safe thickness, these also become adventurous ski opportunities. As you might guess from the lack of mountains, downhill skiing is not abundant; however, there are some options close by where you can get your fix.

Cross-Country Skiing

MADISON NORDIC SKI CLUB
www.madnorski.org

The club welcomes old pros or absolute beginners and meets monthly in the winter and organizes trips, races, and other activities. The Web site is a great resource for where to go and what the snow conditions are like at each park. Parks with hiking trails often will groom those trails in the snowy season. Dane County Parks and the Wisconsin Department of Natural Resources maintain lists of parks with ski trails. Here is a list of the best options within the city or a short drive away.

Cherokee Marsh Conservation Park South Unit, 5002 School Rd., 3 miles classical

Elver Park, 1301 South Gammon Rd., 6 miles skating and classical

Governor Nelson State Park, 5140 County Hwy. M, Waunakee, 4.5 miles skating and classical

Lake Farm County Park, 2862 Waubesa Ave., 8 miles mostly classical

Lake Kegonsa State Park, 2405 Door Creek Rd., Stoughton, 6 miles classical

Odana Hills Golf Course, 4635 Odana Rd., 3.4 miles skating and classical

Olin-Turville Park, 1155 East Lakeside St., 2 miles classical

Owen Conservation Park, 6021 Old Sauk Rd., 1.6 miles classical

Pleasant View Golf Course, 1322 Pleasant View Rd., Middleton, 5 miles skating and classical

Token Creek County Park, 6200 US Hwy. 51, DeForest, 3.8 miles

The University of Wisconsin Arboretum, 1207 Seminole Hwy., ungroomed

Warner Park, 1511 Northport Dr., 2.5 miles

Downhill Skiing & Snowboarding

CASCADE MOUNTAIN
W10441 Cascade Mountain Rd., Portage
(608) 742-5588 or (800) 992-2754
www.cascademountain.com

Snowboarders and skiers have 36 trails and five terrain areas to choose from including some expert mogul challenges. Lifts total 10. Kids under 13 ski for free with a paying adult. Tubing is also available for the nonskiers in the group. The property makes its own snow so even when the grass may be showing in Madison, it is possible to hit the slopes. Here's a nifty plan: ski part of the day and then head to nearby Wisconsin Dells for some water park fun. Cascade Mountain and area indoor water parks often offer package deals including lodging.

TYROL BASIN
3487 Bohn Rd., Mt. Horeb
(608) 437-4135
www.tyrolbasin.com

Sixteen trails run down from a height of 300 feet and are serviced by three triple chairlifts and three surface tows. Snowboarders have several rails, jumps, and even a propane tank to work off of. Equipment for both skiers and snowboarders is available for rent.

WINDSURFING & KITEBOARDING

As unlikely as it may seem, Madison offers some good wind-driven water recreation. When the weather offers up something more than a breeze, enthusiasts run to places such as Tenney Park, James Madison Park, Warner Park, and the Memorial Union Terrace to seize the day and the wind. See the outfitters under Kayaking & Canoeing for rental equipment.

Madison School and Community Recreation (MSCR)

MSCR is a department of the Madison Metropolitan School District and for over 80 years has been providing recreation options for residents within the Madison Area School District. All ages are welcome and events run year-round. The summer program calendar comes out in Mar while the winter edition is printed in Nov. The catalog is online as a download, but also appears as an insert in the *Wisconsin State Journal* and is mailed out to all residents. For adults there are leagues for soccer, baseball, basketball, and volleyball. Kids' choices are extensive. MSCR is set up in Warner Park Community Recreation Center (1625 Northport Dr.; 608-245-3669) and Meadwood Neighborhood Center (5734 Raymond Rd.; 608-467-8360) Open weekdays. Contact MSCR, 3802 Regent St.; (608) 204-3000; www.mscr.org.

YOGA STUDIOS

BLISS FLOW YOGA
2981 Cahill Main, Fitchburg
(608) 273-3569
www.blissflowyoga.com
Owner/instructor Angela Gargano has been in national publications. Her professional instructors offer a variety of hour to hour-and-a-half long sessions and classes including yoga introduction, pre-natal, and candlelight yoga. Massage is also offered.

INNER FIRE YOGA
5003 University Ave.
(608) 661-0167
www.innerfireyogacenter.com
This spacious, green-design studio offers instruction in both group and private sessions. Along with Bikram yoga, Power Flow, Inner Fire Fusion, and Yin yoga, hot yoga is available with 100-plus degree temperatures to accelerate the cleansing of the body. Every Sat a community yoga class is offered for a low drop-in rate. Massage therapy and workshops in meditation and nutrition are also offered.

THE PERFECT KNOT
409 South Few St.
(608) 848-2339
www.perfectknot.com
This laid-back east-side studio almost seems reluctant to call itself a business. The primary purpose is yoga not marketing, and instructors are independent and enthusiastic. Courses run the gamut and include Bikram Method Hatha yoga, Kundalini yoga, Vinyasa yoga, Odissi Dance, Scaravelli-inspired yoga, deep flow, and pre- and post-natal yoga. This is a friendly place to start (and continue!). Drop in rates are around $10. Passes make prices even cheaper.

YOGA CO-OP OF MADISON
812 East Dayton St., Suite 200
(608) 446-9642
www.yogacoop.com
The co-op offers a variety of levels of Iyengar method classes from an introductory course to more advanced poses, as well as classes designed especially for women and children. The hourlong sessions cost around $10 with passes available for co-op members and nonmembers as well.

YOGA IN THE GARDENS
Olbrich Botanical Gardens
3330 Atwood Ave.
(608) 246-4550
www.olbrich.org
Olbrich Botanical Gardens makes a nice setting for Yoga in the Gardens, a weekly morning and evening event. In spring, summer, and fall the activity is held outside when conditions are favorable. A certified Kripalu Yoga teacher leads each session. Call or check the Web site to confirm days and times. Bring your own mat and water bottle. Open to walk-ins. Comes with a fee of about $12.

KIDSTUFF

Madison is a city that's active for all ages and the menu of options for kids is quite extensive. Whether you are looking for some quiet time, an educational moment, sports, or summer camp, Madison has something to offer. Watch for Kids Stuff in "The Guide," *Isthmus'* weekly arts and entertainment section. This is also available online at www.thedailypage.com/theguide.

The abundance of public parks means an abundance of free playgrounds. However, not too many kids around here are unfamiliar with the Wisconsin Dells Water Parks. Once your child hears about this magical place, they may be driven to fits until you take them. For more information about the all-season "Water Park Capital of the World," check out the Day Trips chapter. The Kidstuff chapter is broken down into the following sections: Artsy Stuff, Fun Stuff, Nature Stuff, Smart Stuff, Splish Splash,Tasty Stuff, and a few listings for Shopping and Story Time. Close-ups focus on Summer Day Camps, Nature Passports, and Fall Fun.

Not every idea is confined to this chapter; there are many activities kids can enjoy with the adults. Explore the Recreation chapter and, for example, consider taking a bike ride as a family along one of Madison's marvelous paved multiuse paths or hike along the trails of the Arboretum.

ARTSY STUFF

ART CART
Madison Museum of Contemporary Art
(608) 257-0158
www.mmoca.org
This is art on wheels. Sponsored by the Madison Museum of Contemporary Art, the Art Cart visits city playgrounds, beaches, and parks, and sets up shop and allows kids and their families to participate in free art making activities. The program lasts from June through Aug. The age focus is really from three through eight, but all ages are welcome. When you consider what your child should wear (besides sunscreen of course) just remember that this may involve finger paint. Activities are held during the day and the evening. Watch the Web site to see what's coming up.

CHILDREN'S THEATER OF MADISON
228 State St.
(608) 255-2080
www.ctmtheater.org

Not only is the focus of the productions about kids, but the organization also trains young actors. Classes for children five and older are available in acting, improvisation, musical theater, and even stage combat. Summer drama school consists of one-week and three-week sessions, the latter of which conclude with a production. Check the Web site for upcoming auditions as well as course schedules and costs. Each production description on the Web site or brochure comes with age recommendations. Some plays are for all ages while others might appeal more to children eight years of age or even older. This helps families decide who might like it and who might squirm in their seat for two hours. Also see the CTM listing under Performing Arts, page 93.

KIDS IN THE ROTUNDA
Overture Center for the Arts
201 State St.
(608) 258-4141
www.overturecenter.com/community/
kids-in-the-rotunda

In the basement theater at the Overture Center's rotunda, kids can enjoy a series of performances by artists that include musicians, magicians, storytellers, actors, and jugglers. The events are free and occur on Sat afternoons from Oct until May. Snacks and refreshments can be purchased at the cafe on-site.

WISCONSIN CHILDREN'S CHOIR
1706 Norman Way
(608) 233-1227
www.wisconsinchildrenschoir.org
Children with an interest in singing have a marvelous opportunity to learn and experience more. The Wisconsin Children's Choir is an audition-based organization with three levels of choirs: Concert Choir for children entering grades 3 through 8, and Chorale and Chamber Choir for the more advanced middle- and high-school aged children. Auditions are held in Aug, Jan, and May. Rehearsals are scheduled regularly throughout the academic year with concerts in the winter and spring and some possible touring for the older students in June.

FUN STUFF

ANGELL PARK SPEEDWAY
300 Park St., Sun Prairie
(608) 837-5252
www.angellpark.com
How about a night at the races? In nearby Sun Prairie Angell Park Speedway hosts midget auto racing. Kids 12 and under are offered free admission, and there are occasional promotions and activities aimed at the little ones.

> **i** Though the Madison Marathon may sound like an adult sort of race, the Memorial Day Weekend event also sponsors a race for kids. Read more in Annual Events–May, page 167.

BUCKY'S BUDDIES KIDS CLUB
www.buckysbuddies.com
Bucky Badger is the mascot of the University of Wisconsin Badgers and is always a big hit with the kids. Get those Badger fans started when they are young. Join Bucky's Buddies by logging on to Bucky's Badger Den. Fans receive newsletters, free general admission tickets to specially selected UW athletics events, and notification of upcoming events aimed at children. There are also a few simple games on the Web site.

CIRCUS WORLD MUSEUM
550 Water St., Baraboo
(608) 356-8341
www.circusworldmuseum.com
The Ringling Brothers Circus was born just north of Madison in Baraboo and this collection of historic buildings and museum exhibits commemorates the glory days. Besides the obvious interest kids have for the animals on-site and some of the colorful displays, they also have access to KidsWorld Circus. Twice a day this children's program lets kids star in their own circus acts. Inside the original circus elephant house, a ringmaster takes volunteers from the audience to don costumes and face paint and be part of the show. From the magic tricks to tiger kids jumping through hoops, each show is recorded and burned on DVDs, which are available for purchase soon afterward. Baraboo is about a 45-minute drive north on US 12 from Madison. Open daily from mid-May through most of Oct and then on weekdays for the rest of the year. Admission is about $7 for adults, half that for kids under 12 and free for those under 5.

> **i** Watch for the Kids' Expo, an annual event hosted in Nov at the Alliant Energy Center. See Annual Events, page 177, for more information.

DUCK SOUP CINEMA
Overture Center for the Arts
201 State St.
(608) 258-4141
www.overturecenter.com/community/duck-soup-cinema
It is remarkable to watch, in this age of attention deficit disorder and high-speed digitized this or that, as an old black-and-white silent film still

manages to reach a modern audience and tickle some funny bones. Scheduled several times each year are some old silver-screen classic works of the likes of Charlie Chaplin, Harold Lloyd, and Buster Keaton. An organist fires up the Grand Barton organ for accompaniment and sound effects, and an emcee introduces Vaudeville-style acts before the moving pictures start moving. Tickets are around $6 but half-price for kids 12 and under. All seats are reserved.

i When school is out for the summer watch for kids' movie series at the local movie theaters. These are very cheap or even free matinee showings of family friendly entertainment. Check Entertainment for a list of cinemas.

FAST FORWARD
4649 Verona Rd.
(608) 271-6222
www.fastforwardskate.com

It's remarkable that roller skating hasn't changed much over the years. Rent skates, skate to music, fall down on occasion. Besides the open skating, however, Fast Forward offers in-line skates and hockey as well. Admission prices are $4–7 per person depending on the time with a couple dollars more for skate rental. Birthday parties can be hosted here with pizza and ice-cream cake in a private party room plus of course a bit of skating.

LAKESIDE KIDS
Monona Terrace Community and Convention Center
1 John Nolen Dr.
(608) 261-4000
www.mononaterrace.com/community/all-programs

Lakeside Kids, a summertime children's program held on Wed mornings in June and July, is hosted at Monona Terrace and takes place on the rooftop. Entertainment is provided by local performers, from musicians and storytellers to yoga and martial arts instructors, and is moved inside the convention center when weather isn't cooperating. Events are intended to be fun, educational, and provide some

hands-on involvement aimed at children between ages four to eight. Free. See the Annual Events chapter, page 163, for Celebrating Youth!, an event hosted by the Monona Terrace in Jan.

i MSCR (Madison School and Community Recreation, www.mscr.org) often offers free pontoon boat and canoe rides from Tenney Park (1500 Sherman Ave.) in the summers. In the past this has been the fourth Sun of the month. No reservations necessary, just show up.

LITTLE AMERRICKA
700 East Main St., Marshall
(608) 655-3181
www.littleamerricka.com

"Twenty smiles" from Madison's east side, this small-town amusement park makes a nice day trip. The park's 29 attractions include gas-powered go-karts, minigolf, and an assortment of rides for various ages and heights. Some of the rides, such as the Whiskey River Railway are good for the entire family to enjoy. The schedule varies and it is always best to call or consult the Web site. Generally, Little Amerricka is open on weekends starting in late May, most (but not all) days in June, July, and Aug, and then back to weekends in Sept. The Pumpkin Train is the only ride operating on weekends in Oct. There is no general admission. Unlimited ride passes are sold to children based upon their height as some rides are not available to children under 36 or 42 inches. Individual tickets are available for minigolf and all rides including the go-karts. But some rides and attractions require multiple tickets and so the unlimited day pass is often a better deal. Concessions sell the usual carnival fare—hot dogs, burgers, popcorn, cotton candy, and frozen treats.

MADISON MALLARDS BASEBALL
2920 North Sherman Ave.
(608) 246-4277
www.mallardsbaseball.com

Remember when a trip to the ballgame was a family event? Major League ticket and vendor prices have made a trip to the stadium a serious investment. But the Mallards have brought the family out to the ballpark with affordable pricing, a convenient location, and parking, and with interactive fun. In between innings something is always going on, whether it's the antics of team mascot Maynard G. Mallard or a foot race around the bags for kids from the stands. Watch the game calendar for kids' days, sports clinics, and other promotions. The parking lot is perfect for a bit of pregame tailgating, and the vendors inside the park offer the usual assortment of delicious food. Birthday parties can be hosted with bleacher seats, hot dogs, soda, and cupcakes, and a visit from Maynard. Call the box office at least one week in advance if you are considering a birthday bash.

i Known as the Waterpark Capital of the World, kids in the know perk up at the mention of Wisconsin Dells. The 21 water parks—three of them outdoors, the rest indoors—are just part of the total Dells experience. Other theme parks, go-kart tracks, minigolf courses, and attractions abound. Educational and natural attractions are also numerous from wildlife preserves and petting zoos to boat tours and hiking. To find out more, look in the Day Trips chapter.

SCHWOEGLER'S PARK TOWNE LANES .
444 Grand Canyon Dr.
(608) 833-7272
www.schwoegler.com
With 36 lanes and bumper bowling capabilities, Schwoegler's makes a good outing. Bowling birthday parties are always popular and there are a variety of packages available, clearly priced, which offer bowling, a party room, refreshments, pizza, and a bowling pin for the birthday child. Open daily from 9 a.m.

ULTRAZONE
680 Grand Canyon Dr.
(608) 833-8880
www.playlasertag.com

Sledding

The hill at **Heistand Park** on the east side at 4302 Milwaukee St. is quite nice for sledding offering a long run, a bit of steepness, and good open space at the bottom. However, the big daddy of Madison's park hills is at **Elver Park** at 1250 McKenna Blvd. The hill is wide and long and gets plenty of use, which can make it pretty fast as well. Because there is also ice-skating, hockey, and cross-country skiing here, park patrons also have access to a shelter house.

Be careful of other sledders and look ahead to see what's at the bottom of the hill where you're heading. Don't linger at the bottom of the hill, but make way for the next sled. Always go up the side of the hill and not up the middle of the run.

Laser tag came on the scene in the 1980s with rather pricey game units that could only be fun if all the kids in the neighborhood also had them. The game seemed like a flash in the pan. But since 1995 Ultrazone has been quite successful keeping the sport alive and its popularity with kids is notable. Much less painful and messy than paintball it is a laser-based shoot-em-up version akin to capture the flag where teams of friends or often strangers work together to take out the enemy and their bases. Each 15-minute game costs about $7.50 with discounts for buying several games at once. Ultrazone specializes in birthday parties. Let the kids run around here for a while and sit back and let Ultrazone do the planning. The Web site even offers downloadable invitations. Decorations, pizza, soft drinks, a cake, and two games in the arena are all included in

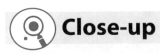 **Close-up**

Fall Fun

Summer ends and the kids go back to school, but activities in and around Madison are never better than in the fall. Consider the options as the leaves turn and the Halloween decorations go up. From apple picking to trick or treating, the autumn fun has begun. Who would have imagined there are over 600 corn mazes in the United States and Canada each fall? Thankfully there is a directory for them: www.cornmazedir.com. Another great Web site, www.pumpkin patchesandmore.org, tracks apple and pumpkin picking by county in Wisconsin. (Madison is in Dane County.) As the field corn dries up, the corn mazes appear. Area farms set up labyrinths that are open to the public often up until around Halloween.

Dr. S. Cary's Corn Maze & Pumpkin Patch
Jellystone Park of Fort Atkinson
N551 Wishing Well Dr., Fort Atkinson
(920) 568-4100
www.drscaryshauntedhouse.com

Hit the corn mazes by day or the haunted house by night. Take a pumpkin home or paint one on-site. Admission is around $12 for the haunted house. The mazes are cheaper and family rates are available.

Eplegaarden Orchard
2273 Fitchburg Rd., Fitchburg
(608) 845-5966
www.eplegaarden.com

Just south of Madison, the Norwegian-themed farm offers pick-your-own apples, raspberries, and pumpkins as well as hayrides, farm animals, and a haunted barn. The fun lasts until about Thanksgiving.

Schuster's Playtime Farm
1326 Hwy. 12/18, Deerfield
(608) 764-8488
www.schustersplaytimefarm.com

The farm is open in spring, summer, and fall for tours, hayrides, and meeting farm animals up close and personal. The corn maze in the fall runs through Oct. You can choose to simply visit the barnyard, take a hayride, or explore one of the corn mazes. Admission fees start at a few dollars and head up to $10, depending on activities included.

Treinen Farm Corn Maze and Pumpkin Patch
W12420 Hwy. 60, Lodi
(608) 592-3481
www.treinenfarm.com

This 15-acre corn maze is the largest in the state and located just 20 miles north of Madison. With miles of trails it is nothing to sneeze at—unless you have hayfever. See the aerial shots of the mazes and be a-mazed. A horse-drawn hay wagon hauls guests to the pumpkin patch to choose their future jack-o-lanterns or pumpkin pies. Admission is charged separately for the patch or the maze with a discount for doing both. You can also skip the pumpkins and just take the hayride. Open Aug through mid-Nov.

the birthday package. Ultrazone is open daily from mid-June to Sept, but then closed for private parties on Mon and open with shortened hours from Sept until the next summer. Some may prefer to go on weeknights when the place is not as busy.

i Watch for Ultrazone laser tag free games for good grades specials. Students bring in report cards for game credits.

VITENSE GOLFLAND
5501 Schroeder Rd.
(608) 271-1411
www.vitense.com

Golfland offers much more than the name implies and some may want to make a day of the place. That's fine because Golfland offers day rates that include time with all of the activities. On-site are batting cages with both hardballs and softballs

HALLOWEEN

State Street has become the center of a growing Halloween celebration that attracts costumed revelers from around the country. In the past, these events ended on sour notes in the wee hours of the mornings as drunken celebrants confronted police when it was time to go home. The organizers and the City of Madison law enforcement have a much better handle on things these days, and rather than banning it altogether, the event has been expanded to include concerts and entertainment at various locations along the length of State Street. Even during the troubled years, the early evening hours were enjoyable for whole families who came downtown—with or without costume—to stroll up and down the street, taking photos of the best and most memorable costumes. Be aware, however, that some may find certain costumes a bit risqué for youthful eyes. Nothing illegal, but just saying.

Downtown Madison Family Trick or Treat
State Street & the Capitol Square
(608) 266-4711
www.visitdowntownmadison.com
www.cityofmadison.com/parks/hayrides
.html

During Halloween participating businesses in downtown Madison—on State Street and around the Capitol Square—offer trick or treating for children 12 and under during the business day. Shops are marked with flyers in their storefront windows and a list of all who are participating can be picked up at any one of the stores themselves or at the Madison Children's Museum at 100 North Hamilton Street. Madison Parks offers Trick or Treat Hay Rides on the Capitol Square at this time as well. The trick or treating is free but there's a nominal fee for each person getting on the hay ride.

Halloween at the Zoo
Henry Vilas Zoo
702 South Randall Ave.
(608) 266-4732
www.vilaszoo.org

Halloween at the Zoo is open to the public and offers free Trick-or-Treating, a Fun House, and live music in the zoo's Education Pavilion. The event gives parents some relief from door-to-door concerns and since 1987, when the event was first held, it has raised hundreds of thousands of dollars to support the Henry Vilas Zoo.

Mallatt Pharmacy and Costume
3506 Monroe St.
(608) 238-3106 or (877) 687-5287 (ext. 7)
www.mallatts.com

Get a bottle of wine for the adults, your child's amoxicillin for the ear infection, mail a few letters, and rent the Halloween costumes. The 1941 corner drugstore has been selling costumes since the 1980s. For masks, hats, theatrical makeup, prosthetics, fangs, tails, wigs, and even whole gorilla suits, Mallatts has the full collection. Expert advice is also readily available.

and pitching at a variety of speeds. Helmets and bats are provided. Bring swimsuits if you want to play Water Wars. Participants use rubber tubes and funnels as giant slingshots to launch water balloons at opponents in an aluminum cage 40 feet away. Water balloons are purchased by the bucket. Climb the five different routes of the 24-foot rock wall, or play HiBall, a trampoline game akin to basketball and volleyball where

players bounce in the air while trying to shoot baskets over the head of their opponents.

Vitense's minigolf has some fun obstacles and challenges and can be played year-round. Two 18-hole courses, themed as Wisconsin and California, are located outside, while another 18-hole course featuring miniaturized Madison landmarks is inside the main building. An arcade there offers a variety of games as well. For the older kids—and really, how old was Tiger Woods?—golf lessons are available. A superb driving range and a nine-hole par-3 course lighted for night play are on the property. When the kids get hungry, the clubhouse's Green Tree Grill menu has children's portions of various items such as mini-corn dogs, grilled cheese, chicken tenders, and burgers with sides of fries and apple sauce. Smoothies, slushies, and ice cream are also offered. Vitense is located just south of the Beltline Highway at Schroeder Road and Whitney Way and is open daily. Discounts for groups of 10 or more are available. Golfland does birthday parties.

NATURE STUFF

**ALDO LEOPOLD NATURE CENTER—
EDNA TAYLOR CONSERVATION PARK
300 Femrite Dr., Monona
(608) 221-0404
www.naturenet.com**
Named for the famous Wisconsin conservationist, the center itself exemplifies green building practices by using recycled and natural materials and renewable energy systems. On either side of the property are local conservation parks with hiking trails. The center overlooks a pond often occupied by Canada geese, prairie restoration, and its own Web of short trails. The award-winning Leopold Interpretive Trail takes hikers through habitats native to Wisconsin and offers in-depth signage with thought-provoking questions. Look for the 200-year old hickory tree on-site. The center is open weekdays during business hours, but the trails are open from sunrise to sunset. Pets are not allowed in the park. Tours and programs are by appointment only so call the center (608) 221-4038 or register online to either join one or in some cases get on a waiting list. Most of the events have fees per person or per family and members of the nature center receive discounts. Adjoining the nature center to the east is the 56-acre Edna Taylor conservation park that contains 1.3 miles of trails through oak savanna, forest, meadows, and restored wetlands and includes a bit of boardwalk through the cattails

therein. It's a lovely place to spot some wildlife and wildflowers. Only the forest trails are partly shaded otherwise expect to use sunscreen.

**CAPITOL TREE TREK
State Capitol
2 East Main St.
(608) 266-0382
www.wisconsin.gov**
A tour of the State Capitol is a common school field trip in Wisconsin but can be done on your own with free daily tours. But another great activity that combines an educational/naturalist element with an outdoor treasure hunt activity is the Capitol Tree Trek. There are 30 different species of trees on the Capitol grounds, and a map of them can be found at the information desk on the 1st floor under the dome. The back of the map has line drawings of the different leaves of these trees. Certain bur oaks are original to the property and estimated to be more than 150 years old. The map and leaf key may also be downloaded from the Department of Natural Resources Web site above.

**HENRY VILAS ZOO
702 South Randall Ave.
(608) 266-4732
www.vilaszoo.org**
This is Madison's best free attraction for families. Enjoy a petting zoo, a conservation carousel, and an electric zoo train that circles the grounds. The gift shop sells an abundance of educational items and toys such as stuffed animals. Parking is right outside the zoo entrance on either end. The adjoining Vilas Park offers some shaded picnic areas and pavilions, perfect for a post-zoo visit picnic. Just outside the zoo is also Lake Wingra and a small sandy beach often with a lifeguard. Also nearby is the University of Wisconsin Arboretum with walking trails through forest and prairie and a visitor center with abundant information.

**OLBRICH BOTANICAL GARDENS
3330 Atwood Ave.
(608) 246-4718
www.olbrich.org**

The gardens make for a lovely stroll all by themselves, but the center also offers a variety of workshops and events such as a gardening class for kids and Blooming Butterflies, the last half of July and beginning of Aug, when the butterflies leave their cocoons in the Bolz Conservatory.

SMART STUFF

MADISON CHILDREN'S MUSEUM
100 North Hamilton St.
(608) 256-6445
www.madisonchildrensmuseum.org
In 2007, the museum was rated as one of the top 20 in the country by *Grand Magazine*. This was before it moved to its new digs. As of Aug 2010, the new and improved Children's Museum has three times the amount of space it had before, with room to expand even more, and occupies an entire city block touching on the Capitol Square. The exhibits have been redesigned and on-site parking has been added. Parents and their children can participate in more educational programs and see performances. Check out the interactive water vortex in the welcome center and put a ball inside to watch it whirl. A special area is reserved for the smallest of the bunch, the five and under crowd, and shows bridges and themed huts all well lighted and colored. An art studio and Possible-opolis have an interactive paint wall and a loom on the wall. The LEED-certified, environmentally responsible building also has a rooftop terrace which affords a Capitol view, gardening opportunities, and a space for evening events. This will be open for all seasons. The museum aims at kids 12 and under. A small cafe is on site for snacks and the building is wheelchair accessible. There is an admission fee. Open daily.

Educational at the UW

One doesn't need to be old enough for college to get some education at the University of Wisconsin. Several departments at the UW offer outreach programming especially aimed at children. The small departmental museums are great for curious little minds and some offer hands-on exhibits.

L. R. INGERSOLL PHYSICS MUSEUM
University of Wisconsin
2130 Chamberlin Hall
1150 University Ave.
(608) 262-3898
www.physics.wisc.edu/museum
The exhibits here are begging to be touched, and in doing so kids get a chance to learn the basic concepts of physics. Particle Physics Pinball and Earthquake Simulator sound as much like games as they do educational contraptions. Open weekdays. Free.

MADISON GEOLOGY MUSEUM
University of Wisconsin
1215 West Dayton St.
(608) 262-2399
www.geology.wisc.edu
Full-size models and castings of various dinosaurs and Ice Age mammals, including a mastodon and the skull of a Tyrannosaurus rex, are sure to impress children. The mock-up of a limestone cave and a black light exhibit are part of the interactive educational experience. The museum's self-guided tour booklet contains a variety of information about the exhibits as well as Geo Explorer activities aimed at engaging children. This booklet is available on the Web site and is best downloaded so that museum visitors can make notes and write down answers to trivia and treasure-hunt-style questions. Free admission. Closed Sun.

UNIVERSITY OF WISCONSIN–DAIRY CATTLE CENTER
1815 Linden Dr.
(608) 262-2271
www.dysci.wisc.edu/facility/dcc.htm
As this is the Dairy State, a visit to see the cows at the University of Wisconsin seems appropriate. Milk is an important product in Wisconsin, and the University has a long history of making advances in dairy technology. Parents and their children can watch and learn as the approximately 90 cows of the research dairy herd are milked each day at 4:30 p.m.

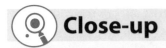 # Close-up

Nature Passports and Wisconsin Explorers Booklets

There's nothing quite like a treasure hunt or a checklist. Two local programs offer the find-and-seek experience with an educational/naturalist element to them. Both programs offer free booklets or passports that a child can take to nearby parks and nature centers.

Parents can get their kids involved with some educational exploration of the wonderful green world around Madison and the rest of the state.

THE NATURE PASSPORT

Nature Passport is a project of Nature Net: the Environmental Learning Network. This affiliation of nature centers around Southern Wisconsin is dedicated to providing good (and fun) educational experiences for teachers and families. The passport program was organized by the Aldo Leopold Nature Center (see above). Ringo Raccoon is your guide through the natural world of Madison. The passports are a means for children and their parents to share in the discovery of outdoor exploration and offer educational opportunities while encouraging excitement for the natural world. Users can write, draw, and sketch what they see and learn during each visit to a nature center. The Nature Passports are free and available at participating sites from Memorial Day through Labor Day. They may also be ordered online at www.naturenet.com. Spanish and Hmong versions are available. Look for the passports in Madison at the Aldo Leopold Nature Center, Cherokee Marsh, Henry Vilas Zoo, Lussier Family Heritage Center, Madison Children's Museum, Olbrich Botanical Gardens, the University of Wisconsin Arboretum (Visitor Center), and the UW Geology Museum. Outside of the city, pick them up at the Aldo Leopold Foundation or International Crane Foundation in Baraboo, the MacKenzie Environmental Center in Poynette, or Bethel Horizons near Governor Dodge State Park just north of Dodgeville.

WISCONSIN EXPLORERS

The state park system in Wisconsin is phenomenal. No matter where you are, several parks are always just a short drive away and home to a plethora of animals and plants. Park rangers are

UNIVERSITY OF WISCONSIN–SPACE PLACE
University of Wisconsin
2300 South Park St.
(608) 262-4779
www.spaceplace.wisc.edu
The UW Space Place isn't on campus but rather located on South Park Street in the Villager Mall just north of the Beltline Highway. This is the public outreach and education center for the UW astronomy department and as such involves children with activities, demonstrations, presentations, and lectures by faculty and staff from that department. Exhibits include a gravity well, an explanation of how the seasons work, and comparison information about our solar system. Some of the instruments on display have been on space flights. Exhibits also feature projects that the UW has worked on and is working on, such as the world's largest telescope being built at the South Pole or images from the Spitzer Space Telescope. Local schools often take field trips here. Watch for children's workshops, aimed at children 6–10, on Sat mornings at 10 a.m. The center is open by appointment only or during scheduled events.

SPLISH SPLASH

CRAWDADDY COVE WATERPARK
Madison Holiday Inn Hotel and Suites
1109 Fourier Dr.
(608) 826-0500
www.wiscohotels.com/water-parks.php

helpful and informative, have a passion for what they are doing, and understand the importance of preserving our parks and making them pleasant destinations for everyone, especially families. The next time you visit a state park, forest, trail, or recreation area, ask for a free Wisconsin Explorers booklet. These booklets engage young people with scavenger hunts, arts and crafts, games, and a multitude of hikes and educational nature activities. (Participating children were once known as Junior Rangers but since 2009 the program is called Wisconsin Explorers.) Kids record their observations and experiences in these nature journals and can be rewarded for their efforts. Children can earn collectible patches by completing booklet requirements. The explorer books come at three levels: for ages three to five, six to eight, and nine and older. The booklets are free and available at participating state parks. Upon completing the booklet's checklist, kids (or their parents) can turn in an evaluation sheet to the park office in person or by mail and receive the commemorative patch. For more information visit www.dnr.state.wi.us/org/land/parks/interp/we or call (715) 365-8966.

The closest participating parks to Madison are:

Blue Mound State Park
4350 Mounds Park Rd., Blue Mounds
(608) 437-5711

Devil's Lake State Park
S5975 Park Rd., Baraboo
(608) 356-8301

Governor Dodge State Park
4175 Hwy. 23 North, Dodgeville
(608) 935-2315

Governor Nelson State Park
5140 County Hwy. M, Waunakee
(608) 831-3005

Lake Kegonsa State Park
2405 Door Creek Rd., Stoughton
(608) 873-9695

Mirror Lake State Park
E10320 Fern Dell Rd., Baraboo
(608) 254-2333

New Glarus Woods State Park
W5446 County Rd. NN, New Glarus
(608) 527-2335

Rocky Arbor State Park
US Hwys. 12/16, Wisconsin Dells
(608) 254-8001 or (608) 254-2333

For wet fun out of the sun this Louisiana bayou themed water park fits the bill. A large shrimp boat and a 55-foot open slide are the main attractions and sit amid a kiddie pool with geysers, shooting fountains, and an activity pool with basketball hoops. A game room and snack bar are also on-site. Holiday Inn guests receive five wristbands for water park admission with each room booked. This indoor water park is not just for guests though guests do have quick and intermittent access for a whole day and the next morning. Day passes for nonguests are also available from Sun through Thurs but are subject to availability. The park is open year-round so can be a good option on rainy summer days as much as freezing winter ones. A 48-inch height minimum is enforced for the water slide, and all children must be accompanied by an adult although there are lifeguards on duty. There are changing facilities but no storage lockers; guests simply leave valuables in their rooms or where they can see them. Children two and under play for free, while children 3 to 12 pay around $10, and anyone older pays about $15.

i Crawdaddy Cove Waterpark offers group discounts and might make a good destination for a birthday or other party.

GOODMAN POOL
325 Olin Ave.
(608) 264-9292
www.cityofmadison.com/parks/pool

Madison long talked about a need for a public pool. With a tremendous gift from Irwin A. and Robert D. Goodman and the cooperation of the city and many citizens from all walks of life, this pool came to fruition in 2006. With room for 1,000, two waterslides, diving boards, and an eight-lane lap area it's a beauty. Toddlers and other small children have shallow areas and there are also concessions, a sandy play area, changing rooms, deck chairs, umbrella tables, and shade structures. The pool is open daily for the summer. Daily and seasonal passes are available for children, adults, and whole families, and Madison residents are charged a slightly lower rate. Swimming lessons, using the American Red Cross Learn to Swim program, are also offered. For questions about lessons, call (608) 266-4711. The pool's competitive swim team, the Sharks, is open to Madison kids six years and older who have had swimming lessons and are comfortable swimming at least two lengths of the pool. Swimmers get expert coaching to improve swim strokes and racing techniques and then compete in swim meets throughout the summer.

SUN PRAIRIE AQUATIC CENTER
920 Linnerud Dr., Sun Prairie
(608) 837-7433
www.cityofsunprairie.com

The aquatic center offers a zero-depth entry pool with a 210-foot water slide, fountains, diving boards, and a sand volleyball pit on the side. Admission is open to the public and costs $3.50. Kids can bring pool toys and floatation devices on certain evenings of the week. Check with the center for the schedule. All children under eight years of age must be accompanied by someone 16 or older.

WALTER R. BAUMAN OUTDOOR AQUATIC CENTER
2400 Park Lawn Place
(608) 836-3450
www.middletonrec.org

This outdoor facility has a zero-depth pool entrance, an eight-lane competition pool, and a diving area. Two 134-foot waterslides, interactive water play equipment, a sandy playground, and concessions make this more than just a swimming pool. Capacity here is 724 people. The pool is open to the public for a nominal fee. Middleton residents and Middleton-Cross Plains School District residents receive discounts. Seasonal passes are available. Times are set aside for swimming and diving lessons, adult swims, and swim/dive team events and practice. The pool opens for the summer season around mid-June and closes around the end of Aug/beginning of Sept.

i Check the Recreation and Parks section for beaches in Madison!

TASTY STUFF

BEAN SPROUTS CAFÉ
6719 Frank Lloyd Wright Ave.
Suite 101, Middleton
(608) 826-6986
www.beansproutscafe.com

Imagine a kids' snack place and cafe where nothing is fried and no soda pop is served. With all the junk food out there aimed at kids, Bean Sprouts comes as a welcome relief for parents trying to "trick" their kids into eating healthy. The menu offers gluten-free, dairy-free, and casein-free options. The standard menu lists healthy drinks such as juice spritzers, smoothies, and soy milk; uncommon appetizers such as fruit salsa with baked cinnamon chips or hummus with broccoli; and creative sandwiches, wraps, and pastas that all come with one healthy side. (No french fries!) Meals are designed for the smaller tummy but portions come in larger adult sizes as well for a couple bucks more. This is the only restaurant in the country to make its own organic baby food. Food can be ordered ahead for carry-out and they'll even bring it out to your car when you pull up to spare you the unpacking and repacking of the kids. The property itself is created with the smaller set in mind: tables without sharp edges, a play area, a stepping stool at the front counter to enable the pint-size to order like the full-size do. There is even a kid-size toilet in the family bathroom. The cafe hosts birthday parties, tea parties, and story times, and cooking classes for kids and parents encourage patrons to take some of the food wisdom home with them. Open daily.

CAFÉ LA BELLITALIA
1026 North Sherman Ave.
(608) 243-1200
www.cafelabellitalia.com
This lovely little Sicilian restaurant features a family menu, serving up spaghetti and meatballs or ravioli for a family of four for a very reasonable price. The pizza is also quite nice. (See more under Restaurants–Italian page 58.)

ELLA'S DELI AND ICE CREAM PARLOR
2902 East Washington Ave.
(608) 241-5291
www.ellas-deli.com
The decorations in this classic deli are in constant motion and the adults may be as entranced with them as the kids. A separate menu aims toward kid-size portions with a variety of healthy choices such as soups and vegetable sides, as well as the usual hits like hot dogs, PB&Js, and chicken strips. Ice cream anyone? There's even a listing of spoon-size portions for the one and under crowd such as apple sauce, peas, and mandarin oranges. (See more under Restaurants–Delis and Sandwiches page 55.)

HUBBARD AVENUE DINER
7445 Hubbard Ave., Middleton
(608) 831-6800
www.foodfightinc.com/hubbard.htm
The diner is a nice family-friendly environment and has a decent kids' menu. Service is good and if the kids like pies, this is the place to be. The fresh-baked pies are legendary. (See more under Restaurants–Breakfast Joints page 47.)

SHOPPING

CAPITOL KIDS
8 South Carroll St.
(608) 280-0744
www.capitolkids.com
With a play area in the middle of the store, this is downtown's best place to shop for the kids

while the kids are in tow. Locally owned, Capitol Kids offers an outstanding selection of games, books, toys, and clothes. One-hour street parking is limited on the square. The Capitol Square South parking ramp is just over a block away on the corner of Main and Fairchild Streets. A visit here is combined nicely with a visit to the Sat morning farmers' market across the street or the Children's Museum, also on the square. Open daily.

> **i** Got some clothes the kids have grown out of? Or maybe you're looking for some hand-me-downs for a child growing too fast to keep up with? Watch for Madison's Semiannual Half-Pint Resale event. Parents can buy affordable resale clothing or sell some on consignment for a little extra cash. (halfpintresale@gmail.com, http://halfpintresale.googlepages.com)

PLAYTHINGS TOY STORE IN HILLDALE
Hilldale Shopping Center
702 North Midvale Blvd.
(608) 233-2124
www.playthingstoystore.com
Their motto is "Entertain, educate, and fascinate." Since 1986 this locally owned specialty toy store has been introducing the Madison community and their children to toys that stimulate the young mind. Items range from games and books to mobiles and art projects and ages served are from infants to 12 year olds. Staff is involved in choosing what is stocked and quite knowledgeable about this market. The staff post their recommendations online and are happy to share their ideas in person as well.

WILD CHILD INC.
1813 Monroe St.
(608) 251-6445
www.wildchildclothes.com
In 1981, Renee West opened the original Wild Child store on East Johnson Street. Her partner Bill West joined her (and she has had two more boys) and moved into the near west side location on Monroe Street just down the road from the stadium. The trademark Wild Child clothes are

mix-and-match with tops, bottoms, hats, dresses, and accessories and can be personalized in-store. The fabrics use natural fibers, often organic cotton, and offer a wonderful variety of colors. Sizes range from infant to toddlers. The mission of Wild Child is to provide quality natural clothing without resorting to sweat-shop labor. If you like to buy American, this is a good place to patronize for clothes. Toys, games, and accessories such as diaper bags are also for sale. Toys are often from Canada or Europe. Open daily. Wheelchair accessible. Street parking is metered until 6 p.m. or you can park on a side street.

STORY TIMES

BARNES AND NOBLE BOOKSELLERS EAST
1 East Towne Mall
(608) 241-4695
www.bn.com (search on Madison, WI)
The bookstore has a great selection of children's books, but also hosts a series of events. Story time takes place on Mon at 10:30 a.m. year-round. Weekend story times are offered occasionally and typically center around themes or holidays such as Halloween and Thanksgiving. A costumed character visits once a month to entertain the kids and grant photo opportunities. Other activities join the mix in summer and for special occasions; for example, there's a bilingual story time for Hispanic Heritage Month. More specific information is available on the Web site. Free.

i Watch for Reid Miller's Paw Paw Puppet Theater. Miller, a freelance storyteller, appears from time to time at various local establishments including Java Cat Coffee (www.javacatmadison.com) on the east side. Check his Web site (www.myspace.com/reidmillershow) for where to see him next.

BARNES AND NOBLE BOOKSELLERS WEST
7433 Mineral Point Rd.
(608) 827-0809
www.bn.com (search on Madison, WI)

The Madison Public Library System

For its wealth of activities, events, and resources aimed at children the Madison Public Library really can't be beat, and the only plastic you need to pull out for it is a library card. Check your local library branch for scheduled story times, presentations, and other entertainment. A list of upcoming events can be seen on the online calendar at www.madisonpubliclibrary.org/calendar. For the busy parent who perhaps wants a couple of children's books or a DVD of the latest Disney film, the library system offers online access to the catalog. Go to www.linkcat.info to search for items and then place them on hold for pick up. If the closest branch does not offer a particular item that you are looking for, you can mark it for pick up at your preferred branch; wherever that book or CD is located in the system—across town, out in Verona, or even as far north as Wisconsin Rapids—a librarian has it shipped to the waiting location. This can take as little as a day or two if the item isn't already checked out, otherwise the hold is put on a waiting list. The libraries all provide free wireless Internet connection and a number of computers that can be reserved. The various free databases within the system are gold for the young student on a research project. Having a knowledgeable librarian's guidance can be a lot more focused, productive, and of course personal than time on Google. For more info, check out www.madison publiclibrary.org.

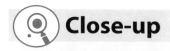

Close-up

Summer Camps

School is out and unless your child is now enrolled in swim lessons, soccer league, piano lessons, yoga, and taekwondo every week, he or she probably has some free time. Summer camps are wonderful opportunities for kids to meet new friends, experience new activities, and have some fun while freeing up a parent's schedule a bit. **Madison School and Community Recreation (MSCR)** has a variety of good programs year-round but particularly in the summer (www.mscr.org). Also look for nature-based programs organized by the **Aldo Leopold Nature Center**.

SUMMER DAY CAMPS AND AFTER SCHOOL PROGRAMS

Wisconsin Youth Company
(608) 276-9782
www.wisconsinyouthcompany.org

Since 1974, the nonprofit Wisconsin Youth Company has served Dane County by organizing a variety of fun and educational events and programs. Its After School program (www.afterschoolwi.org) hosts Summer Day Camps, weeklong professionally supervised camps for children in one of two age groups: 5 to 7, and 8 to 12. With over 70 themes and specialties, choices are numerous and the weekly fee is around $150. An inexpensive care program is available both before and after the camp hours making the 9 a.m. to 4 p.m. program hours more convenient for working parents. The school-year program offers supervised activity at various area schools both before and after the school day. Locations total 24 with several in Madison as well as some in surrounding communities Middleton, Mount Horeb, Stoughton, Verona, and Waunakee. Watch for January's annual Celebrating Youth! event as well. Check out the Wisconsin Youth Company Web site for more detailed information on programs and links for kids.

Earth Focus Day Camp
University of Wisconsin Arboretum
1207 Seminole Hwy.
(608) 263-7888
http://uwarboretum.org

Aimed at children aged 3 to 14, this ecological programming has been offered for close to 20 years now. Kids get hands on experience with native plants and animals and learn about the different habitats of Wisconsin. Attendees learn about their potential impact on the world around them. There are three programs, each serving a different age group. The camps are offered from about mid-June to mid-Aug. Registration deadlines are two weeks before the selected camp date.

Summer on Prairie Farm
Kids Express Learning Center
3276 High Point Rd.
(608) 845-3245
www.kidsexpress.com

The center operates year-round with all-day and after-school programming but also operates a summer program. Located on an 8-acre mini-farm just south of Elver Park on Madison's southwest side, the camp offers a whole variety of learning and play opportunities. The grounds have a wooded playground, and kids enjoy arts and crafts, nature study, and gardening activities as well as up-close experiences with a variety of domesticated animals such as llamas, sheep, goats, and birds. Lead teachers have degrees in early childhood development and teach a variety of subject areas from literature and math to music and art. Enrollment for new students is in Feb each year and there may be a waiting list. The program accepts children ages six weeks through grade 3.

YMCA of Dane County
www.ymcadanecounty.org

For children from ages 2 to 14 the YMCA camps provide a wide range of activities from swimming and other sports to arts and crafts sessions and nature/environmental programming. Club Wannago and Discovery Day Camp are full-day experiences and offer different themes each week throughout the summer. Locations serve the Madison area: east, north, and northeast. Registration starts in March, and it's a good idea to apply early as these programs are quite popular.

Much like the east side location, this bookstore, which is considerably larger, also offers story times. So as not to conflict with the east side events, these are held on Tues and Thurs at 10:30 a.m. Saturdays frequently offer either storytelling or costumed characters. Free.

BORDERS BOOKSTORE EAST
2173 Zeier Rd.
(608) 240-0080

BORDERS BOOKSTORE WEST
3750 University Ave.
(608) 232-2600
www.borders.com
Both Borders locations offer regular story times for the kids. Check with each location for its specific schedule and upcoming kids' events. These activities are free.

THE UNIVERSITY BOOKSTORE
Hilldale Mall
702 North Midvale Blvd.
(608) 238-8455
www.uwbookstore.com
Watch for weekly story times aimed at children two to five years old. The stories are told in the bookstore's basement level where there is also a sizeable children's book section. The events are free.

ANNUAL EVENTS

It seems something is always going on in Madison. Summer is like one continuous moveable feast of neighborhood festivals, expos, musical extravaganzas, and Capitol Square events. And winter be damned; when the snow flies Madisonians go outside and have festivals anyway, and in the past have flown kites on a frozen lake.

Annual events include big sporting challenges such as the Ironman Triathlon and Madison Marathon, foodie fests such as The Taste of Madison, or musical celebrations such as Capital City Jazz Fest or the World Music Fest. Be sure not to miss the more unusual moments as well such as the Wisconsin Cow Chip Throw in nearby Prairie du Sac or Brat Fest, an incredible weekendlong gorging of the wurst kind. Wash that down at one of the nation's best beer fests, August's Great Taste of the Midwest. Some events become weekly during the summer or between Memorial Day and Labor Day. Often these relate to concert series and a round-up of them is in this chapter's Close-up.

The calendar in some cases is a bit loose here. Certain events repeat like clockwork on a designated date or weekend each year while others may not be so predictable. The Madison Marathon is pretty much always going to be Memorial Day Weekend, while an annual music festival might be "sometime in August" or switch months altogether due to conflicting events, changes in sponsorship, or any number of reasons. So it is always good to look ahead and double check dates and ticket availability. For the events held at the Alliant Energy Center it is important to note that parking is on the center's grounds and in most cases incurs a fee of a few dollars. In cases where it is free, this is noted in the listing.

JANUARY

CELEBRATING YOUTH!
Monona Terrace Community and Convention Center
One John Nolen Dr.
(608) 276-9782, ext. 23
www.celebratingyouth.org
This family-friendly celebration partly sponsored by Dane County's Wisconsin Youth Company (www.wisconsinyouthcompany.org) includes youth stage performances as well as an art exhibit, hands-on activity stations, and exhibitors with resources for youth and families. A nominal donation of around $1–2 is recommended.

WEDDING PLANNER & GUIDE BRIDAL SHOW
Alliant Energy Center
1919 Alliant Energy Center Way
(608) 233-7001
www.wedplan.com

This is the big event for all things wedding related and exhibitors include formal wear stores, bakeries, jewelers, florists, travel agents, music providers, and more. Tickets are around $10 and can be bought at the door or in advance for a discount.

FEBRUARY

BOCKFEST
Capital Brewery and Bier Garten
7734 Terrace Ave., Middleton
(608) 836-7100
www.capital-brewery.com
The last Sat in Feb, beer fans don their mittens and mufflers and head to a beer garden for the day no matter what the temperature is. This is the release of Capital's Blonde Doppelbock, and patrons line up for T-shirts and special drinking mugs. Live music entertains the crowd, and the event's climax is when Brewmaster Kirby Nelson

gets up on the roof of the brewery and throws mildly explosive smoked chub (fish) into the crowd below. Anyone recovering an intact fish head is rewarded with a beer. Admission is free but the beer isn't.

MAD CITY MODEL RAILROAD SHOW
Alliant Energy Center
1919 Alliant Energy Center Way
(608) 836-1747
www.alliantenergycenter.com
Figure this: over 90,000 square feet of laid out miniature scenery with trains of several different scales meandering through them. A train lover's dream. In addition to the classic trains hundreds of tables exhibit collectibles, books, art, apparel, and tools for the hobby. Prizes are given out through the event. Tickets are around $10 per day for the two-day event.

MADISON FISHING EXPO
www.madfishexpo.com
First held in 1985, this is the largest show of its kind in the Midwest with attendees numbering more than 20,000 over the course of its three days. Shop for tackle, fishing trips, and boats. A variety of kids' activities includes a trout fishing pond. Tickets are sold at the door, and parking at the Alliant Energy Center lots exacts a fee as well. Watch for the fest in late Feb.

MADISON RV AND CAMPER SHOW AND SALE
Alliant Energy Center
1919 Alliant Energy Center Way
(608) 222-1507
www.madisonrvshow.com
Local RV dealers come together to show the very latest vehicles and features for living on the road. The show boasts of having over 1 mile of RVs and campers. Tickets for the three-day event are around $8 plus parking. Children enter free with a paying adult.

MADISON WINTER FESTIVAL
Capitol Square
www.winter-fest.com

This snowy event began in 2004 as a cross-country skiing sprint race up around the Capitol. The Square becomes the site of snow sculptures, cross-country skiing, snowboarding, and snow-shoeing events for an entire weekend. Biking and a frosty run/walk are also on the event list as is speed-skating on Lake Monona. This is typically the only chance one gets to go cross-country skiing on the street around the Capitol. Local businesses and museums host special events as well and make good places to warm up a bit. Watch for this in Feb but keep an eye on Jan each year as well.

i For several years Madison hosted an event called Kites in Ice, where kite flyers would brave the winter chill and get out on the frozen lake ice to send color into the sky on a string. The event was extremely popular, but funding it apparently was not as much. Considering the Madison independent spirit, a reappearance of this event, possibly coinciding with Madison Winter Festival, should not be ruled out. Check local listings.

MIDWEST GARDEN EXPO
Alliant Energy Center
1919 Alliant Energy Center Way
(608) 262-5256 or (800) 253-1158
www.wpt.org/gardenexpo
Wisconsin Public Television and the University of Wisconsin Extension/Cooperative Extension Horticulture Team put together this superb three-day expo of seminars, hands-on workshops, and demonstrations for gardening, lawn care, and landscaping. Over 400 exhibitors are on hand and attendees number close to 20,000. Tickets are under $10 and discounts are available for advanced purchase or multiday entry. Children 12 and under enter free.

ORCHID QUEST
Alliant Energy Center
1919 Alliant Energy Center Way
(608) 267-3976
www.orchidguild.org

This dazzling display of flowers is a welcome event in the heart of winter. Presented by Orchid Growers' Guild of Madison, the two-day event features orchids from all over the world and presentations about orchids and how to grow them. Tickets are around $6 and about half that more for both days.

ZOR SHRINE CIRCUS
Alliant Energy Center.
1919 Alliant Energy Center Way
(608) 256-0281
www.shrinecircusinfo.com
An annual Madison tradition, the family-owned three-ring circus delights crowds with elephants, acrobats, tigers, and the usual clowns. Tickets are general admission with a slight extra charge for reserved seats, but all are around $15. The circus is in town for three days with twice-daily performances.

MARCH

BIKE-O-RAMA SALE
Alliant Energy Center
1919 Alliant Energy Center Way
(608) 251-8413
www.bikeorama.com
As the name suggests, this is the big event for cyclists. Bike sales representatives are on hand offering discount prices on the upcoming year's models. Compare models, test ride them, and shop for accessories. Admission is free.

CANOECOPIA
Alliant Energy Center
1919 Alliant Energy Center Way
(608) 223-9300
www.rutabaga.com/canoecopia
This is the largest paddlesport exposition in the world. Hosted by local outfitter Rutabaga, the event includes over 100 exhibitors. Paddlers and teachers host educational sessions and professional guides and outfitters are on hand with expertise on distant destinations as far away as the Arctic Circle. The best and latest gear is for sale at good prices as well. Admission is around $10 per day or a bit more for a three-day ticket.

MABA HOME PRODUCTS SHOW
Alliant Energy Center
1919 Alliant Energy Center Way
(608) 288-1133
www.maba.org/home-products-show/
Since 1980 Madison Area Builders Association has sponsored this expo of hundreds of exhibitors displaying the latest trends and products in the home building and remodeling world. The three-day event includes seminars and product/service promotions. Admission is typically free though parking at the center is not.

OVERTURE CENTER'S INTERNATIONAL FESTIVAL
The Overture Center
201 State St.
(608) 258-4141
www.overturecenter.com
Song and dance, food, and crafts are featured from a variety of cultures from around the world but shared by Madison's residents of varied international origins. They call it "Local Goes Global." The Sat event typically celebrated in Mar or late Feb is free often with a related ticketed performance in the evening in one of the Overture Center's halls.

APRIL

CAPITAL CITY JAZZ FEST
Quality Inn and Suites
2969 Cahill Main St., Fitchburg
(608) 850-5400
www.madisonjazz.com/jazzfest
Usually held the last weekend in Apr, the jazz fest has been bringing quality artists to Madison since 1989. Four sessions occur over a three-day period. Tickets for each event cost around $35 while an all-sessions ticket offers a bit of a discount. The venue is limited to about 200 attendees. Tickets go on sale in Jan.

CRAZYLEGS CLASSIC
(608) 261-5347
www.crazylegsclassic.com
Since 1982 this annual run/walk has raised money for the University of Wisconsin Athletic

Department and now sees close to 18,000 participants each year. Named for Elroy "Crazylegs" Hirsch, a former UW athlete and athletic director, the 8K run (2K walk) begins at the Capitol Square and ends on the football field at Camp Randall Stadium. Runner's World has rated it one of America's 100 best events. Preregister online or check the Web site to see where you sign up on the day of the race.

MIDWEST HORSE FAIR
Alliant Energy Center
1919 Alliant Energy Center Way
(608) 267-3976
http://midwesthorsefair.com
Over 1,500 horses and 500 vendors come from around the United States to this annual equine expo. This three-day event is one of the best of its kind in the nation. Expect demonstrations, workshops, rodeo, and a Kid's Korral. Daily ticket fee with a discount for a three-day ticket or advance tickets. Tickets for the Fri evening rodeo and the Sat jumping grand prix are sold separately through Ticketmaster and also require the general admission ticket.

RETURN TO TRADITION POW-WOW
Madison Area Technical College (MATC)
Truax Campus–Redstem Gym
3550 Anderson St.
(608) 246-6458
http://matcmadison.edu
First celebrated in 1991, this spring pow-wow celebrates Native American culture and tradition with food and educational opportunities as well as the pow-wow itself. Nominal fee. This is typically held on a Sat afternoon in Apr.

VARSITY BAND SPRING CONCERT
Kohl Center
601 West Dayton St.
(608) 265-4120
www.badgerband.com/concert
Professor Michael Leckrone started this tradition in March 1975 when he put on what was to be a final concert of the year and a little party to follow. Four hundred and fifty people showed

up and it was considered big. Now, the three-day annual event sees in excess of 25,000 attendees and features professional lighting and pyrotechnics. Tickets go on sale in Feb.

WISCONSIN FILM FESTIVAL
www.wifilmfest.org
Documentaries, animation, shorts, feature length-films are what you can expect from this statewide film fest. Directors or other commentators may be on hand for presentations and discussions. Films are voted on by attendees and juries. Venues include various University of Wisconsin locations, the Orpheum Theatre, the Madison Museum of Contemporary Art, Bartell Theater, Majestic Theater, and the Monona Terrace. The festival is presented by the UW–Madison Art Institute and its Department of Communication Arts. Look for the four-day event in early Apr. (The event gets pushed back in the case that the university's spring break coincides with the early Apr dates.)

MAY

BRATFEST
Alliant Energy Center
1919 Alliant Energy Center Way
(608) 267-3976
www.bratfest.com
Well, it's not Wisconsin if there aren't any brats. This four-day festival contends that Madison is the Brat Capital of the World. Bratwurst can be credited to the abundant German immigrants who settled in the Badger State starting in the mid-1800s. The event is held every Memorial Day Weekend. It began in 1983 as a customer appreciation event for Sentry Foods in Hilldale Mall, but eventually evolved into a charity event so massive it had to be relocated to the more spacious Willow Island at the Alliant Energy Center. Two stages host live music on all four days, and there is a midway with carnival rides and a variety of other activities. The brats are provided by Wisconsin's own Johnsonville Sausage. The Johnsonville Big Taste Grill is 65 feet long and cooks 750 brats at a time. In the past, special

appearances have been made by the Budweiser Clydesdales and the Oscar Mayer Weinermobile. Over 200,000 brats are consumed and world records are often touted.

BURGERS AND BREW
Capital Brewery Bier Garten
7734 Terrace Ave., Middleton
(608) 217-2987
www.reapfoodgroup.org
Farmers and brewers get together for this celebration of local food and drink. Tickets cost around $25 and grant you three mini-burgers and a small glass of beer. Some popular area chefs contribute their culinary skills. The event raises money for REAP Food Group's Buy Fresh Buy Local program, which connects area restaurants with area farmers. Besides the host brewery, several other area brewers are on hand as are some cheesemakers.

GALLERY NIGHT
Madison Museum of Contemporary Art
227 State St.
(608) 257-0158
www.mmoca.org
Held twice annually the event allows the public to meet local artists in either their studios or at one of their exhibits. Various galleries and other Madison businesses take part in this and host tours and receptions. Check with the museum or that week's *Isthmus* newspaper for information on artists and venues. The other gallery night occurs in Oct.

MADISON CLASSIC HORSE SHOW
Alliant Energy Center
1919 Alliant Energy Center Way
(608) 267-3976
www.alliantenergycenter.com
Come see the finest American saddlebreds and hackney ponies around in this judged competition. Benefits go to Junior Exhibitor Scholarships and the Breast Cancer Recovery Foundation. Parking is free.

MADISON MARATHON AND EXPO
Alliant Energy Center
1919 Alliant Energy Center Way
(608) 267-3976
www.madisonfestivals.com/marathon
Not only is this a USA Track and Field–certified race and qualifier for the Boston Marathon, but it is also a very nice, if exhausting, tour of the best parts of the city. The route, which begins and ends at the Alliant Energy Center, takes runners along the shores of Lakes Mendota, Monona, and Wingra, past the Capitol and the Governor's Mansion, and through the University of Wisconsin campus and the university's Arboretum on the south central side of the city. As the charity-affiliated event is not an all-or-nothing affair, runners can also opt for a half- or quarter-marathon. There is also a kids' race. All finishers get medals, and awards are given to best times according to gender and age groups. Around 1,500 participants try to tackle the 26.2 miles each year, while double that run the half-marathon. The race takes place the Sun morning of Memorial Day Weekend. Race packets are handed out at the Madison Marathon Expo at the Alliant Energy Center on Sat. Participants can register online at www.marathonguide.com starting in Nov and continuing up until just a couple days before the race. Registration is also possible at the expo but for increased fees.

MIFFLIN STREET BLOCK PARTY
This street party found its roots during the 1969 student protests of the Vietnam War and at that time ended in three days of violent conflict between students and police. (See more about this in the History chapter.) Traditionally held the first Sat of May, the party—read "the drinking"—starts early in the morning and continues into the night. Live bands play on porches and front yards. Anywhere from a few hundred to a few thousand students take part in what is one giant house party. Problems with misbehaving drunks and a riot in 1996 have forced the city and students to work harder at keeping things in line. Glass containers are completely prohibited whether on public or private property, and drinking alcohol is only legal on private property—one cannot even

take one step on the sidewalk or off the curb into the street. Arrests are immediate and often total over 200. Every once in a while a reveler tests this no-tolerance policy and comes away from the weekend with that story about "just one step on the sidewalk!"

UNIVERSITY OF WISCONSIN COMMENCEMENT
The Kohl Center
601 West Dayton St.
(608) 262-3956
www.secfac.wisc.edu/commence
Though commencement is generally attended by people who have a direct connection to someone participating in it, other Madison visitors need to be aware that every hotel in town is likely to be booked solid. The three-day event (that's a LOT of students) takes place on a weekend in the middle of May and each round of degree conferral lasts about two hours and is open to the public.

JUNE

BLUES PICNIC
Warner Park
www.madisonbluessociety.com
The Madison Area Blues Society hosts its annual picnic blues celebration at Warner Park on the north side. Food vendors are on-site and beer is for sale. The event is great for families. Blues Kids is a short workshop to teach kids how to play harmonica and compose songs when their baby done left 'em. Bring a blanket or chair if you are so inclined. The organizers often host a raffle and promote a food drive for a local food pantry. The event is free.

i Keep up with all the area blues festivals and other goings-on by checking in with the Madison Blues Society (www.madisonbluessociety.com).

COWS ON THE CONCOURSE
Capitol Square, Main Street, and Martin Luther King Jr. Boulevard
www.danecountydairy.com/dairycows

Every June, the cows come out on the first Sat to take over a couple of streets just off the Capitol Square. The event, sponsored by Dane County Dairy Promotion Committee, kicks off the statewide June Dairy Month. Pet some cows and their calves, talk to dairy farmers, learn more about the dairy industry and, of course, sample some dairy products such as grilled cheese sandwiches, cream puffs, and some ice-cold milk. Live music is also on the schedule. The event is free.

DOWNTOWN WORKS WEEK
(608) 261-4747
www.downtownworksweek.com
This weeklong celebration of working downtown offers lunchtime concerts, Madison's Largest Coffee Break, T'ai Chi, and more. The venues include the Capitol Square, the rooftop at Monona Terrace Community and Convention Center, Madison Area Technical College's downtown campus, and the Overture Center. The event has pages on Facebook and Twitter (@DowntownWorks). Free.

ISTHMUS JAZZ FEST ON THE TERRACE
Memorial Union Terrace
www.isthmusjazzfestival.com
With Lake Mendota as the backdrop, this two-day festival celebrates jazz in a variety of styles including Dixieland, swing, bebop, Latin jazz, as well as fusion forms. Most of the acts perform on the Union Terrace and attract quite a crowd for the free shows. The headline act, however, is a ticketed event held inside at the Wisconsin Union Theater. Those tickets are on sale at the theater's box office (www.uniontheater.wisc .edu). UW–Madison students can purchase discounted tickets. The fest takes place around the first weekend in June.

MARQUETTE WATERFRONT FESTIVAL
Yahara Place Park
(608) 241-7143
www.marquette-neighborhood.org
Set in the park next to where the Yahara River empties into Lake Monona this two-day festival is another popular neighborhood fest. Celebrated since 1990 in mid-June, the fest features a live

music stage with nearly a dozen bands, various food and drink vendors (including beer), a co-ed volleyball tournament, and a paddling race on the Yahara. Hayrides and kids' games, including a fun run for the little ones, are also typically part of the production. Shade is provided by some lovely cottonwoods. Some "warm-up" concerts can be expected one or two days before at a couple of local bar venues. The event is free.

MIDDLETON'S BIG EVENT
(608) 831-6350
www.middletonbigevent.com

The city springs into action with this event. Look for sidewalk sales around Greenway Station and lots of children's activities such as crafts, games, and face painting. Expect citywide garage sales, live music at multiple venues for a nominal fee, and Taste of Middleton, which features dozens of local restaurants offering sample-size portions of their signature dishes. A fun walk/run, hiking, biking, geocaching, and much more are part of the festivities. Free shuttles work their way around Middleton so it is easy to park and ride through the entire festival. The day ends with fireworks.

MOUNDS DOG FEST
Angell Park, Sun Prairie
(608) 825-9800
www.moundspet.com

This fest is as much for the dogs as the owners themselves. Formerly held at the Alliant Energy Center, the event moved to nearby Sun Prairie. Expect demonstrations for the owners and contests for the dogs. The local K-9 police dogs are often in attendance. Entry and parking are free.

PRAIRIE STATE CLASSIC HORSE SHOW
Alliant Energy Center
1919 Alliant Energy Center Way
(608) 267-3976
www.midstatesmorgan.org

The annual equestrian event brings Morgans and several other breeds for judged competition. The three-day event in early June is open to the public.

RHYTHM AND BOOMS
(See July for this annual fireworks extravaganza. Some years it is held the last Sat of June.)

WEDDING PLANNER & GUIDE SUMMER BRIDAL SHOW
Alliant Energy Center
1919 Alliant Energy Center Way
(608) 233-7001
www.wedplan.com

A bit more relaxed than its Jan counterpart, the event nevertheless offers the same: exhibitions from formal wear stores, bakeries, jewelers, florists, travel agents, music providers, and more. The two-day event is in mid-June. Tickets are around $10 and can be bought at the door or in advance for a discount.

JULY

ART FAIR ON (AND OFF) THE SQUARE
On the Capitol Square
(608) 257-0158
www.mmoca.org/events/artfair/index.php

This outdoor art exhibit/sale has been going on since 1959. The Madison Museum of Contemporary Art sponsors the event, which features live music and entertainment, as well as food vendors spread throughout the tents of nearly 500 artists. Media range from photography and painting to ceramics, furniture, glass, jewelry, and so much more. The streets of the Capitol Square are closed to traffic during the two-day event. A kids' area offers games, art activities, and face painting. Art Fair Off the Square (www.artcraftwis.org/afos .html) hosts around 140 Wisconsin artists and occupies Martin Luther King Jr. Boulevard extending from the square to the rooftop terrace of the Monona Terrace Community and Convention Center. This event is free and open to the public and usually held the weekend after the Fourth of July weekend.

ATWOOD SUMMERFEST
(608) 241-1574
www.goodmancenter.org

Atwood Avenue's local street fair features a couple of stages (a blues stage and a rock stage) for live performances during the Sat event. The street along the 2000 and 2100 blocks is closed off and vendors line the edges. The event is free. Food and beverages are for sale from several local vendors. Many other local items are for sale (or resale) and the event is typically well attended with people ready to dance a bit. This is a fundraiser for the Goodman Community Center.

DANE COUNTY FAIR
Alliant Energy Center
1919 Alliant Energy Center Way
(608) 267-3976
www.danecountyfair.com
The first agricultural fair was held in 1851 in Madison. Today, the county version is the fourth largest of its kind in the state. Along with carnival rides and food, the fair also offers live music, entertainers, and commercial exhibitors, and displays the accomplishments of youth involved with 4-H Club, Future Farmers of America, and other organizations. Tickets for the five-day event in July are around $7 and a pass good for all five days is just about double that. Parking is free.

LA FETE DE MARQUETTE
www.marquette-neighborhood.org
This annual neighborhood festival coincides with Bastille Day (July 14) and brings four days of food, drink, games, and music to the near-east side's Central Park (or nearby). The styles of the live music come from French-speaking or French-influenced parts of the world, from North Africa and Haiti to Quebec and New Orleans. The event is free and carry-ins are not allowed. Central Park is under development and will be located along the railway corridor near East Main Street. Until it is complete, this fest location may float around a bit.

MAXWELL STREET DAYS
State Street and the Capitol Square
www.maxwellstreetdays.org
From 1871 to 1994, Chicago's Maxwell Street was home to an outdoor bazaar. In 1975, Maxwell Street Days was started as a way to put downtown Madison businesses in the spotlight. Now an annual shopper's delight, the weekend sale brings over 80 downtown stores out on the sidewalks with bargains. Food vendors and musicians join the mix. The three-day event is typically the weekend after Art Fair on the Square around mid-July.

OLBRICH HOME GARDEN TOUR
(608) 246-4550
www.olbrich.org/events/homegardentour.cfm
Private gardens on Madison's north side become public for one weekend each year. Tickets run between $12 and $15 and can be purchased in advance. The tour around the Maple Bluff community is self-guided but the owners/gardeners and landscapers are on hand to talk about what they've created and how.

OPERA IN THE PARK
Garner Park
Madison Opera
(608) 238-8085
www.madisonopera.org
www.madisonopera.blogspot.com
Since 2002, the Madison Opera has offered a free summer evening performance. Opera fans or the opera curious, be sure to bring lawn chairs or a blanket. Attendance is often up around 13,000.

PADDLE AND PORTAGE
(608) 226-4780
www.paddleandportage.org
This is what you get when you put together two lakes, an isthmus, and a competitive spirit in an outdoors kind of town. Held on a Sat in mid-July often coinciding with Maxwell Street Days, this canoe and kayak race starts from James Madison Park on Gorham Street with a loop into Lake Mendota, passes overland via the Capitol Square, and then ends at Olin Park on John Nolen Drive after crossing Lake Monona. Registration is possible on-site. Paddlers must complete the course in less than 1 hour and 40 minutes to be listed in the results. The registration fee is around $30–35.

RHYTHM AND BOOMS
Warner Park
(at Northport Drive and Sherman Avenue)
www.rhythmandbooms.com

This Independence Day extravaganza includes food, live music, children's events, carnival rides, F-16 flyovers, skydivers, bingo, and other activities. But what makes it more than just your local Fourth of July festival is the amazing fireworks display. Lasting about 35 minutes and setting off about 15,000 shells, this is the largest in the Midwest. The whole production is synchronized to a musical program that is broadcast by a local radio station. So whether you brave the massive crowds estimated at 300,000 that congregate under the booms or find a quiet spot on the opposite side of Lake Mendota, you can listen along. In order to avoid conflicting with Elver Park's and other area fireworks displays on the actual 4th, Rhythm and Booms is scheduled for the Sat before July 4. Sun is the rain date. Anyone with a boat might want to consider viewing the show from the water. Beer gardens are on-site, but carry-in alcohol is not allowed. Pets are not allowed nor are grills or personal fireworks. Pack mosquito spray and sunscreen if you are coming early. Parking can be tricky and attendees may have a long walk to the park. Locals may sell spots on their yards. Madison Metro buses run here and Madison Area Technical College charges a few dollars for parking and a few more for a roundtrip shuttle. Tune in to WOLX 94.9 FM.

i The Memorial Union Terrace at the University of Wisconsin is a great remote place to watch the Rhythm and Booms show and listen to the music with it. Tenney Park on Sherman Avenue isn't bad either.

WILLY STREET FESTIVAL
(608) 257-4576
www.cwd.org

Live music is played on as many as seven stages, various performers wander the street, and food, games, beer, arts and crafts, and a parade on Sun are all part of this neighborhood fair first cel-ebrated in 1978. A community raffle offers a ton of prizes. The festival is celebrated in the 800 to 1000 blocks of Williamson Street. Bring a costume and join the parade. Some acts from the concurrent Madison World Music Fest perform here as well. The event benefits Common Wealth Development and the Wil-Mar Neighborhood Center.

AUGUST

AFRICA FEST
Warner Park
2930 North Sherman Ave.
(608) 258-0261
www.africanassociation.org

Music, dancing, food, and other vendors representing the diverse cultures of Africa meet at the park for this free event in mid-Aug.

GOOD NEIGHBOR FEST
Fireman's Park
7400 Lee St., Middleton
www.goodneighborfestival.com

Since 1964 Middleton has been celebrating its small-town neighborly spirit and recognizing members of the community who have been "good neighbors." The three-day Aug event includes a craft fair, 5k run, raffle, carnival rides, lots of games for the kids and families, and live music. A parade makes its way down University Avenue on Sun. The event is free.

GREAT TASTE OF THE MIDWEST
Olin-Turville Park
www.mhtg.org

The Madison Homebrewers and Tasters Guild puts on this amazing craft beer festival—certainly one of the best in the nation—the second Sat of Aug. Tickets for this festival go on sale May 1 and sell out in about an hour. Attendance is capped at 6,000. Over 100 brewers showcase their beers under three large tents in Olin–Turville Park along the shores of Lake Monona. The festival is finely organized, fresh water is ample, commemorative sample glasses are provided, and even transportation is arranged. Various buses start at designated meeting points around the

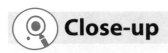 **Close-up**

Free Music in the Summertime

The best things in life are free. In Madison that includes a lot of music. Each summer a variety of community music events head outdoors and they don't cost you anything but your time. The lakeside terrace at the Memorial Student Union at the University of Wisconsin becomes a magnet for people looking to catch a sunset and a band in the evening. Acts from across the country play there on Fri and Sat nights. **Behind the Beat** is the Fri evening sunset jazz series. The music actually can vary a bit even within the jazz genre but generally this is a laid-back experience. **The Terrace** has an abundance of tables and chairs and a few picnic tables for seating. These can fill up, however, on the nicest of days and definitely will do so when a popular act is on the bill. Grilled food, soda, and a variety of beers are served here.

Concerts on the Square
Wisconsin Chamber Orchestra
State Capitol
www.wcoconcerts.org

It's one of Madison's best loved summer traditions: a bit of classical music and a picnic in the park. But in this case the music is provided by a full orchestra set up on the steps of the State Capitol building and the park is the Capitol grounds. Attendees often set down blankets before work in the morning to mark a spot and return at the end of the day to have a picnic dinner and perhaps a bit of wine. Vendors are on-site. Beginning in June and ending in July, the free concerts are on six consecutive Wed nights. The music starts at 7 p.m.

Jazz at Five
100 block State St.
(608) 310-4462
http://jazzat5.org

A tradition since 1994, Jazz at Five is a free concert series featuring local and national performers at the top of State Street where it meets the Capitol Square. The turnout is always pretty good so it is best to get there a little early. Bring your own chair. If weather is not cooperating, look for these events to continue as scheduled but in the lobby at the Overture Center just a block away at 201 State St. Call the information line above to be sure.

Monona Terrace Summer Concert Series
Monona Terrace Community and Convention Center
One John Nolen Dr.
(608) 261-4000
www.mononaterrace.com

With Lake Monona on one side and the Capitol on the other, this rooftop venue offers one of the best views in town. Add a little song and dance and you can't go wrong. The summer series consists of two parts. The first is **Concerts on the Rooftop**, a series of live music events held on Thurs evenings from June through July. The second is **Dane Dances**. A local D.J. sets up before and after a live band. The aim for these shows is to get people up and dancing. These shows are on Fri evenings in Aug. Shows in both series are free and family friendly. The rooftop has very little seating so it is a good idea to bring your own lawn chairs. The center's **Lake Vista Café** offers food in a "casual gourmet" style. Picnics are allowed but carry-in alcohol is not permitted.

Capitol City Band
Rennebohm Park
115 North Eau Claire Ave.
(608) 835-9861

Through July and Aug the Capitol City Band plays free concerts on Thurs nights at 7 p.m. Bring a picnic and a lawn chair if you're inclined.

city, carrying ticketholders to and from the fest. Points of origin are typically brewpubs, taverns, or restaurants. Afterward, free cab rides from the fest are also available.

JJO BAND CAMP
Alliant Energy Center
1919 Alliant Energy Center Way
(608) 267-3976
www.jjobandcamp.com
Hosted at the Alliant Energy Center's outdoor concert venue Willow Island, this event sponsored by Classic Rock radio station WJJO 94.1 FM features over 30 hard-rock acts. It is an all-ages show but alcohol is served to the 21+ crowd. No carry-ins are allowed, and the event starts in the morning and ends mid-evening. Tickets are sold via Ticketmaster (www.ticketmaster.com). An ATM is usually on-site. Watch for the event on a Sat or Sun in early Aug.

i The Memorial Union Terrace hosted a blues fest in Aug 2009. Blues fans may want to watch and see if that becomes an annual trend.

KING STREET BLOCK PARTY
www.thedailypage.com
Isthmus Publishing puts on a Sat street party at the end of Aug in the 100 block of King Street. Live music, family friendly activities and performers, and food and drink from around the block are on offer.

MADISON ROOTS FESTIVAL
Alliant Energy Center—Willow Island
(608) 255-4646
www.frankproductions.com
In early Aug this one-day concert fills two stages all day and brings in some big names. Previous festivals have included John Butler Trio, Dar Williams, and G. Love and Special Sauce. Parking is free and beer is served. Tickets are sold at the gate but cheaper in advance. The festival was originally held at the Capital Brewery Bier Garten and could return there in the future.

MIDWEST GYPSY SWING FEST
Art in the Barn
5927 Adams Rd.
(608) 835-0454
www.midwestgypsyswingfest.com
Eastern European meets American jazz in this celebration of gypsy swing that brings out some notable local talent and brings in members of the international scene. The two-day event is ticketed.

ORTON PARK FESTIVAL
1100 Spaight St.
www.marquette-neighborhood.org
This neighborhood fest on the near east side is located in Madison's first park. Expect live music over the course of three days as well as food and drink. One of the highlights is an evening acrobatic performance by the Cycropia Aerial Dance Troupe under one of the park's enormous and powerful oak trees. An international dinner is served on Fri night. The music continues with Orton After Dark which moves indoors at the High Noon Saloon (701 East Washington Ave.; 608-268-1122).

SUN PRAIRIE SWEET CORN FESTIVAL
Angell Park, Sun Prairie
(608) 837-4547
www.sunprairiechamber.com
Join over 100,000 others to tackle more than 70 tons of sweet corn. Butter is abundant and salt shakers hang from the trees. Beyond the ears, there are also carnival rides, live music, food booths, a beer tent, arts and crafts, a petting zoo, and a variety of family entertainment. A parade starts off the four-day event on Thurs evening, and the steamed corn is served only on Sat and Sun. Uncooked corn is abundantly for sale to take home. Entry incurs a nominal fee and if you park on the grounds, that fee includes admission.

TOKEN CREEK CHAMBER MUSIC FESTIVAL
4037 Hwy. 19, DeForest
(608) 241-2525
www.tokencreekfestival.org

Established in 1989 and just over a week long, the festival is hosted by artistic directors John and Rose Mary Harbison and includes concerts, recitals, rehearsals, and forums. The setting in a rustic barn is intimate and the performances are of the highest quality. Tickets sell out fast for each event and are available by mail. After Aug 1 it is best to call regarding availability and waiting lists.

TRIANGLE ETHNIC FEST
(608) 256-7808
www.bayviewfoundation.org
The triangular-shaped neighborhood inside Regent and Park Streets and West Washington Avenue was once the heart of Greenbush, a neighborhood populated by a wide variety of immigrants—the most numerous of whom were Italians, Eastern Europeans, and Jews—and African Americans. Much of "the Bush" was leveled for urban renewal in the 1960s. The resulting Bayview community is still home to a diverse ethnic population though the countries of origin have changed to include Laos, Mexico, Vietnam, Nicaragua, Cambodia, Columbia, China, and various nations in Africa. Since 1985, the residents and the Bayview Foundation have been putting together this annual celebration of their various cultures. This fest brings out the food, music, and dance performances and features various vendors of ethnic cuisine.

THE WISCONSIN AIDS RIDE
(608) 252-6540
www.actride.org
The ride spans four days in Aug and covers 300 miles through hilly southern Wisconsin. Riders are pledge-supported and raising money and awareness to fight AIDS and HIV. Each year is listed as ACT 8, ACT 9, etc. (AIDS Network Cycles Together). Register online for a fee.

WISCONSIN CAPITOL PRIDE FEST
Alliant Energy Center—Willow Island
1919 Alliant Energy Center Way
(608) 267-3976
www.wisconsincapitolpride.org

The LGBT community shows its pride during this two-day festival that includes a variety of events—live music and entertainment, family activities, and a community picnic—as well as a pride parade around the Capitol Square. Food vendors and DJs are on hand. Attendees can also expect dancing and perhaps a drag show or two. Much of the event is free although donations are appreciated.

SEPTEMBER

FORD IRONMAN WISCONSIN TRIATHLON
www.ironmanwisconsin.com
The grueling three-part competition includes a 2.4-mile swim in Lake Monona, a 112-mile biking segment, and the 26.2-mile marathon. Spectators avidly cheer participants on at various spots throughout the course. Monona Terrace is a prime viewpoint for the swim. State Street and other downtown streets are good locations to watch the marathon portion. The sign-up to take part in the race often sells out a year in advance and begins for next year right after the race.

FORWARD MUSIC FESTIVAL
www.forwardmusicfest.com
www.myspace.com/forwardmusicfest
In Sept 2008 the FMF was born, and without any sort of prior experience or reputation the creators managed to get some national acts to attend and pull off a very successful festival to rock the isthmus. The next year was bigger and better. The aim is to highlight diverse local and regional talents and showcase the Midwest contribution to the indie music scene. Austin has its South by Southwest, and Madison now has its Forward Music Festival. Venues include High Noon Saloon, Orpheum Theatre, Majestic Theater, The Frequency, and the Overture Center. For a good deal on ticket prices, buy a festival wristband in advance that covers the whole weekend with all its venues and 70+ bands.

HOMECOMING
University of Wisconsin
www.uwhomecoming.com

The homecoming tradition began for the Badgers in 1911, and every fall the campus hosts a week of events including a kick-off celebration in Library Mall, a scavenger hunt, charity run/walk, a parade, and much more. The week culminates with the homecoming football game at Camp Randall Stadium.

MADISON WORLD MUSIC FEST
At the Memorial Union at the University of Wisconsin and at the Willy Street Fair
www.uniontheater.wisc.edu/worldmusicfest
Since 2003 this extraordinary festival has been bringing artists from around the world for free performances, workshops, and lectures. Music starts on a Wed and continues through Sat. The performances are often on two stages—the lakeside Terrace and the Wisconsin Union Theater—and run a staggered schedule so that attendees can enjoy nonstop shows while other musicians are setting up. The free event is funded by sponsors and donations and is scheduled the same week as the Willy Street Fair which provides yet another venue.

MONROE STREET FESTIVAL
(608) 255-8211
www.monroestreetfestival.com
On the near west side, this neighborhood festival runs the full length of Monroe Street. Entertainment varies by block and includes live music, a petting zoo, games for the kids, and sales at local businesses. The Monroe Street branch of the public library (1705 Monroe St.) hosts a book sale. Typically this free event is hosted on a Sat late in Sept unless it conflicts with a Badger football game in which case it might be a Sun.

QUILT EXPO
Exhibition Hall at Alliant Energy Center
1919 Alliant Energy Center Way
(920) 356-6144
www.wiquiltexpo.com
Partly presented by Wisconsin Public Television, this is the big annual event for quilters of every skill level. The expo hosts dozens of stage presen

tations and lectures as well as an abundance of workshops. Prizes are awarded for a juried quilt contest. Admissions fees are around $8 each day with discounts for multi-day and advance purchase. Each lecture also incurs a fee with larger prices for hands-on quilting workshops.

SUN PRAIRIE BLUES FEST
Angell Park
(608) 235-8475
www.spbluesfest.com
This impressive blues festival got its start in 2007 and draws on regional and national acts. Up until now it has billed itself as "10 bucks for 10 hours of blues" which is a crazy good deal. The grounds are sheltered so the show is on rain or shine. Food and beverages are for sale including beer of course. Tickets are cheaper in advance but available the day of show. Proceeds support local Lions Clubs.

TASTE OF MADISON
On the Capitol Square
www.tasteofmadison.com
On the Sat and Sun of Labor Day Weekend, Madison restaurants bring their delicious dishes to the Capitol Square and festival attendees eat their way around the Capitol. Over 200 menu items are offered from 65-plus local restaurants and a map shows where they all can be found. Three stages located on the streets running perpendicular off the square host free live music for both of the festivals days. Benefits go to United Cerebral Palsy of Dane County. The event is free.

WISCONSIN COW CHIP THROW
Marion Park, Prairie du Sac
www.wiscowchip.com
Yes, it's what you think: an event of Olympoop proportions. The two-day festival includes a lot of music, food, arts and crafts, a walk/run, and a parade. But the central event is the flinging of dried cow pies. Hopeful throwers pay a small fee to compete, and onlookers in bleachers alongside the flinging field need to keep their eye on the chips—they don't typically fly straight. Free.

> **ℹ** Pioneers once resorted to cow chips in the heart of winter. The dried dung burns without odor or soot and provides a good heat source!

ZOO RUN RUN
Henry Vilas Zoo
702 South Randall Ave.
www.vilaszoo.org
The 5k and 10k fun runs benefit Madison's free zoo. Founded in 2006, the race attracts fleet-footed zoo fans numbering over 1,000 and raises over $20,000 in pledges.

OCTOBER

APPLE FEST
Warner Park Community Recreation Center
1625 Northport Dr.
(608) 243-5252
www.nescoinc.org
On a Sat early in Oct, the fruit filled fest benefits the local Senior Coalition. Expect a kids' carnival, arts and crafts, bake sale, used book sale, and local music and dance entertainment. There's a nominal entry fee but kids under 12 are free.

FREAKFEST
Halloween on State Street
On the Fri and Sat evenings before or including Oct 31, this now infamous costumed festivity has had some growing pains over the years. Excessive drunkenness and ineffective police supervision turned into small riots and a boon for the pepper spray industry. The official event is Sat evening though revelers often take to the street Fri night as well. In recent years, live music stages featuring local and national acts (such as Third Eye Blind) and an outdoor film showing have been set up. A DJ provides some tunes for the best costume contest. Portable stadium lighting in the street, abundant police on foot and on horseback, and the ticketed gated entryways for the bands seem to have brought the fest under control. Stern warnings of intolerance for hooliganism and a more respectful crowd have surely helped. That

being said, if anything is going to happen, it will happen in the wee hours as the bars close and it's time for everyone to clear out. Earlier in the evening, the unofficial parade of costumed revelers is a sight to behold and, er, a riot to take part in. Whole families come out for people watching fun, though once in a while a costume might push the limits of what some may think of as "family friendly." Attendees number close to 100,000 each year.

FUTURE LIFESTYLES FALL SHOW
Alliant Energy Center
1919 Alliant Energy Center Way
(608) 247-5200
www.50pluslifestylesmagazine.com
Local magazine *50-Plus Lifestyles* organizes this event that provides information, seminars, demonstrations, health screenings, and entertainment for its target audience, the over-50 crowd. The event is free and so is parking.

GALLERY NIGHT
Madison Museum of Contemporary Art
227 State St.
(608) 257-0158
www.mmoca.org
Held twice annually the event allows the public to meet local artists in either their studios or at one of their exhibits. Various galleries and other Madison businesses take part in this and host tours and receptions. Check with the museum or that week's *Isthmus* newspaper for information on artists and venues. The other gallery night occurs in May.

HARVEST MOON FESTIVAL
Lussier Family Heritage Center
3101 Lake Farm Rd.
(608) 224-3604
www.countyofdane.com/lwrd/parks/heritage
Hosted by Friends of Capital Springs Recreation Center, this fall fest takes place at night with various naturalist presentations, a bonfire, and a night hike. Food and beverages are for sale and live music entertains. A nominal fee is charged.

LITERACY NETWORK RUN/WALK

www.litnetwork.org

This fun run benefits the Literacy Network of Dane County, which provides language tutoring and literacy training for low-income adults and families. Lengths of runs are 5K and 10K and the walk is 5K. The course starts at the intersection of State and Gorham Streets then crosses campus along Lakeshore Path before returning to the starting area. Timing chips are distributed to participants and worn around the ankle or foot. Awards are given to participants who collect certain amounts of the tax-deductible pledges. Pre-registration is required and fees are around $30.

MADISON FOOD AND WINE SHOW

Alliant Energy Center
1919 Alliant Energy Center Way
(608) 270-3640
www.madisonfoodandwineshow.com

This three-day gourmet tasting event sponsored by *Madison Magazine* offers samples of the best food and wines from the area as well as cooking seminars and the Dueling Chef Competition. Attendees get goodies in a gift bag and access to over 150 vendors. Patrons must be of legal drinking age to attend. Tickets start at around $35 with discounts for three-day tickets and advance purchase.

WISCONSIN BOOK FESTIVAL

Wisconsin Humanities Council
222 South Bedford St., Suite F
www.wisconsinbookfestival.org

Spanning five days and taking place in several different venues, mostly downtown, this literary event is one of the largest of its kind in the country and attracts over 15,000 attendees. Authors from all over the country come to read from their works, answer questions, and host panel discussions. If you like books at all you are sure to recognize several big names each year. Pre-festival events can occur as much as a month in advance. During the event some of the smaller venues can fill quickly so it is worth planning ahead. Events such as the keynote presenter require a free ticket.

WORLD DAIRY EXPO

Alliant Energy Center
1919 Alliant Energy Center Way
(608) 224-6455
www.worlddairyexpo.com

Attracting nearly 70,000 people from all over the world, this five-day international expo typically leads up to and includes the first weekend in Oct. All the latest in dairy technology and equipment is on display and a Parade of Champions shows off the finest dairy cattle. If there was ever a bovine beauty pageant this would be it. Seven different breeds "compete" for top honors. Free seminars are aimed at those in the trade, and virtual farm tours take visitors around the world.

NOVEMBER

HOLIDAY ART FAIR

Madison Museum of Contemporary Art
227 State St.
(608) 257-0158
www.mmoca.org

Look for something a bit more creative this year for the holidays. The museum puts on a holiday gift shopping sale with fine pieces of ceramics, jewelry, woodwork, glass, and more by artists. There is a Gourmet Gallery and a Rediscovered Art and Treasures sale as well. Admission is a nominal fee and children under 12 are free.

HOLIDAY MARKET IN MADISON

Alliant Energy Center
1919 Alliant Energy Center Way
(608) 278-7990
www.madisonballet.org/market

The shopping season is on and this extravaganza puts together over 120 vendors in one place with items of all sorts including home decor, art, gourmet food, toys, sporting goods, and apparel. General admission pays at the door. The event is hosted by the Madison Ballet.

KIDS' EXPO

Alliant Energy Center
1919 Alliant Energy Center Way
(608) 276-9797
www.kids-expo.com

The expo provides a load of information about family-friendly events, destinations, programs, products and services and the businesses and organizations that provide them. Various educational presentations are intended to give exposure to these organizations and connect parents with options and ideas for the entire year. Entertainment is provided by local dance and gymnastics groups and others. Admission is free.

MADISON WOMEN'S EXPO
Alliant Energy Center
1919 Alliant Energy Center Way
www.madisonwomensexpo.com
Local women's magazine *Brava* hosts this two-day event the weekend before Thanksgiving. It features hundreds of exhibitors and some celebrity guests. From health and fashion to home and family, the topics run the gamut. Information on fitness and career opportunities is also available. No strollers or pets allowed. Tickets are per day or for the whole weekend and cheaper in advance. Check the Web site for possible freebies.

WISCONSIN DOG FAIR
Exhibition Hall at Alliant Energy Center
1919 Alliant Energy Center Way
(608) 267-3976
www.badgerkennelclub.com
The fair hosts vendors, seminars, educational demonstrations, and a raffle. The event lasts one day and tickets are around $7. Check the Web site for free-parking offers.

WISCONSIN ORIGINAL CHEESE FESTIVAL
Monona Terrace Community and Convention Center
One John Nolen Dr.
(608) 261-4000
Dozens of Wisconsin artisan cheesemakers are on hand to talk about their craft and provide sam-ples. The two-day event includes tours of local cheese plants, afternoon seminars, and meals at local restaurants that are paired with specific cheesemakers. All tickets are sold in advance beginning in Sept.

DECEMBER

HOLIDAY CONCERTS
Olbrich Botanical Gardens
3330 Atwood Ave.
(608) 246-4550
www.olbrich.org
Each Sun afternoon in Dec, the Evjue Commons at the gardens plays host to a concert. Music varies from strings, choirs, and light jazz to straight up rock and roll or country. A nominal donation is requested.

THE NUTCRACKER
(608) 278-7990
www.madisonballet.org
It's an annual holiday tradition. Tchaikovsky's classic is performed by Madison Ballet with the accompaniment of the Wisconsin Chamber Orchestra each year starting in mid-Dec.

OLBRICH'S HOLIDAY EXPRESS FLOWER AND MODEL TRAIN SHOW
Olbrich Botanical Gardens
3330 Atwood Ave.
(608) 246-4550
www.olbrich.org/events/holidayexpress.cfm
You may have expected poinsettias at botanical gardens but the holiday surprise at Olbrich is the train show. Large-scale model trains from statewide members of the Wisconsin Garden Railway Society chug through miniature landscapes for all to enjoy daily for most of the month of Dec. There is a nominal fee.

DAY TRIPS AND WEEKEND GETAWAYS

Madison is a great place to be, but let's be honest: everyone needs a break sometime. The area around Madison offers a variety of distractions from pleasant drives through rolling farmland, rock outcrops, and forested bluffs to supercharged touristy water parks. Outdoorsy types can find dozens of places to hike, paddle, birdwatch, or bike within just an hour's drive of the city limits. Milwaukee and Chicago and all those two-metropolitan areas have to offer are easy day trips or weekend breaks, but a number of options are even closer to the Mad City. To the west is the Spring Green area. Set along the Wisconsin River amid some very picturesque countryside, the little community nevertheless offers fine dining, important attractions, and first-rate theater. To the south lies Green County, a region of the state famous for its cheese production and Swiss heritage. To the north lies the Wisconsin River valley and the dominating Baraboo Hills that forced the river's path and just a bit farther north is Wisconsin's most popular tourist destination: Wisconsin Dells.

WISCONSIN DELLS

www.wisdells.com

People love it or they hate it. Those who claim to hate it, however, need to look again, look around the bend, explore a little more. The Dells have more to offer than just the commercial hype aspect. It combines the bells and whistles of a wound-up tourist destination with the natural beauty of the Wisconsin River Valley. Though it bills itself as the "Water Park Capital of the World"—and for good reason, there are over 20 here—it is also home to some remarkable scenery, as pretty as any in the state.

At the end of the last glacial period of the Ice Age, the sheet of ice from the north melted forming the massive Glacial Lake Wisconsin held in by debris deposits and ice dams. In what could only have been a thunderous event of biblical flood proportions, the waters burst forth and carved the sandstone formations and much of the river bed we see today. The Native Americans believed a giant serpent had dragged its belly across the land, and indeed the serpentine path through the Dells captures the imagination in such a way.

The name Dells comes from the French explorers and fur traders who passed this way in the 18th century. They referred to the *dalles* or the narrows of the Wisconsin River. The name stuck despite a period of being officially known as Kilbourn City when a railroad president of that name bridged the river and founded a town there in 1857.

As far as the water parks and attractions go, travelers may have trouble sorting out all the claims, especially in the "largest" department. The largest *outdoor* water park, or the largest water park *and* theme park? In the end it is simply splitting hairs and each of the parks has an attraction visitors swear by as the best.

Getting there is as easy as hopping on I-90/94 and heading north. The drive takes about 45 minutes making the Dells a perfect day trip or long weekend.

Water Parks

CHULA VISTA RESORT
4031 River Rd., Wisconsin Dells
(608) 254-8366
www.chulavistaresort.com

Wisconsin Dells–Lake Delton Strip

Many of the businesses lie along the Wisconsin Dells Parkway, which passes through the two adjacent communities of Wisconsin Dells and Lake Delton. The actual lake in Lake Delton is an artificial creation formed when Dell Creek was dammed. In 2008 the pressure of torrential rains—12 inches in one night—overflowed County Highway A not far from the dam, and the earth let loose allowing the whole lake to drain in less than three hours right into the nearby Wisconsin River. Several million dollars and a new dam later, Lake Delton was filled once again and reopened on June 9, 2009, one year after the disaster.

For travelers looking for the all-inclusive deal, this is one of the more popular. Get a room, suite, condo, or villa at the resort and spend your time exploring the water parks. Some of the suites have themes such as Caribbean pirates or African safaris. There are nine food outlets here including a chophouse, buffet, bar and grills, a pizzeria, and a fresh market. Both indoor and outdoor parks on-site feature almost 30 waterslides and a wave pool as part of a 200,000-square-foot facility. Additionally there is minigolf, an 18-hole golf course, games, and a day spa. Be aware of where your accommodations are located on the property, especially if you want to be just a skip from the water parks themselves. Some rooms are far from the recreation though a shuttle is on call and usually pretty quick.

KALAHARI
1305 Kalahari Dr., Wisconsin Dells
(877) 525-2427
www.kalahariresorts.com/wi

This chain of resorts goes with an African theme on the decor and piped in music. Everything all together is the idea here: water park, hotel room, spa, shopping, and dining. At 125,000 square feet, the indoor park is second in the nation in size to its sister resort in Ohio. The outdoor portion opens for the summer, and both parks offer private cabanas with flat-screen TVs, a safe, lounge chairs, and a refrigerator.

MOUNT OLYMPUS WATER PARK
1881 Wisconsin Dells Pkwy., Wisconsin Dells
(608) 254-2490
www.mtolympuspark.com
Mt. Olympus is rather hard to miss with its colossal recreations of a coliseum and other classical ruins. Formerly known as Familyland, this is not quite as big as Noah's Ark but nevertheless offers a magnificent 156-acre collection of rides, slides, and activities. The indoor and outdoor water parks offer nearly 40 water slides, four children's water play areas, two endless rivers, surfing with nine-foot waves, and much more. On-land activities include go-carts, bumper cars, five roller coasters, and various other rides. Several of these theme park attractions are indoors as well. Zeus' Playground and Neptune's Water Kingdom are the outdoor parks, while The Parthenon and Medusa's Water Park take things indoors. Golf is nearby and there's even a shuttle to the Ho-Chunk Casino south of town. Eight food outlets have Greek-themed names and offer generally snack and lunch-oriented menus from gyros and burgers to pizza and funnel cakes. Fine dining is best done around town. Two on-site hotels offer lodging: Hotel Rome and the Pompeii Motel.

NOAH'S ARK WATER PARK
1410 Wisconsin Dells Pkwy., Wisconsin Dells
(608) 254-6351
www.noahsarkwaterpark.com
Noah's Ark has long been a formidable competitor in the water park scene and has a few of those "greatest" claims to fame: America's longest water coaster, world's largest bowl ride, and the only 4-D theater, which features none other than *Sponge-Bob SquarePants*. Scorpion Tail is the nation's only

looping water slide. Forty-nine water slides, two wave pools and lazy rivers, four kids' areas, and a variety of dry land activities to boot. Annually raising the bar, they remain one of the kings of the scene. Season passes are incredible deals for water park junkies. A single day pass is around $35.

WILDERNESS WATERPARK RESORT
511 East Adams St., Wisconsin Dells
(800) 867-9453
www.wildernessresort.com
Wilderness claims to be America's Largest Waterpark Resort with the largest indoor wave pool. The transparent roof of the three-section facility lets the rays in for the tan seekers so the indoor status doesn't necessarily mean "shaded." Along with a collection of tube slides, lazy river, kids' areas, and waterfalls, the park has the Dells' tallest family raft ride and the Cannonbowl, with its giant funnel. The non-water activities include laser tag, games, minigolf, and a haunted hotel. The outdoor park is open during the summer and includes minigolf and go-carts. Golf is available on two courses and a day spa is also on-site. Five zip-lines as high as 55 feet in the air offer a two-hour adrenaline experience. Lodging options range from standard hotel rooms and suites to five-bedroom cabins. The resort is set among trees on 600 acres, so it arguably has the better view of the big resorts. Three restaurants are on the property including Fields at the Wilderness, the fine dining option.

Other Attractions

EXTREME WORLD
1800 Wisconsin Dells Pkwy., Wisconsin Dells
(608) 254-4111
www.extremeworld.com
You don't have to get wet to have a good time at the Dells. The thrill rides at Extreme World have been featured on the Travel Channel. Bungee jumping, the Ejection Seat, and go-karts are part of the rush here. But The Skycoaster, located across the street at Mt. Olympus, drops riders 100 feet at speeds of up to 65 mph before pulling up and flying them 90 feet into the air. The whole thing is about four seconds and leaves people

breathless. Terminal Velocity offers something that no one else does: a free fall experience without any sort of attachment. They just drop you into a specially designed net—no kidding. It is pricey but then the experience really is like no other. Parking is free and so is ogling the activity. Each thrill is paid for separately. Second rides/jumps are not always possible during peak times.

H. H. BENNETT STUDIO
215 Broadway, Wisconsin Dells
http://hhbennettstudio.wisconsinhistory.org
Henry Hamilton Bennett was born in 1843 and his interest in photography didn't come until after a Civil War injury left his right hand crippled. In 1868 he began to shoot the Dells. You might say what Ansel Adams is to Yosemite and the American West, Bennett is to the Wisconsin Dells. His photos told a story of a place and did much to publicize beauty and drama of the Dells beyond Wisconsin's borders. The photo studio he opened back in 1865 remained in the family for several generations. The Wisconsin State Historical Society restored the studio and curates the collection of prints, negatives, and classic photography equipment. Probably the most famous of the photos is of one of the Dells' most famous sights. Stand Rock is a narrow pedestal of sculpted sandstone with a wider flat rock ledge balanced at its top. Today trained dogs jump the five-foot gap from the nearby cliff, but it was Ashley, the son of H. H. Bennett, who made the leap that was first captured on film, back in 1888. The studio is open daily from May 1 to Nov 1. An admission fee applies. This is wheelchair accessible.

THE ORIGINAL WISCONSIN DUCKS
1890 Wisconsin Dells Pkwy. North, Wisconsin Dells
(608) 254-8751
www.wisconsinducktours.com
It's not often one gets to ride in an amphibious World War II army vehicle. These "ducks" were first brought to the Dells in 1946 by Mel Flath. They barrel along through the woods and then splash into the Lower Dells offering the best scenery of land and water. Be prepared to get a little wet.

POINT BLUFF RESORT
3199 County Hwy. Z, Wisconsin Dells
(608) 253-6181
www.pointbluff.com

The resort offers canoe, kayak, and tube rentals for those who prefer Mother Nature's water park. The Wisconsin River is a beautiful place to paddle, and the carved sandstone is a good reason to bring a waterproof camera. Trips last from about an hour and a half up to five to seven hours, with overnight options as well. The resort runs a shuttle or you can paddle independently. Prices start from about $30.

RICK WILCOX MAGIC THEATER
1666 Wisconsin Dells Pkwy. North, Wisconsin Dells
(608) 254-5511
www.rickwilcox.com

Rick has been doing magic since he was 10. He and his wife/assistant Susan have been around the world with their act and featured in places such as Las Vegas and London. His specialty is up-close performance and this 550-seat theater, which the Wilcoxes opened in 1999, works well for him. Shows are an hour and a half long and appropriate fun for all ages. The Wilcoxes are available after the show for photos and auto-graphs, and the gift shop sells great stuff for the aspiring magician. Fee.

RIPLEY'S BELIEVE IT OR NOT
115 Broadway, Wisconsin Dells
(608) 253-7556
www.ripleys.com

Ripley's has capitalized on the bizarre and this museum of eight galleries spread across two floors delivers as expected. From shrunken heads and torture devices to mutant animals and unaired episodes of the TV show, there are plenty of oddities. The dimly lit halls offer placards for all displays so visitors know what they are looking at. Be aware that some of the weird stuff may scare small children. Open daily from Mar into Oct and then with limited days for the rest of the year. Fee.

TOMMY BARTLETT SHOW AND EXPLORATORY
560 Wisconsin Dells Pkwy. North, Wisconsin Dells
(608) 254-2525
www.tommybartlett.com

What once was strictly a seasonal waterski show—and still a fabulous one at that—now also includes the indoor Exploratory, meaning that Tommy Bartlett has something to offer even in the winter season or whenever weather is not cooperating. The ski show on Lake Delton runs 90 minutes and features professional stunts by ski-ers and boat captains as well as a bit of comedy making for a great family event. With the success of indoor water parks, it made sense to try to find a viable "off-season" attraction. Exhibits are interactive and include a high-wire bicycle ride, an authentic Russian space station core module, a Mercury space capsule, and what remains a simple yet popular item, the static electricity demonstration—a hair-raising experience. The ski shows run from Memorial Day Weekend to Labor Day Weekend, while the Exploratory is open daily year-round.

i Watch for area hotel promotions that often offer free or reduced price tickets to Tommy Bartlett, water parks, or other area attractions.

WISCONSIN DEER PARK
583 US Hwy. 12, Wisconsin Dells
(608) 253-2041
www.wisdeerpark.com

Though the state is actually crawling with deer and you are sure to see some by the roadside—standing or otherwise—it is not often one has the chance to pet one. The deer park offers a four-block-long pathway in a wooded 28-acre preserve. The animals, which have been born and raised in captivity, come right up to the visitors. Other animals occupy the park, from the familiar such as elk and bison, to the more exotic, such as lemurs and emus. Feed specially formulated for the animals must be purchased at the site. Adult entrance fees are $10. Open May through Oct. Wheelchair accessible.

Restaurants

THE DEL-BAR
800 Wisconsin Dells Pkwy., Lake Delton
(608) 253-1861
www.del-bar.com
Since the 1930s this has been the supper club of choice serving naturally aged steaks and a variety of seafood dishes. As many as 500 people dine here each night. The name comes from its location between the Wisconsin Dells and Baraboo. The original restaurant was a log cabin, but an expansion by Frank Lloyd Wright protégé James Dresser gives it its current Prairie-style look. The menu offers prime grade certified Angus beef aged 28 to 35 days as well as seafood, a children's menu, and early bird specials. Much has been written over the years about the Del-Bar and it has made national "Best-of" lists. The average dinner price is from $25 to $35. Open daily for dinner.

HIGH ROCK CAFÉ
232 Broadway, Wisconsin Dells
(608) 254 5677
www.highrockcafe.com
Located on the 2nd floor overlooking the street, the cafe consistently gets raves from locals and travelers alike. In the glut and glitz world of a tourist mecca, this is a fine example of keeping quality at a premium. Soups, salads, appetizers, wraps—the menu is American and represents the traveling "research" of the two owners' quest for the best recipes from around the country. Starters may include hummus, crabcakes, or ahi tuna. Salads don't use iceberg lettuce, pastas and sandwiches are creative, and dinner entrees are varied from prime rib to chicken piccata but include a Friday Fish Fry. Open for lunch and dinner, closed Mon. Prices for most items are under $10, while dinner entrees stay under $20.

ISHNALA RESTAURANT
S2011 Ishnala Rd., Lake Delton
(608) 253-1771
www.ishnala.com
This supper club overlooks beautiful Mirror Lake and its Arrowhead Bar makes a fine perch for a predinner cocktail. The Coleman family built a log cabin here in 1909. When the Hoffman brothers built a restaurant in 1955, they incorporated much of the original structure. The dining room floor shows 76 tons of flagstones quarried locally, a few live pine trees grow up through the floor, and the views from the dining room are wonderful. The menu centers around naturally aged steaks with some surf and turf options. All meals come with salad and potato. The road to the restaurant was used for a scene in the movie *Public Enemies*. Heading west toward Mirror Lake State Park from US 12 (south of the Dells and the Interstate), watch for Ishnala Road and a totem pole on the right (north). The restaurant is open daily for dinner Memorial Day to mid-Sept. Entree prices hover around $35.

MOOSEJAW PIZZA AND DELLS BREWING CO.
110 Wisconsin Dells Pkwy. South, Wisconsin Dells
(608) 254-1122
www.dellsmoosejaw.com
With a big moose sprawled on the roof of the delivery car, you can't miss this place. Decorated as a northwoods lodge and showcasing a copper brew system, Moosejaw has appeal for the eyes as well as the appetite. The beer here is all brewed on site and uses locally grown hops. Open daily for lunch, dinner, and evening drinks. Check the Web site for coupons.

RIVER MOON CAFÉ
770 US Hwy. 12, Wisconsin Dells
Lower Dells Boat Docks
(608) 254-4141
This eatery takes the traveler out of the hectic action of the Dells and offers great fresh food with homemade touches in a comfortable, peaceful place. Expect fresh sandwiches, pastas, soups, and salads. The desserts are exceptional. Eat on the back deck for a great view of the river and dam. Reasonably priced.

State Parks

MIRROR LAKE STATE PARK
E10320 Fern Dell Rd., Baraboo
(608) 254-2333
www.dnr.state.wi.us/org/land/parks/regions/
scr/mirrorlake.html

Just south of the I-90/94 this state park is as placid and peaceful as the Dells are up and running. Bluffs and their carved sandstone cliffs surround an oddly shaped lake whose surface often perfectly mirrors the sky. Activities include hiking, swimming, off-road biking, and boating. There are three campgrounds with 151 sites. In the winter trails are converted for cross-country skiing. Bike, boat, canoe, and kayak rentals are available within the park. A state park vehicle fee applies. One cabin and hiking trail are wheelchair accessible.

ROCKY ARBOR STATE PARK
N381 US Hwy. 12/16, Wisconsin Dells
(608) 254-8001 (from Memorial Day to Labor Day)
(608) 254-2333 (the rest of the year)
www.dnr.state.wi.us/org/land/parks/specific/
rockyarbor

For a trip back 500 million years, stop in at this state park for a picnic or a hike. Just northwest of the Dells and right off the Interstate, the 224-acre Rocky Arbor is a beauty just a few minutes from the action. A 1-mile self-guided nature trail follows a former bed of the Wisconsin River, and along the trail are several species of rare plants and some exposed sandstone carved by flowing water. In the center of this green canyon is an old outcrop, what was once an island in the stream. A nice little playground is in the parking area. Showers and flush toilets serve the park's 89 campsites. A state park vehicle fee applies.

In Nearby Baraboo

CIRCUS WORLD MUSEUM
550 Water St., Baraboo
(608) 356-8341
www.circusworldmuseum.com

The Ringling Brothers circus was created in 1884 by five brothers from Wisconsin. Their first show was held in Mazomanie but they made their home in Baraboo. Their success was great, and in 1907 they even bought their competition, the Barnum and Bailey Show. Many of the old buildings remain on the circus' wintering site there. Visitors can see more than 200 restored circus wagons, a massive collection of posters (including one of Buffalo Bill's Wild West), a documentary about the circus and its founders, and some circus animals as well. KidsWorld Circus takes children from the audience and creates some circus acts with them involving magic and costumed kid-tigers jumping through hoops. This National Historic Landmark is operated by the Wisconsin State Historical Society. Open year-round—daily in the summer and shoulder seasons, but with limited hours and days from about late Oct into Apr.

INTERNATIONAL CRANE FOUNDATION
E11376 Shady Lane Rd., Baraboo
(608) 356-9462.
www.savingcranes.org

The whooping crane was once nearly lost to history with numbers down under 100. The rarest of the 15 species of cranes in the world, the whooping crane is part of an amazing come back with the help of some dedicated and clever volunteers. Each year several young cranes raised in captivity by caretakers dressed in cranelike disguises are trained in the fall to migrate south for the winter following an ultralight airplane. It's an incredible story and both the birds and the history of the project can be found at the ICF. All 15 species are on display here and their calls echo across the grounds. See the mating dances in the spring. Trails on-site pass through oak savanna and prairies. An educational center features interactive exhibits, and a gift shop sells memorabilia. Open daily Apr 15 through Oct 31. Guided tours and audio tours are available. Fee.

Shopping

CARR VALLEY CHEESE STORE
420 Broadway, Wisconsin Dells
(608) 254-7200
www.carrvalleycheese.com

This is the Dells showroom for the award-winning cheese factory headed up by master cheese-maker Sid Cook. Choose from some familiar styles, such as aged cheddars and gouda, or sample one of Sid's American originals, recipes made from goat, sheep, and cow's milk blends and cave aged. Gift boxes are available. Open daily.

SWISS MAID FUDGE
743 Superior St., Wisconsin Dells
(608) 254-7771
www.swissmaidfudge.com
Using copper kettles and marble slabs, this confectioner makes fudge they way it's supposed to be made. A family business since 1962, Swiss Maid is a sweet tooth's dream offering exceptional fudge but also caramels, saltwater taffy, hand-dipped chocolates, caramel apples, and much more. Watch it all being made right there in the shop. Be careful of the free samples. That's how they get you.

TANGER OUTLET CENTER
210 Gasser Rd., Wisconsin Dells
(608) 253-5380
www.tangeroutlet.com/wisconsindells
Located on the north side of I-90/94 at US 12 West/23 North (exit 92), this outlet mall attracts passionate shoppers. Over 60 brand names are represented here including Disney, Polo Ralph Lauren, Crocs, and Old Navy. The Web site offers downloadable coupons.

THE DRIFTLESS AREA

Following US 151 southwest out of Madison takes visitors straight through to Iowa and passing several good attractions. The landscape is characterized by rolling hills and river valleys, and unlike much of the rest of the state there are no natural lakes here. This is called the Driftless Area because it is free from glacial deposits (drift) and was untouched by the last advance of ice 15,000 years ago. The area gave the state its nickname when miners came to dig out the abundant lead, and later zinc, from the land. These same miners initially dug shallow shelters to sleep in at night and the similarity to a badger den didn't go unnoticed.

Blue Mounds

Not much more than a blip on the map, this town nevertheless has two very fine attractions of the natural sort. **Blue Mound State Park** (4350 Mounds Park Rd.; 608-437-5711; www.dnr.state.wi.us) is centered on the tallest hill in southern Wisconsin. The hill is 1,716 feet above sea level and when visitors climb the 40-foot observation towers on the east and west ends of the park, the view is far and wide and includes the Baraboo Hills and the Wisconsin Riverway in the distance. The park contains over 13 miles of hiking trails which are mostly open for skiing in the winter as well. A mountain bike trail circles the hill. The Military Ridge State Trail passes along the park's edge, meaning one could actually bike here from Madison along the former rail bed. Campsites and a swimming pool are also on site.

From high above to deep below, the next site is **Cave of the Mounds** (2975 Cave of the Mounds Rd.; 608-437-3038; www.caveofthemounds.com), a natural limestone cavern that is open for visits year-round. On site is a rock shop, natural trails, and a butterfly farm. Free interpretive programs are available in the Discovery Center. But the main attraction is a guided walk through the stalactites, stalagmites, and beautiful crystal formations of the cave. The cave was formed over a long period of time as acidic water trickled deep into the ground and dissolved limestone, which is over 400 million years old. The path through the cavern is paved and lighted. The temperature remains a cool 50 degrees regardless of the season.

Mineral Point

Mineral Point gets a nod from the National Historic Trust as one of the best places to see. Its preservation has been meticulous and a walk down the street is a step back in time. Settled first by Cornish immigrants, it was a mining town. Look for the visitor center at the intersection of Spruce and Shake Rag Streets. A stop at **Pendarvis** (114 Shake Rag St.; 608-987-2122; http://pendarvis.wisconsinhistory.org) affords a look at the limestone cottages that the immigrants constructed giving the area a bit of an English countryside look. The site is managed by the Wisconsin State Historical Society and guides dressed in period clothing reveal stories of the past.

Another historical structure worth a visit is **Orchard Lawn** (234 Madison St.; 608-987-2884; www.mineralpointhistory.org), a Civil War–era Italianate home that is now the office of the Mineral Point Historical Society. It is open during the summer or by appointment.

While lead brought people in the past, today it is art that draws the crowds. Nearly two dozen art galleries and studios, primarily on High Street or Commerce Street, are open for viewing and purchasing locally made art. The best times to go are the gallery nights held in Apr, June, Aug, and Dec (www.mineralpoint.com/art/index.html). Be sure to eat a Cornish pasty and a figgyhobbin, a pastry with cinnamon, raisins, caramel, and nuts. **The Red Rooster Café** (158 High St.; 608-987-9936) is a good source for both as well as a good hearty breakfast joint.

If you are really in the mood for a drive, head all the way to the Mississippi River and check out the tiny town of Potosi, which has the longest main street without an intersection in the world at 3 miles. In town is **St. John Mine** (129 South Main St.; 608-763-2121) which sells an hour's guided tour into the old mine. Not far past that closer to the river is the old Potosi Brewery. This large brick building has been restored and now not only is it brewing beer again, but it is also home to the **Great River Road Interpretive Center** (www.wigreatriverroad.org) and the **National Brewery Museum** (209 South Main St.; 608-763-4002; www.potosibrewery.com). The brewpub offers a full menu to go along with some Good Ole Potosi and other microbeers.

WISCONSIN RIVER AND HILLS OF BARABOO

Sauk City/Prairie du Sac

The Wisconsin River passes these sister cities on its way to the Mississippi. Before crossing the river into Saul City, go east to **Wollersheim**

Winery, arguably the state's finest. In the 1840s, Hungarian-born Agoston Haraszthy, now considered the "Father of California Viticulture," stopped first in Wisconsin. When he left for the Gold Rush, a German family took over for a couple generations before giving up on wine. The Wollersheim family and their French son-in-law have brought the vineyard back from the dead and the winery has won several awards. Tours and tastings are offered daily.

Exploring the Wisconsin River for a few hours, a full day, or even an overnight stay on one of the many sandbars is a great adventure. Rent a canoe (pickup and drop off shuttle available) at **Sauk Prairie Canoe Center** (500 Water St.; 608-643-6589; www.spcanoerentals.com), which has been an outfitter since 1971.

Baraboo

Farther north just before Baraboo is one of the state's most popular parks, **Devil's Lake State Park** (S5975 Park Rd. Baraboo; 608-356-8301; www.dnr.state.wi.us). Two incredible rocky bluffs rise up on either side of the lake, which was formed when two glacial moraines plugged either end of the gorge. The scenery is stunning, and the hike to the top of either bluff is a challenging but rewarding endeavor. The north and south ends offer swimming areas, and the park has 407 campsites. Miles and miles of trails explore the surrounding terrain and the **Ice Age National Scenic Trail** passes through the heart of the park. Just to the west of the park is **Ski-Hi Fruit Farm** (E11219A Ski-Hi Rd.; 608-356-3695), which sells 35 varieties of apples as well as pies, cider, and turnovers. The season begins at the end of summer and continues into Nov.

In Baraboo visit **Circus World Museum** (550 Water St.; 608-356-8341; www.circusworldmuseum.com) on the site of the original Ringling Brothers Circus. Many of the old buildings remain and the circus train cars have been restored. There is plenty for kids and adults. If you like soup, don't miss **Jen's Alpine Café** (117 Fourth St.; 608-356-4040; www.foodspot.com/jensalpine) which specializes in them. Stop in for breakfast or lunch or get a fish fry on a Fri night. **The Ho-Chunk Casino** (S3214 US 12; 800-746-2486, www.hochunk.com) is just north of Baraboo before the highway reaches the Wisconsin Dells.

WEST TO SPRING GREEN

Spring Green

The small city has a variety of small art shops and makes for a nice weekend escape from Madison. Consider an overnight stay at **Hill Street Bed & Breakfast** (353 West Hill St.; 608-588-7751; www.hillstreetbb.com), a 1904 Queen Anne Victorian home.

One of the principle attractions in Spring Green is Frank Lloyd Wright. Wright was born in Richland Center, WI, in 1867. As a young architect he went to work for Louis Sullivan in Chicago for a few years before leaving to make a name for himself. And that he did. His designs are world famous—the Guggenheim Museum in New York City, the residential Fallingwater in Pennsylvania—and his mark is left in several places in Madison as well (see Attractions). But his estate is the epicenter of the Wright story. The fascinating experimental home and the Hillside Studio where students still study architecture should not be missed and stories of his personal life play out like a soap opera. Tours of the estate begin from the **Frank Lloyd Wright Visitor Center** (5607 County Hwy. C; 877-588-7900; www.taliesinpreservation.org), which has a gift shop and a cafe serving breakfast, lunch, and dinner. Tours include information both on his work and his colorful life. Reservations are highly recommended. The tour season runs from May through Oct.

Not far down the road from Taliesin is another sort of architecture: the **House on the Rock** (5754 State Hwy. 23; 800-334-5275; www.thehouseontherock.com). Alex Jordan, a man apparently with a knack for collecting odd items, began building his own sort of experimental home on a high rocky bluff in the 1940s. An infinity room stretches out over the cliff for a dizzying view. The labyrinthine halls and rooms of the house and several more exhibition halls house an endless series of collections and oddities including rooms full of dolls, antiques, and a massive indoor carousel with 289 exotic creatures and thousands of lights.

A night in the woods with Shakespeare is a memorable Spring Green experience. **American Players Theatre** (5950 Golf Course Rd.; 608-588-2361; www.playinthewoods.org) hosts plays in both indoor and outdoor venues. The focus is Shakespeare and several other classics fall into the mix. This is one of the finest theatrical experiences in the Midwest. If you choose not to picnic at American Players Theatre before the show, consider a dinner at **The Bank Restaurant & Wine Bar** (134 West Jefferson St.; 608-588-7600; www.thebankrestaurantandwinebar.com). The converted 1915 bank offers fine dining and a wine list of 200 or more vintages.

> **i** Not long before Spring Green is the small town of Arena. Look for the big mouse at the side of the highway marking Arena Cheese (300 US 14; 608-753-2501; www.arenacheese.com). This is a perfect stop for fresh cheese curds and a whole variety of other cheeses including cheese gift boxes. A viewing window in the shop lets visitors watch cheese being made.

GREEN COUNTY: CHEESE AND BEER

Green County has a tremendous reputation for its cheese. Several cheese factories still operate through the county and some of the artisan varieties have taken awards in competition. The backroads wind through forest and farmland, and many of the small towns have preserved their historic buildings and yesteryear main streets.

New Glarus

New Glarus has long been known in Wisconsin as America's Little Switzerland, but a more recent arrival than the 1845 Swiss pioneers has given the town name a different sort of notoriety. **New Glarus Brewery** (119 County Rd. W; 608-527-5850; www.newglarusbrewing.com) has two brewing sites, one on either end of town. The older, smaller one brews their specialty beers while the new multimillion dollar brewery on the hill is where the tours are and where Spotted Cow, the flagship beer is produced.

Up the hill in town, the **Swiss Historical Village** (612 Seventh Ave.; 608-527-2317; www.swisshistoricalvillage.org) is a collection of 14 old buildings. Visitors learn more about those Swiss pioneers and the life they created here. Take a tour or stop in the gift shop for imported Swiss products including Schabziger (Sap Sago), a herb-infused hard cheese from the Canton of Glarus. As for the rest of the town you may think you are in Switzerland. Buildings show chalet detailing, Swiss flags flap in the breeze, and most every business with the word "house" in its name seems to spell it "haus." Antique and gift shops are abundant and the restaurants lean toward Swiss cuisine.

A stop for lunch at **Puempel's Olde Tavern** (18 Sixth Ave.; 608-527-2045; www.puempels.com) is common and inside are some 1913 murals (not Swiss, but Austrian). For some Swiss fondue head to **The New Glarus Hotel Restaurant** (100 Sixth Ave.; 608-527-5244; www.newglarushotel.com) or **Glarner Stube** (518 First St.; 608-527-2216). For cheese to take home, **Maple Leaf Cheese** (554 First St.; 608-527-2000; www.mapleleafcheeseandchocolatehaus.com) is a good bet, but the incredible fresh fudge might be more tempting.

i Located between New Glarus and Monroe along WI 69 is Monticello where you should definitely consider a stop for dinner at the award-winning Dining Room (149 North Main St., Monticello; 608-938-4912; www.209main.com).

Monroe

Monroe is the American capital of Swiss Cheese. Just north of Monroe near Monticello, Bruce Workman, Master Cheesemaker at **Edelweis**

Creamery (W6117 County Hwy. C, Monticello; 608-938-4094; www.edelweisscreamery.com) makes 180-pound Emmentaler cheese wheels with traditional copper equipment. Heading into Monroe, the Roth Käse cheese factory's store **Alp and Dell** (657 Second St.; 608-328-3355) makes another cheesy stop for the day with a viewing window for visitors to see the process. For the seriously adventurous, try another local favorite in the cheese department: limburger. The odiferous soft cheese may be an acquired taste, and a good place to make that attempt is **Baumgartner's Cheese Store and Tavern** (1023 Sixteenth Ave.; 608-325-6157), which builds deli sandwiches with several varieties besides limburger and serves locally brewed beer. Downtown shops line the town square which features the photogenic 1891 Green County Courthouse and its four-faced clock tower.

i Green County Cheese Days (www.cheesedays.com), a tradition since 1914, occur in Monroe the third weekend in Sept of even-numbered years. Attendees exceed 100,000 and the event hosts a parade, tractor pull, arts and crafts fair, polka music, yodeling, and absurd amounts of cheese and beer.

Not to be outdone by New Glarus, Monroe too has a beer tradition. **Minhas Craft Brewery** (1208 Fourteenth Ave.; 608-325-3191; www.minhasbrewery.com)—formerly Huber Brewery and founded in 1845 as Blumer Brewery—is the second longest continuously operating brewery in the country. Stop in for a tour and visit the museum and gift store. For something a little different in the age of digitized surround sound stadium-seating cinemas, stick around for an evening at a classic drive-in. The family-run **Goetz Sky-Vu Drive-in** (1936 State Route 69; 608-325-4545) just south of town has been in business since 1954. The double-features cater to families.

Appendix

LIVING HERE

In this section we feature specific information for residents or those planning to relocate here. Topics include real estate, education, health care, and much more.

RELOCATION

Madison was all about promise and potential when James Duane Doty first campaigned for the paper city on an isthmus when the territorial government had to choose its capital. There wasn't even a single cabin on the hill at the center. But modern-day Madison is the promise fulfilled. A beautiful city with lakes and green space, a world-class university, and a Midwestern friendliness that is hard not to like. Since the 1960s when it was touted as the best place to live in the USA, Madison has won hearts and minds and kept Ph.D. graduates in jobs for which they are overqualified. Since its number one rating in *Money Magazine* in 1996, it seems that the number of "best of" listings in publications has grown exponentially to the point of becoming cliché. Not only is Madison one of the tops for bicycling, walking, and recently, for adventure (*National Geographic Adventure Magazine*), it also ranks high for job opportunity, starting a business, healthy living, education, and just being one of the "most livable" cities. Apparently, Madisonians also have the best teeth. Whatever might draw a person to Madison, few will be those who regret the choice.

Within this chapter is information about making that move—a review of some of the popular neighborhoods and nearby communities, listings of real-estate firms, neighborhood libraries, radio and TV stations, and even instructions on how to register to vote or change your driver's license.

NEIGHBORHOODS

Downtown

The area around the Capitol has abundant rental properties, and students have the majority of the territory covered but for some assorted single family homes. Condos, however, are abundant up around the Capitol Square and overlooking John Nolen Drive and sell for some premium prices.

East Side

Williamson–Marquette

The Wil–Mar neighborhood nestles in on the north side of Lake Monona and from the edge of downtown stretches along Willy (Williamson) Street toward the Yahara River. Since the 1960s it has been labeled as the "hippie" part of town, and for some there's no getting over that image despite the growth of some condo projects, a planned Central Park, and the scattering of great restaurants that often attract a hip, modern crowd. Community-supported neighborhood festivals reveal a strong sense of place and are awaited with great anticipation each summer. The ethnic and eclectic eateries, coffee shops, and a few music venues spread throughout make Wil–Mar very walkable. Houses tend to be old multistory affairs or bungalows, the kind with front porches, and they sit rather close together with modest yards and off-street parking (though not always). Rentals are always available and some of the student population is drawn here, often of the graduate level type. The paved Capital City bike path passes through parallel to Willy Street, and the Willy Street Co-op attracts foodies and shoppers concerned about where their food comes from. Farther east from here is Schenk–Atwood.

Tenney–Lapham

Located opposite East Washington Avenue from the Williamson–Marquette neighborhood,

Tenney–Lapham also runs east to the Yahara but borders on the other lake, Mendota. It includes the fabulous Tenney Park popular for shoreline fishing, ice-skating in winter, and swimming and water sports in summer. A bike path connects it across the isthmus to the Capital City path. At its eastern end close to downtown lies James Madison Park another lakeshore green space with an outfitter for recreational rentals. Several blocks of local shops and eateries make up the East Johnson Business District, the small commercial center of the neighborhood. Housing varies from expensive and historic lakeside mansions, to modest apartment and condo complexes.

Schenk–Atwood–Starkweather–Yahara

Schenk's Corners, where Atwood Avenue meets Winnebago Street, takes its name from a family-owned general store opened here in 1893 and lies to the westerly side of this area south of East Washington Avenue bounded by the Yahara River, Lake Monona, and Starkweather Creek. The small commercial zone spread along Atwood Avenue functions as a sort of "downtown" for the neighborhood. The spirit of this area of town isn't much different from Wil–Mar. Once a blue-collar neighborhood, it is characterized by modest revitalized single-family homes with the porch-and-yard neighborly feel to them. Jenifer Street Market though not a co-op still has a local-business appeal, and the restaurants and bars along Atwood Avenue and surrounding the popular concert venue the Barrymore Theatre are popular hangouts. At the easterly end are the lovely Olbrich Gardens and the city park of the same name with Starkweather Creek sneaking through to Lake Monona. The Goodman Community Center is the important social heart for the neighborhood, especially for youth and seniors, and offers a fitness center and food pantry. Atwood Summerfest, the annual neighborhood festival, raises money to support it. Community activism is abundant, and the residents have invested a lot of effort into improving and maintaining the quality of the neighborhood.

West Side

Vilas–Greenbush

With Vilas to the west and Greenbush to the east, these two neighborhoods fill in the area south of downtown toward Lake Wingra and Wingra Creek. Along the west side is the popular Monroe Street with a variety of great local shops and restaurants and the diminutive but nevertheless highly convenient Monroe Street Branch Library. Houses in the Vilas area tend to be larger and include a variety of well known styles such as Victorian, Queen Anne, and Craftsman. The Wingra Park National Register Historic District is established in a portion of the neighborhood: a federal tax credit program to assist property-owners in renovation costs of their historic properties. Camp Randall is close to the north while the zoo, Lake Wingra, and Vilas Park are walking distance to the southwest. Greenbush was once home to many Italian and Eastern European immigrants. Mixed apartment complexes have since replaced the old buildings at its east side near Monona Bay. St. Mary's and Meriter Hospitals are in this neighborhood. The bungalows and more modest houses closer to Vilas are slightly less pricey, while the same attractions and parks that Vilas enjoys are just a slightly longer walk away.

Dudgeon–Monroe

With so many lakes it is not surprising to have so many neighborhoods bordered by water and this is a gem on that list. Monroe Street heads west from Camp Randall Stadium, passing through two walkable neighborhood commercial zones with fine restaurants, quaint shops, and a few good taverns (plus a Trader Joe's). Down side streets shaded with plenty of old trees, you will find an abundance of big old-school midwestern homes as well as the more modest bungalows and Cape Cods. Wingra Park and the northern portion of the Arboretum are just part of the abundant green space perfect for walkers and joggers. The extremely popular Southwest Commuter Path passes through the backyards just off Monroe Street. The preschool through college campus of Edgewood is also part of the neighborhood as is the Glenway Children's Park.

Regent Neighborhood/ University Heights

This neighborhood lies west of Camp Randall Stadium along Regent Street and south of University Avenue. The University Heights portion is a historic district and many houses were built at the end of the late 19th century. The area has the advantage of being at once peaceful and just off the main thoroughfares to get around town. Homes along Regent Street have traffic to contend with, but the size and quality of the houses is often worth the trade off for homebuyers. Randall Elementary and Madison West High School are in the area.

Midvale Heights/Westmorland

Bounded Mineral Point Road to the north, Odana Road to the south, Glenway Golf Course to the east, and Whitney Way to the west, the two neighborhoods are divided by Midvale Boulevard. These were the suburbs in the 1950s, and houses radiate the idyllic coziness from that decade, but some homes from the earlier settlement years, large Victorians, and some luxury properties round out the mix. The new Sequoya Library sits at the center and the Beltline Highway is just a few minutes down Midvale, while University Avenue and Hilldale Mall are just a bit farther in the opposite direction making this location enviable.

North Side
Maple Bluff

Though some may imagine it is a Madison neighborhood, Maple Bluff (www.villageofmaplebluff .com) is actually a village by itself and often referred to as a suburb though it begins just about at the Tenney Lock and ends at Warner Park completely engulfed by Madison. Very fine homes line the shore of Lake Mendota on the west with houses becoming more modest with distance from the lake. Sherman Avenue serves as the border to the east providing quick access to a few small shopping complexes. In the past it has been characterized as conservative and wealthy but changing times have given the area

a bit more diversity. The area is known for some residential gardens that open to the public once a year.

Northport–Warner Park– Sherman Neighborhoods

East of Sherman are modestly priced often modestly sized single-family homes in quiet neighborhoods. Heading across Northport one finds an area of multiunit apartment complexes and then larger single family homes farther west near Cherokee Marsh.

South Side

Areas south of the Beltline run the gamut from the Allied Drive region in the southwest plagued by a negative reputation and crime/poverty issues to the affluent Arbor Hills just south of the Arboretum. Neighborhoods are constantly changing and it is good to consult current real-estate material about prices and trends. Farther out at the edges of the city and on into Fitchburg, new development continues.

NEARBY COMMUNITIES

FITCHBURG
www.city.fitchburg.wi.us
Fitchburg can be somewhat elusive for anyone looking at a map. The land just south of Madison on both the end of Park Street, Fish Hatchery Road, and Verona Road falls under its purview. Depending on what direction you are coming, you might just see farmland behind the roadside sign. Much of Fitchburg is just 10 minutes from downtown. Especially along the south side of Madison, the typical traveler wouldn't know where the town ends and the city begins but for a road sign. But Fitchburg is hardly an extension of the city. The city offers some chain restaurants and shops as well as some very good locally owned eateries and its own brewpub. State multiuse trails including the Capital City, Military Ridge, and the most recent, the Badger State, pass right through Fitchburg making the city a magnet for cyclers.

MCFARLAND

www.mcfarland.wi.us

The Village of McFarland has its own school system with schools that have seemed to hit the optimum size of not too big, not too small, and with a bit of diversity. Being just a couple minutes south of the Beltline Highway on Stoughton Road/US 51 gives it a not too far location as well. The population is about 7,500, and the village has its own library.

MIDDLETON

www.ci.middleton.wi.us

Heading west, University Avenue heads right into the city of Middleton, which seems to blend right into Madison. When the city was ranked as the Best Place to Live in the United States in 2007, however, it removed all question that this was its own community. With a population of just under 20,000, Middleton has the appeal of a small town but is just minutes from the center of its much larger neighbor. The Good Neighbor City, as it calls itself, has done much to revitalize its downtown including a remodeling of a Victorian-style train depot from the town's railroad beginnings. Some of the fine restaurants in the Restaurant chapter make their home here and a variety of boutique shops as well. Its proximity to Madison's west side, and its own areas of strip malls, make it convenient for shopping. Other public resources include the library—which has been acknowledged as one of the state's best by the Wisconsin Library Association—a farmers' market, the Walter R. Bauman Outdoor Aquatic Center, a performing arts center, and a network of trails through several very nice parks and a nature conservancy. The community falls under the jurisdiction of the Middleton–Cross Plains Area School District.

MONONA/COTTAGE GROVE

www.monona.wi.us

www.village.cottage-grove.wi.us

They share the same school district but Monona lies nestled into Madison along the east shore of Lake Monona, while Cottage Grove is a short drive east into the country. Whereas Monona has older neighborhoods rich with old trees and developed parks, Cottage Grove is a city on the build. The multiuse Glacial Drumlin State Trail, which passes on an old rail bed all the way to Waukesha, has its western terminus in Cottage Grove. Plans are to connect the path into Madison and the Capital City Trail. Both towns have their own established commercial zones and don't rely on Madison for much other than the big box stores and the larger job market.

OREGON

www.vil.oregon.wi.us

Surrounded by farmland and about a 15-minute drive south of Madison along US 14, Oregon is a community of just under 10,000 but is growing fast. Its small downtown area has been restored to its historic look and offers a handful of restaurants and shops. It has its own high school and is part of the Oregon Area School District, which includes the tiny town of Brooklyn.

SUN PRAIRIE

www.cityofsunprairie.com

To the east of Madison just 10 miles and with a population of over 28,000, Sun Prairie is its own city. The community has one high school, two middle schools, seven elementary schools, and three parochial schools. A second high school is in the planning stages. Its proximity to Madison is convenient for employment on the east side, and the lower home prices are tempting people to commute.

VERONA

www.ci.verona.wi.us

This city of just over 12,000 is growing fast as a bedroom community to Madison. Located southwest of the city and separated from it by farmland, Verona is about a 15-minute commute from the Capitol Square and downtown. Epic Software Systems built its enormous campus here and funded its own Madison Metro bus for commuters. Verona's school system receives high marks. Other facilities cater to the youth such as the 40-acre, 15-field Reddan Soccer Park, a natatorium, University Ridge Golf Course, and the Eagles Nest Ice Arena, which offers year-round skating and hockey programs on an Olympic-size rink. US 151 passes along the edge of the city with several access points making a trip into Madison quick and easy.

REAL ESTATE

At the end of 2009 the average home price for Madison was $250,000, and buyers had the advantage with an abundance of houses on the market and sale prices coming in at 5–10% off the asking price. The most envied neighborhoods are generally the near east, such as Wil–Mar and Schenk–Atwood, and near west such as Dudgeon–Monroe, Westmorland, or Vilas—well established neighborhoods with older houses, some of them historic, and plenty of old trees. Some sellers don't go through the traditional real estate firms and there is a healthy market of FSBO's (For Sale By Owner) that you can find online at www.fsbomadison.com. You can sort by price and neighborhood. Also have a look at the South Central Wisconsin Multiple Listings Service (www.scwmls.com) where you can find the property listings of more than 500 real estate firms.

Popular Real Estate Firms

BUNBURY & ASSOCIATES
6180 Verona Rd.
(608) 310-5777
www.bunburyrealtors.com

CENTURY 21 AFFILIATED
221 West Beltline Hwy.
(608) 221-2121
www.c21affiliated.com

COLDWELL BANKER SUCCESS
2927 South Fish Hatchery Rd., Fitchburg
(608) 276-3161
www.cbsuccessrealty.com

FIRST WEBER GROUP
5250 East Terrace Dr.
(608) 443-2277
www.firstWeber.com

KELLER WILLIAMS REALTY
3 Point Place
(608) 831-0800
http://madisonwest.yourkwoffice.com

RE/MAX PREFERRED
2970 Chapel Valley Rd.
(800) 236-4411
www.madisonpreferred.com

RESTAINO & ASSOCIATES
2970 Schroeder Ct.
(800) 637-1178
www.restainohomes.com

STARK COMPANY REALTORS
2980 Arapaho Dr.
(608) 256-9011
www.starkhomes.com

Apartment Living

This is a university town so don't be surprised if some of the apartment rentals seem a little high priced in the downtown area. Often large houses show two or three flats. In some cases houses down around the UW campus rent out one room at a time with shared facilities. Returning students will often get together with a group of friends or place ads for roommates to rent an entire house. Condos around the Capitol have some attractive views and prices that rise as high as the buildings themselves. Young professionals working in the downtown area might prefer these. Some apartment complexes are also scattered within the residential neighborhoods near there. But moving out from the isthmus rents start going down quickly especially in the cases of aging buildings and distances not entirely convenient to campus. Something very important to consider when renting downtown is the parking situation. Neighborhoods have parking permit stickers, and in winter the plowing of snow means a lot of shuffling cars in limited space. Off-street parking in these neighborhoods is as good as gold (and may cost you some). Leases vary from month-to-month to full year deals. Anything student-related will likely run one-year leases beginning Aug 15 and during the summer months sublets are abundant.

The **Tenant Resource Center** (1202 Williamson St., Suite A; 608-257-0006) offers great free advice and good information about the ins and outs of renting. The center often mediates housing-related disputes and publishes a useful self-help guide for renters and landlords. University of Wisconsin students can consult the **Campus Assistance Center** (The Red Gym, 716 Langdon St.; 608-263-2400) about off-campus housing matters and a housing listing.

Craigslist (http://madison.craigslist.org) and the local classifieds (especially in the weekly *Isthmus* or on www.madison.com) are good resources for apartment listings. **Start Renting Inc.** (102 North Franklin Ave.; 608-257-4990; www.startrenting.com) has searchable listings for the greater Madison area or you can go online and order your free copy of www.madison.com's *Apartment Showcase Magazine* (http://aptshowcase.madison.com) which explores Madison and Dane County options.

VOTER REGISTRATION

Voters can register until 5 p.m. 20 days before an election at any Madison Public Library, any Madison Fire Station, or in the City Clerk's Office. This is the "open registration" period and no proof of residence is needed. Registration can also be done via mail. Voter registration application forms are available in English, Spanish, and Hmong. Register by downloading an application from the City Clerk Web site, completing it, and mailing it to City Clerk, 210 Martin Luther King Jr. Blvd. #103, Madison, WI 53703. The registration form must be *postmarked* 20 days or more before any election you plan to vote in. First-time Wisconsin voters must include a photocopy of one form of proof of residence. This can be a current and valid Wisconsin driver's license or Wisconsin identification card, or other official Wisconsin ID, an employer-issued photo ID, a real-estate tax bill (or real-estate tax receipt for the current year or

the year before the election), a student photo ID from University of Wisconsin–Madison or Edgewood College, a utility bill dated within 90 days of the election, or a current bank statement, paycheck, or government-issued statement. The State of Wisconsin requires an original signature on a voter registration form, so faxes and e-mails must be followed up with an original copy being delivered to the City Clerk's Office.

Once registration closes at 5 p.m. 20 days before an election, voter registration can only be done in person in the City Clerk's Office with proof of residence until 5 p.m. the day before the election. Any of the previously mentioned proofs of residence can be used or a corroborating witness can accompany the voter to the Clerk's Office. The witness must be eligible to vote in the City of Madison, have proof of residence, and be able to verify the registering voter's residency information. And as remarkable as it may seem, voters in Wisconsin can register right at the polls on Election Day using the same proofs of residence. Where one votes depends on one's address. Call the City Clerk's Office (608-266-4601) or consult the City Clerk Web site (www.cityofmadison.com/clerk) under "Where Do I Vote?" in the left column menu to find out the appropriate polling place.

DRIVER'S LICENSES AND VEHICLE REGISTRATION

Driver's licenses and tests of course must be taken care of in person. License plate renewal and vehicle registration are possible by mail and on the Internet. The centers accept only cash or checks. Credit cards can only be used on the Web site (www.dot.wisconsin.gov).

MADISON EAST SERVICE CENTER
2001 Bartillon Dr.
(608) 266-1466

MADISON WEST SERVICE CENTER
Hill Farms State Transportation Building
4802 Sheboygan Ave.
(800) 924-3570

**MADISON EXPRESS SERVICE CENTER–
RENEWAL OFFICE**
302 Westgate Mall (at Whitney Way and
Odana Road)
(608) 266-2353

LIBRARIES

The **Madison Public Library System** (www
.madisonpubliclibrary.org) is often taken for
granted. The Central Library at 201 West Mifflin
St. is across the street from the Overture Center
and eight other branches are spread throughout
the city. There are plans in the works to create a
$47 million flagship library facility on the other
side of the block, but the current building still
functions well as a place for those downtown to
pick up a book or movie, get on the Internet, or
consult a librarian. The superb reservation system,
which can be accessed online (www.linkcat.info),
allows users to have their held items sent to their
local library branch anywhere in the city. This
eliminates a trip to a faraway branch or the downtown location with its traffic and parking issues.
The reservation system can call up items from
libraries throughout the South Central Library
System (SCLS) including Verona, Baraboo, DeForest, and Stoughton among others. Interlibrary
loans are delivered every working day. Anyone
with a library card within the SCLS can use that at
Madison libraries as well.

All libraries offer magazines and newspapers,
DVDs and videos, CDs, and a reference section,
and of course plenty of books including the latest bestsellers often in numerous copies. Latest
releases of bestsellers and films on DVD also
typically have copies for low-price rental to try
to satisfy the demand. In the online reservation
system one can see how far down the waiting
list he or she is. Computers are available for word
processing, searching the library catalog and
databases, and Internet use. Wireless Internet
is free. To obtain a library card requires proof
of residence such as photo I.D. with a current
address or a photo I.D. and a current lease, check,
or dated piece of mail with a current Madison
address on it. All libraries are closed on Sun with
the exception of the Central and Sequoya Branch,
which open Sun afternoons during part of the
academic year.

Madison Library Locations

ALICIA ASHMAN BRANCH
733 North High Point Rd.
(608) 824-1780

CENTRAL LIBRARY
201 West Mifflin St.
(608) 266-6300

HAWTHORNE BRANCH
2707 East Washington Ave.
(608) 246-4548

LAKEVIEW BRANCH
2845 North Sherman Ave.
(608) 246-4547

MEADOWRIDGE BRANCH
5740 Raymond Rd.
(608) 288-6160

MONROE STREET BRANCH
1705 Monroe St.
(608) 266-6390

PINNEY BRANCH
204 Cottage Grove Rd.
(608) 224-7100

SEQUOYA BRANCH
4340 Tokay Blvd.
(608) 266-6385

SOUTH MADISON BRANCH
2222 South Park St.
(608) 266-6395

Other Libraries Nearby

MIDDLETON PUBLIC LIBRARY
7425 Hubbard Ave., Middleton
(608) 831-5564
www.midlibrary.org

MONONA PUBLIC LIBRARY
1000 Nichols Rd., Monona
(608) 222-6127
www.mononalibrary.org

WORSHIP

Considering the melting pot of Madison's population, one can expect a corresponding spectrum of spiritual beliefs. Christians, especially Lutherans and Catholics, may be the largest population, but does not even begin to summarize the scope. Even within the Christian community are faith-free churches, Greek Orthodox, and African American congregations. Islam, Judaism, Buddhism, and even Wiccan are represented. Many religious-based foundations contribute to local charities and causes. The Freedom from Religion Foundation (www.ffrf.org) is a group of atheists and agnostics that focus on keeping church and state separate with attention to detail and a passion that approaches the religious itself. Watch around Dec when the battles over holiday decorations begin down at the Capitol.

Grace Episcopal on 6 North Carroll St. opened its doors back in 1858 and today is the only church on the Capitol Square. Lutheran churches are the most abundant. Arguably the best known—possibly for its size or its reputable outreach programs—is Bethel Lutheran at 312 Wisconsin Ave. What started as an 1855 Norwegian Lutheran congregation now also offers service in Spanish and with signing for the deaf. The Wisconsin Lutheran Chapel and Student Center at 220 West Gilman St. is active on campus for worship, Bible study, and other social programs, as is St. Paul's University Chapel at 723 State St. Holy Redeemer Church at 120 West Johnson St. is a German Catholic church dating to 1869, the second oldest in town. With a congregation dating back to before Wisconsin became a state, First United Methodist Church at 203 Wisconsin Ave. offers youth ministries programs and outreach including a food pantry. The largest Catholic churches are St. Dennis on the east side at 313 Dempsey Rd., and Our Lady Queen of Peace on the west side at 401 South Owen Dr. Blessed Sacrament on the west side at 2116 Hollister St. is also rather popular. Mount Zionist Baptist at 2019 Fisher St. is the largest African American congregation in town.

Synagogues include the Beth Israel Center at 1406 Mound St. and Temple Beth El, which is a Reform congregation, at 2702 Arbor Dr. The B'nai N'rith Hillel Foundation near campus at 611 Langdon St. is also a good resource for the Jewish community. The Islamic Centre of Madison can be found at 21 North Orchard St. and the Society of Friends Quaker Meeting House is located at 1704 Roberts Ct. Buddhists have resources at Deer Park Center, a Buddhist monastery in nearby Oregon, WI. The Dalai Lama seems to be a regular visitor to Madison, drawing admirers from a variety of faiths to his speaking engagements. If you are Greek Orthodox, or if you haven't seen the ornate Byzantine style, stop in at Assumption Greek Orthodox Church at 11 North Seventh St.

The First Unitarian Society of Madison has some interesting digs at 900 University Bay Dr. Frank Lloyd Wright was the architect behind its design. Circle Sanctuary welcomes others of the Shamanic Wiccan tradition and has a 200-acre nature preserve in the hills near Barneveld, WI (www.circlesanctuary.org).

> **i** Madison has its own Catholic diocese with over 130 parishes in 11 counties.

MEDIA

TV Channels

Since the move to digital transmission, the CBS, NBC, and ABC channels are offering a second embedded channel of alternative programming. WMTV 15 offers a regular transmission of weather-related news. WHA 21 actually offers two extra signals including a "Create" channel with programming focused on cooking, gardening, and DIY, and a "Wisconsin" channel that features many history and travel programs about the Badger State. Charter Cable is the primary cable provider often making temporary offers of bundled cable, phone, and Internet service.

(Watch your bills carefully and understand many offers expire after a designated time period.) Other satellite transmissions are available such as DirecTV. Since all stations broadcast in the immediate Madison area, most are easily picked up by antennae depending on the surroundings (i.e., basements, concrete, or brick walls, etc.)

WISC 3 CBS affiliate www.channel3000.com

WMTV 15 NBC affiliate www.nbc15.com

WHA 21 Wisconsin Public Television www.wpt.org

WKOW 27 ABC affiliate www.wkowtv.com

WMSN 47 FOX affiliate www.fox47.com

WBUW 57 The CW affiliate www.madisonscw.com

Newspapers and Magazines

It seems there is something for everyone in the vestibules of your local grocery stores and other establishments. Stacks of varying periodicals, some magazines, some tabloid-style newspapers, reach out to every age and interest, from *Dane County Parent*, *Sustainable Times*, and the fifty-plus *Dane County Lifestyles*, to *Asian Wisconzine*, *Capital City Hues*, and the LBGT *Our Lives*. These are all free for the taking.

Subscription Magazines

BRAVA

www.bravamagazine.com

The first issue of this magazine ran in 2002, and in 2009 it was purchased from its Madisonian founder Kristin Ericksonby Brave Enterprises, LLC, which is still local. Aimed at Madison women, the monthly magazine presents interviews and profiles of local women, fashion spreads, and features tending toward style, health, home, and family. The company hosts the annual Women's Expo each Nov.

INBUSINESS

www.ibmadison.com

InBusiness focuses on the stories and successes of regional businesspeople, and its subscribers are often area executives. Each year the magazine lists Dane County's top 100 businesses.

MADISON MAGAZINE

www.madisonmagazine.com

The monthly magazine covers dining, area travel, style, art and entertainment, and business features. The Best of Madison reader poll is watched for at the end of every summer. The Web site offers a lot of useful content as well such as a dining guide.

PROGRESSIVE

www.progressive.org

Hardly just a Madison publication, *The Progressive* reaches readers across the country and even beyond the borders. The monthly magazine began in 1909 as the weekly newspaper of Progressive former governor and senator Fighting Bob La Follette. Features include investigative journalism and commentary. The political viewpoint of the content is right there on the cover.

Newspapers

ISTHMUS

www.isthmus.com

www.thedailypage.com

This weekly paper runs feature stories on topics of pertinence to Madison and Dane County residents. Some topics may be controversial or investigative journalism pieces. Also included is a variety of movie, art, entertainment, and dining

---

Student Newspapers

Several student newspapers come out of the University of Wisconsin, two of them officially published by the university. *The Daily Cardinal* was founded in 1892 and *The Badger Herald* was founded in 1969. The left-leaning *Madison Observer*, founded in 2003, and the conservative *Mendota Beacon*, founded in 2005, are also produced by students. All of them are free.

reviews, plus classified ads, and arguably the best weekly calendar of events from movie listings to knitting clubs. Their Web site is the source for what's going on in local entertainment and events. The latest print issue comes out every Thurs. Free.

CAPITAL TIMES
www.madison.com/tct

The newspaper was founded in 1917 by William T. Evjue, a former editor for the *Wisconsin State Journal*. He supported then U.S. Senator Robert Marion "Fighting Bob" La Follette's Progressive ideas and opposed the growing public interest in entering World War I and felt his new newspaper would be more effective in that ambition.

WISCONSIN STATE JOURNAL
www.madison.com/wsj

This newspaper began in 1839 as the weekly *Madison Express*, which went daily 13 years later as *Wisconsin Daily Journal*. The paper took its current name in 1860.

MAXIMUM INK
www.maximumink.com

This monthly newspaper, based in Madison but distributed throughout the state, covers all things musical including interviews, reviews, previews, and features on bands from the local to the international in all styles. The events calendar follows live music around the state. The Web version has a sortable calendar and archived material. Free.

THE ONION
www.theonion.com

America's Finest News Source. This is a Madison original. Founded by a couple of University of Wisconsin students in 1988, the weekly paper prints "fake news" often of a hilarious, political, or borderline offensive nature. In 2001 the *Onion* moved the head office to the Big Apple and its Chicago office is its largest, but it remains near and dear to Madisonians and as always, free. Pick up a copy for a good laugh. The Web site, which nabs over 4 million readers each month, presents some different content and includes audio/video

Madison Newspapers

Madison Newspapers (www.madison .com) is a partnership between two competing newspapers formed in 1948 to cut down on operating costs. The *Wisconsin State Journal* agreed to be a daily morning paper and Sunday newspaper, while the *Capital Times* delivered in the afternoons Mon through Sat. The right leaning *Wisconsin State Journal* and the left-leaning *Capital Times* continued independently under the same roof. On Apr 26, 2008, the *Capital Times* stepped into what appears the future of print journalism and went primarily online. Now a Wed insert in the *Wisconsin State Journal,* the *Capital Times* still offers some in-depth local news and commentary with a progressive bent. The *Capital Times* is also available for free as a stand-alone paper on newsstands. The Web site www.madison.com is the online home of both papers plus *77 Square* and provides up-to-the-minute local news, blogs, forums, and classifieds.

material as well. The paper's A.V. Club insert reviews movies, music, and previews upcoming concerts in an irreverent but honest style. Free.

77 SQUARE
www.madison.com

This weekly newspaper reports on art, culture, and entertainment in the city and provides a few in-depth features on news subjects relevant to Madison. The paper is produced by the *Capital Times* but replaces the Rhythm section in the *Wisconsin State Journal*. The new issue comes out every Thurs and is available as a stand-alone or as an insert in the *WSJ*. Free.

Radio

WERN 88.7 FM	University of Wisconsin Public Radio
WORT 89.9 FM	Progressive Community Radio, talk and music
WJWD 90.3 FM	Christian, Religious
WSUM 91.7 FM	University of Wisconsin College, Alternative music
WXXM 92.1 FM	The MIC 92.1 Madison's Progressive Talk Radio
WHIT 93.1 FM	The Lake 93.1 Classic Rock
WJJO 94.1 FM	Hard rock
WOLX 94.9 FM	Oldies
WBKY 95.9 FM	Country
WMAD 96.3 FM	Mad Radio Alternative, new rock
WMGN 98.1 FM	Magic 98, Adult Contemporary and 70s, 80s
WJVL 99.9FM	Country
WDDC 100.1 FM	Country
WTLX 100.5 FM	Sports
WIBA 101.5 FM	Classic Rock, Packer football games
WBDL 102.9 FM	Adult Contemporary
WZEE 104.1 FM	Z104 FM Top 40
WNFM 104.9 FM	Country
WBZU 105.1 FM	Charlie FM, variety contemporary and classic hits
WMMM 105.5 FM	Triple M, Adult Album Alternative
WKPO 105.9 FM	Hot 105.9, Hip-Hop
WWQM 106.3 FM	Q106 FM, Country
WKCH 106.5 FM	Oldies, Radio
WNNO 106.9 FM	Mix 106.9 Top 40 Variety
WSJY 107.3 FM	Adult Contemporary

EDUCATION

Madison schools are rated high in national publications. Yet the spirit of independence remains strong in the city, keeping a healthy population of private schools—both religiously affiliated and independent—running waiting lists. The surrounding communities have nothing to be ashamed of either. When moving to the Madison area, consider what schools correspond to your new neighborhood. But also be aware that according to state law, parents can send their children to a school in another district. Applications for doing so are available at the Wisconsin Department of Public Instruction's Web site (www2.dpi.state.wi.us) and must be completed by the posted deadline, typically in late February of the academic year before the intended start date. Higher education includes the state's enormous University of Wisconsin–Madison, the flagship of a strong statewide system that was founded at the same time Wisconsin became a state. Other options include a private liberal arts college and a fine technical college system, as well as a variety of options for working adults seeking to complete degrees on evenings and weekends.

PUBLIC SCHOOLS

MADISON METROPOLITAN SCHOOL DISTRICT
545 West Dayton St.
(608) 663-1879
http://drupal.madison.k12.wi.us
The district serves around 26,000 students and has 31 elementary schools, 11 middle schools, four standard high schools, and one alternative high school. Alternative and early childhood programs are also offered for grades 6 through 12. Other than Madison itself (both the city and the town), the district also includes the communities of Fitchburg, Maple Bluff, Shorewood Hills, Blooming Grove, and Burke. The racial mix for MMSD is 50% Caucasian, 24% African American, 15% Hispanic, 10% Asian, and 1% Native American. Forty-seven percent of the student body is considered low income, 15% have special education status, and 16% have English Language Learner status. Based on graduation rates and test scores MMSD gets very high marks nationwide including a top 1% nationwide rating from *Expansion Management Magazine*, a business journal. Several other magazines rate it near the top as well. Madison students perform higher than the national and state averages for SAT and ACT exams, and for its modest size has an inordinate number of National Merit Scholar Semifinalists. Madison has a 4 to 1 student-to-computer ratio and spends just over $11,000 per student, about $2,000 higher than the state average. District schools have a licensed instructional staff member for every 10.8 students. As recommended by the state's SAGE (Student Achievement Guarantee in Education) program, kindergarten through third grade classes have 15 or fewer students for reading and math in 22 of the district's 32 elementary schools.

MCFARLAND SCHOOL DISTRICT
5101 Farwell St., McFarland
(608) 838-0430
www.mcfarland.k12.wi.us
McFarland serves 2,100 students in its six schools. The district includes one high school, one middle school, two elementary schools dividing grades 1 through 5, an early learning center, and a charter school. Over 70% of their K through 8 students participate in the summer school program. The district has frequently been acknowledged for achieving the highest score in reading at the third-grade level

in the state. McFarland got a mention in the book *The Power of Smart Goals* by Anne Conzemius and Jan O'Neil as an example of a district being successful in institutionalization of its goals.

MIDDLETON–CROSS PLAINS AREA SCHOOL DISTRICT
2429 Clark St., Middleton
(608) 829-9040
www.mcpasd.k12.wi.us
The district serves eight communities both rural and urban just west of Madison. Enrollment totals about 5,800 students. The district includes six elementary schools with all-day kindergarten, two middle schools, and one standard and one alternative high school. Special programs address special education needs, alternative settings, work experiences, and gifted and talented students. SAT and ACT test scores exceed state and national averages, and students perform in the top 1% of the state in proficiency tests. Minority enrollment is at 7.9%, students receiving free or reduced lunch total 8.3%, and students with disabilities are at 14%.

MONONA GROVE SCHOOL DISTRICT
5301 Monona Dr., Monona
(608) 221-7660
www.mononagrove.org
Monona is tucked in right under Madison on the east side of Lake Monona and has its own school district for just under 3,000 students both in Monona and the community of Cottage Grove. Cottage Grove has its own three schools offering grades pre-K and 1, 2 through 4, and 5 through 8 in separate buildings. Monona has a prekindergarten through grade 2 school, a grade 3 through 6 location, and both a standard and alternative high school. The district also operates Together 4 Kids, an early learning program offered for four-year-olds at five locations throughout the two communities.

VERONA AREA SCHOOL DISTRICT
700 North Main St., Verona
(608) 845-4300
www.verona.k12.wi.us
This quickly growing bedroom community to the southwest of Madison has four elementary schools, two middle schools, two charter schools, and one high school. Students total over 4,500 with minority students representing 27% of the student population. Composite ACT scores at the high school average about a point higher than the state average.

PRIVATE SCHOOLS

There is a wide variety of private independent and religious schools, and many of them have waiting lists, so it is important to plan well in advance. Several schools use the Montessori program in the Madison area. This is a selection of but a few schools.

ABUNDANT LIFE CHRISTIAN SCHOOL
4901 East Buckeye Rd.
(608) 221-1520
www.alcs.us
Founded in 1978, the school's mission is academic achievement with a Christian context. This ministry of Madison's Lake City Church enrolls about 300 students from prekindergarten through grade 12. Over 60 different churches are represented. The multimillion dollar facility has 24 classrooms, two gymnasiums, two music rooms, a computer lab, art room, library media center, science lab, weight room, and cafeteria. The 28-acre campus includes fields for football and baseball/softball, sand volleyball courts, as well as playgrounds.

BLESSED SACRAMENT SCHOOL
2112 Hollister Ave.
(608) 233-6155
http://school.blsacrament.org
This Catholic school is well attended by students from other backgrounds. Grades 1 through 3 are multiaged and mixed into units, as are grades 4 through 6, and 7 and 8. Kindergarten is self-contained. Units move from classroom to classroom throughout the day for different teachers.

EDGEWOOD CAMPUS SCHOOL AND HIGH SCHOOL
2219 Monroe St.
(608) 257-1023
http://campus-school.edgewood.edu
www.edgewoodhs.org
Founded in 1881 by the Dominican sisters, Edgewood is a complete education package offering schooling from age four on up. (See more about the college under Higher Education on the next page.) The grade school has two levels of kindergarten for four- and five-year olds and continues up through 8th grade. Edgewood High School is the only full-size Catholic high school in the area. One quarter of the students are not Catholic and almost 12% are minorities. This is a college preparatory school offering over 130 courses including Accelerated, Honors, and Advanced Placement courses. A majority of the teaching staff of about 60 have earned advanced degrees. The school offers a complete range of subjects, which includes fine-arts courses, 18 science courses, three foreign languages, and 12 AP courses. The school's enrollment of just under 700 students insures good student-teacher ratios and small class sizes. Nearly all students are involved in one or more extracurricular activities. Many students receive financial aid.

HIGH POINT CHRISTIAN SCHOOL
7702 Old Sauk Rd.
(608) 836-7170
www.highpointchristianschool.org
Christian-based but nondenominational, High Point teaches around 200 students from kindergarten through grade 8 as well as preschool. The school was founded in 1975.

HOLY CROSS LUTHERAN SCHOOL
2670 Milwaukee St.
(608) 249-3101
www.holycrossmadison.org
Holy Cross is a member of the Evangelical Lutheran Synod. The church operates a preschool and K through 8 school as well as an after-school program. Enrollment is just over 100 students.

MADISON CENTRAL MONTESSORI SCHOOL
4337 West Beltline Hwy.
(608) 274-9549
www.madisoncentralmontessori.org
Founded in 1972, the school enrolls almost 150 students in three primary classrooms for ages two-and-a-half to six years, two lower elementary classrooms for the six- to nine-year olds, another classroom for nine- to 12-year olds, and still another for 12- to 14-year olds. They also provide care for before and after school and a summer camp for kids three to nine years old.

OUR LADY QUEEN OF PEACE SCHOOL
418 Holly Ave.
(608) 231-4580
www.qops.k12.wi.us
This Catholic grade school was founded in the 1940s on Madison's west side. Enrollment approaches 500 for the K through 8 program. Kindergarten class sizes are under 20 while approaching 30 in the other grades. Enrollment is open to all students regardless of religious background.

ST. AMBROSE ACADEMY
602 Everglade Dr.
(608) 827-5863
www.ambroseacademy.org
The academy, founded in 2004, is run by lay-people and independent of any parish though it operates within St. Thomas Aquinas Parish. Students are taken from 6th grade through high school. The student body was initially small but is growing very quickly in the past couple years. The first students to take all four years of high school graduated in 2007.

WALBRIDGE SCHOOL
7035 Old Sauk Rd.
(608) 833-1338
www.walbridgeschool.com
Walbridge aims to personalize instruction and keep student-teacher ratios low in order to reach students with learning differences. This may mean learning disabilities, ADD, or just frustration with traditional methods and settings. Grades K through 8 are served.

WINGRA SCHOOL
3200 Monroe St.
(608) 238-2525
www.wingraschool.org

Since 1972, this independent progressive school has been educating kids aged five through 14. Part of the mission is to "teach tolerance, conflict resolution, appreciation for different points of view, self advocacy, negotiation, and listening." The teaching approach focuses on student interests and the important experience of being a child. Classes mix ages, the enrollment is around 135, and the student-teacher ratio is 7:1. Before- and after-school programs are offered.

HOMESCHOOLING

Madison's independent spirit shows in a modest but growing community for homeschoolers. Homeschool programs must meet state Department of Public Instruction criteria and information for that purpose are available at www.dpi.wi.gov/sms/homeb.html, but forms must be ordered by phone at (608) 266-5761 or toll free at (888) 245-2732, extension 1. For more information consult this useful Web site: http://homeschooling-wpa.org/.

HIGHER EDUCATION

EDGEWOOD COLLEGE
1000 Edgewood College Dr.
(800) 444-4861
www.edgewood.edu

This private liberal arts college set in a residential neighborhood on the near west side just north of Lake Wingra is part of a full education experience from preschool to Masters programs. The college, founded in the Dominican tradition, offers both traditional undergraduate and graduate studies as well as accelerated or flexible schedule degrees for returning students. Class sizes are small, on the average 15 students.

Postgraduate relevant job placement has a high success rate. The college offers more than 60 majors and 40 minors and is flexible on personalizing programs. Total enrollment is about 2,400 and about a quarter of those are graduate students. The school participates in NCAA Division III sports. Graduate studies are in areas of business, education, nursing, family therapy, religious studies, and sustainability. Dormitories are on campus.

MADISON AREA TECHNICAL COLLEGE
3550 Anderson St.
(608) 246-6100
www.matcmadison.edu

MATC offers a wide variety of educational and professional development programs from short bartending courses to full technical and professional certifications including graphic design and areas of IT and nursing. Associate degree and professional certificate programs total over 140. The college also has a liberal arts transfer program by which a student can finish the required classes toward a bachelor's degree and transfer to the UW–Madison or other four-year colleges. MATC has eight Madison campuses including one downtown near the Capitol. The Truax campus on the northeast side is the largest of them.

UNIVERSITY OF WISCONSIN–MADISON
716 Langdon St.
(608) 263-2400
www.wisc.edu

The UW–Madison is the flagship of the state public university system and was founded the same year Wisconsin took statehood, 1848. Within the university are 20 colleges and schools covering a wide array of disciplines including education, business, law, medicine, and engineering. Enrollment is typically up around 30,000 undergraduate students and another 10,000 or so graduate and professional students. Degrees are granted in 135 undergraduate majors, 151 masters programs, and over 100 doctoral programs. The university is a member of the NCAA's Big Ten Conference and competes in 25 sports as the Wisconsin Badgers. This is categorized as a research university and often has spent nearly $1 billion in an academic year. It ranks in the top five for science and engineering research investment and number one for nonscience areas. The

"Wisconsin Idea" was born here, a philosophy that the work and learning of the university should reach and benefit all the citizens of the state of Wisconsin. The university is consistently ranked high both nationally and abroad. The UW is located to the west of the Capitol along the shore of Lake Mendota and occupies nearly 1,000 acres. UW–Madison has a longstanding reputation for high academic achievement, political activism, and alcohol consumption.

Other Higher Education

CARDINAL STRITCH UNIVERSITY
8017 Excelsior Dr. # 140
(608) 831-2722
www.cardinalstritchumadison.com
Founded in the Franciscan tradition, Cardinal Stritch is a Milwaukee-based college. Its College of Business and Management operates this satellite campus, which provides degrees for working adults including an associates degree in business and bachelor's degrees in public safety management, human services management, strategic management and information systems, and business administration.

CONCORDIA UNIVERSITY
2909 Landmark Place, Suite 101
(608) 277-7900
www.cuw.edu/madison
This is a satellite campus run by the Milwaukee-area liberal arts college. Degree options include areas of business management, criminal justice management, education, health care management, human resource management, and graduate studies in administration, counseling, curriculum and instruction, reading specialist, and an M.B.A. program. Teacher certification in elementary or secondary education is also available.

HERZING COLLEGE PROFESSIONAL DEVELOPMENT CENTER
5218 East Terrace Dr.
(608) 249-6611
www.herzing.com/madison

Founded in 1948 as one of the oldest electronics schools in the country, Herzing now offers associates and bachelor's degrees in areas of technology, business, design, public safety, and health care. Degrees can be taken in as little as three years and schedules are accommodating.

LAKELAND COLLEGE
3591 Anderson St., Suite 101
(608) 244-2725
www.lakeland.edu
The Madison campus of this Sheboygan-based college offers classes for adults on a once-a-week schedule to help them complete undergraduate and graduate degrees. Areas of study are accounting, business management, computer science, criminal justice, education, health care or hospitality management, and marketing. Some courses are also available online.

UNIVERSITY OF PHOENIX
2310 Crossroads Dr.
(608) 240-4701
www.phoenix.edu
The University's Madison campus offers programs in business, management, finance, global business management, hospitality management, public administration, and others. Also available are M.B.A.s with focuses on accounting, global management, health care management, human resources management, marketing, or technology management. Classes are typically in the evening and once a week.

UPPER IOWA UNIVERSITY
4601 Hammersley Rd.
(608) 278-0350
www.uiu.edu
Ideal for the working adult, Upper Iowa offers M.B.A. and Masters of Higher Education Administration programs as well as degrees and professional training in areas of accounting, business, criminal justice, emergency and disaster management, health services administration, human resources management, psychology, public administration, and technology and information management.

HEALTH CARE

The quality of health care in Madison runs quite deep. Five hospitals serve the community as do more than 20 clinics and urgent care locations. Medical foundations and associations are abundant as are alternative medicine practitioners. Meanwhile the University of Wisconsin–Madison's medical, nursing, and pharmacy schools plus the groundbreaking research done in the University Hospital and on campus bring the amount and quality of care options to a level unexpected in a community of Madison's modest size.

HEALTH DEPARTMENT

MADISON AND DANE COUNTY PUBLIC HEALTH DEPARTMENT
210 Martin Luther King Jr. Blvd.
(608) 266-4821
www.publichealthmdc.com
Serving almost 500,000 people in the 1,200 square miles of Madison and Dane County, the government department works with partners in the community to provide information on health and disease issues. Check here for information on a wide variety of matters that affect health and living in the area, including local beach conditions, water and air quality issues, tobacco matters, and communicable diseases and immunizations.

HOSPITALS

AMERICAN FAMILY CHILDREN'S HOSPITAL
See University of Wisconsin Hospital, page 207.

MENDOTA MENTAL HEALTH INSTITUTE
301 Troy Dr.
(608) 244-3262
www.dhs.wisconsin.gov/mh_mendota/index.htm
Opened in 1860 as the state insane asylum, it was renamed Mendota State Hospital in 1935 and then its current name in 1974. The Wisconsin Department of Health Services operates the facility, which treats patients with complex psychiatric conditions. The facility is secure for certain legal and behavioral necessities. Mendota also operates outpatient treatment services for individuals in the community. Mendota is one of the first such mental health facilities accredited by the Joint Commission.

MERITER HOSPITAL
202 South Park St.
(608) 417-6000
www.meriter.com
The fifth largest hospital in the state, Meriter is staffed by over 1,100 physicians covering all areas of specialties. Operated as a not-for-profit hospital, it has 448 beds and provides a broad range of services from basic care to surgeries. It acts as a teaching affiliate for the University of Wisconsin. Three of the hospital's specialties stand out: cardiovascular care, women's health, and the area's only community-based Child and Adolescent Psychiatric Hospital. Meriter also operates clinics in Middleton and on Madison's west side.

WILLIAM S. MIDDLETON MEMORIAL VETERANS HOSPITAL
2500 Overlook Terrace
(608) 256-1901 or (888) 478-8321
www.madison.va.gov
This 87-bed facility provides comprehensive tertiary care in medicine, surgery, neurology, and psychiatry. The hospital employs 1,400 personnel and serves over 34,000 veterans each year. The hospital is affiliated with the University of Wisconsin School of Medicine and Hospital and

shares some of the hospital's resources. Special programs include open heart surgery, CT scans, MRIs, angiography, substance abuse rehabilitation, organ transplants, women's stress disorder treatment, and mental health care.

ST. MARY'S HOSPITAL
707 South Mills St.
(608) 251-6100
www.stmarysmadison.com

St. Mary's humble beginnings in 1912 as a 75-bed Franciscan "Sister's Hospital" are a far cry from the expanded complex we have today. Now boasting new inpatient and outpatient facilities, the hospital holds 440 beds, almost as many as its 441 active and associated physicians. A sky bridge connects the Dean and St. Mary's Outpatient Center with the rest of the complex. Areas of specialty include a cardiac center, family birth center, pediatrics, neuroscience, geriatrics, orthopedics, and emergency services. St. Mary's serves the University of Wisconsin School of Medicine as a site for three-year family practice residency programs. St. Mary's Hospital is affiliated with St. Louis' SSM Health Care, which is sponsored by the Franciscan Sisters of Mary. St. Mary's also has an Adult Day Health Center at another location, home care services, and a nursing facility (St. Mary's Care Center) on Madison's southwest side. Together with its affiliated physician group, Dean Health System, St. Mary's manages more than 22 primary-care clinics, the Davis Duehr Surgery Center, and the Surgery and Care Center in Madison.

UNIVERSITY OF WISCONSIN HOSPITAL
600 Highland Ave.
(608) 261-5628
www.uwhealth.org

The hospital was established as Wisconsin General Hospital in 1924 by the Wisconsin Legislature but moved to its current location in 1979. The 471-bed facility is one of the best academic medical centers in the nation. The hospital can often be found listed in annual lists of the top medical facilities and is a national leader in cancer treatment, pediatrics, ophthalmology, surgical specialties, and organ transplantation. The main hospital has nearly 1,000 physicians. The cancer research done here makes it one of the best places in the country to be treated. It is one of only two organizations in the state with Level One adult and pediatric trauma centers. There are six intensive care units. UW Hospital also operates the American Family Children's Hospital, which opened next door in 2007. The complete medical and surgical center is designed for family comfort and has a pediatric intensive care unit, a highly reputable transplant surgery unit, and a cancer center. Additionally, 80 outpatient clinics are operated by UW Hospital and Clinics.

AREA CLINICS AND URGENT CARE FACILITIES

CONCENTRA URGENT CARE
1619 North Stoughton Rd.
(608) 243-3962

358 Junction Rd.
(608) 829-1888
www.concentra.com

DEAN EAST CLINIC AND URGENT CARE
1821 South Stoughton Rd.
(608) 260-6000

752 North High Point Rd.
(608) 824-4000
www.deancare.com

UNIVERSITY OF WISCONSIN–HEALTH CLINIC
20 South Park St.
(608) 287-2000

UW Health East Towne Clinic
4122 East Towne Blvd.
(608) 242-6865
www.uwhealth.org

INDEX

Travel Like a Pro

To order call 800-243-0495 or visit thenewgpp.com

gpp
travel

The Cheap Bastard's Guide® to
NEW YORK CITY
MORE THAN 1,000 **FREE** LISTINGS

100
B E S T
Resorts of the Caribbean

OFF THE BEATEN PATH®
VIRGINIA A GUIDE TO UNIQUE PLACES →

The Luxury Guide to
Walt Disney World® Resort Second Edition
How to Get the Most Out of the
Best Disney Has to Offer

shifra stein's
day trips®

from kansas city
fifteenth edition

JOHN HOWELL S III
NINTH EDITION
CHOOSE COSTA RICA
FOR RETIREMENT

FUN WITH THE **FAMILY**
Hundreds
of Ideas FOR
Day Trips
WITH THE
Kids
Connecticut

INSIDERS' GUIDE
Florida Keys
and Key West

SCENIC DRIVING
COLORADO
STEWART M. GREEN

INSIDERS' GUIDE ®

The acclaimed travel series that has sold more than 2 million copies!

Pointing You in the Right Direction

Santa Barbara
Including Channel Islands
National Park

Glacier
National Park

Columbus

INSIDERS' GUIDE
Columbus

INSIDERS' GUIDE
North Carolina's Outer Banks

INSIDERS' GUIDE
The Twin Cities

INSIDERS' GUIDE
Pittsburgh

INSIDERS' GUIDE
Savannah and Hilton Head

Now with a fresh new look!

Written by locals and true insiders, each guide is packed with information about places to stay, restaurants, shopping, attractions, fun things for the kids, day trips, relocation tips, and local history. For over twenty years, travelers have relied on *Insiders' Guides* for practical and personal travel and relocation information.

To order call **800-243-0495**
or visit www.InsidersGuides.com